SO-AIZ-822

Columbia University Contributions
to Anthropology
Volume XXVI

KWAKIUTL TALES

NEW SERIES

BY

FRANZ BOAS

KWAKIUTL TALES

NEW SERIES

BY

FRANZ BOAS

PART I — TRANSLATIONS

AMS PRESS
NEW YORK

Reprinted with the permission of
Columbia University Press
From the edition of 1935, New York
First AMS EDITION published 1969
Manufactured in the United States of America

Library of Congress Catalogue Card Number: 79-82367

AMS PRESS, INC.
New York, N. Y. 10003

398.2
B66 K

pt.1

78-1397

TABLE OF CONTENTS

PREFACE

The following tales, unless stated otherwise were collected by the writer at Fort Rupert during the winter 1930—31. The translation of most of the texts is quite literal. Instead of the constantly recurring quotation "it is said" I have used *q*.

The following alphabet has been used:

E

i e, î ê, a, ô, o u

ī ē, ë, ä, ā, â, ō ū

E	obscure e, as in flower.
i e	are probably the same sound, intermediate between the continental values of i and e.
î	i in hill (= ι).
ê	e in fell.
a	has its continental value.
ô	German o in voll.
o u	are probably the same sound, intermediate between the continental values of o and u.
ë	a somewhat doubtful sound, varying greatly in its pronunciation among different individuals between ē and êi.
ä	German ä in Bär.
â	aw in law.
u	indicates that the preceding consonant is pronounced with u position of the mouth,

	Sonans.	Surd.	Fortis.	Spirans.	Nasal.
Velar	g̣	q	q!	x	—
Labialized velar	g̣w	qw	q!w	x^u	—
Palatal	gw	kw	k!w	x̣^u	—
Anterior palatal	g·	k·	k·!	x·	—
Alveolar	d	t	t!	s	n
— Affricative	dz	ts	ts!	—	—
Labial	b	p	p!	—	m
Lateral affricative	ʟ̣	ʟ	ʟ!	—	—
Lateral fricative	l	ɫ	—	—	—
Glottal Stop	ε	—	—	—	—

h, y, w, ḥ (faucal)[1]

Comparative notes have been added to the tales, but these are intended only to bring together the Kwakiutl versions contained in

---

[1] Used only occasionally by a *Gwa'waēnox^u*.

various publications. When the tale has been discussed in my general comparative treatment of Tsimshian material, the reference to this discussion has also been given. The following abbreviations have been used in quotations:

Ts Tsimshian Mythology. 31st Annual Report of the Bureau of American Ethnology, Washington, 1916.

S Indianische Sagen von der nord-pacifischen Küste Amerikas, Berlin, 1895.

M The Social Organization and Secret Societies of the Kwakiutl, Report of the U. S. National Museum for 1895, Washington, 1897.

C Kwakiutl Tales, Columbia University Contributions to Anthropology, Vol. II, 1910.

III Kwakiutl Texts, Jesup North Pacific Expedition, Vol. III, 1902—05.

X Kwakiutl Texts, second series, Jesup North Pacific Expedition, Vol. X, 1906.

CX The Religion of the Kwakiutl Indians, Columbia University Contributions to Anthropology, Vol. X, 1930.

Bella Bella, Bella Bella Texts, Columbia University Contributions to Anthropology, Vol. V, 1928.

Q!ā'neqe^εlak^u

Told by *Ō'mx·^εid.*

Hungry were *q Q!ā'neqe^εlak^u*[1] and his father and his stepmother and his younger brother at the village *K·!ē^εyaī'ł.* Then *q* the father of *Q!ā'neqe^εlak^u* made a salmon weir in the river for salmon. Then *q* the father looked at his salmon weir. They were two in the canoe, (he) and his wife. He did not allow *Q!ā'neqe^εlak^u* and his [5] younger brother to go aboard. The father of *Q!ā'neqe^εlak^u* came back. The children became hungry. The father of *Q!ā'neqe^εlak^u* said *q* shouting to his children, "Warriors are paddling," said *q* the father of *Q!ā'neqe^εlak^u*. Then *q Q!ā'neqe^εlak^u* and his younger brother became hungry. Behold! *q* his father only lied when he [10] said to him that warriors were seen by him. Behold *q* his father only said so that he alone might eat the salmon he had caught, the two, *q* he and his wife. Then *q* his father hid the salmon to starve his child *Q!ā'neqe^εlak^u* and his younger brother. "We tried to get game," said on his part *q* his father. Then *q* he gave a small [15] piece of roasted salmon to his child. Then *q Q!ā'neqe^εlak^u* was angry, "I knew that you got salmon," said *q Q!ā'neqe^εlak^u*. "Really badly your wife hates us. Now I shall take revenge on you, *Mā'q!ŭns,*" said *q Q!ā'neqe^εlak^u*. Then *q* he took up his father and threw him out of the house. "You will go as the heron of later [20] man," said he *q* to his father. And so *q* immediately his father became a heron. Then *q* he took up his step-mother and threw her against the post of his house. "You will be the woodpecker of later man." Then *q* his step-mother became a woodpecker, and *Q!ā'neqe^εlak^u* showed that he was not an ordinary man, (he) and his [25] younger brother.

"Let us move," said *q* on his part *Q!ā'neqe^εlak^u* to his younger brother. "Let us go to *Ăx^udɛ'm* and make a house there to be our house." — "Let us go," said *q* on his part his younger brother. Then *q* they just went, going to *Ăx^udɛ'm*. Then *q* he saw a double- [30] headed serpent. Then *q Q!ā'neqe^εlak^u* killed the double-headed serpent to have it for his belt.[2] Then *q* they arrived at *Ăx^udɛ'm*. Then *q* he built a house[3]. Wind-Blowing-from-End-to-End *(Yū'yu-balag·ilis*[4]*)* was the name of the house of *Q!ā'neqe^εlak^u*. Place-of-

[1] S 194, no. 2; C 187; X 185; p. 5: lines 1—90.
[2] S 195, no. 3; C 193; X 192, no. 2; p. 7: lines 91—100.
[3] S 195, no. 5; C 193; 192; X 192, no. 3; p. 7: lines 100—122.
[4] Called at another place *YEwi'balis.*

³⁵ Rolling-Down-in-the-House *(Ġwā′gwɛk·îmlilas)*, q was the name of
the house of his younger brother. "Now you will be sitting here.
Keep on sitting in our house. Now your name will be Only-One
(ᵉnɛmō′gwis)," said q *Q!ā′neqeᵉlakᵘ* to his younger brother. "Now
I will go and work for your provisions," said q *Q!ā′neqeᵉlakᵘ¹*.
⁴⁰ Then q *Q!ā′neqeᵉlakᵘ* started. Then q he threw a whale with a sling
stone. Four q whales were thrown with sling stones for provisions
for Only-One. Then q he went home. He told his younger brother,
"Here come your privisions, Only-One, these four whales. Do not
leave our house. Remain and stay here. Wait for the time of my
⁴⁵ return. Now I will go and set things right in the world," said q
Q!ā′neqeᵉlakᵘ. "Good-bye," said q on his part Only-One. Then
q *Q!ā′neqeᵉlakᵘ* started.

Then q he saw a man. The man was sharpening q a shell². Then
q *Q!ā′neqeᵉlakᵘ* asked him, "What is being done by you?" said q
⁵⁰ *Q!ā′neqeᵉlakᵘ.* Then q the man laughed. "Are you the only one
who does not know what is known by us? It is said, that he will
set everything right, Lord *Q!ā′neqeᵉlakᵘ.* With this I will make
my fighting tool," said q on his part the man. He did not know
that it was *Q!ā′neqeᵉlakᵘ* who asked him. "Come that I may see
⁵⁵ what is being sharpened by you," said q on his part *Q!ā′neqeᵉlakᵘ.*
Then q he gave what was being sharpened by him to *Q!ā′neqeᵉlakᵘ.*
Then q he took it and stood it on his ears. "You will be the deer
of later man," said q *Q!ā′neqeᵉlakᵘ.* Then the one who had been a
man became a deer. These mussel shells are on the ears of the deer.
⁶⁰　　Then q *Q!ā′neqeᵉlakᵘ* started. Then q he met, as he was walking,
a man who was sharpening his lance.³ Then q he went towards
him and asked him, "What is being worked by you, friend?"
said q *Q!ā′neqeᵉlakᵘ.* Then q the man laughed. "Are you the only
one who does not know what is known by us? It is said that he
⁶⁵ will set everything right, Lord *Q!ā′neqeᵉlakᵘ,*" said on his part
q the man. He did not know that it was *Q!ā′neqeᵉlakᵘ* who was
asking him. "Come here with your work," said on his part q
Q!ā′neqeᵉlakᵘ. Then q the man gave him what was being sharpened
by him. Then q *Q!ā′neqeᵉlakᵘ* took him and turned his head the
⁷⁰ other way. Then q he put it on his backside and smeared the
dust from sharpening on him and painted his backside and his
face. "You will be the raccoon of later man." Then q he became
a raccoon.

---

¹ S 195, no. 4; C 193; X 193; p. 8: lines 122—140.
² S 200, no.23; C 201; X 211, no.10; Bella Bella 32; p.9: lines 146—166.
³ S 200, no. 24; C 203; X 212, no. 11; compare Bella Bella 10; p. 10:
lines 182—188.

Then *q* *Q!ā'neqeᵉlakᵘ* started again. Then *q* he saw very many houses[1]. Not one man *q* was there. Just one *q* little child was [75] outside. Then *q* the little child called *Q!ā'neqeᵉlakᵘ*, and gave him to eat. Then *q*, she finished giving him to eat. And so *q* she never gave any water to drink to *Q!ā'neqeᵉlakᵘ*. Then *q* he said that he wished to drink water. "Don't say that, my dear," said on her part *q* the child. "That is the cause of the death of our [80] former tribe," said, on her part *q* the little child. "Don't be in vain afraid. You will just go my double-headed serpent belt being put on to you," said on his part *q* *Q!ā'neqeᵉlakᵘ*. "Go ahead," said on her part *q* the child. Then *q* *Q!ā'neqeᵉlakᵘ* put his belt on the child. "Go and draw water," said, on his part *q* *Q!ā'neqeᵉlakᵘ*. [85] Then *q* the child waded into the lake. And so *q* as soon as she went seaward wading, the sea monster opened its mouth and devoured the child. Then *q* *Q!ā'neqeᵉlakᵘ* said, "Snake in belly, snake in belly, snake in belly, snake in belly." Then *q* the sea monster opened its mouth again and vomited very many bones [90] of men. The child came last *q*. The child was not dead *q*. "Help me," said on his part *q* *Q!ā'neqeᵉlakᵘ*, "to gather the bones that we may revive them," said *q* *Q!ā'neqeᵉlakᵘ*. "Go on, take pity on them," said, on her part, *q* the child. Then *q* they worked. Then *q* they gathered all the bones. Then *q* *Q!ā'neqeᵉlakᵘ* sprinkled [95] his water of life on the bones. Then *q* all came to life who had only been bones, and they became a tribe again. Many *q* now had short legs and short arms. Perhaps the one arm and the one leg were not right. There was no way *q* in which they were not, when they arose. Then *q* *Q!ā'neqeᵉlakᵘ* took his belt from the child. [100] These *q* are the first of the Koskimo who were pitied by *Q!ā'neqeᵉlakᵘ*

Then *q* he started again. Then *q* he saw a man who was sharpening something *q*[2]. Then *q* *Q!ā'neqeᵉlakᵘ* went towards him and questioned him. "What is being done by you, friend?" Then *q* the man laughed. "*Ha, ha, ha, ha.* Are you the only one who [105] does not know what is known by us? It is said he comes to set everything right, our Lord *Q!ā'neqeᵉlakᵘ*." He did not know that behold! it was *Q!ā'neqeᵉlakᵘ* who questioned him. "Bring it to me that I may see what is being worked by you." Then *q* the man gave him what was being sharpened by him. Then *q* *Q!ā'neqeᵉlakᵘ* [110] took it. "Turn the other way," said *q* *Q!ā'neqeᵉlakᵘ* to the man. Then *q* the man turned the other way. Then *q* he put it into his backside. "You will be the land otter of later man," said on his

---

[1] S 196, no. 6; C 201; X 217, no. 16; p. 10: lines 204—246.
[2] X 213, no. 12; Bella Bella 32; p. 10: lines 189—191.

part *q Q!ā′neqe^εlak^u*. Then *q* the one who had been a man became
115 a land otter.

Then *q Q!ā′neqe^εlak^u* started again. Then *q* he met some women[1].
The four women *q* could not see. They had no eyes. The women
only *q* felt of what they were steaming. They were steaming
q clover roots. Then *q Q!ā′neqe^εlak^u* went towards them and stole
120 one of what was being steamed by the women. Then *q* the women
tried to find the clover root that was being steamed by them. Then
q the women smelled *Q!ā′neqe^εlak^u*. "Hm," said *q* the women, "What
would bring to this beach our Lord *Q!ā′neqe^εlak^u?* Hm, it smells
of *Q!ā′neqe^εlak^u*." Then *Q!ā′neqe^εlak^u* went towards them and
125 rubbed with the thick of the thumb the eyes of the women that
they should come to see. And so *q* the women began to see. Then
q Q!ā′neqe^εlak^u took them and threw them up. "You will be the
ducks of later man." Then *q* the women became ducks. And
so *q* that is the reason why ducks do thus being thrown up when
130 they first start to fly.

Then *q Q!ā′neqe^εlak^u* started again. He just *q* went inland of
Ha′yalik·awē^ε[2]. He did not dare to meet him, for *Q!ā′neqe^εlak^u*
was secular in the winter ceremonials. Only the *Nō′nlεm* was
known by *Q!ā′neqe^εlak^u*.
135 Then *q* he started again. Then *q* he saw a canoe on the water.
A man lay on the back with knees drawn up, wearing red cedar
bark around his head. He was singing *q:*

"Do not touch me on the water, *Ō′lala* uninitiated.
Hai, I am made to be a thrower, *Ō′lala* uninitiated, *Hai*,"

140 said *q* the one who was lying on his back in the canoe. Then *q*
Q!ā′neqe^εlak^u became afraid. "O friend, you must be a shaman,"
said *q Q!ā′neqe^εlak^u*. "And so I just wish to be a shaman. I just
feel good because it is easy traveling," said on his part *q* the one
who was lying on his back in the canoe. Then *q Q!ā′neqe^εlak^u*
145 called him. "Come ashore, friend," said *q Q!ā′neqe^εlak^u*. The
man came *q* shoreward. Then *q Q!ā′neqe^εlak^u* took him and streaked
down his body to the tail and threw him into the water. "You
will be the codfish of later man," said *q Q!ā′neqe^εlak^u*.

Then *Q!ā′neqe^εlak^u* started again. He arrived at Nimkish. He
150 arrived and saw a man[3]. And *Q!ā′neqe^εlak^u*'s word to him was,
"I am *Q!ā′neqe^εlak^u*," said he *q*, "I am going to set you right.
What do you want to be?" said *q Q!ā′neqe^εlak^u* to *Gwa^εnā′lalis*.

---

[1] S 202, no. 28; C 203; X 215, no. 14; Bella Bella 32.

[2] S 167, 197, no. 13; C 207; X 196, no. 6; 223, no. 20; Comox S 63;
compare Ts 685.

[3] S 135; X 228, no. 25.

"Let me be a large river," said on his part *q Gwaᵉnā′lalis*. "Now you
will be that way," said on his part *q Q!ā′neqeᵉlakᵘ*. Then *q* he took
Gwaᵉnā′lalis and pushed him down on the ground. "You will be ¹⁵⁵
a great river. You will never run dry the length of daylight (as
long as the world lasts)," said *q Q!ā′neqeᵉlakᵘ*. Then *q* he was
a large river and its name is *Gwa′ ᵉnē* when he was a large river.
    Then *Q!ā′neqeᵉlakᵘ* went back to *Áxᵘdᴇ′m¹*. His younger brother
was not there. Only *q* bones. Then *q Q!ā′neqeᵉlakᵘ* sprinkled them ¹⁶⁰
with his water of life and Only-One revived. Then *q Q!ā′neqeᵉlakᵘ*
spoke, "Only-One," said he *q*, "let us become a tribe," said *q
Q!ā′neqeᵉlakᵘ*. Then *q* Only-One asked the post of his house that
men should come out of it. Men came *q*. They went out of the
post of the house of Only-One. And so *q* just sufficient was the ¹⁶⁵
number of the men when he told his post to stop, when enough
were the men who came out of the post of his house. "These will
be a tribe and you will stay in our country," said *q Q!ā′neqeᵉlakᵘ*.
"Now you will go north, I will go south of our world," said *q
Q!ā′neqeᵉlakᵘ* to his younger brother. "You will not always keep ¹⁷⁰
on with bad things, else I should have too hard work when I try
to set right your bad things," said *q Q!ā′neqeᵉlakᵘ*. "I will do so,"
said *q* Only-One. And so *q* that is the reason why bad sickness
comes from the north end of our world. That is its length.

(Recorded by George Hunt)

Heron² *q* lived at Whale-Beach *(gwē′gwak·!awaᵉlis)*. *Q!ā′neqeᵉlakᵘ*
came into the house of Heron, and so Heron said to him at once,
"Welcome, child, for you have come into my house," said he to
him. And now Heron never asked him where he came from, and
he also never questioned him. "Who are you?" he never said to ⁵
him, for he just said that he had him for his son and treated him
well. Now *Q!ā′neqeᵉlakᵘ* and Only-One *(ᵉnᴇmō′gwis)*, the other
child of Heron loved each other. Now Heron made a salmon
weir, a salmon weir for getting sockeye salmon in the river *K·ēᵉyaῑ′ł*.
As soon as the salmon weir was finished he went back to his ¹⁰
house, for Only-One and *Q!ā′neqeᵉlakᵘ* always stayed at home.
As soon as day came in the morning Heron and his wife went to
look at their salmon trap. Then *q* one sockeye salmon was in the
inside of the salmon weir. Then *q* said Heron to his wife, "What
shall we do that we may conceal the sockeye salmon from our ¹⁵
children, else they will ask us for food," said he *q*. Then *q* said

¹ S 199, no. 18; C 199; X 229.
² S 194, no. 2; C 187; X 185; p. 1: lines 1—47.

his wife, "Go on and scare them when we arrive at the point
of land. You will say, 'Leave children, ghosts are here!'" Then
he said so when he saw his children and they ran into the woods.
²⁰ Now Heron paddled strongly and ran ashore on the beach of his
house. And so *q* immediately Heron carried the sockeye salmon
and entered his house. Then *q* Heron quickly made roasting
tongs while his wife cut the sockeye salmon, and she roasted it.
As soon as it was done they ate it quickly. And so *q* as soon as
²⁵ it was done they hid the remainder of bones. And so *q* as soon as
it was finished their children came into the house and sat down.
Now said Heron that his children had done right when they ran
right inland "to hide yourselves for I am always expecting the
warriors of the ghosts to come," said he. And so, as soon as day-
³⁰ light came in the morning he went to look at his salmon weir.
Then *q* he took two sockeye salmon out of his salmon weir. He
came *q* home. And so *q* as soon as Heron came to the point of land
he said, "Leave, children, ghosts are here!" said Heron. And
now *q* he saw his children as they were running right inland into
³⁵ the woods. Then *q* Heron paddled and ran ashore on the beach
of his house. Then *q* Heron at once carried the two sockeye salmon
and carried them into his house. Then *q* his wife at once cut open the
sockeye salmon. Then Heron made roasting tongs, two roasting tongs.
And so *q* as soon as they were roasted, they ate quickly what was
⁴⁰ roasted. And so, as soon as the food was all gone they quickly threw
the remains of bones into the fire. And so *q* as soon as this was done
Q!ā'neqeᵋlakᵘ and Only-One came into the house and sat down.
And so *q* they looked angry; and now *q* they did not speak. Then
q day came in the morning and Heron went to look at his salmon
⁴⁵ weir. Then *q* he took three sockeye salmon out of his salmon weir.
Then *q* he went home. Now he arrived at the point of land and
said, "Leave children, ghosts are here!" said he and he saw his
children running into the woods. Now Heron paddled strongly
and ran ashore on the beach of his house. And so *q* immediately
⁵⁰ Heron carried the three sockeye salmon and went into his house
and put down the salmon. Now he quickly made roasting tongs,
three roasting tongs while his wife quickly cut open the three
salmon. As soon as they finished they roasted them by the side
of the fire. And so *q* as soon as the roasted sockeye salmon were
⁵⁵ done they quickly ate them. And so *q* as soon as it was all gone
they hid the remains of bones. *Q!ā'neqeᵋlakᵘ* and Only-One came
q in and sat down. Now *q* they looked really angry while Heron
and his wife were happy, for they were satiated. Then *q* daylight
came in the morning and Heron with his wife went to look at their

salmon weir. Then *q* four sockeye salmon were in it. Then *q* [60]
he took them out and carried the four sockeye salmon out of his
small canoe and went home. And so, *q* as soon as he arrived at
the point of land he said, "Leave children, ghosts are here!"
said Heron. And now *q* he saw his children running right inland
into the woods. Then *q* Heron paddled strongly and ran ashore [65]
on the beach of his house. Then *q* he carried the four sockeye
salmon and went into his house. And so *q* immediately his wife
cut them open while Heron made roasting tongs, four roasting
tongs. And so *q* as soon as they were done he placed them upright
by the side of the fire. And so as soon *q* as they were roasted [70]
they ate the roasted food, each two roasted ones. And *q* Heron
did not know that *Q!ā'neqeᵋlakᵘ* was peeping through at the side
of the house watching his parents when they were eating the
roast. Then *q* *Q!ā'neqeᵋlakᵘ* heard the words of Heron when he
told his wife to eat quickly, "else we might be seen by our children [75]
and we will hide quickly these remains of bones," said *q* Heron.
And so *q* they had almost eaten the roast when *Q!ā'neqeᵋlakᵘ*
came into the house. Then *q* he said, "That is what you are doing,
confounded (dead) ones," said he, and he took Heron, tore his
body in two and threw it up. "You will be the heron of later [80]
generations," said he, as the heron went away flying. Then *q*
he took the wife of Heron, tore her body in two and threw her up.
Then *q* he said, "Now you will be the woodpecker of later generations," said he as the woodpecker flew to the post of the house
and pecked the post and it flew out of the house with Heron, who [85]
was now a heron.

Now *q* *Q!ā'neqeᵋlakᵘ* began to wish to know what to do in this
our world. Then *q* he said to Only-One, "I will go not far from
our house," said he as he went out of the house and started
to go to the point of land. And so *q* as soon as he arrived there [90]
he saw a large bird pecking at what was being pecked at by it. Now
he saw that behold! it was the Thunderbird what *Q!ā'neqeᵋlakᵘ*
saw and it flew away. Now *q* it left behind what was being
pecked by it. Then *q* *Q!ā'neqeᵋlakᵘ* started to look at what had been
pecked by it. Now he saw that it was a double-headed serpent. [95]
Now *q* *Q!ā'neqeᵋlakᵘ* skinned off a narrow strip from the back
of the double-headed serpent, which had the name snake on back,
to be his belt. Then *q* he took the two eyeballs; and *q* he added
to his supernatural power when he kept the snake on the back
and the eyeballs of the double-headed serpent. Then *q* he started[1] [100]

---

[1] 1 S 195, no. 3; C 193; X 192, no. 2; p. 1: lines 30—32.

and went to *K!wā′nēᵋ*, a sandy beach, and sat down there. Then
q it occurred to him to make a large house[1] to be the house of
his younger brother Only-One. Then q *Q!ā′neqeᵋlakᵘ* arose. Then
q he said, "Come Swell-Striking-Beach *(t!ō′xᵘtoᵋwalis)* to be the
105 post of my future house here!" said he q. Then q a man came
out of the swell and stood at the place referred to by *Q!ā′neqeᵋlakᵘ*
as his standing place. Then q he said again, "Come Sound-of-Rolling-
Gravel *(qālqap!alālis)* to be the post of my future house here!"
said he q. Then the man came q out of the groundswell and stood
110 at the place referred to by *Q!ā′neqeᵋlakᵘ* as his standing place. Then
q he spoke again and said, "Come Angry-Face *(bē′bekŭmlisila)*
to be the post of my future house here!" Then q the man came
and stood at the place referred to by *Q!ā′neqeᵋlakᵘ* as his standing
place. Then q *Q!ā′neqeᵋlakᵘ* spoke again and said, "Come, Standing-
115 on-Edge-on-Top *(k·!ᴇt!oqâlis)* to be the post of my future house
here." Then the man came and stood at the place referred to by
Q!ā′neqeᵋlakᵘ as his standing place. Now q the four men were
the posts of the long house which has two names Blowing-from-
One-End-to-the-Other *(Yŭwē′balīl)* and Place-where-Faces-are
120 Indistinct *(Gwā′gwᴇk·ᴇlīlas)*. I do not know from where *Q!ā′neqeᵋlakᵘ*
got the two beams and the roof boards. And now q the house
he built was finished. Then[2] q he went back to his house and q
Only-One was just sitting on the floor while *Q!ā′neqeᵋlakᵘ* was
working at the house. As soon q as *Q!ā′neqeᵋlakᵘ* entered the
125 house of Heron, q he said to Only-One that he had built a house
for him at *K!wā′nēᵋ*, "for your house for the time when I will
be gone. Now I shall get provisions for you in the morning,"
said he q. And as soon as day came in the morning, *Q!ā′neqeᵋlakᵘ*
and Only-One arose and they went to *K!wā′nēᵋ*. As soon as q as
130 they arrived at the house they sat down outside in front of the
house. Then q *Q!ā′neqeᵋlakᵘ* saw a whale spouting. Then q he
took his sling and one eyeball of the double-headed serpent and
laid it into his sling. Then q he threw the slingstone at the whale.
Then q *Q!ā′neqeᵋlakᵘ* said, "Snake move inside! Snake move
135 inside! Snake move inside!" Then q the whale ran ashore and
lay dead not far from the house. Then q *Q!ā′neqeᵋlak* took the
eyeball of the double-headed serpent out of the whale. Then q
four whales in all were killed with the sling by *Q!ā′neqeᵋlakᵘ* to be
provisions of Only-One. Now he changed the name of *K!wā′nēᵋ*
140 after this. Now it has the name Whales-Between *(Gwēgwak·ᴇlis)*.
Now q he told Only-One that he would go and see the princess

---

[1] S 195, no. 5; C 193; 192; X 192, no. 3; p. 1: lines 33—36.
[2] S 195. no. 4; C 193; p. 2: lines 36—45.

of *Gwa⁼nā'lalis*. "That is the reason why I took these four whales for you as your provisions and this house to be your house. Now I shall start, for I do not know the length of time it will be," said *Q!ā'neqe⁼lakᵘ* as he started. **145**

Then[1] *q* he saw a man sitting on the ground sharpening what was being sharpened by him on a sandstone. Then *q Q!ā'neqe⁼lakᵘ* went towards him. Then *q* he went suddenly near the man and questioned him. "What indeed, is being sharpened by you, friend," said he to him. Then *q* said the man to him, "For who are you **150** that you do not know that *Q!ā'neqe⁼lakᵘ* is coming to set things right? I am sharpening my shell knife to fight with him, in case he should hurt me," said he *q*. Then *q Q!ā'neqe⁼lakᵘ* said, "Give it to me that I may look at it," said he *q*. And so *q* at once the man gave the two shell knives to *Q!ā'neqe⁼lakᵘ*. Then *q* he took **155** him. Then *q* he said, "This is good! But this will be better," said he as he put one shell knife on each of the two sides of the head of the man. Then he also said *q* "Go and turn your backside this way!" said he *q*. And so *q* at once the man turned his backside towards him. Then *q Q!ā'neqe⁼lakᵘ* rubbed the grinding dust of **160** the shells on the sandstone and rubbed it on the backside of the man; that is the reason why the backside of the deer is white. Then *q Q!ā'neqe⁼lakᵘ* said, "Now you will be the deer of later generations," said he *q*. Now *q* the deer jumped and went inland into the woods. Now he had the two shells of the large mussels, which the early **165** people called shell knives.

Then[2] *q Q!ā'neqe⁼lakᵘ* started. Then *q* he saw a man sitting on the ground sharpening what was being sharpened by him. Then *q Q!ā'neqe⁼lakᵘ* went towards him and questioned the little man. Then he said to him, "What is being sharpened by you, friend?" **170** said he *q* to him. Then the man said to him, "This will be a spear that I may fight with *Q!ā'neqe⁼lakᵘ* for it is said he will come to set us right," said he *q*. Then *q Q!ā'neqe⁼lakᵘ* said to him, "Give me for a while your spear that I may look at it," said *q Q!ā'neqe⁼lakᵘ* to him. And so *q* at once the man gave it to him. Then *q Q!ā'neqe⁼-* **175** *lakᵘ* took the spear. Then *q* he said, "This is good! Turn your backside this way, friend!" said he *q*. And so *q* immediately the little man turned his backside to *Q!ā'neqe⁼lakᵘ*. Then *q* he stuck the spear into his backside as a tail. Then *q Q!ā'neqe⁼lakᵘ* said, "You will be the mink of later generations," said he. Now was **180** his tail when he went inland what had been his spear.

---

[1] S. 200, no. 23; C 201; X 211, no. 10; Bella Bella 32; p. 2: lines 48—59.
[2] X 214.

2

Then[1] q Q!ā′neqeᵉlakᵘ started coming. Then q he saw a man
sitting on the ground and he also sharpened what was being
sharpened by him. Then Q!ā′neqeᵉlakᵘ again put on the backside
185 of the man the spear marked with rings. Then q he marked his
face with the dust of grinding. Then q Q!ā′neqeᵉlakᵘ said to him,
"Now you will be the raccoon of later generations," said he to
him q. Then the raccoon went into the woods.

Then[2] q Q!ā′neqeᵉlakᵘ started coming. Then q he saw a man
190 sitting on the ground, sharpening what was being sharpened by
him. Then Q!ā′neqeᵉlakᵘ made him become a land otter.

And so, as soon as he had finished, he started and he heard many
men talking. Then q he saw the man with mouths on the body.
Then q Q!ā′neqeᵉlakᵘ questioned him, "Is it you who is heard by
195 me talking like many people?" said he q to him. Then the many
mouths on the body of the man replied at the same time, "I was
the one heard by you," said they q. Then Q!ā′neqeᵉlakᵘ said to
him, "It is bad that you are in this way of your many mouths.
Now I shall set you right, so that you may have one mouth as I have
200 one mouth," said he q and he spat on the palm of his hand and
pressed it on the body of the man .Then q all the mouths of his
body closed up after that. Now the man had only one mouth
after that.

And so q as soon as he had finished he started[3]. Now q Q!ā′neqeᵉlakᵘ
205 saw many houses on the west side of the river of Ǥō′sēᵉ. Then q
he saw that one house had a little smoke. And q it seemed strange
to Q!ā′neqeᵉlakᵘ. Then q he entered in it. Then q he saw a child
sitting on the floor. Then q Q!ā′neqeᵉlakᵘ questioned the child.
Then q he said to him, "Where are the house owners of these
210 many houses?" said he to him q. Then q the child answered him.
Then q it said, "O my dear! A monster there caused the death
of my tribe in this pond behind the village, for as soon as a man
goes to draw water he is swallowed by the hā′naq!ăts!ă. Look at
me! for I really want to drink water, for although there is a little
215 water in my bucket, I endure it, and I shall only drink it when
I shall really want to drink water," said he q. Then Q!ā′neqeᵉlakᵘ
said to him, "Drink your water here and go to draw water. I shall
just follow you to see what will be done to you by the one to whom
you refer as hā′naq!ăts!ă," said he to him q. And so q immediately
220 the child took the bucket and drank the water. Then q he invited

---

[1] S 200, no. 24; C 203, X 212, no. 11; compare Bella Bella 10; p. 2:
lines 60—73.

[2] X 213, no. 12; Bella Bella 32; p. 3: lines 102—115.

[3] S 196, no. 6; C 201; X 217, no. 16; p. 3: lines 74—101.

Q!ā'neqeᵋlakᵘ to follow him. And so *q* as soon as they almost reached the pond *Q!ā'neqeᵋlakᵘ* said to the child, "Stand still for a while that I may belt you with this belt," said he *q*. And so *q* he belted the child. And so *q* as soon as he had finished *Q!ā'neqeᵋlakᵘ* said to (the child), "Go and draw water!" said he to him *q*. ²²⁵ And so *q* immediately the child drew water. Now the *hā'naq!āts!ă* took him into his mouth. And so *q* at once *Q!ā'neqeᵋlakᵘ* said, "Snake move inside! Snake move inside! Snake move inside!" Then the *hā'naq!ăts!ă* vomited all he had eaten. That *q* was when first *Q!ā'neqeᵋlakᵘ* sprinkled the child with his water of ²³⁰ life and he revived. Then he asked him to put together the bones of the people who had long been dead. And so *q* as soon as he had gathered the bones of each person *Q!ā'neqeᵋlakᵘ* took the water of life and sprinkled it all over the bones. Then *q* all revived. Now *q* many men and women were sitting (and some) ²³⁵ with one leg short and (others) hermaphrodites. Now *q* the hermaphrodites wished to keep together for their ways were like those of women when they were working. Then *q* their voice was like that of women when they were talking, and also they did not like to be near men, for they are weavers of mats and they cut ²⁴⁰ open salmon and they dig clover roots. Their work is not men's work. And also hermaphrodites have neither husband nor wife. That *q* is the reason that only one tribe, the Koskimo have many hermaphrodites, that *Q!ā'neqeᵋlakᵘ* put together quickly the bones of the dead people vomited by the *hā'naq!ăts!ă* at *Ǧō'sēᵋ*. Now ²⁴⁵ I shall stop talking about *Q!ā'neqeᵋlakᵘ*. That is the end.

Łexx·ā'lix·ᴇlayu, the son of *Nōmasᴇ'nxeᵋlis* who lived at *Tsē'ltsᴇqalā'lis* saw *Q!ā'neqeᵋlakᵘ* coming. He went into the house and said to his father, "There is a man coming towards our house." His father replied, "I have been expecting him, our Lord, who is ²⁵⁰ setting the world right. I shall ask him to transform me into a small island on the point of *nᴇᵋwē'dēᶜ* (Sutil Pt.) and *xŭsbaᵋlī's* (Fort on point). The name of the island shall be *Hă'nxstālis* (Shining on the water), so that I may be seen by the canoes passing by." Soon *Q!ā'neqeᵋlakᵘ* arrived. When he entered *Nōmasᴇ'nxeᵋlis* spoke ²⁵⁵ and said, "Welcome, Lord! I wish to be transformed into an island, so that I may never die." *Q!ā'neqeᵋlakᵘ* did not molest *Łexx·ā'lix·ᴇlayu* for he was afraid of his power. He had full supernatural power *(lā'x·sâ nau'alakᵘ)*, being a thrower of supernatural power *(mā'maq!a)*. ²⁶⁰ After *Q!ā'neqeᵋlakᵘ* had built a house for his brother *ᵋnᴇmō'gwis* and created the people who were to live in it, he saw that they all

were downcast. Therefore he invited them in the evening to a
Nō'nlɛm ceremonial. In doing so he used "backward talk," that
265 is he said the opposite of what he meant. He said, "I am not
inviting you. Do not come at once" *(k·!ē*ᵉ*s*ᵉ*ɛn Lē'lalōL. wä, las*
*k·!ē*ᵉ*s hā'lag·iliLōL).* When he said, I am going to gather Fritillaria
(lāLɛn x·ō'kwaL) he meant, that he was going down to the beach.
He told the people that the *Nō'nlɛm* would last four days and during
270 this time they would be foolish and unable to speak properly. Then
he showed the *Nō'nlɛm* masks, first the killerwhale, then the
Merman and last the *Q!ō'mogwē*. In each of these dances the dancer
appeared first, moved around the fire and ran out of the house.
After this the mask appeared[1].

Ō'ᵉmäl

(Told by *Kwā'kwaano*, a *Nā'k!wax·da*ᵉ*x*ᵘ)

It is said *Ō'ᵉmäl* lived at *Ōᵉstō'wa*. And so *q* he searched for a
wife[2]. Then *q* he went to the grave and asked, "Are there no twins
here, graves on the rock?" — "We here are that way on the
rocks." Then *q Ō'ᵉmäl* asked the grave, "Are there no twins here,
5 graves on the rock?" — "I am a dead twin." Then *q Ō'ᵉmäl*
took her for his wife, and he went home after this. Then *q* he
called his younger brothers to make a salmon weir in his little
river. And so *q* his younger brothers made a salmon weir and so
as the salmon weir was finished he went to call his wife to go and
10 wade in the water. *Ō'ᵉmäl* followed (?) his wife and she waded.
Many salmon went up the river (?) when the twin woman waded
in the water. Then the basket of the salmon weir was full. There
were no salmon in the salmon weir of Deer, for he was foolish. It
was closed all around. Then the woman cut a great many salmon.
15 There were a great many heads and middle pieces and fins. Now
his houses were full of dried salmon and he got fuel to dry it. It is
said, *Ō'ᵉmäl* came (back) carrying on the shoulder firewood. Then
q the middle pieces hooked in his hair. Then *q Ō'ᵉmäl* said, "You
funny things, you catch me and you come from the ghosts."
20 Then *q* the woman, his wife, said, "What did you say, *Ō'ᵉmäl?*
What did you say, *Ō'ᵉmäl?*" Then *q Ō'ᵉmäl* said, "I did not say
anything, my dear mistress." (But) *Ō'ᵉmäl* had said, "You are
from the ghosts, you are from the ghosts." And the twin woman
became angry and also the dried salmon. Then *q* the dried salmon

---

[1] See p. 143.
[2] S 174; III 323; C 217, 491; Rivers Inlet S 209; Bella Bella 6.

came back to life, all her tribe, and *Ō'ᵉmäl* held his former wife ²⁵ when all went into the water in the little river, and there was none of the salmon left, when all went out of the house, and he cried with his children because they had no food, and they were hungry.

And *Ō'ᵉmäl* called in his tribe. He was going to woo the princess of ³⁰ the salmon chief.¹ He launched his unfolding canoe and *Ō'ᵉmäl* went aboard with his younger brothers. No women and children went and they started paddling. Deer stood in the canoe paddling when they came to be on the water. It is said they came in sight of *Kwā'wä*. Then *q Ō'ᵉmäl* said, "Do let us take some stones at ³⁵ *Xᴇxᵘdᴇᵉma'* in Knight Inlet," and they took four stones at *Xᴇxᵘdᴇᵉma'*. They came out of the inlet. And so *q* they just struck the horizon of our world searching for the house of the chief of the salmon; and they reached a nice country, a living place where there were many houses. Then *Ō'ᵉmäl* said, "Do not let us go right ⁴⁰ ashore and haul up the canoe." They and the houses were invisible to each other. It was not long before someone came paddling out of the village. An old man *q* was paddling along. Then *q* he was looking for trees and the old man did not see *Ō'ᵉmäl*, for he had gone into a nice (piece of) firewood which was known to him ⁴⁵ as to be taken for firewood by the old man. Then *q* he took out his wedge, and he did not know about *Ō'ᵉmäl* that he was sitting in the (piece of) wood standing on the ground. And he began to chop the butt of the tree. Then the old man drove in one of his wedges and *Ō'ᵉmäl* bit off the point of the wedge, and the ⁵⁰ wedge jumped out. Then *q* the old man took his wedge and looked at it. Again he took another wedge and he wedged it in again and again *Ō'ᵉmäl* just bit the point of it. The old man took it to look at it. Then again he took out another wedge to drive it in and again it jumped out. Then *q* he took the wedge and looked and ⁵⁵ he began to cry. "Oh, probably I shall be scolded by my master (on account of) the wedge, that existed when first our world became light," and *Ō'ᵉmäl* came out of the tree. Then *q* he said, "What is the reason of your noise about your plans, old man? Give me your wedge." Then *q* he took the wedge and put the point ⁶⁰ in his mouth, for he was still holding in his mouth the pieces bitten off in the middle of the wedges, and he stuck the tip of the wedge to the place where it had been. It was just whole (as) he did so. All the wedges were made alive by *Ō'ᵉmäl* that he might be quick with his wooing. And *Ō'ᵉmäl* threw over the tree on the ground. ⁶⁵

---

¹ S 175, no. 12; III 330; C 169, 217; Comparative notes Ts 671.

Then q it broke into pieces and the old man carried the firewood
aboard his small canoe. Then q $\bar{O}'$ $^\varepsilon m\ddot{a}l$ questioned the old man, "Does
not the daughter of the chief come down to get this at the beach ?"
Then q the old man replied to his words. "She will come and
70 will come down as soon as I arrive at the beach, to take the smallest
piece I obtained by getting firewood." Then q $\bar{O}'$ $^\varepsilon m\ddot{a}l$ said, "Let
me go into this firewood!" and $\bar{O}'$ $^\varepsilon m\ddot{a}l$ went into the inside of the
firewood. Then q the old man piled up the firewood in his canoe
and went home. He arrived at the beach of his house. Then
75 q the old man threw out of the canoe the firewood when the
little pretty daughter came. And so q it was there on the beach
when the girl took in her arms the firewood in which $\bar{O}'$ $^\varepsilon m\ddot{a}l$ was.
And so q as soon as the girl started $\bar{O}'$ $^\varepsilon m\ddot{a}l$ stretched out his hands
from the firewood to embrace the girl. And so q immediately
80 the girl threw it down on the beach and she looked at it and took
it up. Then q the girl took up again the firewood and tried to
start and again $\bar{O}'$ $^\varepsilon m\ddot{a}l$ embraced her. Then the girl threw it down
on the beach and stared at it, and q $\bar{O}'$ $^\varepsilon m\ddot{a}l$ called to the old man.
"As soon as I have been thrown four times by the girl, you will
85 take the firewood in which I am and place it in the corner of the
house. Do not let me be near the fire, else I might be set on fire."
Now it was night and the mother of the woman took the firewood
in which $\bar{O}'$ $^\varepsilon m\ddot{a}l$ now was and threw it on the fire. He came (to
be) across the middle. He was across the middle of the fire, for
90 the woman did not know that $\bar{O}'$ $^\varepsilon m\ddot{a}l$ was in the firewood. Now
night came when the girl lay down in her room. Then $\bar{O}'$ $^\varepsilon m\ddot{a}l$
started and went to her. $\bar{O}'$ $^\varepsilon m\ddot{a}l$ said, "I am $\bar{O}'$ $^\varepsilon m\ddot{a}l$. I am going
to have you for my wife." — "Come, my dear, my father always
kills those who from time to time try to be my husbands for, behold!
95 is he not the chief of the salmon ? Behold! here are the killerwhales," and the killerwhale who had been sea hunting came
making a noise. And so q as soon as day came the father of the
girl said, "Arise, my dear, with your husband and come to break-
fast," said he q. Then the girl said to $\bar{O}'$ $^\varepsilon m\ddot{a}l$, "Now you will take
100 care, my dear, my ᐧfather tries to kill all those who try from time
to time to become my husbands." And $\bar{O}'$ $^\varepsilon m\ddot{a}l$ sat down. His
wife did not go. Then the whole tribe came in. The ends were
adzed sharp, and poles were driven into the floor at the end of
the fire, and when it was ready the chief called his son-in-law
105 $\bar{O}'$ $^\varepsilon m\ddot{a}l$, "Come, $\bar{O}'$ $^\varepsilon m\ddot{a}l$, stand up." Then $\bar{O}'$ $^\varepsilon m\ddot{a}l$ was tied to a
post which stood on the floor and he was roasted and his father-
in-law made a (strong) fire. And so, his father-in-law did not
know that $\bar{O}'$ $^\varepsilon m\ddot{a}l$ went into (the post) driven into the floor. Then

they went out. Then q the tribe went home. Again night had
come. Now $\bar{O}'\,{}^{\varepsilon}m\ddot{a}l$ q did not lie down that night with his wife. [110]
He did lie down the next night with his wife. Then the chief called
his tribe and $\bar{O}'\,{}^{\varepsilon}m\ddot{a}l$ and all the women. And all came in. Now
posts were driven in the middle of the floor. As soon as it was
done the father-in-law said, "Come $\bar{O}'\,{}^{\varepsilon}m\ddot{a}l$." $\bar{O}'\,{}^{\varepsilon}m\ddot{a}l$ came. $\bar{O}'\,{}^{\varepsilon}m\ddot{a}l$
arose and stood on the floor, (next) to the (post) driven into the [115]
floor. And he was thus with stretched arms as he was tied with
cedar ropes. Then a porpoise was taken and put next to the fire.
Now the fire blazed up. Then it was not noticed that $\bar{O}'\,{}^{\varepsilon}m\ddot{a}l$ went
into the (post) driven into the floor and again he just disappeared
because he was supernatural. And again the tribes went out. [120]
Then q the younger brothers of $\bar{O}'\,{}^{\varepsilon}m\ddot{a}l$ talked among themsleves,
being out of sight. And q Deer said he would go and make war,
for he had not thrown his spear. And it came to be night again.
$\bar{O}'\,{}^{\varepsilon}m\ddot{a}l$ was still in the (post) driven into the ground. Then he lay
down with his wife that night. Then q day came, when the chief [125]
said, "Rise, my dear, that we may take breakfast." And again
the father of the girl called his tribe to come and sit near by in
the house. Then q the chief said to his son-in-law, "Are you a
supernatural man, $\bar{O}'\,{}^{\varepsilon}m\ddot{a}l$?" Then q $\bar{O}'\,{}^{\varepsilon}m\ddot{a}l$ said, "Yes, I am
supernatural." — "Let me try you", said q on his part, the chief. [130]
"Please," said $\bar{O}'\,{}^{\varepsilon}m\ddot{a}l$, "let my brothers come." Then q the chief
said, "Call your brothers to come and watch your wife." Then q
he started paddling to go and call his brothers. And so q as soon
as he reached his brothers he took out of the canoe the four stones
from Knight Inlet. And, behold! q his younger brothers launched [135]
their paddle-side canoe, and $\bar{O}'\,{}^{\varepsilon}m\ddot{a}l$ took along some ocher which
also came from Knight Inlet and also clay, also eagle down and
charcoal. They came q pushing the paddle side canoe, and Deer
threw his lance at one man. The Deer was laughed at by his
tribe. Then they were called in by the chief, into his house, and [140]
q four killerwhales were put in line on the beach; and q they
just went out of the house who had all gone into the house. They
were to go at once to Knight Inlet and $H\ddot{e}'lala$ was to go to Skeena
River $(Ts!_{E}x\cdot\bar{\imath}na)$. And the killerwhales went seaward which
were to be the traveling canoes of $\bar{O}'\,{}^{\varepsilon}m\ddot{a}l$, going to Knight Inlet. [145]
Then q $\bar{O}'\,{}^{\varepsilon}m\ddot{a}l$ pretended to make a mistake, when he swam. He
was rocking about on the water. And so q $\bar{O}'\,{}^{\varepsilon}m\ddot{a}l$ just went ashore
so that he might not be seen by the tribe.

The $N\bar{a}'k!wax\cdot da^{\varepsilon}x^{u}$ obtained their $N\bar{o}'nt_{E}m$ ceremonial at
$Y\ddot{a}xwa\bar{e}'sd_{E}m$ when $\bar{O}'\,{}^{\varepsilon}m\ddot{a}l$ painted all the birds which had been [150]

white before. After they had been painted they danced with the following song[1]:

yîxwa'ēs,	*yîxwa'ēs*	*ts!ets!äsâgag·anᴇmx·st!aʟē*
		(?)
Dance on beach,	dance on beach	it might be as though it were

155   *lânukŭmeǧa hā'daǧa, ha ya ya*

Head owner of world women, lady woman, ha ya ya.

Hā'daǧa[2]

Told by *Yā'qoʟas*

Hā'daǧa was a sister of *Ō' ᵉmäł*. They lived at *Wa'edzēᵉ*. *Ǧaᵉwaxē'l*, that is *Ō'ᵉmäł*, lived at *ʟᴇ'nʟᴇnʟaakᵘ*. From there he went to *Wa'edzēᵉ*. His princess was *Hā'daǧa*. *Hā'daǧa*, his princess, was eating sea eggs with all the children of the village. When she did so the
5 Crow called out, "*K·āx, k·āx, k·āx.* The princess of *Ǧaᵉwaᵉēnoxᵘ* is eating sea eggs. *K·āx, k·āx, k·āx.*" When *Ō'ᵉmäł* heard this he was ashamed on account of his sister. He ordered the people to break up their houses and to leave her. They loaded their canoes with the house boards, left, and built a house at *Wa'edzēᵉ*. *Hā'daǧa* was
10 left all alone. She had two dogs. She looked around for old mats and old boards and made a small shelter for herself. When this was done she spoke to the dogs and said, "I wish you were men so that you might help me to get cedar which I might split." Then the dogs said, "We are men." They went into the woods to bring
15 cedar twigs. She said to the one dog, "I wish you were a man so that you could get spruce roots for me." He went and brought them in his mouth. She split the roots and made a fish basket. When it was done she ate and then she put the basket into the water at *Nā'x·a* (a place near the light house). She said, "I wish
20 you would catch the son of *Q!ō'mogwa.* Soon she pulled up the fish basket and it was full of kelp fish. Three times it was full of kelp fish. The fourth time she repeated saying that she would like to catch the prince of *Q!ō'mogwa.* When she pulled it in a fourth time she saw a small man sitting on a box in the fish basket.
25 She tore the basket. He came out, went ashore and told her to carry the box. She was unable to lift it. Then he himself took it up and carried it up to the high water mark. When he opened

---

[1] When this dance is performed the women have their blankets pinned around the neck and spread out from the neck down to the feet, the arms and hands extending the blanket. They dance slowly.

[2] S 183; C 245; Comparative notes Ts 184.

it there were two whales in it. Then he married her and built a
house. They tried out the oil from the whales. While they were
doing so a gull came. *Hā'daqa* called it in and said, "Come here ³⁰
that I may give you some blubber. Here is a piece of boiled blubber
which I want to send to my grandmother. You will find her.
She is always mending cedar bark blankets." The gull took the
blubber and flew away. It flew very low over the village. Then
it saw an old woman mending a cedar bark blanket and thought, ³⁵
"This must be the one." It alighted next to her and said, "This
is sent to you by the one whom you deserted." Then the old woman
arose and went into the house. She sat down there in front of her
work, with her face to the back of the house, and secretly she
bit off a piece of the blubber. *Ō'ᵉmäl* heard the noise when she ⁴⁰
was chewing it and said, "What are you doing there? What are
you biting?" The old woman said, "I am biting the cedar bark
on which I am working." When she bit off again a piece secretly
Ō'ᵉmäl saw it. He said, "It sounds as though you were eating
something." He arose and threw her down and in her mouth he ⁴⁵
found the blubber. Then she struck his face with it and said,
This blubber was sent to me by the one whom you deserted." —
"*Â â â â,*" said *Ō'ᵉmäl.* Then he went out to get mussels for his
sister and they went back to the place where *Hā'daqa* had been
deserted. He carried his basket full of mussels to her, hoping ⁵⁰
to appease her. He said, "*HadzEgō', hadzEgō', ts!ēts!ExᵘbEsā'qa-
k·asaaqōs yaq!wŭlwadzEs g·iadzō' g·iadzō!*" *Hā'daqa* told her husband
to open the door and to let him in. He came in and sat down.
Hā'daqa boiled a seal and gave to her brother a small grease dish
which she took out of her room. She put it in front of her brother, ⁵⁵
filled with oil. When *Ō'ᵉmäl* saw it he thought, "It is too small."
He thought if he should dip once into the grease dish the oil would
all be used up; but when he began to eat he could never empty it.
Then he was eating greedily and the oil was just running through
him. Then he said, "My blanket is making a crackling noise." ⁶⁰
(*ā'leg·ak·!Eg·alg·in ᵉnExᵉŭna' ᵉyē*). Then *Hā'daqa* became disgusted and turned him out. After the feast all the people unloaded
their goods and stayed with *Hā'daqa.*

Ō'ᵉmäl and Grizzly Bear
Told by *K·!ä'maxalas*, a *Gwa'waēnoxᵘ* woman, father Nimkish
Recorded by George Hunt
Story of the numaym *Kwē'kwäᵉnoxᵘ* of the *Gwa'waēnoxᵘ*

Ō'ᵉmäl q and his younger brothers, Deer and Raccoon-Made-to-
Go-up and Land-Otter-Made-to-Go-up and Mink (Sun-Maker) and

Squirrel-Made-to-Go-up and Wren lived at $G\cdot_Ey\bar{o}'x^u$, at the head
of the bay near $H\bar{e}'g_Ems$. Then q $Q!\bar{e}q!awat$ who is referred to by
5 the Kwakiutl as Wren made a salmon weir in the river of $G\cdot_Ey\bar{o}'x^u$.
It is said his salmon weir was made in this manner. And so q

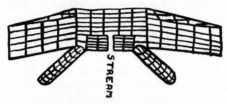

as soon as he had finished his salmon weir which he made for the
sockeye salmon $Q!\bar{e}'q!awat$, the Wren, went home to his house.
And so q as soon as night came he lay down on his back and went
10 to sleep. And so q immediately he dreamed about his salmon
weir. (He saw) in his dream (that) the two fish baskets were broken
(it has two names also round-bodied baskets for sockeye salmon).
Then q he dreamed also about his salmon weir. In his dream it
talked to him and in his dream q the salmon weir asked Wren to
15 take care and rise early every morning to take out the sockeye that
was in the trap. On account of the grizzly bear *(mō'dog·ila* who
is called by the Kwakiutl *g·ila)*, "if the grizzly bear should know
about me," said q the salmon weir. "Now he will always come and
break me up and take out the sockeye that is in me and eat it,"
20 said the salmon weir in his dream to Wren. And so q as soon
as day came in the morning, Wren awoke, took his cape and his
drill *(s_Elō'dayu* which is called by the Kwakiutl, *ănk^u)*, and
shredded cedar bark. Then q he awakened his mother. Then q
he said, "I just wish you to know I will go and take out the sockeye
25 that is in my salmon weir, for I worry that the grizzly bear may
break my salmon weir," said Wren q to his mother, Heaven-Maker-
Woman *(L_E^εwag·ilaogwa)*. Then q Heaven-Maker-Woman replied
to her child Wren. Then q she said, "Go child, only take care of
your ways so that you may not get hurt," said q Heaven-Maker-
30 Woman to her child. Then q Wren started going up the river.
Then q he arrived at his weir for catching sockeye salmon. And
q he saw the two fish baskets that were filled to the mouth with
sockeye salmon. Then q Wren spoke. Then q he said, "That is
what I wish that you may always be filled to the mouth with
35 sockeye salmon, for you are a salmon weir. Thank you, supernatural one. Now you have taken pity on me," said he q and
took out the sockeye salmon. And so q as soon as he had taken
out his sockeye salmon, he broke off four cedar twigs. Then

q Wren twisted the four twigs and made a hauling line to haul the
sockeye salmon he had caught. And so q as soon as he had finished [40]
twisting the four-twisted cedar withe hauling line he strung the
sockeye salmon on it. And so q as soon as he had finished he
hauled them down the river. And so q as soon as he arrived at
the beach of his house, his brothers $\bar{O}'\,{}^\varepsilon m\ddot{a}l$ and Deer and Raccoon
and Land Otter and Mink and Squirrel all were sitting on the [45]
summer seat outside of Wren's house, for $\bar{O}'\,{}^\varepsilon m\ddot{a}l$ was expecting
Wren to come home as he had gone to look at his salmon weir.
And so, that is the reason why $\bar{O}'\,{}^\varepsilon m\ddot{a}l$ saw at once Wren coming
to the beach of his house; and so q immediately $\bar{O}'\,{}^\varepsilon m\ddot{a}l$ asked his
younger brothers to go and meet Wren on the beach; and so q [50]
all went down the beach, $\bar{O}'\,{}^\varepsilon m\ddot{a}l$ and his younger brothers, and
they hauled up the four strings of sockeye salmon and put them
down on the ground on the seaside of the house of Wren. And so
q immediately Wren asked $\bar{O}'\,{}^\varepsilon m\ddot{a}l$ to request his younger brothers
to make a fire on the seaside of his house and to put many stones [55]
on the fire to steam all the four strings of sockeye salmon, said
he to him q. And so q immediately the ancients made a fire outside.
Then q the others picked up the stones and threw them on the
fire on the ground. And so q as soon as the stones on the fire were
ready, $\bar{O}'\,{}^\varepsilon m\ddot{a}l$ asked his younger brothers to go inland to get many [60]
skunk cabbage leaves. And so q immediately all his younger
brothers went, but q it was not long before all came back carrying
in their arms much skunk cabbage and put it down on the ground
alongside the fire on which the stones were. And so q as soon
as all the stones were red hot they raked up all the fire. And [65]
so q as soon as this was finished they took the sockeye salmon
and put them on the red hot stones. And so q as soon as all the
sockeye salmon were on the stones they took skunk cabbage
and spread it around what was being steamed. And so q as soon
as this was finished Raccoon and Deer each took one large bucket [70]
full of water and poured it at the same time over what was being
steamed. And so q immediately they covered it with much skunk
cabbage; but it was not long before the sockeye lying on its belly
was cooked. And so q immediately $\bar{O}'\,{}^\varepsilon m\ddot{a}l$ just asked his younger
brothers to take off the covering of skunk cabbage. And so as [75]
soon as it was all off $\bar{O}'\,{}^\varepsilon m\ddot{a}l$ asked his younger brothers to sit
around the sockeye that was now cooked and they ate. And so
q they had eaten all the steamed sockeye salmon, when Wren came
out of his house. And q he was going to eat with his brothers.

On his part q Wren had no word (that he said) to his brothers, [80]
for he presumed that sockeye would be again in his salmon weir.

Then q night came. Then q Wren[1] went to lie down early in his
bed, for he wished to rise early in the morning. And so q as soon
as day came in the morning he arose and took his cape and put
85 it on. It is said he also took his fire drill and shredded cedar bark
and took it when he started out to go up the river. And so q
as soon as he reached his salmon weir he saw that it was broken
and there was not one sockeye salmon in it. And so q immediately
Wren patched his salmon weir. And so q as soon as he had finished
90 patching it he left it when it was nearly evening. And so q $\bar{O}'$ $^\varepsilon m\ddot{a}l$
and his younger brothers all went to sit on the summer seat on the
seaside of the house of Wren, for all of them, $\bar{O}'$ $^\varepsilon m\ddot{a}l$ and his younger
brothers, expected that Wren would have caught many sockeye
salmon. And so q as soon as Wren came in sight on the beach
95 of his house $\bar{O}'$ $^\varepsilon m\ddot{a}l$ saw that he had not caught one sockeye
salmon, and q the hearts of $\bar{O}'$ $^\varepsilon m\ddot{a}l$ and his younger brothers
were bad, for they never ate that day, for they depended on
what was to be obtained by Wren. And so q that was the reason
why $\bar{O}'$ $^\varepsilon m\ddot{a}l$ and his younger brothers were really hungry. Wren
100 q came and went into his house. He just q lay on his back in his
bed and went to sleep, and q he never ate on his arrival, for his
heart was really bad on account of the one who had damaged
his salmon trap. And so q day had not come in the morning before
Wren arose. Then q he put on his cape. Then q he took his fire
105 drill and shredded cedar bark. Then q he went out of his house when
daylight had not (yet) come in the morning. Then q he walked
up the river; and so q it was getting daylight when he arrived at
his salmon weir; and q he saw Grizzly Bear breaking up his
salmon weir; and q Grizzly Bear took out the sockeye salmon
110 and put them down inland from the past (destroyed) salmon weir.
And so q as soon as Wren reached him Wren spoke. Then q he
said, "O Grizzly Bear, what is the reason that you damage my
weir, you ugly hollow stomach, you ugly one whose food goes
from end to end," said he to him q. Then q Grizzly Bear replied
115 to the speech of Wren. Then q he said, "Oh, what is it, indeed, you
little one, indeed, you cannot compete with anyone, you come
with an angry face to me. Look! I'll suck you in. Look! I'll
crush you with my paws. Look! I'll take you in my mouth, because
you dare to come and scold me," said he q. Then Wren said to
120 Grizzly Bear, "Go on, try to suck me in, try to crush me," said
he to him q. Then q Grizzly Bear opened his mouth and sucked
Wren in. And so q Wren just went from end to end through the

---

[1] See Ts 718 for comparative notes; also Bella Bella 30; Kutenai Tales,
Bulletin 59, Bureau of American Ethnology, Washington, 1917; p. 171. See also
Quileute Texts, Columbia University Contributions to Anthropology, XII 123.

intestines of Grizzly Bear and jumped out of his anus. And *q*
Grizzly Bear did not notice that Wren jumped out of his anus
and *q* Grizzly Bear said, "But just again you did not beat my [125]
strength," said he *q* when Wren spoke behind him. Then *q* he
said, "O Grizzly Bear, what do you mean saying that I am beaten
by you, for I am still alive," said he to him *q*. Then *q* Grizzly
Bear said, "I'll suck you in," said he to him *q*. Then *q* Wren said
to him, "Go on! do suck me in! Then I'll drill inside of you," [130]
said he to him *q*. And so *q* immediately Grizzly Bear opened his
mouth and sucked in Wren. And so *q* as soon as Wren was in
his stomach he drilled with his drill, but *q* he had not been drilling
for a long time before the shredded cedar bark caught fire. Then
q Wren took off his cape and tucked it into the smouldering cedar [135]
bark. Then *q* Wren jumped out of the anus of Grizzly Bear and
q smoke came in sight from the nose of Grizzly Bear and his mouth
and his anus, and *q* Grizzly Bear coughed. "Cough, cough, cough,
cough, Grizzly Bear! Cough, cough, Grizzly Bear!" Then *q* Wren
spoke. Then *q* he said, "Serves you right, Grizzly Bear, serves [140]
you right. Why are you coughing? Although I am a small man
you cannot overcome me. Although you are big I am not afraid
of you. Go on! Keep on coughing! Serves you right!" said
Wren to Grizzly Bear. But *q* he had not been coughing a long
time before Grizzly Bear was dead. And so *q* as soon as Grizzly [145]
Bear was dead Wren went home at once. And so *q* as soon as he
reached the beach of his house he saw *Ō'ᵋmäł* and his younger
brothers sitting on the summer seat on the seaside of his house,
and *q* Wren just went past *Ō'ᵋmäł* and his younger brothers and
went into his house; and *q* *Ō'ᵋmäł* noticed that Wren was not [150]
wearing his cape, for Wren was always wearing his cape. And
so *q* as soon as Wren had gone into his house he spoke. Then *q*
Wren said, "Mother! engage, engage, mother! Engage, engage,
mother! to carry on the back, mother! Verily, he is lying on
his stomach, mother! the dead Grizzly Bear, mother," said *q* [155]
Wren to his mother. Then *q* (his) mother did not believe the words
of Wren. And that was the reason why (his) mother said to him,
"O naughty boy, it would be impossible to be (so) daring. You
would just be taken into the mouth by Grizzly Bear," said *q*
his mother. Then *q* Wren said to his mother, "It is true, mother, [160]
Grizzly Bear is really now dead," said *q* Wren to his mother. Then
q Wren went out of his house and called *Ō'ᵋmäł* and his younger
brothers. And so *q* as soon as they were all inside Wren engaged
them all to go and help him, for he was going to skin the Grizzly
Bear, said he *q*. And so *q* immediately *Ō'ᵋmäł* asked his younger [165]

brothers to go and take their knives in their houses. And so q
at once they went to get their knives. But q it was not long before
they came back. Then q they started. Then they arrived at a
deep canyon. And so q as soon as they had passed it they arrived
170 at the place where Grizzly Bear lay dead. And so q they all skinned
it at once and it was not long before it had been entirely skinned.
Then q they butchered the meat. And so q as soon as all the meat
had been butchered Wren spoke. Then q he said, "You are the
one, Squirrel, whom I want to carry on his back the skin," said
175 he q. Then $\bar{O}'{}^\varepsilon m\ddot{a}\dot{t}$ and his younger brothers said all together,
"No don't, Squirrel is not strong enough to carry it on his back,
for it is (too) heavy, for Squirrel is flabby-handed," they said q.
Then q Wren said again that he wanted Land Otter to carry the
skin. Then q again $\bar{O}'{}^\varepsilon m\ddot{a}\dot{t}$ and his younger brothers all said to-
180 gether, "Don't, Land Otter is not strong enough to carry it on
his back, for it is (too) heavy, for he is very short-legged," they
said q. Then q Wren said again, "Let him, Mink, carry this skin
on his back," said he q. And so q immediately Mink spoke. Then q
he said, "Not I, not I wish it, I am not strong enough. Let $\bar{O}'{}^\varepsilon m\ddot{a}\dot{t}$
185 carry it on his back," said he q and all the younger brothers of
$\bar{O}'{}^\varepsilon m\ddot{a}\dot{t}$ agreed to the words of Mink; and q $\bar{O}'{}^\varepsilon m\ddot{a}\dot{t}$ carried the
skin on his back; and q $\bar{O}'{}^\varepsilon m\ddot{a}\dot{t}$ did not wait for his younger brothers,
and started. His younger brothers came q and started; and so
q as soon as his younger brothers passed the deep canyon they
190 did not see the tracks of $\bar{O}'{}^\varepsilon m\ddot{a}\dot{t}$. And so q his younger brothers
kept right on walking. Then q they arrived at their house. And
so q immediately Wren asked his mother, "Has $\bar{O}'{}^\varepsilon m\ddot{a}\dot{t}$ not arrived?"
said he q. Then q his mother said that $\bar{O}'{}^\varepsilon m\ddot{a}\dot{t}$ had never come
to the house. Then q Wren said that they would all together
195 go to look for their elder brother $\bar{O}'{}^\varepsilon m\ddot{a}\dot{t}$. Then q the six brothers
went all together. And so q as soon as they had almost arrived
at the deep canyon, Mink saw $\bar{O}'{}^\varepsilon m\ddot{a}\dot{t}$ come walking and he carried
nothing on his back. And so q it was he, $\bar{O}'{}^\varepsilon m\ddot{a}\dot{t}$, who was the first
to talk, "I had an accident with the skin I was carrying, I fell
200 into a deep hole in the canyon," said q $\bar{O}'{}^\varepsilon m\ddot{a}\dot{t}$. Then q Deer spoke.
Then q he said, "I guessed already the reason why $\bar{O}'{}^\varepsilon m\ddot{a}\dot{t}$ left us,
when he came carrying the skin on his back, for he wished to eat
it alone, that greedy one," said he q and jumped on his body,
and q the fat of the bear came through on both sides, from his
205 mouth and from his anus; and q $\bar{O}'{}^\varepsilon m\ddot{a}\dot{t}$ became angry on account
of what his younger brothers were doing to him. Then q he said
to Wren, "What you have done to me is good, younger brothers,
for you have done harm to me on account of the bear skin. Now

Q!ēq!āwat, you will be the Wren of future generations; and you,
Deer, will be the deer of future generations; and you, Raccoon, 210
will be the raccoon of future generations; and you, Land Otter,
will be the land otter of future generations; and you, Squirrel,
will be the squirrel of future generations; and you, Mink, will
be the mink of future generations," and q all the younger brothers
of Ō'ᵋmäł became quadrupeds. Only Wren became a wren. And 215
q the five kinds of quadrupeds scattered along the banks of the
river, and so q only the wren at once scratched for food on the
ground. And q Ō'ᵋmäł was alone.

Then q it occurred to him to change his body and become a
young man so that he might not be known to the mother of Q!ēq!awat 220
who was now a wren. And so q as soon as he had finished he
started, Ō'ᵋmäł being a young man and went to the house of
Q!ēq!awat who was now a wren and entered it. And so that was it
q when Ō'ᵋmäł was the first to speak. Then q he said to the mother
of Q!ēq!awat, "Why are you alone in the house?" said he q. And 225
so q Heaven-Maker-Woman, the mother of Wren replied to him
at once. She said q, "Ah, who are you, good man? Where do you
come from? Did you not meet Ō'ᵋmäł and his younger brothers,
for they went to carry on their backs the meat of Grizzly Bear
who was killed by Q!ēq!awat, my child," said she q. Then q Ō'ᵋmäł 230
said that he had never met them, "for I came from the north
side and I knew that you have no husband and that is the reason
why I came to get you for my wife, Heaven-Maker-Woman, that
I may have you for my wife," said he q. And so q immediately
Heaven-Maker-Woman agreed to his words and q they were 235
married. Then q Ō'ᵋmäł asked his wife not to think about her son
and the others. And so that q did his wife, for she never once
thought of her son from the time she had for her husband the
unknown man who however was Ō'ᵋmäł. And q her husband
asked his wife always to steam the meat of the grizzly bear, "for 240
I am always hungry," said he q. And so q that was what his wife
did. It was not long before all the meat was gone. And so q as
soon as all the meat was gone Ō'ᵋmäł, the handsome man, got
ready and said to his wife that he was going hunting in the morning
and q went out of the house. Then Ō'ᵋmäł left his wife after that. 245

That is the end of the story told by K·!ä'maxalas whose father
is a Nimkish and whose mother is a Gwa'waēnoxᵘ.

Ā'dag·ilis

Told by *G·ī'qalas*, a *Gwa'waēnox^u*

Ā'dag·ilis and the wolf were playing q on the ground.   Then
q *Ā'dag·ilis* and the wolf threw each other with quartz at the place
called *Kwăxō'ʿ*.   Then q the wolf became angry with *Ā'dag·ilis*
because he was overdoing it on the ground, playing on the ground
5 with the wolf. He took his death bringer and swung it at *Ā'dag·ilis*.
And so q for a short time *Ā'dag·ilis* was dead. Then he was revived
by the ermine. Then q *Ā'dag·ilis* was helped by the ermine. He
was given the cause of being alive a long time by the ermine.
Then q the wolf did not q keep ready. His wolf tail was pulled
10 out q. Then q it was hidden by *Ā'dag·ilis*. Then the wolf asked
him for his wolf tail. "I will show you a good way for salmon.
You will not eat the death bringing jaw[1] of the salmon." Then
q he was answered by *Ā'dag·ilis*, "We'll continue not to understand your words. But we shall know that this your wolf tail will
15 go. You will not hurt our later generations." — "I shall bring to
life every now and then those who will purify themselves among
those who will take your places. Now you will call me wolf." —
"Now we have finished and so I shall not eat the death bringer
jaw with which the salmon lie on logs." Then q a crying sound
20 was heard. And so that q was the speech which he tried to give
to you, "Ha, ha, ha. Your teeth keep on eating the death bringing
jaw of the salmon."

The Wolf.

Told by *G·ī'qalas*, a *Gwa'waēnox^u*

The wolf *(G·īlā'lalit)* q invited all the animals. The animals were
going to have a winter dance together, the wolf, wolverene, black
bear. They had for their chief q the woodman. Now they had
a winter dance together in the inside of a rock. The place q is a
5 large cave. They had for their drum a wonderful thing. The drum
q is just seen. It is the root q of a cedar. And so q they were dancing.
Quartz q was the plaything of the wolf. Then q they danced the
war dance. The wolverene q danced the war dance. Then q they
had for their secrets q little birds which were their supernatural
10 treasures. Then q the woodman showed his strength as a man.
He took the double-headed serpent and put the double-headed

---

[1] i. e. the lower jaw.

serpent on as a belt. The chief came *q* and spoke about the ways
of the other men. He struck at their character as a tribe. "Let us
stay this way and do not let us assemble. Let us just scatter over
this world. What shall we do with our sacred room? Do not in [15]
vain say this shall be the story of this place, wantonly left behind
in our country. This will be the story of those who will take our
place."

Mink[1].

Told by *G·ī'qalas*, a *Gwa'waēnox^u*

Mink was taking care of his salmon weir. Then *q* his salmon [1]
weir was finished. Then *q* it was asked, "What is your catch,
salmon weir?" — "For what little thing should it be? a little
bullhead." — "Yä, throw it into the water!" And he said again,
"What is your catch, salmon weir?" — Now the salmon weir [5]
replied, "A little flounder." (Then in succession a kelpfish, dogfish
red cod, *q!wä'k·ela*, spring salmon, steelhead salmon, dog salmon,
silver salmon, trout, *k·!āma* [a very small fish]; a little double-
headed serpent). "That is it!"
He cut it open. Then *q* mink sent an invitation and all the animals [10]
came in, the wolves, black bears, wolverenes. Then he danced
with his song:

> Mink wears on his head the hat of the
> dead princes of the wolves, yahä.

The sparrow came *q* and danced: [15]

> Our friend carries one in each hand, the sparrow.

The robin came *q* and danced:

> Ahäi, ahä, let our friend robin dance a little more, ahäi, ahä.

The raccoon came *q*:

> The little one has a mark across the eyes, [20]
> ahaha, ahahä, ā ahä, ā ahä.

The *(gaō'x^usē)* came:

> He tries to cure me; curing the nose. You came
> trying to cure me.
> There is now no cause of fear curing the anus. [25]

Mink and the Ghosts[2]

(Recorded by George Hunt)

Mink lived *q* at Crooked Beach *(Qā'logwis)*. On his part *q Ā'Lēk·e-
lels*, the chief of the *Hō'sdalag·imux^u* and the *Lā'laēnox^u*, lived

---

[1] See S 149; M 538; X 103; CX 57; Comox S 75; Seshelt, Journal Royal
Anthrop. Society of Great Britain and Ireland, 34:57; Squamish, Report
British Association for the Advancement of Science, 1900:543.

[2] Compare S 159, no. 8; X 113.

3

at the place which has the name Stench Beach (*ᵋya′ x·p!ōsdēsᴇla*)
to the north of Crooked Beach. Then *q* Mink always went every
5 night to steal sea eggs at the houses of the *Hō′sdalag·imuₓᵘ* and
the *Lā′laēnoxᵘ* for only that was their food, sea eggs. And Mink
also liked very much just to break (eat) all the time sea eggs, for
that was the real food of Mink, the sun-maker. Then *q* for a long
time Mink had been doing that; he stole sea eggs every night, and
10 *q* the many tribes, the *Hō′sdalag·imuₓᵘ* and the *Lā′laēnoxᵘ*, did
not know about the stealing of the sea eggs every night. Then
q the chief *Ā′ʟēk·ᴇlᴇls* spoke to his tribe and *q* he said that four
young men should watch every night for the one who would come
to steal the sea eggs from the house, for it was really light, for
15 it was full moon, and so *q* it was past midnight when Mink came
paddling along close to the beach. He came quietly *q* as he came
to the beach. Then *q* he stepped out of his small canoe carrying
in one hand a basket. He came *q* quietly coming up the beach
and now the four young men were just hiding on the ground,
20 and so *q* Mink did not see them as he went past them. Then *q*
he went into the house of *Ā′ʟēk·ᴇlᴇls*; and so, as soon as Mink
had gone into the house the four young men started and barred
the door of the house of *Ā′ʟēk·ᴇlᴇls*, and now *q* Mink was locked
in the house and so *q* two young men were watching the door.
25 Then *q* two went to the beach where the small canoe of Mink
was left and broke it up; and after they had finished breaking
the small canoe they came up the beach and sat on the ground
at the rear door of the house and *q* they were watching in case
Mink should go through there. And so *q* day came in the morning
30 when the four young men opened the door of the house of their
chief *Ā′ʟēk·ᴇlᴇls* and went in. Then *q* they awakened their chief
and *q* they told him that they had locked in the one who used to
steal the sea eggs, Mink. Then *q* the chief said that the whole
tribe should go into his house, and so the four young men called
35 all the men aloud saying, "We are calling on behalf of our chief
Ā′ʟēk·ᴇlᴇls, that each of us may strike Mink who is locked up
here in the house of *Ā′ʟēk·ᴇlᴇls*," said they *q*. And so immediately
q all the men went into the house, and so *q* as soon as they had
all gone in, the door of the house was barred. Then *q* in vain
40 Mink was searched for. He was never found *q*, and so *q* all the
men just went out of the house. And so *q* they had just all gone out
of the house when someone said at the other end of the village,
"Ah! In vain you went into this house of *Atsetsᴇyîlts¹*. Ah, you

------

¹ Mink's pronunciation. He speaks like a child.

cannot catch me," said Mink. And so *q* immediately all the
men launched their war canoes and started paddling, going to the [45]
place where he called. Then *q* the warriors saw Mink running
among the rocks that were rolled together at the foot of the high,
steep rock. Then *q* Mink had no time to go to the end when one
of the canoes reached the place where he was. Then *q* Mink went
under the rocks that were rolled together. The men *q* went out [50]
of the canoes carrying sharp poles to go and stick them under
the place where Mink was. Then *q* Mink saw a starfish sticking
on a rock where he was hiding. Then *q* he took the starfish and
cut it open. Then *q* he took its guts and put them at the end of
a pole. Then *q* the man pulled out the pole. Then *q* he saw the [55]
guts at the end of his pole. Then *q* the man said, "Now Mink
is dead. Look at the guts here which came sticking at the end of
what I used to spear him with," said he. And so *q* immediately
all the warriors went home, and so *q* the warriors nearly arrived
at the beach of their houses when *q* Mink came out of his hiding [60]
place. Then *q* he stood on the rock and cried aloud saying to the
warriors, "O warriors, those are the guts of the starfish which
you got in war. I am still Mink," said he as he ran along the rocks
and went to one end of the high cliff, and Mink *q* had saved himself
after that, and he went home to his house. And so *q* the warriors [65]
went back in vain to where Mink had been standing on the rock
and they searched for him in vain, and so *q* they all just went
home to their houses and that was the time when Mink had gone
out of the rear door of the house when he heard the sound of the
breaking up of his small canoe, and that is the end.   [70]

The Origin of the *Xwē'xwe* Dance.

Told by *Yā'qoɭas*

Wä'qē^ɛ was paddling about near *X̌ŭlk^u*. He went up northward
until he came to *K!wä'nē^ɛ*. There he went ashore, unloaded his
canoe and stayed there for a long time. He built a small house
there. One evening when he was sitting in the house he heard
a rumbling noise and the talking of people. Then he purified [5]
himself because he thought that this was something supernatural.
He heard it again and he went on to look for it. He came to *Ȧx̌^udɛ'm*
and saw a house. Sparks were flying out through the roof. The
noise came from this house. Suddenly it stopped and he heard
people talking. He looked through a knot hole and saw the *Xwē'xwe* [10]
dancing. When a certain word was pronounced in the song they
fell down and were transformed into red cod. Their tails struck

3*

the ground and made the noise. They must have been secular because they did not notice when a stranger approached them. ¹⁵ For four nights he went to look at their dance. Then he thought, "I am going in to see what they are doing." He went in. Nobody took notice of him. Then he stood up and said, "I have obtained you as my supernatural treasure. I want you for my supernatural dance." They agreed. The following is their song which is in a ²⁰ foreign language:

Hayamēnä yeheheya yeheheya nōgwa^εm
hayamēnä yeheheya yeheheya memeqeya yeheya

Note: According to the Fort Rupert people the *Xwē'xwe* dance came from Comox.

Told by *Lā'bit* in 1912.

Wä'qē^ε was living *q* at *X̌ŭlk^u*. Then *q* he wished to paddle at sea to Trail-ahead-of-inlet *(Ts!ē'qŭmē^ε)* and to see the place where *Q!ā'neqe^εlak^u* had come down. And so *q* he started paddling in the morning. And so *q* it was evening when he came at Whale ⁵ Beach *(Ĝwē'gwak·awa^εlis)* and he hauled up his canoe. Then *q* he built a house. And so *q* as soon as he had finished building his house he went *q* in and built a fire when it was getting dark. Then *q* he ate after his arrival. And so as soon as he had finished *Wä'qē^ε* lay down and tried to sleep. Then *q* he could not go to ¹⁰ sleep, for something was troubling him with troubles. And so *q* it was late at night when he was startled by a rumbling sound that was heard by him. Then *q* the floor of his house was shaking as in an earthquake. But *q* it did not last long before it became quiet. Then *q* he heard the rumbling sound; then *q* the floor ¹⁵ of his house shook again. Then *q* it was that way four times. Then *q Wä'qē^ε q* arose, went out of his house and sat down on the ground in front of his house. Then *q* he heard a sound of many people talking at *Ăx^udɛ'm* on the north side of his house. Then *q Wä'qē^ε* went into his house and lay down on his bed. And ²⁰ *q* he heard plainly the sound of many people talking. Then *q* he went to sleep. Then *q* he dreamt of a man who came into his house and said to him, "Don't sleep, friend, but go and purify yourself and wash with hemlock branches in this river and try to get tomorrow night what was heard by you. You will go again ²⁵ into the water in this river when daylight will first come in the morning; and so, as soon as it gets dark you will go and sit down on the ground inland from *Ăx^udɛ'm;* and so, as soon as the ground has quaked four times go into the winter ceremonial house and sit down at the right hand side inside the door. Don't be afraid," said the man as he went out. And so q immediately $Wä'qē^ɛ$ arose [30] and went to the river and broke off hemlock branches and sat down in the water in the river and rubbed his body with hemlock branches. And so q as soon as he finished he went into his house and went to sleep. And so q as soon as daylight came in the morning he went to the river and was sitting in the water while he was [35] rubbing his body with hemlock branches. And so q as soon as he had done so he entered his house and lay down on his bed and went to sleep when it was daylight. Then q he dreamt of a man who came into his house. Then q the man spoke to him. Then q he said, "I come again, friend $Wä'qē^ɛ$ to tell you that [40] there is no reason to fear us; and just go right into our winter ceremonial house tonight, when the fire in the middle of the house is not (yet) built, and sit down at the right hand side of the door; for you have really succeeded in purifying yourself immediately when I told you last night to go and sit in this river and to rub [45] your body with hemlock branches," said the man as he went out of the house. And $Wä'qē^ɛ$ never ate that day. And so, as soon as it was evening he went into the river and sat in the water and rubbed his body with hemlock branches. And so, as soon as he had finished he started to go to $Äx^udɛ'm$. And so, as soon as [50] he had arrived at the cleared ground he sat down among the bushes. And so q he had not been sitting there very long before it came to be dark. Then q $Wä'qē^ɛ$ saw a large house built on the ground seaward from him, and there was no fire on the floor. Then q $Wä'qē^ɛ$ arose from the ground at the place where he was [55] sitting on the ground and went into the doorway of the house and he sat down on the right hand side inside the door. And q $Wä'qē^ɛ$ did not hear one man walking about in the house. Then q he saw glowing coals. Then q (the fire) blazed up in the middle of the house. Then came q many men and women walking in; [60] and q the men sat down in the rear of the house, and the women sat down on the sides of the house. And so q as soon as all had sat down on the floor a man came in and stood on the floor in the rear of the house. He was q the speaker of the house. Then q he spoke. Then q he said, "We have all come in, supernatural [65] ones, now take care when the supernatural power comes to you, women, for I'll call it," said he q as he sang the sacred song which said:

$^ɛā$ $^ɛā$ $hā$ $^ɛā$ $^ɛā$ $hā$ [70]

Magic spirit,

$^ɛā$ $^ɛā$ $hā$ $^ɛā$ $^ɛā$ $hā$

Magic spirit,

said he as he ran around the fire in the middle of the house reaching
the place from which he had come. Then all the women became
75 red codfish and kicked about. That made the rumbling noise
all over the ground. But it was not very long before they turned
again into women, those who had been red codfish. Then the
speaker of the house sang his sacred song again, the same again
as he had sung first. And so, as soon as it was again ended, the
80 women turned into red codfish and kicked about. Then he
had done so four times, when four men came into the door of the
house, on their faces *xwē'xwe* masks. They had long tongues and
eyes standing out of the *xwē'xwe* masks. And four times they
went around the fire in the middle of the house walking with quick
85 steps, and those who were now red cod women just kept on kicking
about while the four *xwę̄'xwe* went with quick steps around the
fire in the middle of the house. And so, as soon as they had gone
around four times the song leaders sang their songs, which said:

Hāᵉyamena ye ne he ya ye he hê yā hāᵉyamena
90 *ye he he yā ye he he ya ye he ya he he*
Hāᵉyamena ye he he ya he I am *hāᵉyamena*
ye he he ya ye he he ya he I am *hāᵉyamena*

And *q* the four *xwē'xwe* danced carrying in each hand the scallop
shells strung on a ring of cedar withes. And so *q* as soon as the
95 song was at an end the song leaders sang again one song which
said:

Go away, ugly ones, go away ugly ones, *ha ha ha ha haa*
Ha, ugly ones with lolling tongues, ugly ones with
lolling tongues *ha ha ha ha haa*
100 *Ha*, ugly ones with protruding eyes, ugly ones with
protruding eyes *ha ha ha ha haa*.

And *q* the *xwē'xwe* danced around the fire in the middle of the
house and they danced out of the door. And *q* the singing stopped
after this and *q* all the red codfish turned into women again in
105 the house and they sat down on the floor. Then *q* the speaker
of the house spoke. Then *q* he said, "O friends, now you have
done well for this one who came here to sit among us, our great
friend *Wä'qēᵉ*. Now you have obtained as supernatural treasure
this great ceremonial, the *xwē'xwe*, for I am the Red Cod and this
110 is my house which has black sealions as the carvings of the
four posts. Now you will have the name *Wä'qēᵉ*, friend. What
are you going to do with this house? Do you wish it to remain
here or do you wish to go to *X̣ŭlkᵘ* where you come from?" said
he. Then *Wä'qēᵉ* said to him, "Thank you, friends, I really got
115 a supernatural treasure. In the past could not be seen the great

ceremonial, the *xwē'xwe* and this winter ceremonial house, for I wish this house to be on the ground of my village site *X̣ŭlkᵘ*," said *Wä'qēᵋ*. Then said the speaker of the house, "Now go, friend *Wä'qēᵋ*. Go home tomorrow morning. I and my tribe will follow you after four days. Your house will be taken and put up where [120] you wish the house to be put on the ground in the night when I arrive. And so, as soon as the house will be finished I will tell you, and go at once and call your tribe that all may go into this house to sit down on both lower sides of the house in this manner and I will sit at the upper end of the house, and you will stand [125]

REDFISH SEAT

PEOPLE SEAT

at the place where I stand in the rear of the house when you sing my sacred song for calling (the spirits), for you will not see me and my tribe, for we shall be invisible when we come," said he. Then *Wä'qēᵋ* said, "Now I will go home in the morning and I shall be [130] expecting you. Thank you for your words, friend," said he as the fire in the middle of the house disappeared. Then all the men and women and the house disappeared. *Wä'qēᵋ* just went back to his house and slept a little while. And so, as soon as it got daylight in the morning he started by canoe and. so *q* [135] it was not yet evening when he arrived at *X̣ŭlkᵘ*, and so *q* he went right into his house and lay down on his bed. Now he was lying down for four days. And so, as soon as he had stayed in the house four days he arose early in the morning to invite his whole tribe with women and children to go and eat breakfast in his house. [140] And so, as soon as they had all come in, *Wä'qēᵋ* gave them food, and so, as soon as they had finished eating *Wä'qēᵋ* spoke. Then he said, "Welcome, tribe, and all of you listen to what will be my word to you, for I wish all of you to go into the water of this river today. Don't ask me what I mean, just guess it," said he. [145] And so *q* immediately his whole tribe went out of the house and went into the water in the river while *Wä'qēᵋ* also went into the water in the river and rubbed his body with hemlock branches. And *q* his tribe guessed that he had obtained a supernatural treasure where he had been. And so *q*, as soon as the whole tribe [150] had washed themselves *Wä'qēᵋ* said to his tribe, "O tribe! now you are ready for what I am expecting tonight. Take care and stand up right away when I call you; and that, do not be afraid of what will be heard by you, tribe," said *Wä'qēᵋ* to his tribe. And so, as soon as it was evening the whole tribe was ready, [155] and so as soon as it was dark in the night *Wä'qēᵋ* heard whispering which said, "Come, friend *Wä'qēᵋ*, and go into your house," said it. And so immediately *Wä'qēᵋ* followed what was only heard

walking; for he did not see a person. They went into the house
[160] and there were only glowing coals in the fire in the middle of the
house. Then the noise of talking asked *Wä'qēᵉ* to invite his tribe, that
all should come in. And so, immediately *Wä'qēᵉ* invited his tribe.
And so all came in and sat down on the floor at the lower sides of
both sides of the house. Then *Wä'qēᵉ* stood up in the rear of the
[165] house. Then he said to his tribe, "Now come, tribe, and look
at my supernatural treasure," said he as he sang the sacred song
of the speaker of the house. And so, as soon as the sacred song
was ended, there was a rumbling sound on both sides of the house
and the floor was shaking. But it was not very long before the
[170] rumbling sound stopped. Then also the shaking of the floor became
quiet. Then it was a while before *Wä'qēᵉ* sang again the sacred
song. And so, as soon as the sacred song was at an end there
was again a rumbling sound and the floor was shaking as in an
earthquake. Three times it did so. But that was now the fourth
[175] time when the four *xwē'xwe* masks came. Their song was sung
by the invisible ones and the four *xwē'xwe* danced. And so, as
soon as the song was ended their other song was sung. Then the
four ·*xwē'xwe* danced again and danced into the bedroom. Now
they finished. And *Wä'qēᵉ* spoke. Then he said, "O tribe, now
[180] you have seen the supernatural treasure which I received from
the Red Cod and the great winter ceremonial house with the carved
posts which are black sealions (which are pictured on page 379,
Figure 20, the four posts of the house and the four *xwē'xwe*[1]),"
said he as he went into the bedroom. And he saw the four *xwē'xwe*
[185] masks and four large drums and also four notched round cedar
poles, one fathom long, (in this way:
these are sawed along the tops of the
drums for making the rumbling sound
of the floor); and that, the four scallop
[190] shells strung on a ring of cedar withes which are carried by the
xwē'xwe when they are dancing. These were put into the room, for
there is no food and property that was obtained as a treasure by
Wä'qēᵉ from the Red Cod. That is the reason why it is said that
the red codfish are stingy. And that is the end.

ʟ!ā'lamin.

Told by *G·ī'qalas*, a *Gwa'waēnoxᵘ*

A house *q* was built on top for ʟ!ā'lamin. He was a slave at the
lake of *G·ᴇyō'x̣ᵘ*. And so *q* all were just fed by his master. He did

---

[1] M 379.

not want *q* to be a slave again. Behold! ʟ!*ā'lamin* finished going
to do thus, that ʟ!*ā'lamin*. For three years he was in the house,
then he was taken out by his master. Then *q* ʟ!*ā'lamin* went [5]
up the river. He saw his master. He tried to believe that he
really left him. Then *q* he believed he was left. He launched
the canoe and loaded it while his master was lying on his back
on the ground. Then he carried across his carvings. Then he stole
everything. He took everything that was in the boxes. Now they [10]
are the privileges of the Nimkish obtained by the running away
of ʟ!*ā'lamin*. And so *q* the boxes just became stone, left when
they were taken by ʟ!*ā'lamin*.

Origin Story of the *G·ī'g·ĭlgăm*, Nimkish[1]
Written by Dan Cranmer

A salmon was named *X̱wā'x̱was*. Now he swam up in the river
to *Gwa'nā'lalis* and he tried to go up the beach at *Ōdzâ'ᵋlas* and he
became a man. He was the only one on the ground before the deluge.
Long ago the deluge came and he went back to his former shape
when he was a salmon. Now the flood stopped at the mountain [5]
inland at (the place) to which the sea went. The sea went down
and he came back to *Ōdzâ'ᵋlas*. He became a man again. And
so, it is said, long ago he built a house at *Ōdzâ'ᵋlas*, a thick beam.
He had for his tool, it is said, this, like this adze. Now he was adzing his beam. "Now he was going to put into the ground his posts. [10]
(He made) the beam. Now his beam was finished. It is said, a large
bird, the Thunderbird came and sat on a rock, or a stone that has
now the name Thunderbird Place. Then *q* he spoke to the Thunderbird, "Oh, indeed, supernatural spirit, I have you for a treasure, for
this has been worked on by me in vain." Then *q* replied the Thunder- [15]
bird. He lifted his Thunderbird mask and spoke. He said, "This is
the reason of my coming, to help you. I pity the way you are." Then
he soared and alighted on the beam and took it up in his talons from
the ground and put it on what was already on the ground. He came
down *q* and took off his Thunderbird dress. Then *q* he spoke to him, [20]
advising him, "You will not often speak. That will only be the time
when you make a noise moving whenever I reach my descendants."
Now he made his Thunderbird dress fly away and it returned to
where it came from above. Then he asked *X̱wā'x̱was*, "Go on, point out
the place for my house, brother. Where shall be my place ?" This will [25]
be my place down river, brother, for you came later to be a man in the

---

[1] S 147; C 83, 471, 472.

world." Then he made a house below that of $\underaccent{.}{X}w\bar{a}'\underaccent{.}{x}was$. Now he was his younger brother for he came later to be a man in the world. Therefore their name is $G\cdot\bar{\imath}'g\cdot\hat{\imath}lg\breve{a}m$ on account of $Kun\bar{o}'sila$ who came down.

Origin Story of the $Ts!\bar{e}ts!\bar{e}l^{\varepsilon}w\bar{a}lag\breve{a}m\bar{e}^{\varepsilon}$

Our Lord, Coming-Right-Down-River came and arrived at $Gwa^{\varepsilon}n\bar{a}'lalis$. It is said he asked him, "What do you wish to be? Do you not wish to be a mountain?" — "O, then everything might always roll off from me." — Would you like to be a large hard
5 stone lying on the beach?" — "O, then I might break in two in future times when there would be light in this world." — "Go on be a river which will never stop in future times when light comes into the world." — "Let me be a river." Then it is said he was pushed down on the beach and became a river. Then he was told, "You will be
10 the place to which salmon will come. Then $Gwa^{\varepsilon}n\bar{a}'lalis$ became a river, therefore it has the name $Gwa'^{\varepsilon}n\bar{e}$.

And so the deluge came and that was the time when a man came up from the sea on the edge of the sea monster $^{\varepsilon}n_Emxx\cdot a'lig\cdot iyu$. He had the name Only-One-Coming-Up who came up who came
15 out of the sea coming from the seamonster from below. Now he had $\underaccent{.}{X}\breve{u}lk^u$ as his country, the country of $Gwa^{\varepsilon}n\bar{a}'lalis$. Now Only-One-Coming-Up had a child, Mountain. Then Mountain came to have a child $Ts!\bar{e}l^{\varepsilon}walag\breve{a}m\bar{e}^{\varepsilon}$. Now he started. He did not know the way he went in this country. Now he obtained a supernatural treasure.
20 And it came down it is said spoke a wise man, the one who takes care of the Nimkish that he should go ahead and imitate the mythical animals beating time and dancing. And that he should invite to his place wherever it might be and that he should come and go there again. It is said he danced the whole night. Then it is said
25 the wise man worried. It is said he sent two supernatural ones to go out of the house to the seaside to try to listen to what was expected to be heard when they beat time. Then it is said the supernatural ones came in again and one man spoke and said, "Let us just give up I have not heard anything." Then it is said spoke the one who
30 went along and he said it is said, "I hear very indistinctly" and so it is said day almost came and it is said the wise man worried, the one who took care of the Nimkish. Then he said, they should invite him even without knowing his place wherever it might be." Then he invited his tribe and they all said together, "O, you are coming, super-
35 natural one, all around the world. Four times they sang. Then it came and approached the sound of the Nimkish according to the way of calling of the wise man. Now they finished what they were doing

in the house. Four times they sang. Then came the sound of
wolves. They were many it is said came and brought down the one
who had gone astray a long time. Now a large wolf was seen. It was [40]
coming up on the beach. It is said the canoes were launched. Four
planks were laid on four canoes tied together. Then they were going
to take him. Now the Nimkish went aboard the four canoes which
were tied together. They were going to take what was seen by them.
Now they were at sea at the place where the large wolf had first been. [45]
When they were in front of it the body of the great wolf squeaked.
Then the wise man went out of the canoe to question him. "What
is your supernatural treasure?" Then the supernatural one said, "My
treasure reaches from end to end of the world. My treasure reaches up
to the sky. My treasure is famous, the wolf treasure." Now he had the [50]
name *Ts!ēts!ēl*ᵉ*wālagămē*ᵉ. Then he was asked by the wise man. Now
go on and ask how you are to act. Then he howled four times. When he
howled then it is said he was answered by howling by the Kayoquath.
Then it is said he howled again. Then he was answered by the Bella
Coola. Then his song was sung. They were four lines long. In this way [55]
the song of the Nimkish came to be known in our times.

Story of the $^{\varepsilon}n\bar{e}'{}^{\varepsilon}n_Elk\cdot!\bar{e}nox^{u}$[1]
Written by Dan Cranmer

He came to be a man in the world and had the name Unattainable
(*Wāwigustâlag·ilitsogwi*ᵉ*lakē*). It is said he poled up the river with
his family and went to look for salmon at $^{\varepsilon}n\bar{e}'{}^{\varepsilon}n_Elg\cdot as$. Then one
child among the other children went to play with him giving each
other some things. Then it is said they finished playing. He went [5]
home to his house. Late at night he was hungry. Therefore, he
awakened his parents and asked for food. He was only scolded by
his parents. "Just pick up something from the floor and be fed.
I am not in favor of what is being learned by you." Then he just
helped himself and he was fed. He put a stone on the fire for [10]
roasting his food. It is said the stones became hot, then he took
them off. He cleaned them so that the ashes came off, then he
poured the salmon roe on it. Then it is said it burst. Now it burst
on his face and his body. Now it hurt. He was only ridiculed by
his parents. Then the child just lay down and he did not eat for [15]
four days. He lay down and he did not eat. Then his parents
became worried on account of the time he had not eaten. Then he
dressed himself. He wore a sewed blanket and ear drops of abalone
shell. The child never ate when they tried to give him food. Night

---

[1] S 151; C 97.

20 came again, he arose and went bathing. At once his face and his
body became good. He bathed twice that evening, then he started.
Now he was going to kill himself. He went inland walking along
the bank of the river. He bathed again and hung one blanket on
the ground. Then he went inland. Again he bathed and put on the
25 ground his other blanket. Then he started again. He went far
and again he bathed and he hung on the ground his abalone shell
of one side. He started and went inland and bathed again. Now
he hung on the ground his other abalone shell. He went inland and
came to the foot of a large mountain. Then he bathed again in the
30 water running down the mountain. As soon as he finished bathing
something came flying in front of him that was like a bird. Now
it is said he felt different; he just bathed again. As soon as he had
finished, the one that was flying in front of him flew down. Now
it carried him from the ground and went up the mountain. Four
35 times he was taken up. Then he took him to the top of the mountain.
Now he knew that he flew. He went just as it pleased him to go.
Then he said he wished to be able to go round viewing the tops of the
mountains. Then, it is said, he thought his way was not good, since
he had no wings. Then it is said he went down river where he had
40 got (the power of flying) before. Now his body was that of a bird,
but his face was the face of a man. For four days he walked to his
former place down the river. For four days he went and he came
back to the place from which he had come. It is said that he landed
here at this river of the Nimkish. He came flying along, soaring with
45 his wings. He was seen by the Nimkish who were fishing in the
river. Then he sat down on top of a tree. Then he spoke, sitting
on top of the tree. He sang his sacred song. He sang. The Nimkish
just fled when they heard the bird singing. Now they were afraid
of the bird singing. Then, it is said, he landed at the place where
50 he started from when he went to kill himself. He came sitting on
top. His friend came walking along. In vain he looked for his
tracks. In vain he searched. Then the one who sat on top spoke,
he said, "Is it you?" In vain his friend looked on the ground to
discover him there. Then he lifted his face, what should it be?
55 There a bird was sitting on top of a tree and only his face was a
man's face. At once he spoke to his friend, he said, "Let me know
right away about our parents, — "O, my dear." said his friend when
he replied to him, "What about our parents? Am I now really a
man? Indeed, my dear, I only come every now and then, that
60 I may know what may happen, whether it may get bad. I always
come to be fed in the way you are at your place. Go tell our
parents, I am your brother, I have come home. Now you will ask

them to go on and purify themselves, only let them pull their
heads into the water, if they should not be strong enough." At once
his friend ran and went to tell his parents. He said, "Slaves, do not 65
stay thus in the house. Our Lord has come. He has come home."
Then it is said they pulled their heads under water in the river and
purified themselves. At once the old people began to be strong and
they themselves took hemlock branches and rubbed their bodies.
Now it is said the friend of the one who was now supernatural went 70
back and went to talk with his friend. Now it is said he flew. He
said to his friend, "Go to our parents and they shall give a winter
dance in our village. A house shall be built and then I shall arrive."
Then it is said his friend told his parents. At once they gave a
winter dance. Then he discovered his child flying along. "Slave, 75
look at our child here. He is flying along." Then it is said his hands
were trembling in the dance. "Stop now doing so, else he might
upset in this river. You will do so for a long time." Then it is said
he arrived at his village site. At once it is said he put up his house.
His tribe was surprised when they began to be strong. Then it is 80
said they gathered boards which were just scattered. Then it is
said he was to be held by his tribe to be played with. The child of
our chief came here, coming back. Then his father's house was
finished on the ground. Then it is said night came. Now it was
late at night for a long time. Then he came and the supernatural 85
one spoke flying along. Now he was near the end of the village.
The tribe awoke at once when they heard the sound, as he came
and made a noise. "Slaves", said all the men. At once it is said
all the men and women and children arose at night and all went
into the water. They bathed and purified themselves. Then in the 90
morning they saw him coming sitting inland of the village. At
once they tried to catch him but he just flew up. On the next day
they tried to snare him, every time he just stepped out of the
snare. Now, however, what he had planned with his friend was
going to be finished. He advised him what to do when they were 95
going to try to get him. It was late when he came making a noise,
flying along near the end of the village. At once the tribe awoke.
"He has come, slave," said all the men. At night they arose and
all went into the water to bathe, all with their wives and children.
Then in the morning he was seen sitting inland from the village. 100
At once they tried to take him. He only flew away going up. On
the next day they tried to snare him but every time he stepped out
of the snare. Now, however, he was going to finish what he had
planned with his friend. He advised him what to do. Then he went
to the house of his father. Then his friend sat on the roof and 105

snared him. The boards were ready below in the house. They were
to be the *mā'dɛm* boards. Then his friend was at the side of the
mā'dɛm. Now it was pushed into the ground. Then it was said
he had a sacred room. He was always watched. He was tied every
110 time he went to sleep, for they were afraid that he might walk off
again. Now summer came. Then it is said he would take care of
him and they finished tying him in the house. Then he himself
took off the dress he had, the bird dress of his body. Then he put
down his dress. Now they finished tying him in the house. Now
115 he became a human being as we are. It came to be summer and
(the upper edge of the sky) came to be fall. Then he tried to paddle
down with his friends. They launched a good, new canoe. His
mother came carrying a new mat and spread it aboard the canoe.
Then they poled. They had not gone far seaward when the small
120 canoe capsized on a small shallow place. Then it is said his friends
tried to look for him. He was never found. He had disappeared
again. It was not long, however; after three months he came back.
Then his tribe worried that he might feel down-cast and do so again.
Then it is said they were playing quoits behind the houses. He
125 came it is said he came out of the ground and the earth moved
greatly. He came it is said out of the ground different on account
of his treasure. At once it is said he was pushed into the ground.
It was not long before he became secular. All his treasures went
back.

The Story of *Ō'xsɛm*[1]

Written by Dan Cranmer.

Ō'xsɛm had for his father *Nɛɡ·ä'*. His mother was an *A'ᵋwa.iₗɛla*
woman. He had a cousin *Yäkwil* who was the child of *Q!ǔ'mx·ɛ-
laɡ·ilis*. Now *Nɛɡ·ä'* owned a copper and *Yäkwil* talked about
the copper of *Nɛɡ·ä'*. Behold! he finished his plan as to what
5 to do. Then he sent a messenger to the *A'ᵋwa.iₗɛla* to help in
killing. *Yäkwil* sent a message that *Ō'xsɛm* should come with
his father and uncles that they should come to *Ōdzâ'ᵋlas*. *Ō'xsɛm*
came with his father and uncles drifting down the stream, and
they came to *Xǔlkᵘ*. He came with his copper. Then *Ō'xsɛm* had
10 a woman relative, one of the wives of *Yäkwil*, and so she told
him that he would be killed on account of his copper. As soon
as he landed the woman went down to the beach to go and tell
Ō'xsɛm that he should just go quickly and go back. His father and
uncle just went up the beach. Then the woman untied the painter

---

[1] C 85, 473; S 150.

of the canoe, said good-bye to *Ō'xsɛm* and he went back. Then [15]
Ō'xsɛm poled and went across to the other side, jumped out of
the canoe and ran up the river and was about to arrive at *Ōdzâ' ᵉlas*.
Then it is said he heard about his father and uncles, that they
had been killed. They tried to pursue him. Then *Ō'xsɛm* carried
on his back the copper wrapped up. He was being pursued. How- [20]
ever, he was never overtaken, for he was very swift. His hair
was long. It almost touched the ground. His hair was blond,
therefore he was called *Ō'xsɛm* but his real name was *Lalā'k·înis*.
He went up river and arrived at *Ōdzâ' ᵉlas* and so his copper slipped
out of his pack. He did not know where it slipped out as he was [25]
walking with his copper. Then he arrived at *Ōdzâ' ᵉlas*. "What
should it be, my dear ones ? My fathers and uncles were killed.
Get ready and let us escape!" Then his mothers and aunts gathered
up their valuables and started. "Your younger brother is fishing
below." Then *Ō'xsɛm* ran down river. What should it be ? His [30]
younger brother was floating about on the water. He took him
by the feet and threw him over the shoulders. Then he ran up.
He had not gone very far when he began to cry and he came to
life again. And he arrived at *K·ak·atîdɛq*. Then he made a raft
of driftwood tied together, and went across, for there were four [35]
of them. He almost arrived at *ᵉmɛgŭnō'ts!ɛxsdēᵉ* when the weather
got foggy and the fog lifted from the water. Then he was seen by
the warriors. "That is *Ō'xsɛm*," said the warriors. Then the friends
of *Ō'xsɛm* in the canoe said, "It is a seal. Look it rushed into the
water. Look it is a cormorant sitting on a rock." Then *Ō'xsɛm* arrived [40]
at *ᵉmɛgŭnō'ts!ɛxsdēᵉ*. He was going to go into the inlet. What should
it be ? There were parts of wrecked canoes. There were three in all.
He gathered them and sewed them. He also found the wing of an
eagle. Now he made a drill for the canoe of that wing bone. He took
cedar withes and twisted them for sewing. Then he repaired the [45]
canoe by sewing. He caulked it. Then he also found three paddles.
Then he also made a bailer. Now he launched the canoe and
paddled. His younger brother steered the canoe with thin boards.
They paddled very quickly. They paddled and travelled at night.
Then they arrived at *Tā'yaǥoƚ*, the village of his relatives on his [50]
mother's side. When day nearly came, he knocked at the door
of the house of his uncle. His uncle opened for him and gave him
to eat. Then his uncle said to his men, namely his warriors, to
see to it what to do to give them something. Then *Qoƚqaxᵘsto*
gave him his club of solid stone. "Go on and see what you are [55]
going to do with it." Then he clubbed one man in the house
and the man died at once. Then *K·ēk·ɛlax·stōƚ* also gave him his

stone club and he clubbed another man in the house. That is
what he will do with it. The men had only time to hide when the
⁶⁰ warriors came ashore. The men quickly went into hiding. Then
Ō'xsɛm hid in the corner of the house when they came in. The
uncle of *Ō'xsɛm* invited the warriors when they arrived. Then
they put much wood on the fire. The men just slept in the house,
for they were tired, for they had not slept for two days, Then
⁶⁵ *Ō'xsɛm* hit them one by one and destroyed all the warriors. Then
Ō'xsɛm went into Knight Inlet. Then *Ō'xsɛm* invited all the tribes.
He arrived at the village site of his father's side, the Nimkish. All
the tribes came ashore. *Wä'qēᵋ* also went to Knight Inlet. But
Wä'qēᵋ had a daughter. She was wooed by all the different tribes
⁷⁰ but nobody was accepted. Then *Lalā'k·înis* also wooed that
woman. He sent a messenger to *Wä'qēᵋ*. At once *Wä'qēᵋ* accepted
Lalā'k·înis. Then *Lalā'k·înis* was told by his messenger; he was
told that he had been accepted. *Lalā'k·înis* arose from among
the others and went out. The others in the house just said he was
⁷⁵ going to get something, but, behold! he went to bathe and purify
himself. Now it was known all over that the princess of *Wä'qēᵋ*
was digging roots on the meadows with one hundred slaves. Then
Lalā'k·înis dressed himself up. He wound his hair around his head
and put (eagle) down on it and went to the place where she was.
⁸⁰ He just found the place where she was. Then he talked to her.
He helped her digging roots. Then the heart of the woman was
really glad. *Lalā'k·înis* asked her, "To whom is it agreed that
you are to be engaged to?" The woman just smiled. Then *Lalā'k·înis* asked her again and the woman told him, "*Lalā'k·înis*
⁸⁵ has been accepted by my father." — "What kind of a man is
Lalā'k·înis?" — "There are few like *Lalā'k·înis* among the tribes."
Then *Lalā'k·înis* let down his hair. "I am *Ō'xsɛm*," said he. The
woman just fell back and fainted. *Ō'xsɛm* just left her and went
home. He went up to the roof of his house and sang his sacred
⁹⁰ song. Now his heart was good because he was now accepted by
chief *Wä'qēᵋ*. That was that *Wä'qēᵋ* said that now he was equal
to *Lalā'k·înis* in the beginning of the myth. The slaves of *Wä'qēᵋ*
gathered around in a circle around the woman. For four days he
came to the same place on the meadow. Then *Wä'qēᵋ* worried. He
⁹⁵ asked that she should go home that she should come and dress
herself up to marry *Ō'xsɛm*. Then the woman went home. Then
she was carried to *Ō'xsɛm* with one hundred slaves. These were
given away by *Ō'xsɛm*. He gave the slaves to all the tribes. *Ō'xsɛm*
was the first one who came to do such a thing, when he gave
¹⁰⁰ away slaves and the rest. Then all the tribes scattered and went

to their villages. The Nimkish came and went home to *X̌ŭlkᵘ*
Lalā′k·inis was the last one to load his canoe. He came with
his heavily laden canoe. Then the Nimkish knew that he was
going home.

Now *Yäkwil* sent his men to go and try to paddle after *Ō′xsɛm* [105]
to kill him. As soon as *Ō′xsɛm* discovered them coming towards
them he stood up in his canoe holding his stone club and watching
to see if he should be struck. He never budged in the canoe. They
were never able to strike him. Now he went ashore at *X̌ŭlkᵘ*.
His load was a large amount of food bought by *Wä′qēᵉ* for him. [110]
Yäkwil had his house on the beach at the foot of *X̌ŭlkᵘ*, for he
was always lying in wait to kill *Ō′xsɛm*. As soon as he arrived
many Nimkish ran down to carry up his canoe with the men and
the load and they put it down outside of the house of his father.
At once *Yäkwil* poled up the river to go to *Gwa′ᵉdzēᵉ*. *Ō′xsɛm* [115]
continually gave to eat to his tribe from his load of food. Now
it was the season for salmon fishing. The Nimkish poled up
the river. It was not long before *Ō′xsɛm* poled up. Then he sent
word that he came to be poled up the river and *Yäkwil* sent his
men to go and pole after *Ō′xsɛm*. That was the reason that he [120]
sent them that he wished to kill him but again they never succeeded
in killing him. That was again done by his tribe, they carried
up his canoe, men and load, for he was respected by his tribe.
Now he thought that he would go after *Yäkwil* and kill him. From
time to time he went in vain to see him at his living place at *Gwa′ᵉ-* [125]
dzēᵉ. He was told by his sweetheart, one of the wives of *Yäkwil*
that he should watch when he was bathing the following day.
"Then you will go and look through a hole and that is the time
when you will enter when he is drying his hair. I shall not bar
the door. When he is done I will wind his hair around my hands [130]
so that he may not be able to stand up." On the following day
he went across on the opposite side and hid behind him when he
was bathing. Now *Yäkwil* went into the water. He did not stay
in the water a long time before he went out. Then his wives spread
a new mat on the floor. His wives dried his hair. He lay on his [135]
back. On one side was the sweetheart of *Ō′xsɛm* at the door.
She had pretended to bar the door. Then *Ō′xsɛm* jumped in
holding his club. In vain *Yäkwil* tried to stand up. The sweetheart of *Ō′xsɛm* just held him on the floor having his hair wound
around her hands. Then *Ō′xsɛm* clubbed him with his club. He [140]
killed him at once. Then *Ō′xsɛm* killed his rival. Then he went
back home to his house.

However, he was a rival of *Wā′xɛwid*. *Wā′xɛwid* had for his

4

wife the aunt of *Ō'xsɛm*. And *Wā'xɛwid* had two adopted children.
145 The children would go upstream looking for salmon in the salmon
traps carrying their spears. Then they threw their spears ahead.
Then the spears struck something and it gave a metallic noise
and so the children considered it important and looked at it.
What should it be? A copper. Now they found what had slipped
150 out of the pack of *Ō'xsɛm*. Then they made a model of the copper.
The copper was imitated. They stuck up the copper between two
trees and only the imitation copper was taken home. In the
evening they arrived at their house. "You have come, masters,"
was said by their mother. Then they were given to eat. After
155 they had eaten they told of their find. "Look at this, our treasure.
This is its likeness. It is that big." And their mother said, "Oh
masters, is it not indeed a treasure what you have found. This
is the copper of your late grandfather. And where may it go?
May be it will go to your uncle here." The younger brother replied
160 at once, "This fool said in vain that it would go to our uncle.
For what should we plan? You will be the one to whom we give
it and you will give it to your husband, for we feel that he has
pitied us. He has made deerskin blankets to be our blankets
and he did not deny us his canoe, therefore we are grateful."
165 And the mother replied and said, "Thank you for what you said,
children."

The numaym *G·ī'g·ilgäm* had a feast. Then *Wā'xɛwid* sat
among them on the floor. His wife called one youth, "Go and
call *Wā'xɛwid*. Say, you should go quickly to your wife. You
170 shall come quickly. She fainted." Then *Wā'xɛwid* arose quickly
in the house. He left his blanket on the floor when he went to
his wife. "You have come, my dear. This is not my way. I only
wanted you to come quickly to the great words of our children.
They found the copper of their late grandfather. Look at this.
175 That is its size. Now these adopted children wish to be grateful
to you for your kind heart to these adopted children; for only
you kept them protected." — "Thanks for these words of our
children. I will honor them even more on account of this, on
account of my kind feeling for them." — "Be quick and go and
180 take it. Take two youths to accompany you." Then she split
boards for light and torches. Then she lighted a long slow match.
Then the wife of *Wā'xɛwid* took a mat and they travelled at
night. After a long time she arrived at *Q!a'ᵋwa*. Then she lighted
what was to be her torch. They used light going inland. "Stay
185 here," said the child to their companions. Only the children
went right into the woods to get the copper. They came with

it and gave it to their mother. Immediately their mother took
a mat and wrapped it around the copper and carried it aboard
when they poled. They just arrived going along. "You have
come," said *Wā'xɛwid* to his wife, "Thank you." *Wā'xɛwid* [190]
could not contain himself, for his heart was glad. He went at
once up to the roof of his house and sang his sacred song. This
was the reason why his tribe was surprised. "What might be the
matter with our chief? Why is he singing at night?" — "The
copper of our late chief has come to him and has been handed [195]
to him." It is said *Ō'xsɛm* in vain barred his door when he heard
the noise of the words of *Wā'xɛwid*, and he became sick at heart.
He was jealous when he heard the noise of the words of *Wā'xɛwid*
when he got the copper. Now *Wā'xɛwid* sold his copper. It was
sold for all kinds of things, the property of the early Indians. [200]
Now *Wā'xɛwid* gave a potlatch to the tribes. Immediately he
did in the same way as was done by *Ō'xsɛm* when he gave away
many slaves to his tribes. Nobody came to do so before, only
Ō'xsɛm and *Wā'xɛwid*. First they did so giving away to all the
tribes. Then he went again to *Ōdzā'^εlas*. And he often gave away [205]
gladly. It was a great potlatch. Then he sent across some
of his servants to go across to the other side to answer his future
words. Then one of the speakers of *Wā'xɛwid* was sitting on the
other side and said, "Who really are chiefs, trees?" Then replied
the one who was hiding on the other side, "That one in the house [210]
above, that *Wā'xɛwid* he is chief." Now he made sick his rival
Ō'xsɛm.

Ō^εmaxt!ā'laʟē^ε[1]

Told by *Nɛg·ā'dze* (Charlie Wilson), a *G·ī'g·îlg̓ăm*.

A country was named *G·ina'ēs*. That is one name of *Wäk·a'-
wa^εyaas*. That was the place where Only-One (*^εnɛmō'gwis*)
lived. That was the reason why he had the name Only-One because
he was really alone at his living place. He had no canoe. A miserable
little house was his house. Then *q* his heart was poor because [5]
he had no clothing. Then *q* he always heard (that there was)
always a noise. They were growling at one another on an island.
Then *q* it occurred to him to go there and learn about the noise
which was always on the island. Then *q* he tried to make a fire
at the end of a log on the beach, to try to make thin the log and [10]
its ends. Then *q* the wood became a little flat at the ends. Then

---

[1] See S 166; M 383; III 271; X 36.

4*

q he just waited for the tide to come up on the beach to what
he was going to use for traveling. Then *q* the tide came up to it.
Then *q* he went on the body (of his log) and sat down, but he
15 picked up driftwood on the beach for his paddle. And so *q* he
went seaward towards the island. Ah, there was a great noise
when he went there. Then *q* he arrived at the island. Behold!
that was the noise. Behold! many sea otters. Then *q* he struck
them with his paddle. He got four sea otters *q*. Then *q* he went
20 back to his house, and *q* the heart of Only-One was good because
he had as his treasure the way of getting many sea otters. Behold!
the island was the place where the sea otters were born. Then
q he arrived at his house. Then *q* he unloaded his game and he
started to skin the sea otters. And so *q* he finished and he made
25 clothing of the sea otters for bed covers and shirts, for he had
no clothing. Twice he would go to the island and club sea-otters
to make clothing [for his clothing]. On his part *q* for a long time
he did not go to the island. Then *q* Only-One thought that he
would walk about inland. Then *q* he started inland. He had
30 not been walking long before he saw a little child crying. Tears
were in the eyes of the little child. "What are you, treasure?"
said *q* Only-One to the child. Then *q* he turned around and put
his arms under the child and went home to his house. And so
he named his child. "You are a treasure from above on the beach,
35 child," said *q* Only-One and he named his child, "Treasure-from-
above-on-the-Beach *(ᴸōgwaᵋyaxalis)*". Now the child in the
story was growing up rapidly. Quickly Treasure-from-above-
on-the-Beach grew up. Now he could walk and go some distance.
Then *q* the child spoke, "I shall go to the inland ground," said
40 *q* Treasure-from-above-on-the-Beach. "Go, master, only be
careful, child," said *q* Only-One to his child. Then *q* the child
started inland. He walked *q*. He walked *q* for a long time walking
in the direction of inland. Then *q* the child heard a sound of
adzing. It was as though adzing was heard by him. Then *q* he
45 kept on walking towards the noise. Then *q* he was coming near
to the place of the noise. Then *q* the child stood on the ground.
Very near *q* was the place of the noise heard by him. Then *q* he
started again. It was as though the noise was in a round salal
patch. He did not see *q* the noise on account of the many salal
50 bushes. No person was seen by him. Then Treasure-from-above-
on-the-Beach thought that he would go ahead and jump to look
through the salal bushes. Then *q* the child jumped and *q* the
child just saw something round lying on the ground. "What,
indeed, may you have come to and stepped among on the ground?"

said q the child. Then q the child thought, "It might not be good [55] if you would just tell your father," said q the child. Then q he picked up from the ground the adze and the various tools. Then q the child went towards the beach. He went home to show to his father what had been found by him. "What, indeed, may it be that I have found?" said q the child to his father. "That [60] was the sound of adzing towards which I went when it sounded. I on my part have never seen the owner, whoever it may have been." — "Heh," said on his part q the father of Treasure-from-above-on-the-Beach. "Master, did you not get it as a super-natural treasure? These are the tools of the one called grouse," [65] said he q on his part to his child. "Thank you for your super-natural treasure, child. Now we will work with this at the canoe which I am trying to make." Then q he went down the beach with his son and he took the tools of the grouse. He put them down on the beach at both ends of a log. Then just by itself q [70] became it a canoe where the wedges were lying on the beach and q the pretty canoe q was finished and q it was done and the hearts of the father and the son were good. Then q they made ready. "We will go," said he q to his child. "We will go seaward to Shell Island $(Q!\varepsilon'ms\varepsilon x \cdot l\ddot{a})$. Not easily obtained will be the [75] work of our child," said he q. Then q they went seaward to Shell Island to club sea otters. Then q their canoe was full of sea otters. Then q they went home. And so q they arrived at their house and began to unload their game and to skin it to make clothing [for clothing] (for himself) and his child. Then q Only-One made [80] a spearshaft for his child. And so q he became the owner of a spearshaft. Then q Only-One said that they would move and leave their dwelling place. He came q paddling with his child, the spearshaft lying in the bow of the canoe and Only-One steered for his child. Then q they went to the far end at $K \cdot !\bar{a}'q!a$. "That [85] is it," said the father and the son. "We will go ahead and make a house here." Then q he went back to his house to go and load a few canoe loads. And so q they went back to $K \cdot !\bar{a}'q!a$. "Let us go ahead," said q Only-One, "and try to get many sea otters and let us make a house." Then q they went aboard their canoe [90] to go again to Shell Island. "You will not go, child, and club them. Now they will be worked with your tool, the spearshaft. Go on and spear the sea otters. You will try to get many." Then q Treasure-from-above-on-the-Beach speared the sea otters. He tried to get many sea otters. And so q his traveling canoe was [95] full and so q they went back to $K \cdot !\bar{a}'q!a$. Then q they unloaded their game. "Let us go ahead, master, and skin our game." Then

q they skinned the sea otters. Then q all the sea otters were skinned. And so q they stretched the sea otter skins, all, the
100 whole number. And so q all the sea otters were dry. "Go ahead, master, and let us look for a place for a house." And so q his child looked. "Let us take this place right in the middle, right in the middle of the fort." And so q they made a house. It had walls of sea otter skins and a roof of sea otter skins. And so q
105 the house was finished. The house was pretty all over q of sea otter skins. "Now our house is finished on the ground, master," said Only-One to his child. "Now we will go paddling, child," said q Only-One to his child, that we may go and get meat from the sea." And so q father and son got ready to go paddling, hunting
110 at sea for meat. That was called meat, seal and porpoise and large porpoise and whale. Then q his child saw a seal. "What is it that is swimming about there? said he q to his father. "This is a seal, my dear," said he q to his son. "Go on and spear it," said he q. Then q the child speared the seal. It was not long q
115 before the traveling canoe was full. "Let us go," said q Only-One to his child. "Now ours is full." Then q they went home and threw out of the canoe their game. "For whom are we planning, master?" said q Only-One to his child. Then the seals were just scattered q because nobody ate them. Then q Only-One said
120 to his child, "Do let us paddle along to his far side." And so q they paddled to $\bar{O}'x{\scriptstyle L}a^\varepsilon lis$ and so q Treasure-from-above-on-the-Beach saw a house. And so q Treasure-from-above-on-the-Beach said to his father, "There is a house on the land side from us." Then q spoke his father, "Yoh, my dear," said q Only-One, "you are
125 my brother." — "It's I, my dear," said on his part q $Dz\varepsilon'nx{\cdot}q!ayo$. His little house had a post in the entrance. "Do try to come near. Come, brother, and enter the house I made on account of our son." The heart of $Dz\varepsilon'nx{\cdot}q!ayo$ was good on account of the speech of his brother. "But you will stay awhile and let me
130 go on paddling to see whether there may be others." Then q father and son started paddling. Then q they happened to meet paddling, $M\bar{a}'tag{\cdot}i^\varepsilon la$. That q his house was also in the same way at $K{\cdot}!\bar{o}'$-$daga^\varepsilon la$. "Yoh, my dear, are you my brother?" — "It's I, my dear," said on his part q $M\bar{a}'tag{\cdot}i^\varepsilon la$. "You are the one who is
135 being looked for by me, brother," said q Only-One, "that you may come to the house I made on account of our child." And so q $M\bar{a}'tag{\cdot}i^\varepsilon la$ also said, "Will I not go according to your speech, brother?" said q $M\bar{a}'tag{\cdot}i^\varepsilon la$. "I have met our brother $Dz\varepsilon'nx{\cdot}q!ayo$ although, behold, he is nearer my house. Come that we may go.
140 Now you will go invited by our child, and our brother $Dz\varepsilon'nx{\cdot}q!ayo$."

Then q Mā'tag·iᵉla came flying. And so q Dzɛ'nx·qǃayo just went aboard the traveling canoe of Only-One. They came q to K·ǃā'qǃa. Then q Only-One butchered for his brothers. And they came and sat in the house. And so q he gave the limbs to his brothers. Their hearts q were good because they came to eat seal. And so q [145] Dzɛ'nx·qǃayo just expressed thanks on account of the way it was in the house of Only-Onė. "Thank you, for what you have done, brother, said q Dzɛ'nx·qǃayo to Only-One who had obtained the canoe. "Do I not get rich because I am your brother?" said q Dzɛ'nx·qǃayo. Then q Mā'tag·iᵉla spoke next. He spoke and this [150] q also was his speech, the speech of Dzɛ'nx·qǃayo when he expressed thanks for sitting in the house of his brother. And q they finished eating the seal. Their hearts q were good and they finished in the house. "You will come again, brothers," said Only-One. And so q they went out of the house to go home to [155] their houses. Then q said Only-One that they should go again to spear sea otters on Shell-Island. They obtained many. Then q their canoe was full. They came q and unloaded their game at their house. Then q they went round again to take sea otters and so q again their canoe was full. Then q they went home. [160] Then q they unloaded their game. Then q they skinned, skinned, skinned. Then q all the sea otters were skinned. Then q they dried the skins. Then q there were very many sea otters all dried. Then q Only-One spoke to his son, "We will go again sea hunting, master," said he q to his son. "Let us go!" so said q his son. And [165] so they paddled and went again spearing seals and porpoises. And so q their traveling canoe was again full of many seals. Then q they went home and so q he again invited his brothers Dzɛ'nx·qǃayo and Mā'tag·iᵉla. And so q his brothers came. Then q they sat down in the house of Only-One. Then q he gave the limbs to his [170] brothers. Then q spoke Only-One. "Come back with what is given by you to your uncles," said he q to his son. Then q his child gave again the chest to Dzɛ'nx·qǃayo and also he gave the legs to Mā'tag·iᵉla. "Now I have made up my mind," said q Only-One, "that I look forward that these may be your ways, [175] brothers," said q Only-One. Then q Only-One took up the chest and set it before Dzɛ'nx·qǃayo. "My dear, brother Dzɛ'nx·qǃayo, now you will be the owner of this dish, the chest. It will never pass in front of you in later times. You will have this seat. And so I will speak again," said q Only-One, took up the legs and set [180] them before his other brother. "My dear, brother Mā'tag·iᵉla, now you will be next to our brother, to Dzɛ'nx·qǃayo. And so I speak, brothers. Now the name of my son will be changed. Now he will

have the name $Ō^ɛmaxt!ā'laₗē^ɛ$. And so I will set this dish before our
185 next brother, $Mā'tag·i^ɛla$. This flipper will go to $Ō^ɛmaxt!ā'laₗē^ɛ$.
And so I shall continue to treat you as my attendants, brothers,"
said q Only-One. Then q Only-One threw the sea otters out of the
canoe and dried them. "My dear, $Dzₑ'nx·q!ayo$," said he q and
gave the sea otters to him. Then q he also gave other sea otters
190 to $Mā'tag·i^ɛla$. Then q again he gave to his son next to $Mā'tag·i^ɛla$
and q he had given all the sea otters to his brothers and his position
as a man became great on account of giving a potlatch to them.
And so q spoke $Dzₑ'nx·q!ayo$, thanking Only-One for what he
had done. Good was his heart because he began to have clothing.
195 And so q they went out of the house and he took his dish and the
sea otters given to him. "Now you will have these for clothing
and others for bed covers." Now he finished the feast given to
his brothers.

Then q Only-One spoke again to his child. "Let us paddle."
200 Then q they made war upon the River's Inlet tribe ($Ăwī'k·!ēnox^u$).
And so that q was the reason why they obtained in war the whale.
The whale came q spouting southward trying to come to $K·!ā'q!a$,
and q father and son obtained as game, standing on the edge
on the beach at $K·!ā'q!a$, coming at the same time when they
205 got the wife which they had tried to obtain. Then q Only-One
told his brothers $Dzₑ'nx·q!ayo$ and $Mā'tag·i^ɛla$ about what he
had obtained.

Then q Only-One spoke again to his son. "Let us woo the
princess of $Qa'wadiliqăla$." And so q they went across to the far
210 side. Then q they met with $Qa'wadiliqăla$ at the mouth of $Gwa'yē^ɛ$.
Then q they took hold of each other's canoe and spoke, "Why
are you traveling at sea?" said q $Qa'wadiliqăla$ to Only-One.
"I am wooing your princess $Hä'qŭlālₑmēga$. Let me speak to you,"
said q Only-One. "What kind of ceremonial have you friend?"
215 said q Only-One to $Qa'wadiliqăla$. Then q $Qa'wadiliqăla$ said, "I
have a great supernatural treasure," said q $Qa'wadiliqăla$. And
he told about his ways. Then q $Qa'wadiliqăla$ asked Only-One
"What kind of ceremonial have you, friend?" said q $Qa'wadiliqăla$
to Only-One. Then q Only-One spoke, "I have the great $xwē'$-
220 xwe," said on his part q Only-One. "Don't let us have in vain
many speeches, friend," said q $Qa'wadiliqăla$ to Great-Only-One.
"Only let us exchange our spearshafts." — "Is that all you give
as a marriage present, that we exchange our spearshafts?" —
"We shall be satisfied," said on his part q Only-One. And so
225 q they exchanged their spearshafts. Then q $Qa'wadiliqăla$ invited
him to go into his house. Then q he entered the house of

Qa'wadiliqăla. "This is your wife," Only-One was told *q.* "This
Hä'qŭlaʟɛmēga will be the wife of your son," said *q Qa'wadiliqăla*
to Only-One. "And so I'll talk to you, friend. Now will go the
ownership of my house. Now will go the ownership of my privileges. ²³⁰
Now you will be the great dance from above. Now you will have
the names *G·î'lg·iya^ɛlis* and *G·î'lgɛma^ɛlis* and *G·îlā'laʟɛla,* and
Gămō'ta^ɛyalis and *Gămōti^ɛlälag·îlis;* and *Nɛg·ä'dzē* and *Nɛg·ä'ēsi^ɛ-
lak^u,* and *Q!ŭ'mx·ɛlag·îlis;* and *Yā'qaxɛlag·îlis;* and *Qwăxō'l;* and
K·!ē'k·!ɛsʟɛn and *Wā'^ɛlagɛmg·i^ɛlak^u.* Nobody will dare to go to ²³⁵
the beams of my house. All the beams of my house are double-
headed serpents. And these posts, look at the speaking post
standing on the floor who greets the visitors which says, 'Go
at those who come into your house, chief,' and the other who
says 'Take pity on them'." And it was obtained by Only-One ²⁴⁰
for his child; and so he went home with the one who was now
his wife. And so they lived for a long time in their house.

Then Only-One spoke again and said that they would go again
to woo on the far side, the princess of *A'naxim. Yā'siłānaga* was
the name of the daughter of *A'naxim.* That is the one to whom ²⁴⁵
Only-One referred as the wife of his son. And so *q* they arrived
in the country of *A'naxim.* Then *q* Only-One saw *A'naxim.* "You
are the one for whom I came, friend," said *q* Only-One. "I came
to woo your princess." Immediately they were married. And
so *Ō^ɛmaxt!ā'laʟē^ɛ* came to obtain the name *A'naxim* and also ²⁵⁰
Yā'siłānaga and *Nā't!ōl.* This was obtained by him far away. They
came home *q* and they came to live. Now he had three wives.

Then *q* Only-One spoke again to his son, "We will go again
wooing," said he *q* to his son. "We will be heading south, child.'
Then *q* they started at sea to woo the princess of *Wā'xap!alasō^ɛ.* ²⁵⁵
^ɛwîlx·sta^ɛsilaōgwa was the name of the princess. And so *q* they
arrived at (the place of) *Wā'xap!alasō^ɛ.* "Why are you paddling
about, friend," said *q Wā'xap!alasō^ɛ.* "I am wooing your princess." — "Come," said *Wā'xap!alasō^ɛ.* "Now you will have this
my child for your wife." Then they were married. "Now you ²⁶⁰
will obtain in war my names. Now you will have the name Great-
Smoke-Owner *(^ɛwā'las Kwax·îlanō'kŭmē^ɛ)* und *^ɛwîlx·sta^ɛsilaōgwa*
and *Kwî'gwalats!ē.*" That is all he got there. And so *q* he came
home. And his wives were sitting in the house, and now they
gave birth. Now they became many. The father and son con- ²⁶⁵
tinued hunting for meat for food for themselves and his wives, and *q*
K·!ā'q!a was just stinking on the beach on account of the large
amount of meat and whales. Sometimes *q* Only-One and *Ō^ɛmax-
t!ālaʟē^ɛ* took some sea otters on Shell Island for dresses for his
wives and for dresses for his uncles *Dzɛ'nx·q!ayo* and *Mā'tag·i^ɛla.* ²⁷⁰

House Story about the Feast of the First Ones[1]

(Recorded by George Hunt)

1   Only-One (*ᵉnᴇmō'gwis*) *q* lived at *Wä'k·awaᵉyaas* and *q* he was alone in the house. Then *q* it occurred to him to walk inland from his house, but, *q* he had not been walking outside for a very long time when he saw a child lying on the ground,, of the size
5 of a child when it is first born by its mother. And so *q* as soon as Only-One saw it he went *q* towards it and went and sat down on the ground by the side of the child. And *q* Only-One waited in vain for its mother to come. And so *q* when Only-One had been sitting on the ground for a long time [when] he gave up waiting
10 for the mother of the child to come [and] when Only-One took up the child in his arms. Then *q* Only-One said, "Thanks, for I got a child by good luck. Now I got you by good luck. And so, you will have the name Supernatural-Treasure-That-Came-Down, great child, for you," said he *q* as he came back home to his house.
15 And *q* the child, a boy, was growing up well. Then *q* Only-One always washed the boy, and so that was the reason why the boy was growing up very quickly, the Supernatural-Treasure-That-Came-Down. And so *q* the boy, Supernatural-Treasure-that-Came-Down, came to be grown up at *Wäk·a'waᵉyaas*. And *q* Only-
20 One really believed that he had Supernatural-Treasure-That-Came-Down as his child. And *q* Only-One and his child, Supernatural-Treasure-That-Came-Down were sitting in his house when a young man came and entered his house. And so *q* immediately Only-One spoke to him. Then *q* he said to him, "Welcome brother,
25 where do you come from?" said he to him. Then *q* the young man answered him. Then *q* he said, "I am *ʟ!ō'ʟ!otsa*, master, I am always together with this Supernatural-Treasure-That-Came-Down," said he *q*; and Only-One never found out where *ʟ!ō'ʟ!otsa* came from; and Only-One and Supernatural-Treasure-
30 That-Came-Down always kept together. Then *q* Only-One came walking along. It is said he came and arrived at Red Bottom Bushes (*ʟ!ā'ʟ!āq!ŭxᴌa*). Then *q* he saw a little house propped up in this manner. Then *q* a man was seated outside of
35 this house. Then *q* Only-One said to him, "Thank you, brother, that we met. Who are you?" said he to him *q*. Then *q* the man said to him, "I am *Dzᴇ'nx·q!ayo*, brother." Then *q* Only-One asked *Dzᴇ'nx·q!ayo*, "But whose is this smoke

---

[1] See S 166; M 326; III 271; X 36.

south of you?" said *q* Only-One. Then *q Dzɛ'nx·q!ayo*, the former *Qō'los*, said, "I have never met with him," said he *q*. Then Only- 40
One came *q* and started and came to *Tā'yaɣoł*.

Then *q* he saw a little house at *Tā'yaɣoł* in this way. Then *q* a sea gull was seated in front, on the seaside of the little house. And so *q* as soon as the sea gull saw Only-One he took off his sea gull mask and *q* he 45
became a man. Then *q* Only-One spoke. Then *q* Only-One said to him, "Thank you that we met, brother. Who are you?" said he to him *q*. Then *q* the man said to him, "I am *Lā'lax·sɛndayo* brother," said he *q*. Then *q* Only-One asked *Lā'lax·sɛndayo*, "But whose is this smoke south of you?" said *q* Only-One. Then *q Lā'lax·*- 50
sɛndayo said, "I have never met with him," said he *q*. Then Only-One came *q* and started and came to the mouth of the river of Fort

Rupert *(Tsā'xis*, Tide-Ripple-Beach). Then *q* he saw a small house in this way and *q* all the boards and the roof were entirely of cedar bark. Then *q* a 55
man was seated on the seaside in front of his house.
Then *q* Only-One spoke. Then *q* he said, "Thank you, that we met, brother. Who are *you*?" said he to him *q*. Then *q* the man said to him, "I am *Ō'dzēᵉstalis*, brother," said he. And so *q* as soon as he finished his speech Only-One started and went to *K·!ā'q!a*. Then *q* 60
Only-One was glad for it is sheltered when the southeast wind is blowing. He came *q* and left it and went home to *Wä'k·awaᵉyaas* and he came *q* and moved to *K·!ā'q!a* with Supernatural-Treasure-That-Came-Down and with *L!ō'L!otsa* and he made a house there. And so *q* as soon as Only-One had finished making the house, 65
then *q* Supernatural-Treasure-That-Came-Down would go and club sea otters and seals on the beach of Fort Rupert, and so, as soon as he had obtained many sea otters and seals, then *q* Only-One was desirous to have what was being seen, the many seals and sea otters on Shell Island *(Q!ɛ'msɛx·Lä)* and he and *L!ō'L!otsa* 70
took a cedar tree which had come drifting ashore on the beach of his house and *q* they burnt it out in the middle so that it was hollow inside. And so *q* as soon as they had finished, then *q* they burnt the sides of the canoe that was being made. And so *q* as soon as it was finished, then *q* immediately Only-One launched the 75
canoe. Then *q* Supernatural-Treasure-That-Came-Down said that he and *L!ō'L!otsa* would go to Deer Island *(Âg·iwalaa')* to try his canoe on the water. Then *q* they started paddling, but *q* it was not long before they came back. Then *q* the canoe was entirely full of sea otters. Then *q* they always went back and *q* every 80
time the canoe was entirely full of sea otters; and *q* Only-One

wished to change the name of Supernatural-Treasure-That-Came-Down and *q* he named him *Ō^ɛmaxt!ā'laʟē^ɛ*; and *q* Only-One sent *ʟ!ō'ʟ!otsa* to go and invite *Ha'yalik·awē^ɛ* at * Łɛ^ɛlā'dē'*.... [1] And so,
85 as soon as he finished giving a feast *Ha'yalik·awē^ɛ* and *Ha'naʟenâ* did not go home. Now *Ō^ɛmaxt!ā'laʟē^ɛ* started inland from *K·!ā'q!a* and *q* he heard the sound of adzing. Then *q* he went into the water in a pond; and so *q* as soon as he had gone into the water four times in four ponds, he saw a canoe and sitting in it a man,
90 a Blue Grouse, and as soon as *Ō^ɛmaxt!ā'laʟē^ɛ* spoke to him the Blue Grouse disappeared. Then *q* *Ō^ɛmaxt!ā'laʟē^ɛ* pushed the canoe, and so *q* the canoe just came by itself out of the woods and came and stopped on the beach of his house at *K·!ā'q!a*, and *Ō^ɛmaxt!ā'laʟē^ɛ* said that he would go paddling far away. Then
95 *q* daylight came when he went aboard his canoe with *ʟ!ō'ʟ!otsa*. Then *q* he steered for *Sā'lots!a*. Then *q* he arrived when he saw (a canoe) which came and paddled from *Yaë'xŭg·iwano* coming along to where *Ō^ɛmaxt!ā'laʟē^ɛ* was staying on the water. And so *q* as soon as it came near, *Ō^ɛmaxt!ā'laʟē^ɛ* paddled and went to
100 meet it and they took hold of each other's canoes. Then *q* *Ō^ɛmaxt!ā'-laʟē^ɛ* spoke. Then *q* he said, "Thank you that we have met, brother. What is the place where you came down, brother?" said *q* *Ō^ɛmaxt!ā'laʟē^ɛ* to him. Then *q* the man answered him. "Thank you that we have met paddling, brother. I am *Qa'wadiliqăla*,
105 brother, and I own the ceremonial, the Great-One-Brought-Down-From-Above. And what is your ceremonial, brother?" said he, it is said. Then *q* *Ō^ɛmaxt!ā'laʟē^ɛ* answered him. Then *q* he said, "I am the great *xwē'xwē*, brother," said he, it is said. Then *q* *Qa'wadiliqăla* spoke again. Then *q* he said,
110 "Go on, pass (the reason) of your paddling, brother," said he *q*. Then *q* *Ō^ɛmaxt!ā'laʟē^ɛ* said, "I came to marry your princess, brother." It is said, he just said [when the sound went of] (when his word went that he would give) his hunting canoe and his harpoon and his harpoon line made of intestines, and his sea
115 otter blanket for covering the knees. And so *Qa'wadiliqăla* just arose in his canoe and said, "Come, brother *Ō^ɛmaxt!ā'laʟē^ɛ*! Come across into this your canoe, now it will be yours, this my traveling canoe, and all my marten skin blankets and lynx skin blankets and marmot skin blankets and goat skin blankets. Now it will
120 all go to you, brother," said he *q* as they each went across into the other's canoe. Then *q* *Ō^ɛmaxt!ā'laʟē^ɛ* said, "O brother, let us go towards my house. That is its smoke, the color that is seen

---

[1] Here follow the invitations M 676.

by us," said *q* *Ō*ᵉ*maxt!ā'laʟē*ᵉ to *Qa'wadiliqăla*. "It is not far."
Then *q* *Qa'wadiliqăla* said, "Don't say so brother, let us go towards
my house that you may quickly see your wife, *Hä'qŭlaʟɛmēga*, 125
my princess," said he *q*. And so *q* immediately *Ō*ᵉ*maxt!ā'laʟē*ᵉ
agreed to his speech. Then *q* they started paddling. And so *q*
as soon as they arrived at the beach of the house of *Qa'wadiliqăla*,
then *q* *Qa'wadiliqăla* spoke. Then *q* he said, "Only you will take
care, brother, when you enter the door of my house. You will 130
step close to my heels," said he *q*. And so *q* as soon as they arrived
at the door, the raven opened (its beak) on the ground, and then
q the four men[1] jumped into the house at the same time, and
*Ō*ᵉ*maxt!ā'laʟē*ᵉ saw that all the posts of the house were alive on
the floor and that the beams of the house were double-headed 135
serpents and *Qa'wadiliqăla* told *Ō*ᵉ*maxt!ā'laʟē*ᵉ to go and sit down
by the side of *Hä'qŭlaʟɛmēga*, his princess who was sitting in the
rear of the great house. Then *q* *Ō*ᵉ*maxt!ā'laʟē*ᵉ started and went
q to sit down alongside of *Hä'qŭlaʟɛmēga* and they were married...[2]
and *Ō*ᵉ*maxt!ā'laʟē*ᵉ finished having a prince's name because he 140
obtained by inviting all the tribes with what he had obtained
from his wife from *Qa'wadiliqăla* and *q* there were many tribes. And
*Ō*ᵉ*maxt!ā'laʟē*ᵉ found out about the chief of the tribe which has the
tribal name *Ma'măleleqăla*, who had the name ᵉ*wā'xap!alasō*ᵉ
who was the rival of *Mā'leleqăla* who lived at *Nū'xdɛ*ᵉ*ma*. Then 145
q *Wā'xap!alasō*ᵉ had the princess ᵉ*wī'lx·staēsɛlaōgwa* and *Ō*ᵉ*maxt!ā'-*
*laʟē*ᵉ wished to go and try to get her for a wife. Then *q* he told
his tribe, and so *q* immediately they went to woo ᵉ*wīlx·staēsɛlaōgwa*.
It came to him in marriage the name, Great-Head-Smoke-Owner
(ᵉ*wā'las Kwāx·ilanōkumē*ᵉ) and the house with a loon on the front, 150
and also a *Dzō'noq!wa* house dish and an eagle house dish and
also many boxes of fish oil and boxes of crabapples and many
sewed blankets. And now *Ō*ᵉ*maxt!ā'laʟē*ᵉ had two wives after this.
Then he invited again all the tribes with what he had obtained
in marriage from *Wā'xap!alasō*ᵉ. Now he had the name Great- 155
Head-Smoke-Owner and he finished having the name *Ō*ᵉ*maxt!ā'-*
*laʟē*ᵉ after this. Then *q* Great-Head-Smoke-Owner wished to
look about on the north side. Then *q* he arrived at Rivers Inlet
(*Wa'nuk*ᵘ). Then *q* he saw *Yā'qaʟɛnāla*, the first chief of the
numaym *Qō'k·axt!ēnox*ᵘ of the River's Inlet tribe. Then *q* *Yā'qa-* 160
ʟɛnāla had for his princess Copper-in-House (*ʟ!ā'qwăl*) and *q*
Great-Head-Smoke-Owner married Copper-in-House, and *q* it
came the privilige that came behind (in marriage) of the Cannibal

[1] That is the chiefs and their steersmen
[2] Here follows the matter on M 679.

Dance with four whistles and red cedar bark, and also the name
165 of the Cannibal dancer *Ǧwā'yokŭlag·îlis* and that was the first
Cannibal dancer who came to the first of the Kwakiutl tribes.
Then *q* the name that came behind (in marriage) was *Yā'qaʟɛnāla*
for the secular season instead of the name Great-Head-Smoke-
Owner. Then *q* *Yā'qaʟɛnāla* said a whale would come to bring
170 all kinds of food, and Great-Head-Smoke-Owner came home
with his wife Copper-in-House to *K·!ā'q!a*, and *q* he had three
wives after this. And so *q* as soon as Great-Head-Smoke-Owner
had stayed for four days at *K·!ā'q!a*, [when] a large whale came
ashore on the beach of the house of Great-Head-Smoke-Owner.
175 That was the marriage gift (of food) of *Yā'qaʟɛnāla* to Great-Head-
Smoke-Owner for Copper-in-House; and *q* he gave a feast with
the whale to the tribes whom he had invited again and Great-
Head-Smoke-Owner had also the name *Yā'qaʟɛnāla* after this.
Now he had the name *Yā'qaʟɛnāla* after this. Then *q* it occurred
180 to him to go and search for a wife on the north side. Then *q* *Yā'-
qaʟɛnāla* started paddling with his numerous tribe. Then *q* he
arrived at the Inlet of the Bella Coola. Then *q* not a man was
seen by him at the head of the inlet. Then *q* he found a broad
trail. Then *q* he went along the trail going inland. Then *q* he
185 arrived at a village. These were the Chilcotin. Then *q* he took
for wife *Yā'silānaɠa* the princess of *A'naxäm*, and *q* the name
(coming behind in marriage) given in marriage to *Yā'qaʟɛnāla*
was *A'naxäm*, and also many lynx skins and marten skins and
marmot skin blankets and the ways of dancing of the Chilcotin.
190 And the names coming behind (given in marriage) were *A'naxäm*
and *Hămā'lag·iyu*. *Yā'qaʟɛnāla* came with his wife *Yā'silānaɠa*
and started. And so *q* as soon as he reached his canoe they went
aboard in it and they came out of the Inlet of the Bella Coola. It
is said *Yā'qaʟɛnāla* was coming and arrived at *K!wā'lna*, when he
195 saw a house there. Then *q* he went ashore there. And so *q* as
soon as he arrived on the beach of the house a man came out
of his house. He came *q* and met him. And so *q* as soon as the
man arrived he spoke to him immediately. Then *q* he said to him,
"Thanks, brother," said he to him *q*. Then *q* the man also said
200 to him, "Thank you, brother, who are you?" said he ‚to him *q*.
Then *Yā'qaʟɛnāla* said to him, "I am *Yā'qaʟɛnāla*. I am *Ō͡ᵋmaxt!ā'-
laʟēᵋ*. I am Great-Head-Smoke-Owner, brother, I came to marry
your princess," said he to him *q*. Then *q* the man spoke. Then
q he said, "I am *Ta'ltɛm*, chief of the *K!wā'lnag·imuxᵘ*. Now
205 come to your wife, my princess, Copper-in-House *(ʟ!ā'qwäl),*"
said he *q*. And so *q* immediately *Yā'qaʟɛnāla* with his Chilcotin

wife and his crew stepped out of the canoe and they all went
into the house of *Ta'ltEm* which had carved posts. And so *q*
as soon as they sat down on the floor *Yā'qatEnāla* married Copper-
in-House; and so *q* as soon as he had finished, *Ta'ltEm* gave [210]
away his coppers, "Cause-of-talk" *(DEnt!alayo)* and Dry-Mouth-
Maker" *(Sē'gExstag·ila)* two expensive coppers, and also the
Cannibal Dance and all kinds of red cedar bark and the name
Around-whom-they-Sit *(K!wä'^εstaak^u)* and his whistles. And so
q as soon as he had finished it was evening. Then *q Ta'ltEm* spoke. [215]
Then *q* he said, "O son-in-law *Yā'qatEnāla*, now I will add chief
names to your names. Now my name coming behind (given in
marriage) will be Getting-Rich *(Q!ōmE^εnakŭla)*," said he *q*. "Now
your wife will go to your country," said *q Ta'ltEm* to *Yā'-
qatEnāla*. And so *q* as soon as day came in the morning *Yā'qatEnāla* [220]
came home with his wives; and so as soon as they arrived at his
house at *K·!ā'q!a* he gave at once away the two kinds of property
obtained from his wives to the tribes. And now he had the name
A'naxäm and Getting-Rich after this. And now end his ways
after this.   [225]

Mā'tag·i^εla[1]

Told by *Â'waxElag·îlis*, chief of the *Maä'mtag·i^εla*

A gull was seen *q*. The gull was walking quickly at *Gwä'dzē*.
It was seen at Long Beach *(G·îldEdzō'lis)*. It was a gull that was
walking quickly. Then *q* the gull spoke, "I am not a gull, I am
a man." — "Who are you?" — "I am *Mā'tag·i^εla*," he said *q* and
took off his gull mask and *q* he became a man. He himself gave [5]
himself the name *Mā'tag·i^εla* and had a child when he became a
man. On his part *q* his child was a boy, his name was *Łe'nstEndzEm*[2].
Then *q* his child thought that it would work. Then *q* he asked his
father what kind of tool was it to snare *(yū'xwa)* with. That
is the kind of thing the child wanted to make, the *yū'xwayo* with [10]
a snare at each end and so *q* he made it. "Come, father, look at
this, father, is that the way I made it? His father came *q* and
looked at it. "That is right, child, what you have made. It is
that way." — "But how will it be put (down) when I go to put
it on the beach, *Mā'tag·i^εla?*" — "It does not matter whether it is [15]
covered by water or whether it is out of the water." — "But what
shall I do, *Mā'tag·i^εla?* Shall I leave it or shall I not sit next to it
on the beach?" — "It does not matter, child, if you sit next to

---

[1] See S 197, no. 14.

[2] Given at another place as ancestor of the *Mā'dilbē^ε* and youngest
son of *Mā'tag·i^εla* (35 th Annual Report Bureau of American Ethnology, p. 950).

it or leave it." — "Then let me leave it and I shall learn whether
20 it will be best if I stay with the thing I am going to work with
so that it will be good." — "It does not matter, child, if you stay
with it when you go to work with it." — "I'll go, father, I'll go
work with it on the beach." Now he worked with it on the beach.
And so q he was sitting next to it according to the words of his
25 father. Nothing of any kind went into it among all the birds
which were to be the food of his father, for that was the reason
why he worked, for his food. On his part q he did so for four days
and he would never leave it q for he wished to get food for himself
and his father. And so q he was sitting next to it again. For a
30 long time nothing came near his *yū'x̣wayo*. Then his heart became
sore because nothing went near to what he had made. "What is
the matter with your tool that they do not go near it?" said he q.
In vain he thought about it. Then q it occurred to him to go and
ask his father *Mā'tag·i*la*. Then q he went to his father. "I just
35 came to ask you, father. What may be the matter with my tool.
Nothing goes near what is worked by me." Then q he was answered by his father, "Go back, child, and go to find out the reason
why it is so, that nothing goes near it. Go and sit near it, child,
and take care that it is not so as though nothing would go near it."
40 Then he went back to the place where he had been sitting and he
was sitting on the beach. He looked at his trap. Then q he turned
his head around. Then q he saw something coming down. Already
he thought it was important. And so q what was seen by him
came right down to his snare and lay flat on his snare and q he
45 arose and took it. He thought already that what he had taken
was important, for it was different in its ways and he looked at
the snare of his tool. "What shall I do with it?" thought he q.
"Maybe it is not good to tell your father, *Mā'tag·i*la*," thought
he q. "Don't tell your father and try to surprise your father with
50 what it may be. What is the best way to do with your snare?
Go on and try to hide it inland (to see) if some kind of thing may
be in your snare." And q he hid it under a cedar tree. For four
days he did not look at it. He never told his father q. He thought
he might just tell if it might be some kind of thing that was hidden
55 inland. Then q after four days he thought he would go and look
at it. Then q his father was wondering that he was not going to
his tool. Then q he questioned his child, "Why don't you go to
your tool?" said he on his part q to his child. "I came and told
you that nothing went near it." And so q he tried to say to his
60 father and he was going to go inland to his snare and he looked at
his snare. And so q as soon as he arrived at the place where it was

lying on the ground where he had hidden it, then *q* spoke the man
who was on the dressed deerskin, "Now you have me for your
supernatural treasure," said *q* on his part the man on the dressed
deerskin, "and this will be your dance," he was told *q*. "You will [65]
be a cannibal dancer and you will have a cannibal pole, and your
name will be *ʟ!ē'x·ɛlag·îlis*. You will be a ghost dancer and this
will be your red cedar bark, this man. Go on and look at it. This
will be your treasure in the house, this dressed deerskin, this
dressed deerskin which never gets empty. Look at it, this your [70]
treasure. You will from time to time do this with your supernatural treasure, from time to time you will turn over your supernatural treasure on its bad side." Then *q* he turned over the
blanket, the dressed deerskin on its bad side, on its death bringing
side. You will not at all not do so (You must do so). You will [75]
go around with what is found by you now, all around the world.
Now he assembled all the people. Now he wished to tell about the
treasure of his child *Łɛ'nsĺɛndzɛm*, and *Mā'tag·i⁵la* gave a winter
ceremonial to show the treasure of his child *Łɛ'nsĺɛndzɛm* and
he had his fort at *Gwa'⁵dzē⁵*. *K·!ō'daga⁵la* was the name of the fort [80]
of *Mā'tag·i⁵la*. Then he gave a winter dance and his child was a
cannibal dancer. *ʟ!ē'x·ɛlag·îlis*, that was his name as cannibal
dancer and *Mā'tag·i⁵la* also showed the winter dance name,
La⁵xʟā'la. Now he showed the ghost dance. Then his sister had
the name *Łɛ'nsɛ⁵widzɛmga*, and *Lōła⁵ya⁵lis* on the other hand [85]
was the winter dance name of *Łɛ'nsɛ⁵widzɛmga*. Then he distributed his supernatural treasure, that dressed deerskin, among those
who were invited. Then his child became a chief and had the name
⁵mā'x̣wă⁵yalidzē. Then he put his child in a seat by himself and
Łɛ'nsĺɛndzɛm changed his name. And that is the end. [90]

Tă'mĺɛls

Told by *Hä'maxodalayugwa*

He came coming down *q* to the beach being a bird. Then *q* he
became a man, that *Tă'mĺɛls* at *Tă'mĺɛls'* Place *(tă'mĺ⁵alis)*.
He came *q* to a great fort like a mountain. Then *q* he had a child
which had the name *Wāx̣wa⁵lenē'ga*. Her other name was *Ts!â'-
laliĺi⁵lakᵘ* and her other name was *Ts!ɛ'ndɛg·îmg·i⁵lakᵘ*. These [5]
were the names of the princess of *Tă'mĺɛls*. That was put on his
face, the *dzō'noq!wa* mask when he became a man, when he had
been a thunder bird. He came and became a man. Now it is said
he took an attendant to be sent. He took one of them and sent
his speaker to bring material for paddles. And so *q* this was a [10]

5

woman who had a name and the name of the woman was *Mō′lē-
ɪɛlayuₓwa*, and there was another one who had the name *wŭₗē′d*.
These *q* were the names of his attendants, that was the attendant
of *Tä′mlɛls*. He had a child *Ā′dag·ilis*. That was the name of
¹⁵ the child of *Tä′mlɛls*. And also one of the names of the child of
Tä′mlɛls as *G·ī′g·ilis*. These were the names of the children of
Tä′mlɛl

<h3 style="text-align:center">*Sē′nₗ!ē*ᵋ</h3>

Told by *Hä′maxodalayuₓwa*

He was a bird when he first came. "Welcome," he on his part *q*
was told. "I will be your treasure when I come. You will just
have a child," said *q Wŭxē′d*. Then he lived in his house. His
house was deep. Then he had for his child *Sē′nₗ!ē*ᵋ. He had on his
⁵ face the thunder bird *(qō′los)*. That was the place where he became
a man. He finished after this. Then *Wŭxēdeq!a*ᵋ*nak*ᵘ arose and
went to the end in his house. And he came to his water. The
water *q* was at the inland end of his house. Then *q* he sat down
at the place of the water. He took the water and lifted the water
¹⁰ to the surface of the water. Then *q* he looked at what was in the
water. That is referred to as Copper-Noise-Woman *(ₗ!ā′qwak·!ālaga)*,
the Great Toad. Now it was his supernatural treasure *q*. "Indeed
it is you." said he *q*. "Now I have you for a supernatural treasure,
my dear," said *q Wŭxē′d*. "Now you really have me for a super-
¹⁵ natural treasure," said on his part *q* the Toad. Then the Toad
said, "Cut this along that you have obtained as your supernatural treasure." He took the copper and went to the place
where *Wŭxē′d* was. "Now you will have these names. And so
this one name will go, Copper-Maker-Woman *(ₗ!āqwag·ilayuₓwa)*,
²⁰ for your child and this privilege, the sheltering dance of the great
chief mask. And you will have the name Shelter for your child
(T!āt!ɛntsīd)." And so *q* he wished to come to Fort Rupert.
And so *q* he came to Fort Rupert.

<h3 style="text-align:center">*Wī′nag·i*ᵋ*lak*ᵘ and *G·ā′malag·i*ᵋ*lak*ᵘ</h3>

Told by *Mɛ′nmɛnlēqɛlas*, a *Nā′k!wax·da*ᵋ*x*ᵘ woman[1].

Recorded by George Hunt.

It is said, *Wī′nag·i*ᵋ*lak*ᵘ was living at *Hē′gɛms*, the first chief
of the numaym *Kwē′kwaēnox*ᵘ of the *Gwa′waēnox*ᵘ, and *q Wī′nag·i*ᵋ-
*lak*ᵘ wished to use the name *Wī′nag·i*ᵋ*lak*ᵘ for his name. That

---

[1] Father *Nā′k!wax·da*ᵋ*x*ᵘ, mother *Gwa′waēnox*ᵘ. See p. 61.

was the reason that he was always going to war where the warriors
of all the tribes were known to be. And so *q Wī'nag·i*ɛ*lak*ᵘ knew [5]
about a supernatural man who had the name *G·ā'malag·i*ɛ*lak*ᵘ,
the root of the numaym of the *G·ē'xsɛm* of the *Nā'k!wax·da*ɛ*x*ᵘ,
the one whose village site was the place *Lɛqō'ma* at the lower end
of *Ǎwē's*. And so *q* right away *Wī'nag·i*ɛ*lak*ᵘ told his son who had
the name *Wā'xo*ɛ*nakŭlas*. Then *q* he said to him, "Let us start [10]
paddling and try to meet Uncle *G·āmalag·i*ɛ*lak*ᵘ," said he *q*. Then
q at once *Wā'xo*ɛ*nakŭlas* got ready and he saw that his father
*Wī'nag·i*ɛ*lak*ᵘ was holding his fire bringer which is this way,

as he went aboard his paddle-side canoe which
was not a large canoe. And so *q* as soon as [15]
*Wī'nag·i*ɛ*lak*ᵘ and his son had gone aboard, the
paddle-side canoe started paddling on each
side of the canoe. On their part *q* they arrived early at *K·!ē'dɛgwis*.
Then *q* they saw a canoe paddling along in the mouth of the river
Xō'qwaēs. And so *q* immediately *Wī'nag·i*ɛ*lak*ᵘ went up to it. Then *q* [20]
he saw it was an old man, very feeble, as the man was paddling sitting
in the stern of his canoe. Then *q Wī'nag·i*ɛ*lak*ᵘ spoke to him.
He said *q*, "What is my friend *G·ā'malag·i*ɛ*lak*ᵘ doing," said he *q*.
Then *q* the old man replied to him. Then *q* he said, "What do
you think he should be doing? He is just sitting in his house," [25]
said he to him *q*. Then *q* the old man started paddling strongly
and the bow of the canoe of the old man struck the cheek (the
sides of the bow) of the canoe of *Wī'nag·i*ɛ*lak*ᵘ. And so *q* the
paddle-side canoe of *Wī'nag·i*ɛ*lak*ᵘ almost capsized. And so *q* the
old man took off the old man mask of the slave. Then *q* behold! [30]
it was *G·ā'malag·i*ɛ*lak*ᵘ who took up his paddle that went right
to the end and put it into the sea. Then *q* once he started paddling
and he almost arrived at *Ǎwē's*. "Ah too bad, behold! that was
*G·ā'malag·i*ɛ*lak*ᵘ," said *q Wī'nag·i*ɛ*lak*ᵘ and he paddled after him.
And so *q Wī'nag·i*ɛ*lak*ᵘ saw *G·ā'malag·i*ɛ*lak*ᵘ when he arrived at [35]
the foot of the steep rock *Lɛqō'ma*. Then *q* a long cedar tree
rested on the rock at the foot of *Lɛqō'ma* and went to the rock
shelf. Then *q* the butt end of the cedar was on the rock shelf
outside of the cave on the face of the bare rock above. That was
the house of *G·ā'malag·i*ɛ*lak*ᵘ, and that was run up on by *G·ā'*- [40]
*malag·i*ɛ*lak*ᵘ, the cedar; and, *q* he pulled up his canoe there. And
so *q* as soon as he had entered his cave house *q* he asked his mother
Q!ɛyō'laga to dress herself and so as soon as his mother was dressed
*G·ā'malag·i*ɛ*lak*ᵘ took eagle down and put the down on his mother.
And *Q!ɛyō'laga* was just entirely covered with (eagle) down, her [45]
head and her whole blanket. And so *q* as soon as he had finished

5*

he warned his mother to take care when she was going to run along
the cedar tree which was reaching down. When he had dressed
his mother *Q!ɛyō'laqa*, he put on his war neck ring. Then *q* he
50 asked his younger brother *P!ā'ʟɛlag·iˁlakᵘ*. "Do listen to me!
When I stand on the rock at the foot of the cedar tree, as soon as
I say, 'Go ahead!' then come out of our house and beat fast time
saying meanwhile, 'Go ahead!'. That is when our mother will
show herself and will run down the cedar tree," said he *q*. And *q*
55 *Wī'nag·iˁlakᵘ* came, his canoe lay on the water seaward from the
lower end of the cedar tree. It is said *G·ā'malag·iˁlakᵘ* came out
of his house. He came and ran down the cedar tree and stood on
the rock shelf. And so *q* as soon as he stood there *Wī'nag·iˁlakᵘ*
arose in his canoe; and *q* he carried his wolf fire bringer. Then *q*
60 he said, as he was swinging it towards the place where *G·ā'mala-
g·iˁlakᵘ* was standing on the rock, "Now take care, friend, and let
us play. It is said that you are a supernatural man," said he *q*
for as soon as *Wī'nag·iˁlakᵘ* swung his carved wolf the whole place
where *G·ā'malag·iˁlakᵘ* was standing caught fire and he was just
65 standing in the midst of the flames. And *G·ā'malag·iˁlakᵘ* was
just standing still on the rock. Then *Wī'nag·iˁlakᵘ* took back the
fire and so *G·ā'malag·iˁlakᵘ* was just standing still on the rock.
He did not say a word. Then *Wī'nag·iˁlakᵘ* again swung his fire
bringer at the place where *G·ā'malag·iˁlakᵘ* was standing. But
70 now, indeed, *G·āmalag·iˁlakᵘ* did not show himself. And so *q* as
soon as it had been burning quite a while *G·ā'malag·iˁlakᵘ* took
hold with both hands of each side of his war neck ring and shook
it. And so *q* its rattling put out the fire. And so *q* immediately
G·ā'malag·iˁlakᵘ looked up towards his house and said aloud, "Go
75 ahead." And so *q* immediately his younger brother *P!ā'ʟɛlag·iˁlakᵘ*
came out of the cave house and he also said, "Go ahead," as he
was beating fast time on the stone front of the cave house. It is
said, their mother *Q!ɛyō'laqa* came out of her house. It is said, she
came down running along the cedar tree and came and stood at
80 the place where *G·ā'malag·iˁlakᵘ* was standing on the rock. And
so *q* as soon as *Q!ɛyō'laqa* was standing on the rock, she said aloud,
"Go on *Q!awētsēwa*, show yourself on account of the one who came
to hurt me, that he may discover that I am also a supernatural one,
friend *Q!awētsēwa*," said she *q*. And so *q* immediately the sea began
85 to whirl about and the tide ran strong, and *q* the tide carried about
the paddle-side canoe of *Wī'nag·iˁlakᵘ*, and *Wī'nag·iˁlakᵘ* saw that
the water was shallow where his canoe lay; and *G·ā'malag·iˁlakᵘ* saw
that *Wī'nag·iˁlakᵘ* was really frightened. And so, that was the
reason why *G·ā'malag·iˁlakᵘ* said to him, "Now take care, friend

Wī'nag·iᵉlakᵘ, don't be afraid too soon, that we may keep on ⁹⁰
playing," said he *q*. Then *q* the tide became quiet and *q* the shallow
place went down. Then *q Q!ɛyō'ḷaga* looked up and said, "Hail!
Hail! Hail on the beach!" Then *q* this our world became dark.
Then *q* there was lightning which almost burned the paddle-side
canoe of *Wī'nag·iᵉlakᵘ*. Now great hail stones were falling, the ⁹⁵
hail stones were of the size of sea gull eggs, and *q Wī'nag·iᵉlakᵘ*
was very much frightened and he began to pray *G·ā'malag·iᵉlakᵘ*
to stop, "for I am beaten by you, Supernatural One," said he *q*.
And so *q* immediately the hail stopped. *G·ā'malag·iᵉlakᵘ* and
Q!ɛyō'ḷaga q were still standing on the rock at the foot of the cedar ¹⁰⁰
tree; and *q Wī'nag·iᵉlakᵘ* and his son *Wā'xoᵉnakŭlas*'s paddle-side
canoe was hardly above water; and *q* they threw the hail stones
into the sea. And so *q* as soon as all the hail stones were out of the
canoe *G·ā'malag·iᵉlakᵘ* spoke. He said *q* "O friend *Wī'nag·iᵉlakᵘ*
why are you very downcast? I suppose we have now finished ¹⁰⁵
playing," said he to him *q*. Then *q Wī'nag·iᵉlakᵘ* answered. Then
he said *q*, "Let us stop, for I will go home," said he *q*. Then
G·ā'malag·iᵉlakᵘ told him to wait. Then *q* he ran up the cedar tree.
Then *q* he went into his cave house. But *q* it was not long before
he came carrying a yew wood clam digging stick. Then *q* he spoke. ¹¹⁰
Then *q* he said, "Oh friend *Wī'nag·iᵉlakᵘ*, now you got as your
treasure this yew wood digging stick, for *q* that your only food are
clams," said he *q*. And so *q Wī'nag·iᵉlakᵘ* came carrying his
digging stick. Then *q Wī'nag·iᵉlakᵘ* thanked him and *q* he went
home to *Hē'gɛms*. Then *q G·ā'malag·iᵉlakᵘ* and his mother ¹¹⁵
Q!ɛyō'ḷaga went up to their cave house. And that is the end.

*G·ā'malag·iᵉlakᵘ*¹
(Told by *Ō'mx·ᵉīd*, a *Nā'k!wax·daᵉxᵘ* story)

They lived *q* at *Ăwē's* having as their fort a steep rock. And
so their house was only a hole in the steep rock. They had only
a ladder when they went out and when they went into their house.
And so *q* as soon as night came they pulled up the ladder so that
warriors might not go up to the house. And so *q* as soon as it was ⁵
morning they pushed down the ladder. Then *q G·ā'malag·iᵉlakᵘ*
started paddling going to *Tsɛᵉlisnukᵘ*. Two q were his paddles,
and his paddles were extraordinary. And so *q* it was this, he
paddled once with his unusual paddles (and his canoe reached its
destination). A large canoe *q* came and showed itself at the point. ¹⁰

¹ See p. 58.

And so *q* at once *G·ā'malag·i^εlak^u* knew that they were warriors. Then *q* *G·ā'malag·i^εlak^u* changed his face. He only *q* became a little old man, for *G·ā'malag·i^εlak^u* was not an ordinary person. The warriors came *q* and took hold of the canoe of *G·ā'malag·i^εlak^u*.
15 Then *q* the chief of the warriors spoke, "What is this chief *G·ā'malag·i^εlak^u* doing?" said *q* the warriors. "What is being done? This chief *G·ā'malag·i^εlak^u* is only sitting in his house," said on his part *q* the old man. But he *q* was *G·ā'malag·i^εlak^u* and the warriors did not recognize him. "We will go and see the chief
20 *G·ā'malag·i^εlak^u*," said on their part *q* the warriors. "Go on," said on his part *q* the old man. Then *q* *G·ā'malag·i^εlak^u* took up in the canoe the extraordinary paddle and when once he had paddled he arrived at his house. "Yaiya," said on their part *q* warriors. "Behold, this one was *G·ā'malag·i^εlak^u*." — "Behold the
25 I have succeeded." The warriors *q* were *Gwa'waēnox^u*. He was named, Made-to-be-Warrior *(Wī'nag·i^εlak^u)*. He was extraordinary. Then *q* he arrived at the beach of *G·ā'malag·i^εlak^u*. *G·ā'malag·i^εlak^u* came down his ladder. "Do not come ashore, else you might come to be a ghost on the beach of my country," said *q* *G·ā'malag·i^εlak^u*.
30 Then *q* he took a very large rock and threw it seaward from the warriors. Then the warriors came *q* drifted shoreward by the waves (made) by the large stone. Then *q* *G·ā'malag·i^εlak^u* took up the traveling canoe of the warriors and pressed down into the water the bow of the canoe of the warriors. Then *q* spoke Made-to-
35 be-Warrior, "Do not act this way, friend *G·ā'malag·i^εlak^u*, I only came to see you." Then *q* Made-to-be-Warrior took out of the canoe a baton and threw it at *G·ā'malag·i^εlak^u*. "Take it, friend. Now my baton will go to you to be the reason of making the right sound for your future generations," said *q* Made-to-be-Warrior.
40 Then *q* *G·ā'malag·i^εlak^u* spoke, "Thank your for this, friend. Stay on the water that I also give something to you," said *q* *G·ā'malag·i^εlak^u*. Then *q* he went into his house. He came *q* holding his clam digging stick. "Take it! Now this, my clam digging stick, will go to you, friend," said on his part *q* *G·ā'malag·i^εlak^u*. Then *q*
45 spoke Made-to-be-Warrior, "Thank you for this, friend *G·ā'malag·i^εlak^u*. Now I will go home," said *q* Made-to-be-Warrior. Then *q* they started paddling and went home. Their paddles were of yellow cedar *q*. Then *q* they met with *Ts!ä'qămē^ε*. *Ts!ä'qămē^ε* was trying to go really fast *q*. And so *q* Made-to-be-Warrior also
50 tried to go really fast. Then *q* split up their paddles. They were just *q* sprinkled over the water, the paddles of Made-to-be-Warrior, for the yellow cedar wood was softer. And so *q* never were spoiled the paddles of *Ts!ä'qămē^ε*, for they were all yew wood. Then *q*

*Ts!ä′qămē*ᵉ went back and took hold of the canoe of Made-to-be-Warrior. Then *q* Made-to-be-Warrior spoke, "What are you going ⁵⁵ to do, *Ts!ä′qămē*ᵉ?" said *q* Made-to-be-Warrior. "I am going to make war on our friend *G·ā′malag·i ⁵lak*ᵘ," said *Ts!ä′qămē*ᵉ on his part *q*. Then *q* Made-to-be-Warrior spoke again, "Do not continue, *Ts!ä′qămē*ᵉ. Behold! He is one whom nobody dares to attack, our friend, *G·ā′malag·i ⁵lak*ᵘ. We are hardly alive here," ⁶⁰ said *q* Made-to-be-Warrior. Then *q* spoke *Ts!ä′qămē*ᵉ, "I will just see our friend *G·ā′malag·i ⁵lak*ᵘ." — "Go, just, try it!" said Made-to-be-Warrior. Then *q* *Ts!ä′qămē*ᵉ started paddling. He arrived at the beach of *G·ā′malag·i ⁵lak*ᵘ. *G·ā′malag·i ⁵lak*ᵘ came *q* down his ladder. "Do not come towards the shore, else you will come to ⁶⁵ be a ghost on the beach in my country," said *q* *G·ā′malag·i ⁵lak*ᵘ. He took up a large rock and threw it seaward from the traveling canoe of *Ts!ä′qămē*ᵉ. Then his canoe came *q* drifted to the shore on top of the waves, drifted by the large stone. Then *q G·ā′malag·i⁵- lak*ᵘ took the bow of his canoe and pulled it ashore. Then *q* he ⁷⁰ took one man and cut off his head and pushed seaward the traveling canoe of *Ts!ä′qămē*ᵉ. And so *q* *Ts!ä′qămē*ᵉ at once just paddled away and went home. He was afraid when the head was cut off of one of his crew. Then *q* he arrived in his country. Then *q G·ā′malag·i ⁵lak*ᵘ started paddling. His wife stayed home with ⁷⁵ her children *P!ā′ʟɛlag·i⁵lak*ᵘ and *Q!ɛyō′ḷaqa*. Then the Bella Bella came *q* to make war. Then *q Q!ɛyō′ḷaga* and *P!ā′ʟɛlag·i⁵lak*ᵘ were taken in war. Then *q P!ā′ʟɛlag·i⁵lak*ᵘ was tied to the thwarts of the canoe. He came *q* being taken out of the inlet. Then *q* the Bella Bella said, "Do fly away, *P!ā′ʟɛlag·i⁵lak*ᵘ! It is said that ⁸⁰ you are not an ordinary man." — "I am going to fly," said on his part *q P!ā′ʟɛlag·i⁵lak*ᵘ. "Do fly away!" said on their part *q* the Bella Bella. They struck with the paddle at *P!ā′ʟɛlag·i⁵lak*ᵘ. Then *q P!ā′ʟɛlag·i⁵lak*ᵘ arose in the canoe and started to fly and went and sat on a rock falling straight down to the water. It just ⁸⁵ has now the name "Precipitous Face" *(Hĕḷgăm⁵laas)*, the place where he was sitting down on a rock. The thwart was just *q* across the back of *P!ā′ʟɛlag·i⁵lak*ᵘ. And so *q* in vain the warriors shouted. They could not get him when he started flying. And so *q* the warriors just started paddling. Then *q* the warriors said, "Do ⁹⁰ sing, *Q!ɛyō′ḷaqa!*" said *q* the warriors. "I am going to sing," said on her part *q Q!ɛyō′ḷaqa*. Then *q* the warriors spoke again, "Do sing, *Q!ɛyō′ḷaqa!* It is said that you are a singer." Then *Q!ɛyō′ḷaqa q* began to sing. Hail was coming down. There came large hail stones, and, as soon as the hail stones hit the heads of the men they ⁹⁵ were at once dead. And so *q* the traveling canoes of the warriors just sank when they were full of hail stones. And so *q* the warriors were just swimming about. Then *q Q!ɛyō'laqa* also started to swim and went towards land. "I am *Q!ɛyō'laqa*, I am *Q!ɛyō'laqa*," 100 she said *q*. She arrived on the land and went along searching for *P!ā'ʟɛlag·i·ɛlakᵘ*. And so *q* she was only seen now and then by the late warriors who were now ghosts. Every now and then they paddle and they were recently seen every now and then. Then *q Q!ɛyō'laqa* met with her brother *P!ā'ʟɛlag·i·ɛlakᵘ*. Then *q* they went 105 home to their country.

Then *q Q!ɛyō'laqa* was playing with a toy canoe on the beach. Then she was pulled under water by a sea monster. *G·ā'malag·i·ɛlakᵘ* came home *q*. Then *q* he was told by his wife, "A great thing happened to our child. She was pulled under water by a sea monster," 110 said *q* the wife of *G·ā'malag·i·ɛlakᵘ*. "I am going to search for her," said on his part *q G·ā'malag·i·ɛlakᵘ*. He took his knife and went down the beach to go and dive. Every now and then he would ask the sea monsters below, "Did you not see my child?" he would say to the sea monsters. And so *q* as soon as a sea monster said 115 that he had not seen his child, *G·ā'malag·i·ɛlakᵘ q* just would cut off the head of the sea monster. Then *q* he saw the one named *ɛnɛ'mxx·alig·iyu*. Then *q* he went into it to look for his head. And so *q* he never found its head, for it was too big. And so *q* he just cut up with his knife the inside of the *ɛnɛ'mxx·alig·iyu*. Then *q* 120 *G·ā'malag·i·ɛlakᵘ* just went home to his house. Then *q G·ā'malag·i·ɛlakᵘ* spoke, "I have given up our child," said he *q* to his wife. "For what can we do about it?" said on her part *q* his wife. Then *q G·ā'malag·i·ɛlakᵘ* started paddling and went to *Wāms*. Then *q* he arrived at Old Man *(Nō'mas)*. The name Old Man was *Q!ā'ga·ɛma*. 125 Then *q* the sea began to boil. Then *q* began to talk the *Wā'wäxē·ɛma* on one side of Old Man. "*Wäqwai'*," said *q* the *Wā'wäxē·ɛma*, "Show yourself for this one," said the *Wā'wäxē·ɛma*. Then *q* the sea began to rise and *q* a sea monster showed itself and was going to devour *G·ā'malag·i·ɛlakᵘ*. Then *q G·ā'malag·i·ɛlakᵘ* thought, "If 130 that might be what has happened to your child," thought *q G·ā'malag·i·ɛlakᵘ*. Then *q* he went into the water and dived. Then *q* he saw two mermen lying on their stomachs below. Then *q G·ā'malag·i·ɛlakᵘ* went towards them and pulled the mermen ashore. What should it be, but bones which were covered (laid on) by the 135 mermen! Behold! that was the late daughter of *G·ā'malag·i·ɛlakᵘ*. Then *q* he took all the bones and went up to his traveling canoe and went home to his house. "I have come and found our late child," said he on his part *q* to his wife. "Thank you," said on her part *q* his wife. Then *q G·ā'malag·i·ɛlakᵘ* sprinkled his water of life

on his child. Then *q* she came to life, who had been *q* only bones. [140]
Then *q* *G·ā′malag·iᵉlakᵘ* spoke to his child when she had come
back to life. "Now you will have the name Cause-of-Killing-Woman
(K·!ē′k·!ᴇlag·idzᴇmga) for I have killed the sea monsters below on
your behalf," said *q* *G·ā′malag·iᵉlakᵘ* to his daughter. Then *q* he
took ashore the heads of all the monsters which he had cut off and [145]
he hung them up on the frame for hanging skulls. And so that is
the reason why the place is called, "Place-for-Hanging-Skulls"
(Xō′qwaēs) and that is the reason why one country has the name
"Having-Hail-on-the-Beach" *(Tsᴇᵉlisnukᵘ)* where the late warriors
were hit by the hail at Having-Hail-on-the-Beach. [150]

Ḥë′ᵉmaᵉnis

Told by *G·ī′qalas*, a *Gwa′waēnoxᵘ*

Mount Stevens *(K!wä)* was sent out of the canoe by those
among whom he was sitting, the mountains. "Go, you will be
Ḥë′ᵉmaᵉnis in your country. You will go and carry this your red
cedar bark. Now you will go. Your cedar bark will be the reason
why they will not dare to go near you. The poles holding the [5]
front boards of your house will be told to go ahead on the ground,
whenever you tell your red cedar bark to go out of the house and
your rattle will shake(?)."
 The child of *Ḥë′ᵉmaᵉnis* came out of the woods *q*. He made a
sparrow blanket. He shot sparrows. Was not the sparrow blanket [10]
which he made right ? *q*. He tried to get enough for a bed blanket.
Then the child went hunting again *q*. He tried to get sparrows.
He arose early in the morning. He went out of his house. He
went straight down to the beach holding his bow. The child
wiped his eyes. He did not recognize clearly *q* what was seen by [15]
him. Then *q* a large bird was seen by the child. Then *q* he went
back into the house. He called his father. "Do come, look at
this large bird, father." Then *q* his father went out and looked
at it. What should it be ? a bird with spread wings. The tips of
the wings *q* reached the middle of the mountain. Then *q* *Ḥë′ᵉmaᵉnis* [20]
saw that the bird took off his blanket pin. A man came out of
his bird dress and turned his face to his mask and spoke, "Now
you will go up again. You will not keep on thundering. Only
sometimes you will sound when my later generations will go (die).
You will speak once at a time when those who will change places [25]
with me will go (die). You will not always blink your eyes. Go!
Now you will go." The bird mask flew away.
 "Do not be this way in the house, *ᵉmā′x̣ŭlaōgwa*. Send your

brother to go and call this wonderful thing because it acted thus,
³⁰ this one who came down. Go and invite him in." Then *q* he
invited the man. He came *q* and entered his house. "Go on and
cook for this one." Then *q* ᵋmā'x̣ŭlaōgwa took her berry cakes
and set before him a dish, and berry cakes were in it and she gave
them to the man to eat. The one named *G·ā'yusdäs* was afraid of
³⁵ the ways of the man. The man had a hooked nose *q*. But on his
part *q* the man did not eat the berry cakes. Then *q* they tried to set
before him also viburnum berries in water. They were given to him
to eat. And so also this *q* he did not eat. Then *q* also crabapples
in water were set before him. They were given to him to eat. And
⁴⁰ so also this *q* he did not eat. Then *q* ᵋmā'x̣ŭlaōgwa asked her
father, "What may be good for feeding him?" Then *q* the man
looked around the roof of the house. Then *q* the man, the bird
man, spoke. The man had a large hooked nose. "Peas," said *q*
the man. "Go on, take it. This, oh wonder, is wanted by him
⁴⁵ for food." Then *q* a drying rack was put down. The man ate *q*
the boiled peas. Then *Ḥë'ᵋmaᵋnis* spoke *q*, "We do not call it peas.
It is named differently by us, for you came to be a man in this
world." Then *q* the bird man spoke, "How do you call it?" —
"We call it salmon spawn. Now listen that I name my names:
⁵⁰ I am Coming-Down *(G·ā'yax̣ᴇla)*, I am Thunder-Bird-Dancer
(Kŭ'nx̣ŭlaɫ). This is my name, Thunder-Woman *(Kŭ'nx̣ŭlaōgwa)*,
Made-to-be-Thunderer *(Kŭ'nx̣ŭlasōᵋgwiᵋlakᵘ)*." These are my
names, Spouting-at-the-Point *(ʟ!āɫbaᵋyā'wis)*. This is my name
Spouting-Woman *(ʟ!ā'ɫᴇmdalaōgwa)*. These will come to be the
⁵⁵ names when I come to take my place in this world, when I come
being a man in this world coming down here."

Told by *G·ī'qalas*, a *Gwa'waēnox̣ᵘ*

And this lord *q* was coming along. He almost arrived. Then
q Ḥë'ᵋmaᵋnis was told, "Take care," said he on his part *q*, "Ḥë'ᵋmaᵋnis, of the poles of your housefront when our lord *Q!ā'neqeᵋlakᵘ*
arrives." And he came *q* and he almost arrived. He came *q* to
⁵ *Ḥē'gᴇms*. There was a noise. It was heard by the lord. There
was howling. Then *q* he was afraid to go to the howling. Then *q*
he passed *Ḥē'gᴇms*. He went along *q* to Mt. Stevens *(K!wä)*.
Then *q* he arrived at Mt. Stevens. "The lord is coming," said on
his part *q Ḥë'ᵋmaᵋnis* to his children. "Take care," said he on
¹⁰ his part *q* to his children, "do not move in the house." Then
ᵋmā'x̣ŭlaōgwa just did so. "Do not look through a hole." She
was a mischievous girl *q*. Then *q Ḥë'ᵋmaᵋnis* went out and beat

time outside for his walking cedar bark. Then *q* he said, "Go ahead." And so *q* he told all the poles of his house front to go ahead. Four times he said so *q*. He said, "Go ahead," and his [15] red cedar bark went out of the house walking. Then *q* the red cedar bark started. The large rattle was made to move by itself. It had the name, Big Rattle. It was moving on the ground by itself and met dancing the lord *Q!ā'neqeᵉlakᵘ*. It was just red cedar bark. Nobody looked after the red cedar bark. Its way was [20] wonderful. Time was just beaten for it. Then *q* the lord threw out of the canoe his stone maker. Then *q* stood up *X·i'lgwīl* and looked through a hole when the lord threw his stone maker. What should it be? Now *X·i'lgwīl* just became a round stone in the house. Then *q* *Ḥë'ᵉmaᵉnis* returned the stone maker of the lord. [25] Then *q* *Ḥë'ᵉmaᵉnis* said, "Go ahead."(?) Then *q* he took his means of playing and threw it at him. And so *q* his canoe just did not capsize on account of the waves made by the means of playing of *Ḥë'ᵉmaᵉnis*. Then *q* he tried to throw out of the canoe his bird maker. The lord threw it. And so *q* *Ḥë'ᵉmaᵉnis* just caught it [30] coming and threw it back again at him. What should it be? They were just birds sitting in the canoe, sitting behind the lord. Then *q* he took it back in the canoe and his steersman became a man again. Then *q* *Ḥë'ᵉmaᵉnis* made waves in the sea of his place. The traveling canoe of the lord just did not capsize. Then *q* the [35] lord spoke forbidding him, "Don't do that, I am beaten. Now these olachen will go behind you. Now this water of life will go to you." — "You have spoken enough. I do not wish the olachen behind me. And so I take the water of life. Go on and run your canoe ashore and come out of the canoe." The fire of *Ḥë'ᵉmaᵉnis* [40] was blazing. Then *q* they were eating and so *q* they almost finished. Then *q* *Ḥë'ᵉmaᵉnis* went out. Then *q* he saw young sawbill ducks. Then *q* he said to the lord, "Very many young sawbill ducks are here." Then *q* *Q!ā'neqeᵉlakᵘ* ran aboard his canoe to paddle after the young sawbill ducks. On their part *q* they were made to [45] turn to *G·ᴇyō'xᵘ*. The lord *q* stepped out of the canoe. He walked up the little river. "Good will be this my little river. This river will be called *G·ᴇyō'xᵘ*." Then *q* he was made to go out. Then *q* he went to one flat place. Then *q* the young sawbill ducks went up the beach. Then he went up the river. "Nice will be this my [50] river. This my river will be called Jumping-Place *(Dᴇx·dᴇᵉmē's)*." Then *q* he was taken upstream. Again *q* the young saw-bill ducks went upstream. "Nice will be this my little river. This my river will be called Squirting-River *(Ts!ē't!āla)*." Then *q* the young sawbill ducks went up again. Again *q* they went up the [55]

river. Then *q Q!ā'neqeᵋlakᵘ* said, "Nice will be this my river.
This my river will be named real river *(Wā'k·as)*." Then *q* again
was he taken across. The young sawbill ducks went up the river.
Then *q Q!ā'neqeᵋlakᵘ* stepped out of the canoe. And so *q* he said
⁶⁰ again, "Really good is this my little river. Buying Place *(K·ᴇ'lwadē')*
will be called this my little river." He came *q* being taken down
the stream. Then *q* the young sawbill ducks went up the river.
"Let us clean it up." Then *q* they cleaned up the place. And so *q*
the young sawbill ducks gave it up. This will be called Cleaned
⁶⁵ *(Sīnkᵘ)*.

G·ā'g·oᵋnaᵋlas

Told by *G·ī'qalas*, a *Gwa'waēnoxᵘ*

G·ā'g·oᵋnaᵋlas was asked *q* at the place *Hē'gᴇms*, "What will
you do?" was said *q* to *G·ā'g·oᵋnaᵋlas*. "Now this world is going
to be different. Now we will flood you." — "What shall I do?
Am I not going to be just in my house under water? If I were
⁵ light of weight I might drift away. I shall just be in my house
under water." Gum was all over his house *q*. He had as com-
panion the wolf. Then his house was under water when his tribe
was drifting about. Then *q* they went up. His tribe just went
gradually to the top of his mountain. Then he made an anchor
¹⁰ and tied in the middle a large rock, but the water reached the top
of Mount Stevens *(K!wä)* and he was tied to his mountain. All
the tribes came and tried to tie (their canoes) to him. Then *q*
the chief named *ᵋmā'xŭlag·ilis* became angry. He said to his elder
brother to go on in the canoe and cut off the tribes. He cut off
¹⁵ his tribe. They drifted about. Then *q* by chance he cut off a
woodworker and they disappeared all around. And so *q* only he
came straight down to his country. It is said, he alone. The past
Gwa'waēnoxᵘ never moved. He came straight down to his country.
The tide went down. He came *q* going to *Wī'dzēᵋq!wālasōᵋ*, to
²⁰ his younger brother *G·ā'g·oᵋnaᵋlas*. He said *q* on his part, "How
are you?", said he *q*. "I am alive," said he *q*. Then he opened.
Now the house site of his tribe did not feel good. The ground was
made bad. The house companions of *G·ā'g·oᵋnaᵋlas* crept out of
the house. Some of the house companions of *G·ā'g·oᵋnaᵋlas* were
²⁵ wolves. Other wolves had human faces. Then *q* he went out and
the wolves stood on one side of him. They took off the animal
masks and went on the water and they made it their country.
"This will be your name, *Hē'gᴇms*." Then they made their skins
into land. And that is the end.

Xŏ'gŭmɢa[1]

Told by *Kwa'xsē˪stāla*

They were fishing on the river at *Q!aˬwak·as.* He was house
owner of the place where the child was sitting on the floor. It was
the house of *Xŏ'gŭmɢa.* And *q Xŏ'gŭmɢa* drove piles for her
salmon weir into the ground on the beach of her house here where
she was taking (the fish) out on the beach of the house of *Xŏ'gŭmɢa.* [5]
Then *q* she would take them out of her salmon trap. She would
cut the fish in it *q* from time to time. Then *q* she would hang
them up to dry in the place where this was done to the salmon.
Now she was drying many and they were put into her house. Then
q she was watching and she was surprised when she saw her drying [10]
salmon, when they just became few. Then *q* she went down to the
beach again to take them out again of her salmon trap. Then *q*
again she cut the salmon and hung them up again and she worried
about the ways of what was happening to what she was hanging
up, for they were just becoming few whenever day came. Then *q* [15]
she made up her mind what to do. Then *q* she made a man and put
it near the mouth of the salmon trap she had made and she imitated
the form of a man and dressed her work with a cape. Then *q* she
also put a hat on it and her work was done. And so *q* she hid in
her house and she watched to learn what was happening to the [20]
fish in the river. And *q* evening came when someone came and
uncovered the door in the rear of the house. And *q* she saw that
first only breasts *q* came through the boards of this house. Then *q*
the breasts were hanging down and *q* a face also came going through
and she became glad. Her hands *q* just came down into the house. [25]
Then she took dry salmon and put them into her basket on her
back. Then *Xŏ'gŭmɢa* worked. She made a bow. Barbed at
the ends *q* were the arrows. These were named barbed pointed.
This kind of arrows were the bones of quadrupeds. Now *q* she
placed again the man she had made outside near the beach at her [30]
salmon trap. She put him near the beach. Now night came.
Then *q* came the *Dzŏ'noq!wa.* And so it was that *q* again she
came from the place she had come from. And so it was that *q*
again as soon as her breasts came through, then *q Xŏ'gŭmɢa* shot
her. She shot her breasts. Then *q* again the breast of the other [35]
side, and *q* the *Dzŏ'noq!wa* rolled down outside. She groaned *q*
and shouted for pain *q.* In vain *q* she moved the shot. She tried
to get out the arrows. Not at all *q* however, had she a way to do so.

---

[1] See III 103; C 442.

Only *q* the arrow shafts were gotten, but *q* the barbed points
⁴⁰ remained inside. And *q* the *Dzō'noq!wa* arrived at her house.
Only *q* she was there on the floor lying dead when *Xō'gŭmga q*
pursued her because she wished to know her house and she saw
what her property was. Oh, there was property! There was no
river food among all these quadrupeds, for she had dried meat as
⁴⁵ means of inviting. Then *Xō'gŭmga* cut off the head of the
Dzō'noq!wa and she carried it out of the woods to her house to be
the wash basin of her child to be. And *Xō'gŭmga* went back to the
house of the *Dzō'noq!wa* to carry her property. There was nothing
from the river on account of the way she was, and she took every-
⁵⁰ thing out of the woods. That is *q* where the *Dzō'noq!wa* lived
(the place) named *K·ā'tâlēᵉ*. Then *q Xō'gŭmga* gave birth. The
husband of *Xō'gŭmga* was Rich Maker *(Q!ō'mg·ila)*. And so *q*
now she was at the mouth of *Hă'nwadēᶜ*. He watched his river so
that he might not be robbed there. That is the reason why he did
⁵⁵ not know that his wife had given birth. And *Xō'gŭmga* took the
head of the *Dzō'noq!wa* and washed her new born child in it and
her child was called *Łā'xᵉŭnāla*. He was the first *q* in the myth.
Then *q Łā'xᵉŭnāla* asked his mother to make a bow for her child.
And so *q* at once *Xō'gŭmga* made a bow. Then *q* the child shot
⁶⁰ little sparrows. Then *q* the child started hunting. He shot bears
up the river from his dwelling place. Then *q* he killed some black
bears. Hai! Then *q* he started again and he went hunting again.
Then *q* he saw a grizzly bear and *q* he shot it also and he also killed
the grizzly bear. Then *q Łā'xᵉŭnāla* started again. He was going
⁶⁵ up the river *q* to the house on the river bank, to the place *Q!aᵉ-
wak·as*. Then *q* he also shot a mountain goat. He just shot up
to it *q* and hit it. Then *q* he just turned back and went and reached
his mother and *q* he stopped shooting with his bow. And so *q* he
questioned his mother and *Xō'gŭmga* talked about the river, why
⁷⁰ the river was bad. Not at all was free of monsters the length of
the river. Then *q Łā'xᵉŭnāla* asked his mother about different
things, "for I think that I will go and explore the bad things to
which you refer." — "Don't, do not say this," said *q* on her part
Xō'gŭmga to her child *Łā'xᵉŭnāla*. "This will not come out right."
⁷⁵ — "Let me go," said he on his part *q* to his mother. Then *q* he was
informed by his mother. "Go aboard now, my dear, only you
will take care," he was told *q* by his mother and she only informed
her child, "As soon as you arrive at *Gwā'gɛmlis* you will see this
point down the river from *Gwā'gɛmlis*." Then he arrived there.
⁸⁰ Then *q* he saw the monster referred to by his mother. For a long
time it was standing on the beach before a really large bear came

standing upright. Its mouth *q* was open as it approached *Łā′x-*
ᵉŭnāla and it wished to eat *Łā′xᵉŭnāla*. And so *q* he just met it.
Then *q* he took a round stone which he had picked up. Then *q*
he threw it at it. It went straight into his mouth as it came with [85]
open mouth towards him and *q* the monster was dead. Then *q*
he threw right through the neck of the bear. Then *q* it fell down
on the other side of the river. And so *q* *Łā′xᵉŭnāla* went right
down the river. He came *q* and arrived at (the place) called
Xᴇxᵘstā′litsōᵉ. Then *q* he saw a seal. That also *q* was a monster [90]
seal and *q* it also came towards *Łā′xᵉŭnāla* with open mouth and
it tried to bite him. Then *q* again he threw a stone into the throat
of the seal and it also was dead. Again *q* he took his stone with
which he had thrown and he started again going down the river
and he went to the mouth of the river. Then *q* again he saw a [95]
monster. Exceedingly wide was the space between the arms of
the devilfish. Now *q* this devilfish is a large stone at the mouth
of the River of *Hā′nwadēᶜ*. Then *q* he threw at it, for he was
almost swallowed (?) by the devilfish, and *q* it also died. He
killed the devilfish. Now he had killed all the monsters of the [100]
river.

Hē′kin

Told by *G·ī′qalas*, a *Gwa′waēnoxᵘ*

Hē′kin was always ill *q*. Sores were on his body while he was
sitting on his mountain. It is named Having-Toads *(Waō′gwat)*.
He went and searched for a place to kill himself, being ashamed
of the way he was. He went inland going to his mountain. Then
q he heard a sound, the noise of a large toad. Then *q* he walked [5]
and went and reached it. Then *q* he saw a large toad. Behold,
it had young ones. Then *q* it stepped out of its nest. It put out
its young ones. Then it talked with *Hē′kin* and they became men
with him. Then *q* the toad advised the poor one, that *Hē′kin*,
what to do. Then *q* he asked that he should take the soft layer [10]
inside (from the nest) of his child. "Do not take it roughly! You
will put it into this pond. This is the water of life. You will wipe
your body with it after you finish sprinkling your body. You will
be well after your trouble. You will go and hold this copper and
you will become a chief. You will put together the cover and your [15]
box. This will be its name. You will have the name Head-Copper-
Maker *(ᴌ!ā′qwag·ilaɢᴇmēᵉ)*. You will have a treasure. This will
be your name, Copper-Maker *(ᴌ!ā′qwag·ila)*." And so *q* he went
seaward. And so *q* he became well. Well had become his body.

20 He was cured by the toad. He was made to bathe in what is the good cause of keeping alive of the toad. That is called the water of life. On his part *q* he was told, "You went to the place of sprinkling your body," he was told *q* by his sister. *ɛna' x·nag·îm* was the name of the woman. "Thanks for the way in which you are now **25** alive, being now well. I am grateful because you are now alive." — — "Now you will carry this copper on your back to your future husband." And that is the end.

Nomasɛ'nxeɛlis[1]

Tradition of the *La'lawilɛla*, told by *Ō'mx·ɛid*

Nomasɛ'nxeɛlis q was living at *Tsē'tsɛqalalis (Tsē'ltsɛqalā'lis)*. Then *q* he put up the princess pole of his princess *Ë'k·ɬawēga*. On top of the princess pole of *Ë'k·ɬawēga* an eagle was sitting *q* and so *q* the eagle was always making noise. It was screeching. "Let us **5** go and pick berries at *Yaqamā'lis*," said on her part *Ë'k·ɬawēga* to her slaves. "Let us go!" said on their part *q* her slaves. Then *q* they launched their canoe. And so *q Ë'k·ɬawēga* went down the beach. She was just led by her slaves, for she was blind. *Ë'k·ɬawēga* could not see. Then *q* they went across to *lɛ'mwas*. Then *q* they **10** paddled for a long time on the sea. Then *q Ë'k·ɬawēga* became uneasy. They never arrived at the place where they were going to pick berries. "Where are we on the water?" said *q Ë'k·ɬawēga*. "The voice of the one who is sitting on top of my princess pole sounds far away," said *q Ë'k·ɬawēga* to her slaves. Then *q* her slaves **15** spoke, "It is very foggy here, my dear. Where may it be that we are steering?" said on their part *q* her slaves. Then *q* she hardly heard the one sitting on top of her princess pole. Then *q Ë'k·ɬawēga* spoke again, "What indeed are my slaves doing on the water?" said on her part *q Ë'k·ɬawēga*. She broke the paddles of her slaves and **20** *Ë'k·ɬawēga* guessed that her slaves were only pretending to paddle. Behold! the slaves *q* just steered seaward into the open sea. Behold! there was no fog. Then *q Ë'k·ɬawēga* stopped hearing her princess pole. "Why do you do so, slaves?" said on her part *q Ë'k·ɬawēga* to her slaves. And so *q* her slaves never spoke. It is said they only tried **25** to paddle quickly steering to the ocean side of the world. But *q* it was four days before they arrived in a country. They came *q* and were met by the tribe at the place where they came to the beach. Then *q Ë'k·ɬawēga* was led and made to go to the house of a man. Then *q* she was given to eat with her slaves. Then *q Ë'k·ɬawēga*

---

[1] See S 188, 196; C 267; also X 195, 221; C 207.

was asked, "What is the reason that you are paddling?" was said [30]
to her *q*. "My slaves paddled away with me. I am *Ë′k·!awēga*.
Evidently my father is poor," said *q Ë′k·!awēga*. "What is your
father's name?" said on his part *q* the man. "He is named *Noma-
sE′nxe*ᵉ*lis*," said on her part *q Ë′k·!awēga*. Then *q* the man spoke,
"I'll have you for my wife. I am Copper-Maker *(L!ā′qwag·ila)*. [35]
I will make you see," said on his part *q* Copper-Maker. "Go on,
have me for your wife," said on her part *q Ë′k·!awēga*. Then *q*
Copper-Maker made her see, for Copper-Maker was not an ordinary
man. And so *q Ë′k·!awēga* could see. Then *q* she became pregnant.
Then *q* she gave birth. A boy *q* was her child. Then *q* she became [40]
pregnant again. Then *q* she gave birth again, and again her child
q was a boy. Then *q* her children were playing in the house and
they came near the little old woman who was sitting on the floor
and they rolled her over on the floor in their play. Then *q* the old
woman became angry. "Do keep still now and then," said on her [45]
part *q* the little old woman. "Is it perhaps known how you came
into this house, children?" said on her part *q* the little old woman.
Then *q* the children became really sad on account of the words of
the old woman. Then *q* the children told their mother, "What were
the words of the little old woman (directed) to us?" said on their [50]
part *q* the children to their mother. "What were her words?"
said on her part *q Ë′k·!awēga*. Then *q* the children repeated the
words of the old woman. "'Is it perhaps known how you came
into this house, children?' said the old woman to us," said on their
part *q* the children to their mother. ,'Oh, very true is her word," [55]
said on her part *q Ë′k·!awēga*. "Long ago my slaves just paddled
away with me. This is not my country," said on her part *q Ë′k·!a-
wēga* to her children. Then *q Ë′k·!awēga* told her husband about
the words of the old woman. Then *q* her husband said that he
would come and take his children. "Go on!" said on her part *q* [60]
Ë′k·!awēga, "that they may go to their grandfather in our country."
Copper-Maker came *q* with his wife and took his children to
*NomasE′nxe*ᵉ*lis*. He came *q* to the beach at *Tsē′tsEqalalis*. Then
q Ë′k·!awēga went up the beach and entered her father's house.
"I am your child, I am *Ë′k·!awēga*. We have come bringing my [65]
children to you," said *q Ë′k·!awēga*. "But I shall go back to the
country of my husband. This, your grandson, will be named
Copper-Maker," said *q Ë′k·!awēga*. "That is the name of his
father." — "Thanks," said on his part *q NomasE′nxe*ᵉ*lis*. Then
q Ë′k·!awēga returned with her husband. Then *q NomasE′nxe*ᵉ*lis* [70]
was near dying. Then *q* he arose and threw into the water the
princess pole of *Ë′k·!awēga*. Its top *q* turned towards *LE′mwas*.

And so *q* that was where was sitting on top *(Wŭpaxʟa*?), the
island on the beach at *ʟɛ'mwas*. And so *q* it is that former princess
[75] pole that the waves strike, that was at *nɛ^ɛwe'dē^ɛ*. And so *q* *Nomasɛ'nxe^ɛlis* just went down to the beach and stood in the water.
"Thus, I shall stand in the water, that I may be seen the (whole)
number of days," said *q* *Nomasɛ'nxe^ɛlis*. Now *Nomasɛ'nxe^ɛlis*
just stands on the rock as a stone at the south end of *Tsē'tsɛqalalis*.

<h3 style="text-align:center">*Hë'lig·iliqăla* and *Lō'ʟɛmaqa*[1]</h3>

Told by *Yā'qoʟas*, a *Naqɛ'mg·ilisala*

Hë'lig·iliqăla was living in *Q!ā'ʟas*. *Lō'ʟɛmaqa* was the sister of
Hë'lig·iliqăla. She was performing a winter ceremonial. *Q!ā'neqe^ɛ-
lak^u* passed behind her because he was afraid of the winter ceremonial. *Hë'lig·iliqăla* was carrying on his forehead the forehead
[5] object for throwing *(mɛqē'wē^ɛ)*. *Hë'lig·iliqăla* threw it first against
Lō'ʟɛmaqa, then *Lō'ʟɛmaqa* threw it back at him. They could
see the means of throwing wherever it went. While they were
playing they were beating fast time. The *Gwa'ts!ēnox^u* came from
the west coast in order to steal the bird's down which had fallen
[10] down from the red ceder bark of the dancers. They had sent a
slave whose name was *Aʟɛ'lak·as*. The slave went around the
house while they were asleep to steal the red cedar bark. But the
house had supernatural power. It discovered that the slave was
going to steal and when he came to the door, it sucked him in.
[15] Then the brother and sister awoke. They heard the slave singing
his sacred song under ground, where the supernatural power had
put him. Then they pulled him up and *Hë'lig·iliqăla* said, "Slave,
what are you doing here? Who sent you?" He replied, "I have
been sent to ask you to send a small piece of red cedar bark and
[20] eagle down to my chief *^ɛmā'xwa*. He asked me to steal it for him."
Hë'lig·iliqăla said, "It is bad, what you are doing. Why didn't
you come and ask us for it?" Then *Hë'lig·iliqăla* took a narrow
piece of bark and a pinch of bird's down and said, "Don't talk
about it. Keep it secret. It is bad that you tried to steal it and
[25] did not come to ask for it. Now go home and do not come back.
This house is supernatural. It is not good what you tried to do."
Then the slave went back to his master. He had a proud face
when he gave the red cedar bark to his master. Then *^ɛmā'xwa*'s
father sang his sacred song.

---

[1] See S 187; X 195, no. 4, 210, no. 9.

Kwe'xag·iᵋla[1]
(Told by *Ō'mx·ᵋīd*)

He wanted to take a wife *q* among the *Yū'ʟ!ēnoxᵘ*, that *Kwe'-xag·iᵋla*. Then *q* he traveled in his unfolding canoe. Not *q* on their part went aboard his daughters, *Hō'ᵋyag·iɫanaqa* and Copper-Smell-Woman *(K·!ē'p!ōsɛlaōgwa)* and Death-Causing-Woman *(Wā'wanɛmg·ilaōgwa)*. Three were his daughters. Then *q*[5] *ʟ!ā'ʟ!axwas* came paddling along below the fort of *Kwe'xag·iᵋla*. Paddle-sided was *q* the canoe of *ʟ!āʟ!axwas*. Then *q* *ʟ!ā'ʟaxwas* spoke, "Are you sitting in the house, friend *Kwe'xag·iᵋla?*" said *q* *ʟ!ā'ʟ!axwas*. "I am sitting in the house," said *q* on her part *Hō'ᵋyag·iɫanaqa*. She imitated the way of speaking of her father[10] when she was afraid of *ʟ!ā'ʟ!axwas* who might have planned to go and have as slaves the children of *Kwe'xag·iᵋla*. And so that was the reason why *ʟ!ā'ʟ!axwas* only left when he became afraid believing that he, *Kwe'xag·iᵋla*, had spoken. But it was she, his daughter, who spoke. [15]

But *Kwe'xag·iᵋla* was going to Triangle Island to woo the daughter of *Yā'qelalag·iᵋla*. And so *q* *Kwe'xag·iᵋla* had her for his wife. He came *q* going home with his wife to the Fort. And so *q* immediately he carried up his canoe on the canoe resting place. Former slaves *q* were the resting place of his canoe. Now the[20] former slaves, the resting place of the canoe of *Kwe'xag·iᵋla* became stones. The father of his wife came *q* to pay the marriage debt. Then *q* a privilege followed (the marriage gift)[2], the potlatch pole. Then *q* *Kwe'xag·iᵋla* was not satisfied with the potlatch pole as privilege that followed (i. e. as marriage gift). *Kwe'xag·iᵋla* *q* said[25] that he wanted that as privilege that followed (i. e. as marriage gift), the louse pole. "Go on, this louse pole will go to you, *Kwe'-xag·iᵋla*," said on his part *q* *Yā'qelalag·iᵋla* to his son-in-law. Then *q* they put up outside the louse pole, in front of the house of *Kwe'xag·iᵋla*. Along its body *q* were crawling big lice, on the post[30] of *Kwe'xag·iᵋla*. These *q* were large crabs. And so *q* every time the lice became hungry they would go down the pole and enter all the houses and go and eat all the men. Then *q* *Kwe'xag·iᵋla* became tired of the lice when they would walk about in his house. Then *Kwe'xag·iᵋla* would take up the tongs and strike among the lice[35] and every time the lice went back to the pole of *Kwe'xag·iᵋla*. Then *q* *Kwe'xag·iᵋla* launched his canoe to go to Triangle Island.

---

[1] S 184.

[2] i. e. the presents given by the father-in-law about a year after the marriage.

6*

Then *q* he said to his father-in-law *Yā'qelalag·i^εla*, "Go on, take
your louse pole. Behold, it is not good. We are too much troubled
40 by the lice who eat our tribe. Many of us are dead, killed by the
lice. That is the reason why I wish that you go and take it back
to you." Then *q Yā'qelalag·i^εla* spoke, "I'll go and take it, that
it may come back. It was you who wished for the louse pole,"
said on his part *q Yā'qelalag·i^εla. Kwe'xag·i^εla q* came back to
45 the Fort and took his canoe ashore.

"Are[1] you indeed sitting in the house, friend *Kwe'xag·i^εla?*"
said *q ʟ!ā'ʟ!axwas.* "I am sitting in the house," said *q* on her part
Hō'^εyag·iłanaqa. Then *ʟ!ā'ʟ!axwas* just left. *ʟ!ā'ʟ!axwas* believed
that it was he, *Kwe'xag·i^εla,* who had been speaking, but it was
50 his child who has spoken when *ʟ!ā'ʟ!axwas* was coming back after
having tried to get feathers at Feather-End.

The *Xoyā'las* move to *Xŭtē's*[1]

Told by *^εnō'la,* a *Koskimo.* Recorded by George Hunt.

The tribe whose name was *Xoyā'las* lived *q* at *Ămā'g·i^εna* and
they had for their chief Made-to-Give-always-Potlatches *(Ămā'-
wayotsogwi^εlak^u).* And so Made-to-Give-always-Potlatches always
took good care of his manhood. He always went into the
5 little river which has the name River-Noise *(wa'k·!āla)* every
morning and evening and he went into the water in the river and
rubbed his body with hemlock branches. Sometimes Made-to-
Give-always-Potlatches visited his other tribe who lived at *G·ō'g·oyo.*
Then he always kept close to the rocky beach at *Xŭtē's.* And that
10 was when it was noticed by him that there was soil heaped up
on the ground that had never been seen before. He just passed
Xŭtē's. Then he arrived at *G·ō'g·oyo* and he was invited by *Â'waade,*
his younger brother, to eat roasted black bass. And so, as soon
as they had finished *Â'waade* asked Made-to-Give-always-Pot-
15 latches to stay for four days. Made-to-Give-always-Potlatches
obeyed his word and Made-to-Give-always-Potlatches always
went inland every morning and evening to go into the water
at the upper end of the river of *G·ō'g·oyo* and he rubbed his body
with hemlock branches. And so, as soon as he had stayed there
20 for four days he said that he would go home to his house at *Ămā'-
g·i^εna* when it would be really evening. And so, as soon as it was
getting dark, Made-to-Give-always-Potlatches went aboard his

---

[1] The following is a repetition of the introductory passage of the tale.
[1] III 377; C 323.

small canoe to drift down with the tide. And so, as soon as he arrived at *Xŭtē's* he heard many men talking and it occurred to Made-to-Give-always-Potlatches that he would just go past [25] by what he heard. Then he arrived at his house at *Ămā'g·i^εna.* And so, as soon as he stepped out of his small canoe he just started and went to the lake of River-Noise. And so, as soon as he arrived at the lake, he immediately took hemlock and balsam fir, the tips of the branches. Then he sat down in the water of the lake. [30] He dived four times. Then he rubbed his body with hemlock branches. After he had rubbed his body with hemlock branches he took the balsam branches and sat down in the water. Then he rubbed his body with the balsam branches. And after he finished rubbing his body with balsam branches his body was [35] bleeding that night. For four days he did this mornings and evenings. And so, as soon as he had stayed for four days at the lake he came out of the woods late at night. And so, he just went to his small canoe and went quietly to *Xŭtē's* late at night. Then he arrived at the lower end of the graveyard on the side of the [40] island at the lower end of *Xŭtē's.* That is where he ran ashore his small canoe on the inland side of the island. Then he tied his small canoe to a spruce standing near the water. And so, as soon as he finished he went into the sea and rubbed his body with hemlock branches. And so, as soon as he had finished he [45] took balsam branches and rubbed his body with the balsam branches. And so, as soon as this was also done he pulled off rock seaweed and rubbed his body with it. And so, this was just finished, and he had washed off the slime of the seaweed, when Made-to-Give-always-Potlatches heard someone who said, [50] "I invite you, Made-to-Give-always-Potlatches, on behalf of Supernatural-of-the-Ground *(Nau'alakŭ^εlɛls),* and also follow me," said the man who was speaking. And so, as soon as Made-to-Give-always-Potlatches saw him he said, "True is your word, friend," and Made-to-Give-always-Potlatches stood up on the [55] rocks and followed the man whom he did not recognize as they were walking on the rocky beach at the lower end of *Xŭtē's;* and Made-to-Give-always-Potlatches saw a high mound, the house place of many houses. Then the man stopped and waited for Made-to-Give-always-Potlatches. And so, as soon as Made- [60] to-Give-always-Potlatches came up to the place where the man was standing, the man spoke to him and said, "Now take care, my dear, I am the one whom you call ghost *(Ha'yaḷilaqas),* for we are the souls of the dead people. I mean this, when you enter this house of our chief Supernatural-of-the-Ground, do not by [65]

any means eat what is given to you, else you will stay away.
And so, as soon as he asks for the reason of your coming, say that
you desire this new village site. Remember my word to you,"
said he. And the man and Made-to-Give-always-Potlatches started
70 together and entered the house. And so, as soon as they entered
the man said, "Now the guest of our chief has also come," said
he. Then another man asked Made-to-Give-always-Potlatches
to go and sit down on the right hand side inside the door of the
house of Supernatural-of-the-Ground. And so, as soon as he was
75 seated, another man took dry salmon and scorched it over the
fire in the middle of the house. And so, as soon as the salmon
was scorched, he took a food mat and broke the scorched salmon
on the food mat. And so, as soon as it was finished he spread it
in front of Made-to-Give-always-Potlatches. And so, immediately
80 Made-to-Give-always-Potlatches took the scorched salmon and
pretended to eat it. But he just kept on hiding it on his chest.
And so, as soon as he had finished eating the salmon, chief Supernatural-of-the-Ground spoke and said, "Go on, friend Made-to-
Give-always-Potlatches, tell me why you came to my house site
85 made by me," said he. And so, immediately Made-to-Give-
always-Potlatches replied to him. Then he said, "This is wished
by me, that I get your house site, chief, that I may come with
my tribe to live here," said he. Then Supernatural-of-the-Ground
answered his words and said, "Now you got your wish. Come
90 with your tribe and build your houses on the ground you got
from me, and let me go with my tribe to the village below this
your village site that we may hear each other when we beat
time in winter. Come tomorrow, for we will go into the ground
tonight. Now go home, friend. We are the souls of the dead
95 of our tribes," said he, as the fire in the middle of the house
was extinguished and disappeared, when, behold! it was getting
daylight in the morning. And so, immediately Made-to-Give-
always-Potlatches looked for a good place on the ground for his
house. And he staked it out so that the stream was to run under
100 the house in the middle of the village site. And so, as soon as he
had finished on the ground he walked on the rocks at the lower
end of *Xŭtē's* and went to where his small canoe lay inside of the
graveyard on the side of the island. And so, as soon as he arrived
there he went aboard his small canoe and started paddling going
105 to his house at *Ămā'g·iɛna*. And so, as soon as he arrived there
he was invited by Place-of-Getting-Rich *(Q!ŏ'mɛɛnakŭɛlas)* by
whom he was to be given food. And so, immediately Made-to-
Give-always-Potlatches stepped out of his small canoe and entered

the house of Place-of-Getting-Rich and he sat down in the rear of
the house. And so, immediately he was given split, dried herring. 110
And so, as soon as he had finished Made-to-Give-always-Potlatches
spoke and said, "Important is what I have done, brother Place-
of-Getting-Rich. I got as a treasure this village site *Xŭtē's*, and
so I wish that we should move all our houses today with all our
tribes and that we should leave this place on which the southeast 115
wind strikes too much. And that will be my house where the
river runs under my house," said he. And so, immediately Place-
of-Getting-Rich agreed to his words. And so, at once Place-of-
Getting-Rich called in his tribe, the *Xoyā'las*, to his house; and
so, as soon as they were all inside Place-of-Getting-Rich told 120
them that he wished them all to move their houses to *Xŭtē's*,
the village site got as a treasure by Made-to-Give-always-Potlatches,
said he. Then all his tribe fellows agreed to his words. And so,
as soon as he had finished his words all the men went out of the
house into which they had been called and all went up to the 125
roofs of their houses and shoved down the roof boards of their
houses and the beams and posts and they put them on canoes
tied together. And so they just piled on their belongings on the
platforms, the belongings of the house, as the tide was rising.
And so, as soon as this was finished they drifted in with the tide 130
running in. And so, as soon as they arrived at the beach of *Xŭtē's*
at high water they quickly hauled up the boards and beams and
posts. Then for four days they built houses and all the houses
of the first of the *Xoyā'las* were finished. And the tribes were
surprised when the firewood was first thrown down at the one 135
end of the village site when all the houses heard a hollow sound
reaching to the other end of the village site. It still sounds thus
at this recent day. Then Made-to-Give-always-Potlatches said
that the reason for the hollow sound was that it is hollow under
the village site of *Xŭtē's* for that is the place where the ghosts 140
live who are referred to as the souls of the dead men. That is
the reason why it is known by the Indians that the village site
of the souls is not far from the village site of the recent living men.
And that is the end after this.

G· î'lgăm

Told by *Ō'mx·ᵉīd*

"I will start," said *q G· î'lgăm* to his parents. "Go on," said
on his part *q* his father. "Take care on the ground, *G· î'lgăm*, and
put on your grizzly bear mask," said on his part *q* the father of

G·î'lgăm. Then *q G·î'lgăm* took his grizzly bear mask and put
⁵ it on. Then *q* he started and went and showed himself at Short
River *(Ts!ā'gwala)* in River's Inlet. Then *q G·î'lgăm* saw many
women picking salmon berries. Then *q G·î'lgăm* carried away
one woman among those of those who were picking berries. Then
q G·î'lgăm thought that he would take off his grizzly bear mask.
¹⁰ Then *q* he took off his grizzly bear mask and put it down.
Then *q G·î'lgăm* started and went to the women who were picking
berries. Then *q* he turned round to look at his grizzly bear skin
on his body. What should it be? It was walking along. Then
q G·î'lgăm took up a branch and threw it at his grizzly bear skin.
¹⁵ And so *q* he just threw down his grizzly bear skin. Then *q G·î'lgăm*
started again going towards the women. Then *q* he reached the
women and took one up in his arms. "I will have you for my wife,"
said *q G·î'lgăm* to the woman. "I am *G·î'lgăm.*" — "Go ahead,"
said on her part *q* the woman. "I will go and tell my father," said
²⁰ on his part *q G·î'lgăm.* "I shall come back quickly," — "Go ahead,"
said on her part *q* the woman. Then *q G·î'lgăm* went to his grizzly
bear skin. What should it be? There was *q* no place where his
grizzly bear skin was. Behold! the grizzly bear skin had started
and gone back by itself to the father of *G·î'lgăm* at Knight Inlet
²⁵ *(Dzā'wadē‘).* Then *q* the grizzly bear skin of *G·î'lgăm* entered the house
of *G·î'lgăm*'s father. And so *q* only the former grizzly bear skin
of *G·î'lgăm* lay in the house. Then *q* the father of *G·îlgăm* and his
wife cried when they knew that *G·î'lgăm* could not return again.
Only his bear skin had returned. And so *q G·î'lgăm* just took a
³⁰ River's Inlet woman for his wife, and he just *q* stayed with the
River's Inlet people. And so *q* he always shot with his arrow.
There was nothing *q* that was not killed by his arrow among the
big animals and even the fierce animals. And so that was the
reason why his name was changed; he stopped being called *G·î'lgăm*;
³⁵ he had the name Archer *(Hă'nʟ!ēkŭnas) q* now. Now his name
was changed when he was a great hunter.

Then *q* he had four children with his wife[1]. Then *q* Archer
became sick. Then *q* he could not see. It is said his children
and his wife were just poor. They had no food now, for Archer
⁴⁰ could not shoot, for he could not see. A bear came *q* and showed
itself near the house. "Archer", said on her part *q* his wife, "this
bear has come and shown itself," said *q* the wife of Archer. "Let
me try to shoot it. You just take hold of the end of this my arrow,"
said on his part *q* Archer. Then *q* he spanned his bow. Then *q*

---

[1] For distribution see Ts 817; C 447; Bella Bella 129.

his wife held the end of his arrow. "Now go on, shoot. Now this ⁴⁵
is straight," said *q* the wife of Archer. Then *q* Archer shot the
bear. "Heh!" said on her part *q* his wife, "It did not touch it,"
said *q* his wife. "Nevertheless, there is noise of groaning," said
on his part *q* Archer. Then *q* his wife and his children went and
skinned the bear. "Do not tell Archer that he nevertheless shot ⁵⁰
the bear." Then *q* his wife boiled the bear. Then *q* it was done.
Then *q* she gave to her children. And so *q* she never gave (anything)
to Archer for she denied that Archer had hit the bear when he
shot at the bear. Then *q* the youngest one of the children hid
some meat of the bear and hid it, to give it to its father. "Never- ⁵⁵
theless, you hit the bear. Our mother only said that we should
not give you of the bear. Eat this," said *q* the child of Archer.
Then *q* Archer spoke, "Keep this, child, and let us go to the lake,
and you guide me," said on his part *q* Archer. "Let us go," said
on its part *q* his child. Then *q* they started to go and reached ⁶⁰
the lake. "This is the lake. Sit down on the ground here," said
q the child of Archer. "Go back to our house, child," said on his
part *q* Archer to his child. Then *q* his child went back. And so
q Archer was alone on the ground. Then *q* a Loon came crying.
Archer *q* heard it. He did not see the Loon for he was blind. ⁶⁵
The Loon came *q*. Then *q* Archer said, "I wish you would become
a man and take pity on me and make me see. I cannot see. I am
blind," said *q* Archer. "And what am I, if I am (not) a man?"
said on his part *q* the Loon. "Come lie down on my back," said
on his part *q* the Loon. Then *q* Archer lay down on his back. ⁷⁰
"Take care," said *q* the Loon, "We shall go around diving in the
lake," said *q* the Loon. "You will just poke me if your breath
gives out as soon as we shall go around this lake, and so you will
begin to see." Then *q* Archer spoke, "Let us try," said *q* Archer.
Then *q* the Loon dived. On his part *q* he had not gone far before ⁷⁵
Archer poked him. Then *q* he raised his head. "Don't act in
this way," said *q* the Loon, "else you might not begin to see." Then
q he dived a again. Then *q* they went to the end of the lake. And
so *q* he just sat on the water. Then *q* he dived again. Then *q*
Archer began to see under the water. Then *q* he poked the Loon. ⁸⁰
Then *q* he raised his head. "How are you?" said on his part *q*
the Loon. "I begin to see a little," said on his part *q* Archer.
"Take care now," said on his part *q* the Loon. "Now we'll go
once (more)," said *q* the Loon. "Go on," said on his part *q* Archer.
Then *q* he dived. Then *q* Archer really began to see underneath ⁸⁵
the water, and so *q* he never poked it. It is said the Loon came up
just by itself, when it had gone around the lake. "How are you?"

said q the Loon. "Now I can see well," said on his part q Archer.
"Now you have found a supernatural treasure," said on his part
⁹⁰ q the Loon. He gave a bow to Archer. "You will make a salmon
of alderwood and put it into the water of the river near your
house. Then you will tell your wife to go and catch the salmon
with a hook. On your part you will not eat with her when your
wife and your children begin to eat the salmon. When they have
⁹⁵ almost finished eating you will go and say to them, 'Yeh! You
are eating alderwood,' you will say to your wife." — "I am going
to do so," said on his part q Archer. Then q the Loon left.

Then q Archer was sitting on the ground. There came q two
in a canoe along paddling, hardly q a little rose their traveling
¹⁰⁰ canoe above the water. Then q Archer called, "Come ashore.
Let me go aboard with you," said q Archer. "Come aboard,"
said on their part q the men. "I am afraid your canoe might
sink," said q Archer. "Ha! Ha! Ha!" said on their part q the
men, laughing. "This my canoe cannot sink. My canoe is (floating)
¹⁰⁵ flat on the water," said q the men. Behold! the two men were
Beavers. Then q Archer went aboard. Indeed q on its part the
small canoe of the Beavers never tilted. Then q they drifted
down the river. "This is near your house," said on their part
q the Beavers. "Now you have for a supernatural treasure this
¹¹⁰ canoe, this our canoe that (floats) flat on the water." — "Thank
you for this," said q Archer.

Then he started and went to the river near his house. Then q
he made a salmon of alderwood and put it into the water in the
river. And so q a sockeye salmon was standing in the water.
¹¹⁵ Then q he went to his house. "Welcome, Archer," said on her
part q his wife. "Welcome," said on his part q Archer. "I have
come to see again. Go and hook this salmon which is swimming
in the river," said q Archer. And so q immediately his wife and
his children went to hook the salmon and they roasted it. Then q
¹²⁰ it was done. And so q immediately the woman and her children
ate it. Then q the roast was almost gone. Then q Archer spoke,
"Heh!" said q Archer, "Eat this alderwood," said he q to his
wife and his children. And so q his wife and his children at once
just became alder trees. Only the youngest one remained alive.
¹²⁵ Now Archer had no wife q.

Then q he went to Long River *(G·î'ldala)* to have a wife among
the Long River people. Then q he went hunting. Then q he saw
very many mountain goats. Then q he shot them with his arrow.
Then q they were all shot. And so q he just went straight down
¹³⁰ to the point on the mountain and hid there. And so q he just

kicked down the mountain goats, and so *q* they just would fall right into the water of Long River. And so *q* he got very many mountain goats. Then *q* he went down the mountain and went home. Behold, the mountain goats just fell down dead at the mouth of Long River. And so that was the reason why he got [135] the name *Gŭ'na* (that means: falling down dead). Now he changed his name and he finished having the name Archer. Now his name was *Gŭ'na*.

"Let us go and try to get sea lions at *Wā'wis*," was said *q* on their part, to *Gŭ'na* by his brothers-in-law, "Let us do so," said [140] on his part *q Gŭ'na*. Then *q* they started paddling to go to *Wā'wis*. Then *q* they arrived there. "Let this one, *Gŭ'na*, be the first to get out of the canoe," said on their part *q* his brothers-in-law. Then *Gŭ'na* stepped out of his canoe on the ground-swell. As soon *q* as he was out of the canoe his brothers-in-law went back [145] and just left *Gŭ'na*. And so *q Gŭ'na* just covered his face with his cape and cried.

"I invite you on behalf of *Ămā'g·iᴌäsᴇlasō͜ᵋ*," was said on some-one's part *q*. And so *q* in vain *Gŭ'na* looked for the one who called him. And so *q* there was nothing on the rock. And so *q* [150] he just cried again. "I invite you on behalf of *Ămā'g·iᴌäsᴇlasō͜ᵋ*," was said on someone's part *q*. And so *q* in vain he looked for the one who called him. And so *q* there was nothing on the rock. Then *q* it occurred to *Gŭ'na* to bite through his cape. Then *q* he bit through his cape in order to look through it. Then came *q* [155] and showed itself Mouse-Woman *(Hä͜ᵋlamâlaga)*. "I call you on behalf of *Ămā'g·iᴌäsᴇlasō͜ᵋ*," said on her part *q* the Mouse to him. Then *q Gŭ'na* spoke, "Do not move about quickly on the rock, supernatural one. I have seen you long ago. Start, that we may go!" — "Come just follow me," said on her part *q* Mouse-Woman. [160] Then *q Gŭ'na* followed her and entered the house of the sealions. Behold! the sealions were men. Then *q Gŭ'na* warmed himself by the fire of the sealions. He came *q* to be looked at by the sealions. "This is the way of *Gŭ'na*. Holes[1] are through the body of *Gŭ'na*," said *q* the sealions. Then *q Gŭ'na* was spoken to by the chief of the [165] sealions. "Why are you doing this?" — "I was left by my brothers-in-law and so I just have to stay for good on the rock on this island," said *Gŭ'na* on his part *q*. Then *q* the chief of the sealions spoke again, "What will you eat?" Then *Gŭ'na* spoke, "This is my food, seals," said on his part *q Gŭ'na*. "Go on," said on their part *q* the sealions, [170]

---

[1] This means that he was sitting with his elbows resting on his knees so that the sealions could look through between the body and the upper arms.

"We do not eat seals; these are our dogs," said *q* the sealions. Then *q* the sealions killed a seal and steamed it. Then *q* it was done. Then *q* Gŭ'na ate the seal. The sealions *q* were really surprised, for they said that the seals were just dogs. Then *q* they
175 finished eating. Then *q* the chief of the sealions spoke, "Is it true that your arrows are fast?" said *q* the sealion. "It is true," said on his part *q* Gŭ'na. "If your arrow will go through the great (sealion-)that-blocks-the-way I'll give it to you for your canoe that you may go back to where you came from," said *q* the chief
180 of the sealions. Then *q* Gŭ'na spoke, "Let me try to shoot the (sealion-)that-blocks-the-way, for my arrow may go through the (sealion-)that-blocks-the-way," said *q* Gŭ'na. "Go on, call the (sealion-)that-blocks-the-way that he may be shot at," said on his part *q* the chief of the sealions. Then *q* the children went
185 and called the (sealion-)that-blocks-the-way. Then the (sealion-) that-blocks-the-way came. "Go on, shoot it!" Gŭ'na on his part *q* was told. "I will try," said on his part *q* Gŭ'na. Then he shot at it. Really *q* his arrow went through the (sealion-)that-blocks-the-way. Then *q* the chief of the sealions spoke, "Behold! Really
190 you are not an ordinary man," Gŭ'na *q* was told. "Really I am not an ordinary man," said on his part *q* Gŭ'na. "Now I'll loan it to you as your traveling canoe," said on his part *q* the chief of the sealions. Then *q* Gŭ'na spoke, "Do take pity on me, that I may go home to my country." Then *q* the chief of the sealions
195 spoke, "Go on! borrow the bladder of the (sealion-)that-blocks-the-way for the canoe of this Gŭ'na," said *q* the chief of the sealions. Then the children came *q* bringing the bladder of the (sealion-) that-blocks-the-way. Then *q* the chief of the sealions spoke, "Get into this bladder. You will not allow the gulls to sit on it, else
200 they might peck open your canoe. You will only name from inside the place you wish, that you may go right to the beach of your country," said *q* the chief of the sealions. "Thank you for your words," said on his part *q* Gŭ'na. Then Gŭ'na went into the bladder. And so *q* his bow was almost too long for the inside
205 of the bladder. "Go on, launch it," said on his part *q* the chief of the sealions. Then *q* the bladder was taken and launched on the sea while Gŭ'na was sitting in the bladder. "Q!ŭlō'ɫ, q!ŭlō'ɫ, q!ŭlō'ɫ, q!ŭlō'ɫ," said *q* Gŭ'na, naming a nice beach on the outside of Calvert Island *(Ăwīk·!edzēᵋ)*. That was named by him that
210 he might go right to the beach there while he was sitting in the bladder of the (sealion-)that-blocks-the-way. From time to time *q* gulls came to be seated on it. And so *q* he would just flip his fingers and they flew away, for Gŭ'na was afraid that the gulls might

peck through his canoe. For *q* four days he drifted about on the
sea. Then *q* he felt that he came to a beach in a country. Then *q* [215]
he let go of what was just squeezed together at the opening of
the bladder. Then *q* he let go of the mouth of the bladder and went
out of the bladder and he recognized the country where he had
gone straight ashore. Then *q* he recognized (it). Behold it was
that, *Q!ŭlō'ł*, where he had gone ashore, not far from the village. [220]
Gŭ'na q was really thirsty for water. Then *q* he searched for a root
and squeezed it and drank the juice. That was what was drunk
by the first (people). Then *q* he discovered a thick root with
water running out at the end on the beach. Then he discovered
the water running out of a hole of a root and he found his treasure. [225]
And so *q* that was now the place where his tribe drew water. Now
Gŭ'na had no hair *q*. His hair was all plucked off, caused by too
much heat in the inside of his bladder. And so *q* he was just feared
by his wife. And so *q* he just left his wife and went to Bella Bella.
Then *q* he saw *Ts!ᴇwŭ́'mqălagas*. And so *q Gŭ'na* said at once [230]
that he would have her for his wife. "Go ahead," said on her
part *q Ts!ᴇwŭ́'mqălagas*. And so *q Gŭ'na* had her for his wife.
He just stayed in the country of *Ts!ᴇwŭ́'mqălagas*. And that is
the end.

Myth of the *Q!ō'mk·!ū́t!ᴇs* of the *Gwaᵉsᴇla*

Told by *ʟ!ā́lĭł*, recorded by George Hunt.

The thunderbird came down *q* at *Ĝă̆ᵉya'xstē̆ᵉ*, the low island at the
entrance at the inlet of the *Gwaᵉsᴇla*, which has the name *Nᴇĝē'ʟē'*.
He had not been sitting long on a rocky place when the Thunderbird
thought it well to take off his thunderbird dress and to let it go
back upward into his house in the upper world. And the Thunder- 5
bird became a man. Now he built a small house to be his house.
And after he had finished building his house he built a platform
of driftwood in front of the house to be his summer seat. And
when this was finished the thunderbird who had turned into a
man was sitting there all the time. Now it was a fine day when he 10
saw Strength-of-Rock. It looked like a bottle seaweed (which is
called by the *Kwā'g·uł wā'wade*). It kept moving *q* below the sea.
Then the Strength-of-Rock came off where it was growing on the
rock and as soon as it came off from the rock the Strength-of-
Rock came out of the sea and became a man. Then he came and 15
sat down on the summer seat. And he, the man, Strength-of-Rock
spoke and said, "Who are you, friend, and what is your descent?"
said he. Then the thunderbird man answered him and said, "I am

T!ā'tǃɛntsǃīd, and my root is the Thunderbird which came from the
20 upper world," said he. Then the Strength-of-Rock man said,
I am *ᵋyā'g·is*, brother *T!ā'tǃɛntsǃīd*, I am *Q!ō'mogwē*. These are
my names. Now look out and go into the sea here so that you will
get as strong as I am. Only try to stay under water," said *ᵋyā'g·is*
to *T!ā'tǃɛntsǃīd*. Immediately *T!ā'tǃɛntsǃīd* arose and went down
25 the beach and waded. And as soon as the sea came up to his waist
he dived. And he did not stay under water a long time when he came
up again. Then *ᵋyā'g·is* said to him, "O brother, is that the length of
your breath? Try and make your breath longer so that you may stay
under water," said *ᵋyā'g·is* to him. Then *T!ā'tǃɛntsǃīd* dived again
30 and he stayed under water a long time before he came up. Then
ᵋyā'g·is said, "Your staying under water is better. Now look,
I mean that you shall stay under water a long time," said *ᵋyā'g·is*,
and he grasped a cedar tree and beginning from the top he twisted
it, and he only stopped twisting when his twisting arrived at the
35 bottom of the cedar tree. He said, "This is the reason why I ask
you to stay under water a long time when you dive so that you
may also be strong. Now dive again so that you may stay under
water a long time." Then *T!ā'tǃɛntsǃīd* dove again and he stayed
down a long time. He came up and for some time he did not dive
40 again until his breath came back. As soon as his breath had come
back he dived. Now he really stayed under water a long time and
came up again. Then *ᵋyā'g·is* called *T!ā'tǃɛntsǃīd* out of the water
to try to twist a spruce tree. And *T!ā'tɛntsǃīd* twisted the spruce
tree and he twisted it easily. Now they were equally strong. Then
45 *T!ā'tǃɛntsǃīd* asked *ᵋyā'g·is* to go into his little house and *T!ā'-
tǃɛntsǃīd* gave food to *ᵋyā'g·is* and after *ᵋyā'g·is* had eaten he spoke
and said, "Am I not going to tell you, brother *T!ā'tǃɛntsǃīd*, why
I came out of the sea? For I wish us to woo the princess of
ʟ!ā'qwag·ila at the north end of the world, to be my wife. We will
50 wait for four days for my canoe to come and lie on our beach to be
our travelling canoe," said he. Immediately *T!ā'tǃɛntsǃīd* replied
to his word and said, "True is your word, brother. To what tribe
belongs *ʟ!ā'qwag·ila?*" said he. Then *ᵋyā'g·is* answered him and
said, "His tribe are the *Ădɛxănē's* who have for their chief *ʟ!ā'-
55 qwag·ila*. Then *ᵋyā'g·is* said, "Now let us go, brother, when your
canoe will come." Now it was four days. Then *ᵋyā'g·is* arose early
in the morning and went out of the house and he saw that his
canoe had come and lay on the beach of his house. Immediately
ᵋyā'g·is went back into his house and awakened *T!ā'tǃɛntsǃīd* to
60 get up and start. And immediately *T!ā'tǃɛntsǃīd* awoke and arose
and took his bed cover and went out of the house with *ᵋyā'g·is*

and they went aboard their canoe. Then *T!ā't!Ents!īd* saw a great
carved box lying in the middle of the canoe filled with sea otter
blankets, the marriage gift for the princess of *L!ā'qwag·ila*, and
also two paddles which were the paddles of *ᵉyā'g·is* as he was 65
steering the canoe, and *T!ā't!Ents!īd* was sitting in the bow as they
started away. Now they went northward. They kept close inshore.
Then *ᵉyā'g·is* saw a sea anemone sticking on the rocks and *ᵉyā'g·is*
pried the sea anemone from the rock with the point of his paddle
(this is called by the *Xaē'sEla* "patch on rock") and he threw it on 70
the beach. Now *ᵉyā'g·is* said, "Now you will become a man and
your name will be *Q!āt!a*, and the name of your tribe will be
Q!at!ē'dExᵘ, of those that are born from you," said he to him.
Immediately the sea anemone became a man, the first man of the
Q!at!ē'dExᵘ. And *Q!āt!a* had *Lēslâs* for his chief who was the head 75
chief of the *Q!at!ē'dExᵘ*. Then *ᵉyā'g·is* and *T!ā't!Ents!īd* paddled.
It was evening when they arrived in the village of *L!ā'qwag·ila*
and his tribe the *ĂdExănē's*. They might be the *G·îdExănē's* who
live in an village called *t!Engās* (Tongass). Immediately *L!ā'qwag·ila*
called *T!ā't!Ents!īd* and *ᵉyā'g·is* to eat in his house and at once they 80
went up the beach to enter the large house which was ten steps
deep. They sat down in the middle of the rear of the house and
immediately they were given food. After they had been given
food *T!ā't!Ents!īd* spoke and said, "We have come and arrived,
chief *L!ā'qwag·ila*, that you may come and treat me and my brother 85
ᵉyā'g·is well. Now you have invited us to come and warm our
faces by your fire. I mean this, we came here paddling to woo your
princess, chief *L!ā'qwag·ila*, for *ᵉyā'g·is*," said he. Immediately
L!ā'qwag·ila spoke and said, "Your words are welcome, *T!ā't!Ents!īd*,
on behalf of this chief *ᵉyā'g·is*, for I was expecting him to come 90
and woo my princess *L!ā'qwag·ilaōgwa*. Now go on, *T!ā't!Ents!īd*,
and marry this evening, that our minds may be at rest." Immediately *ᵉyā'g·is* went out of the house and took hold by its side of the
large box containing the sea otter skins and he put it down inside
the door of the house. Then he called *T!ā't!Ents!īd* to go to the 95
place where he put down the box. And as soon as *T!ā't!Ents!īd*
had gone there he opened the box and took out one sea otter skin.
Then he spoke and said, "Now turn your ear this way, chief
L!ā'qwag·ila, and listen to what I shall say to you. Now I take this
one sea otter blanket," said he and threw it down; and he also took 100
out another sea otter skin from the box and he repeated what he
had said before. As soon as ten sea otter skins had been taken by
him he took out another sea otter skin from the box and he said,
"Now I lift from the floor your princess, chief," said he, "One,

¹⁰⁵ two, three, four, five sea otters," and he took out five sea otters
from the box. And he said, "Now I call with these five sea otters
my wife. Indeed, for I wish my wife to go aboard my wooing canoe,"
said he. Immediately *ʟ!ā'qwag·ila* spoke and said, "Now you got
my princess, chief *ᵋyā'g·is*, now you have her for your wife. Now
¹¹⁰ I give in marriage this house which is ten steps deep and I give
in marriage the name *ʟ!ā'qwag·ila* to be your name and I give in
marriage four house dishes, the grizzly bear, and killerwhale, and
sea lion, and whale, and these seven slaves. (Illustrated on page 627,
figure 194 and the one on page 626, figure 193¹). He is the chief
¹¹⁵ of the seven slaves who dance under your feet, chief *NEg·ä'dzē*.
Now you will be *ʟā'sEla* (*ʟā'sEla* means the *ʟEwE'laxa*) son-in-law.
She, your wife, will teach you the ways of the *ʟā'sEla* and the seven
slaves and their chief will be called by you *ÄdExänē's* dancers,
for that is the dance of my tribe, the *ÄdExänē's*," said *ʟ!ā'qwag·ila*
¹²⁰ to *ᵋyā'g·is*. Now *T!ā't!Ents!īd* and *ᵋyā'g·is* stayed four days; then
they came home to their house at *Ĝäᵋya'xstēᵋ* with his wife *ʟ!ā'qwa-
g·ilaōgwa* and the eight slaves with their chief among them. And
two among the slaves were always paddling. They saw many young
sawbill ducks and the two slaves paddled after them. Then the
¹²⁵ young sawbill ducks went to a river named *T!ō'xsēᵋ*, a river which
has many sockeye salmon and spring salmon and steelhead salmon
and cohoes and humpback salmon. Now the young sawbill ducks
went right up the river of *T!ō'xsēᵋ*. Then the two slaves saw a
house, and immediately the two slaves stepped out of their canoe
¹³⁰ and went into the house. Then the slaves saw an old man lying
on his back by the side of the fire. One of the slaves spoke to him
and said, "What are you doing on my river? To what tribe do
you belong that you come and dare to stay on my river," said
one of the slaves to him. Then the old man answered him and
¹³⁵ said, "I am *Sō'gŭlis* and I own this river. I belong to the numaym
ᵋwā'las of the *Nā'k!wax·daᵋxᵘ*," said he. The slave just threatened
to kill *Sō'gŭlis*, in order to get the river by killing. Therefore
Sō'gŭlis just escaped and came walking through to *Q!Exā'lis* near
the mouth of *Ts!ē'qwēᵋ* (Seymour Inlet). Now the two slaves went
¹⁴⁰ home to their house at *Ĝäᵋya'xstēᵋ*. As soon as they arrived they
reported to *ᵋyā'g·is* and *T!ā't!Ents!īd* what they had done and
immediately *ᵋyā'g·is* and *T!ā't!Ents!īd* and his slaves moved to
T!ō'xsēᵋ. They built a house there. As soon as they had finished
building a house the two slaves paddled again and went to *NEĝē'ʟēᶜ*.

---

¹ This refers to the illustrations in F. Boas "The Social Organization
and Secret Societies of the Kwakiutl Indians; Report U. S. National Museum for 1895. Washington D. C.

This is near the head of the inlet. Now the two slaves saw again [145] a house and at once they wished to go and see the owner of the house. As soon as they arrived on the beach of the house a man came out of his house and came to meet the two slaves. As soon as he came alongside the canoe in which the two slaves were seated the man spoke and said, "Your coming, brothers, is a cause of [150] surprise. Where did you come from? Now come and go into my house," said he. One of the slaves spoke and said, "We come sent by our chiefs, ᵉyā'g·is and T!ā't!ᴇnts!īd to see whether there are traces of men here. Now we have met. Tell me your name," said he. And the man said, "Your word is good. I am Sē'saxâlas and my [155] tribe are the G·ī'g·ilgăm. Where is the village of your chiefs," said he. Then the slave said, "We first lived at Ğă̆ᵉya'xstēᵉ and we came to T!ō'xsēᵉ. Our tribe are the Q!ō'mk·!ūt!ᴇs," said he. Then the conversation ended. Finally they stepped out of their canoe and followed Sē'saxâlas and they went into his house. Now the two [160] slaves saw that the four posts of the house were carved. Then Sē'saxâlas gave food to his visitors. As soon as they had been given food they went out of the house and went aboard the canoe, and the two slaves paddled and went home to their house at T!ō'xsēᵉ. When they arrived at the place near T!ō'xsēᵉ, a country [165] which is named Ǧeg·ägēᵉ, the two slaves saw smoke of a house and at once they went ashore to it. When they arrived on the beach they stepped out of the canoe and stood in the doorway of the house. Then a man was sitting in the house. Immediately he spoke and said to the slaves, "Come right in, masters, and sit down. I am [170] Hai'alk·in, my tribe are the Sī'sᴇnʟ!ēᵉ," said he. Immediately Hai'alk·in gave food to the visitors and after they had been given food Hai'alk·in spoke and said, "Where do you come from, masters?" said he. Then the one slave replied to him and said, "We were sent by our chiefs ᵉyā'g·is and T!ā't!ᴇnts!īd to come [175] and see whether there are traces of men here. Now we have met. The name of the tribe of our chiefs ᵉyā'g·is and T!ā't!ᴇnts!īd is Q!ō'mk·!ūt!ᴇs. Now we have met Sē'saxâlas at Nᴇgē'ʟēˤ whose tribe has the name G·ī'g·ilgăm. Now we will go home to report to ᵉyā'g·is and T!ā't!ᴇnts!īd about our meeting," said he as they went [180] aboard their canoe. Now it was evening. It was not really dark when they arrived at their house at T!ō'xsēᵉ. As soon as they had gone into the house the slaves at once reported that they had met Sē'saxâlas whose tribe had the name G·ī'g·ilgăm at Nᴇgē'ʟēˤ and that the four posts of his house were carved. "And we came to [185] the village of Hai'alk·in who said that the name of his tribe is Sī'sᴇnʟ!ēᵉ and who lives at a place which has the name Ǧeg·ägēᵉ.

7

These are really kind chiefs, for everyone of them invited us in,"
said he. Immediately *T!ā'tǃɛntsǃīd* spoke and said, "Did you
190 hear, *ᵋyā'g·is*, the news of the men of our house that they met
chief *Sē'saxâlas*, chief of the *G·ī'g·ilgǎm*, and *Hai'aɫk·in*, chief of
the *Sī'sɛnⱢǃēᵋ*? Am I not surprised, for I thought we were the
only men in this country. Now welcome, our tribe," said he.
Then *ᵋyā'g·is* spoke and said, "Indeed, the report of the men of
195 our house is good. Now you will call the chiefs *Sē'saxâlas* and
Hai'aɫk·in to come into our house in the morning," said *ᵋyā'g·is*
to the two slaves, said he. As soon as day came in the morning
the two slaves started and they went to invite *Sē'saxâlas* and
Hai'aɫk·in on behalf of *ᵋyā'g·is* and *T!ā'tǃɛntsǃīd*. And it was not
200 yet near evening when they came back. Then *Sē'saxâlas* and
Hai'aɫk·in came. As soon as they came to the beach of the house
of *ᵋyā'g·is* and *T!ā'tǃɛntsǃīd* the whistles of the house sounded,
and now *ᵋyā'g·is* and *T!ā'tǃɛntsǃīd* danced the *Ɫā'sɛla*, the dance
given in marriage by *Ⱡǃā'qwag·ila* to him. And *ᵋya'g·is* made the
205 seven *Ǎdɛxǎnē's* dancers which are illustrated on page 627, fig. 194[1],
and their chief pictured on page 626, fig. 193, dance. (It is a mistake
when the book said that he is *Nō'mas*). As soon as the seven
Ǎdɛxǎnē's dancers finished dancing *ᵋyā'g·is* gave away dressed
deer skin blankets to *Sē'saxâlas* and *Hai'aɫk·in*. And now *ᵋyā'g·is*
210 changed his name and he had the name *Ⱡǃā'qwag·ila* after this.
And he named himself with the name given to him in marriage
by his father-in-law. And *T!ā'tǃɛntsǃīd* also danced with the secular
dancing song and he followed the sunbeam thunderbird mask
of the song which is represented in the book, page 630, fig. 197.[1]
215 And when he finished dancing he gave away dressed deer skin
blankets to *Sē'saxâlas* and *Hai'aɫk·in*. Now the hearts of *Ⱡǃā'qwa-
g·ila* and *T!ā'tǃɛntsǃīd* and *Sē'saxâlas* and *Hai'aɫk·in* were really one
after this and the four chiefs said that they would stay together
and that the name of their tribe would be *Gwaᵋsɛla*. Immediately
220 they built a house in a good country which is called *Ǧwē'k·ɛlis*.
That was their winter village after this.

Ⱡǃā'Ⱡǃaxwas[2]

Told by *Ō'mx·ᵋīd*

Then *q Ⱡǃā'Ⱡǃaxwas* started paddling with his paddle-side canoe.
Then *q* he went to Nass River *(Nās)*. Then *q* he arrived at a village.
Then *q* he was invited to come out of his canoe. Then *q* he was

---

[1] See note on p. 88.
[2] See S 154; III 227.

given to eat. Then q dry salmon was placed before him. Then q
a small grease dish was placed before him which q could not be [5]
emptied of oil. Then q *ᴸ!ā́ᴸ!aχwas* tried to take all the oil. And so
q he never took it all out. Only from time to time it became again
full of oil. Then q *ᴸ!ā́ᴸ!aχwas* wished to go ahead and steal the little
grease dish. Then q he went aboard his canoe and q he had obtained
by stealing the little grease dish. And so q the owner of the grease [10]
dish never moved, and he even saw that *ᴸ!ā́ᴸ!aχwas* had stolen the
little grease dish. Behold! supernatural was the man, the owner of
the little grease dish. Then q *ᴸ!ā́ᴸ!aχwas* started paddling. And
so q as soon as he tried to travel away the man made the sea steep
and so q *ᴸ!ā́ᴸ!aχwas* just came back. Four times q *ᴸ!ā́ᴸ!aχwas* [15]
tried to start paddling, and so q every time the sea was just tilted
up and made *ᴸ!ā́ᴸ!aχwas* come back to the beach of the owner of
the little grease dish. Then q *ᴸ!ā́ᴸ!aχwas* became afraid. And
q he just took the little grease dish out of the canoe and threw it
out of the canoe at its owner. Then q *ᴸ!ā́ᴸ!aχwas* came back to [20]
Ǥwaʾᵋyasdɛ́ms.

Origin of the Chilcotin
Ǥwaʾwaēnoxᵘ
Told by *Ǥ·ī́qalas*, a *Ǥwaʾwaēnoxᵘ*

The *Ǥwaʾwaēnoxᵘ* had a winter dance q together at a place
named *T!ɛ́mχᵘsɛm*. Then their chief spoke (considering as) bad
and too small the island, that he would go across to a real country
and that only there they would have a winter dance together.
Cedar withes q were twisted. Over three hundred fathoms, all [5]
cedar withes. It was tied at the end q by all those inside the whale.
The young men of the *Ǥwaʾwaēnoxᵘ* were all inside the imitation
whale. Then they would pretend to blow. Then the cedar withes
tied to the end of the whale, were pulled. The cedar withes were
tied over three hundred fathoms long. They almost arrived q at [10]
the village site. Then q the cedar rope they were pulling broke
at the end, and so q the many men just sank. They were dead.
Then q the tribes went into the house to talk about what to do.
The chief said q, "Tribes, do not let us just act in vain! for the
talk may never end in our future generations about what happened [15]
to us. Let us just go ahead and do the right way; on account of
our good name we commit suicide of our tribe on account of the
great thing that happened to us. Let us have the name of being
put to shame. Let us go inland." Then q they went inland. Now
a number of years (passed) before they came long ago back to the [20]

7*

sea and built a house on the ground. An attendant of the house jumped into the house, "I am Spouting-in-Front-on-the-Ground *(ʟ!ā′ʟ!alɛnaᵉladzōᵉ)* inland," said he *q.* Another one came *q.* "I am Pried-Up-at-End *(K!wī′diłbēᵉsōᵉ)* inland." — "I am Clear-
²⁵ Sky *(Q!ōᵉxŭlisaᵉwilis)* inland." Then *q* they were all in the house and they ate. Dry deer *q* was their food. And so *q* they almost finished eating when two young men heard shooting and they just went back inland. Then *q* they just built houses again on something. They built their houses *q* on a drift wood jam. Then *q* became
³⁰ different their way of talking from their former way of talking. "Let us go in. We are laughed at by the Kwakiutl tribes." Then their speech was different *q* in the inland country.

The Deluge

Told by *G·ī′qalas*, a *Gwa′waēnoxᵘ*

Chief *Wā′k·as* held a winter ceremonial. When he gave a winter ceremonial long ago the deluge came. They just *q* tied their canoes together and they beat time for the winter dance and sang winter dance songs in the canoes. They went *q* to the top of a great
⁵ mountain. They went on a flat place on a good place on the rocks. Then *q* they went to the top of the mountain and sang four cannibal songs *q* and beat time for the cannibal. They did not know *q* that the deluge had gone down, and so *q* they were still playing on the mountain. Now they just became stone. And so *q* the other men
¹⁰ went right down to their village site and they became a tribe again. Then *q* he made a river. Then *q* he made salmon in the river. Then *q* he blocked out a river canoe. The canoe he was making was self paddling. Then *q* he invited the Rivers Inlet tribe. He invited the *Nō′xŭnts!ī́dɛxᵘ*. All those *q* who were invited came together.
¹⁵ They sang the *lasɛla* (or *ʟɛwɛ′laxa)* songs. Then *q* there were four (songs). Then *q* they were killed by the Bella Coola. They were killed and the tribe had bad luck; and they were killed by the Bella Coola. Their crests were all taken.

Star Story

Recorded by *George Hunt*

The first of the Koskimo lived *q* at *Mɛla′dēᶜ* at the sockeye salmon season and *q* they were catching sockeye salmon at *Mɛla′dēᶜ*; and so, *q* the sockeye salmon had all gone up the river of *Mɛla′dēᶜ* and they finished fishing for sockeye salmon. Then *q* the sea hunters got
⁵ ready to put drift wood across the ends on the beach for their

small hunting canoes, to dry the bottoms, for it was a fine day,
and as soon as this was done they split well-splitting cedar wood,
a fathom and a half in length, for burning the bottoms of their
small hunting canoes. And so, as soon as each hunter had forty
split cedar sticks they evened the ends. Then they took split [10]
narrow strips of cedar bark, tied them together at the near end
of the implement for burning the (canoe) bottoms. Then, it is said,
the implements for burning the bottom were tied in four places
and so, it is said, when they finished it was ready with the small
hunting canoe, when *q* the bottom was dry. Then *q* they lighted [15]
the top end in the fire on the beach and so *q*, as soon as they blazed
up they burned the bottom of the cutwater of the small hunting
canoe and *q* they went towards the stern of the small canoe.
And so, as soon as they had burned the bottom *q* the hunters
went down the beach carrying their implements for burning the [20]
bottom, and threw them into the sea. Then *q* the hunter, when
he threw the implement for burning the bottom into the water,
said, "Now day, be calm, therefore I come to put into the water
this fire that you wish for," said he as he came and left it and
turned over his small hunting canoe. Then *q* he took an old mat [25]
and rubbed off the charcoal on the bottom of the small canoe,
and so *q* as soon as this was finished he righted his small canoe;
and now *q* he had finished when daylight came in the morning
with his (work) as he always rubbed his body with hemlock branches
in the morning and in the evening, the whole number of the many [30]
sea hunters of the first of the Koskimo. And so *q* it began not (yet)
to become daylight in the morning, when the sea hunters all went
to the river *MEla'dē'* and rubbed their bodies with hemlock branches,
all of them with their steersmen, and so *q* as soon as they finished,
they all *q* went home to their houses and had a little breakfast, [35]
and so, as soon as they had finished, the sea hunters took their
canoe boxes in which were the spear points, the harpoon line, and
also four arrows and their bows, and also their paddles and their
harpoon shafts. Then *q* they went down the beach to where the
small hunting canoe was, and so *q* the sea hunters went straight [40]
down to the shore and put down what they carried at the edge
of the sea. Then *q* they came up again on the beach and carried
at each end the small canoe, with their spearsman, and they launched
it outside of where they had put down their belongings. Then *q*
they put them aboard their small canoes. Then *q* all the hunters [45]
went aboard their small hunting canoes and *q* there were three
in one canoe, *Yā'qela* and his two nephews. Then *q* there were
also three in one canoe, *Yā'ᵉyaqExts!a* and his younger brothers,

for *Yā'qela* was the sea hunter of the numaym *Naɛ'nsx·a* of the
⁵⁰ Koskimo. *Yā'ᵉyagɛxts!a* q was the sea hunter of the numaym
Q!ā'ʟ!ēnoxᵘ of the *G·â'p!ēnoxᵘ* and q they started paddling at the
same time, as there were more than twenty small sea hunting
canoes. Then q they arrived at *K·ā'waq*. Then q they would search
for seaotters that might be there, but q none were found there.
⁵⁵ Then q they started paddling and went to *A'ᵉyaax·siwēᵉ* and now q
they found many sea otters all around the island. And q *Yā'qela*
and *Yā'ᵉyagɛxts!a* kept together, and so q the small hunting
canoes of the sea hunters were scattered in the way it is done in
sea otter hunting when they surround the sea otters shouting in
⁶⁰ order to drown them. And so q it was towards evening and q the
other hunters had caught many sea otters. Then q there was no
game now of the two small canoes (of) *Yā'qela* and *Yā'ᵉyagɛxts!a*,
and so q *Yā'qela* and *Yā'ᵉyagɛxts!a* were the first among their
sea hunting fellows, and q it began to be nearly dark. Then q
⁶⁵ *Yā'qela* saw a large sea otter swimming along. On the nape of
its neck q was a ball of fire. Then q *Yā'qela* speared it. *Yā'ᵉya-*
gɛxts!a q also speared the large sea otter, and so q as soon as their
spears had hit the sea otter, the sea otter went out seaward and
went up toward our sky, and q it was dragging behind the two
⁷⁰ small canoes as it was going upward and stuck on our sky. That
was the sea otter, the Pleiades, and so q that is the hunter in the
sky (Orion) *Yā'qela*, and the hunter with him is *Yā'ᵉyagɛxts!a*.
And therefore the hunters know about them, for they all saw them
going up and sticking where the place is of Orion and of the Pleiades
⁷⁵ and of the one who joins in sea hunting. And so, from this these
stars have their names, for the sea hunters told the first Koskimo
all that happened to *Yā'qela* and *Yā'ᵉyagɛxts!a* and the four men
of their crew, and that is the end.

Story of the *G·ī'g·îlgăm* of the *Hăxwā'mis*[1]

(Recorded by George Hunt)

P!ā'sɛlal Hä'qŭlal was living q with his Prince *Yā'qoʟasɛmēᵉ*
and his Princess *Mɛlē't* at *Gwa'yēᵉ*. *P!ā'sɛlal Hä'qŭlal* was the
head chief of the numaym *G·ī'g·îlgăm* of the *Hăxwā'mis*. Then q
the numaym *G·ē'xsɛm* of the *Hăxwā'mis* had for their chief *Lɛlā'-*
⁵ *k·inis*. Then q *Lɛlā'k·inis* asked in marriage *Mɛlē't*, the princess
of *P!ā'sɛlal Hä'qŭlal*. Then q *P!ā'sɛlal Hä'qŭlal* did not wish his
princess *Mɛlē't* to have *Lɛlā'k·inis* for her husband, for *P!ā'sɛlal*

---

[1] See p. 102.

Hä'qŭlał thought that *Lɛlā'k·înis* was too low in rank to have *q* for his wife his princess. Then *q* the mind of *Lɛlā'k·înis* was bad and he was ashamed of the words of *P!ā'sɛlał Hä'qŭlał* to him, [10] and *q Lɛlā'k·înis* bewitched the prince of *P!ā'sɛlał Hä'qŭlał*, namely *Yā'qoᴌasɛmē*ᵉ, for *Lɛlā'k·înis* learned that it was he, *Yā'qoᴌasɛmē*ᵉ and his two younger brothers who did not allow their sister *Mɛlē't* to have *Lɛlā'k·înis* for her husband, and that was the reason why *Lɛlā'k·înis* wished to bewitch *Yā'qoᴌasɛmē*ᵉ [15] so that he might die. And so *q* as soon as *Lɛlā'k·înis* had obtained everything from *Yā'qoᴌasɛmē*ᵉ he worked his witchcraft; and *q Lɛlā'k·înis* put what he used for the purpose of witchcraft into a small canoe box of a seal hunter and he put the canoe box under a thick cedar tree. Then *q* immediately *Yā'qoᴌasɛmē*ᵉ learned that [20] *Lɛlā'k·înis* had bewitched him and so *Yā'qoᴌasɛmē*ᵉ felt at once that he was being bewitched and *q* he became very sick and *q* he was quickly getting emaciated. He was only a heap of bones *q*. Then *q* the two younger brothers and his father *P!ā'sɛlał Hä'qŭlał* had a secret meeting and they said that *Yā'qoᴌasɛmē*ᵉ should [25] pretend to die that night and they would go and pretend to bury him at *Ā'l*ᵉ*ałxō* when daylight would come in the morning, said they. And so *q* as soon as it was nearly daylight the two wives of *P!ā'sɛlał Hä'qŭlał* were crying with the wife of *Yā'qoᴌasɛmē*ᵉ, for the three women believed that *Yā'qoᴌasɛmē*ᵉ had really died, [30] for the three women did not know about the speech of *P!ā'sɛlał Hä'qŭlał* and his three sons when *P!ā'sɛlał Hä'qŭlał* would not allow it to be known why he had done so. And *P!ā'sɛlał Hä'qŭlał* put the past *Yā'qoᴌasɛmē*ᵉ into a large box; and *q* he had this for his coffin. Then *q* they put the coffin aboard the canoe; and the [35] three, *P!ā'sɛlał Hä'qŭlaĭl* and his two sons, besides the late *Yā'qoᴌasɛmē*ᵉ were in the canoe; and *q* they were going to bury him at *Ā'l*ᵉ*ałxō*. And so *q* it was nearly noon when they arrived at *Ōxsde*ᵉ*las* at the lower end of the village site of *Ā'l*ᵉ*ałxō*. Then *q* they took the coffin out of the canoe and put it on the ground where [40] they were going to bury it. Then *q* the two sons of *P!ā'sɛlał Hä'qŭlał* dug up the sand so that there was really a wide (hole); but *q P!ā'sɛlał Hä'qŭlał* took off the cover of the coffin and looked at his prince; and he saw that he was still alive. Then *q* the one who pretended to be dead said that he was getting better, and [45] only this was different that he felt cold, said *q Yā'qoᴌasɛmē*ᵉ to his father. Then *q P!ā'sɛlał Hä'qŭlał* advised *Yā'qoᴌasɛmē*ᵉ not to go out to look when (a canoe) paddling along should be heard seaward from his house. "However, look through a hole so that you may look at it. And as soon as you see that shredded cedar [50]

bark is tied on the heads of the men, go to meet them, for that will
be the way of your younger brothers when they come from time
to time to look after you," said he *q*; for indeed *Yā'qoḷasEmē*ᵉ was
getting well. And so *q* as soon as *P!ā'sElaḷ Hä'qŭlaḷ* stopped giving
⁵⁵ advice to *Yā'qoḷasEmē*ᵉ the two younger brothers of *Yā'qoḷasEmē*ᵉ
came and told that they had finished making the house for their
elder brother. And *Yā'qoḷasEmē*ᵉ went into the ground into the
house dug into the ground. And so *q* as soon as *Yā'qoḷasEmē*ᵉ
went down in his house dug into the ground, then *q* *P!ā'sElaḷ*
⁶⁰ *Hä'qŭlaḷ* asked his two sons to sprinkle water over the sand to
smooth entirely their tracks. And so *q* as soon as they had finished
P!ā'sElaḷ Hä'qŭlaḷ with his two sons went aboard the canoe and
they started paddling and they went home to *Gwa'yē*ᵉ. And so *q*
they had not gone far when they saw *Lelā'k·înis*, the one who had
⁶⁵ bewitched *Yā'qoḷasEmē*ᵉ, paddling along going towards *Ā'l*ᵉ*aḷxō*.
They never talked when they had already thrown into the water
the witchcraft box. Therefore *Yā'qoḷasEmē*ᵉ was getting better.
Then *q* *P!ā'sElaḷ Hä'qŭlaḷ* arrived at the mouth of *Leqwē'*ᵉ, when *q*
P!ā'selaḷ Hä'qŭlaḷ saw a small box floating about. Then *q* he went
⁷⁰ towards it and took it. Then *q* *P!ā'sElaḷ Hä'qŭlaḷ* looked into it.
That was the witchcraft box of *Lelā'k·înis* against *Yā'qoḷasEmē*ᵉ.
And *q* *P!ā'sElaḷ Hä'qŭlaḷ* untied what was tied up in the small box.
Then *q* he threw it into the sea. And so *q* as soon as he had done
so he started paddling and went to *Gwa'yē*ᵉ. It was now salal
⁷⁵ berry season; and *q* the two sons of *P!ā'sElaḷ Hä'qŭlaḷ* always
looked after their elder brother *Yā'qoḷasEmē*ᵉ, once every ten days.
And so that was the reason why *P!ā'sElaḷ Hä'qŭlaḷ* knew that his
son *Yā'qoḷasEmē*ᵉ was getting well. But *q* the salal berries were
nearly over-ripe when the brothers went the last time to see their
⁸⁰ eldest brother *Yā'qoḷasEmē*ᵉ. Now *q* he was not sitting in his dirt-
covered house, and *q* there were no new tracks seen by the brothers;
and they suspected that their eldest brother had been killed by
Lelā'k·înis. And they just went home to *Gwa'yē*ᵉ and they secretly
told their father *P!ā'sElaḷ Hä'qŭlaḷ*. And *q* they did not show
⁸⁵ clearly that their hearts were sorry, and *q* as soon as it was sleeping
time *P!ā'sElaḷ Hä'qŭlaḷ* cried secretly with his two wives and his
two sons. And *q* the two wives of *P!ā'sElaḷ Hä'qŭlaḷ* did not know
the reason why they were recently crying for the past *Yā'qoḷasEmē*ᵉ.
And *q* in vain the women tried to find out why they did so, for
⁹⁰ *P!ā'sElaḷ Hä'qŭlaḷ* had never cried in the morning when he said
that *Yā'qoḷasEmē*ᵉ had died, at the time when he said they were
going to bury him at *Ā'l*ᵉ*aḷxō*, the one who was still alive.

And now, for a while this is finished, and I begin to talk about

Yā'qoḷasɛmē͎ᵋ. And *q* he got strong, but *q* he was very emaciated.
And so *q* he was sitting in his dirt-covered house in the morning, ⁹⁵
thinking about the future way of the speech of his father *P!ā'sɛlaḷ
Hä'qŭlaḷ* and his two younger brothers, when they would come
again to look at the place where he was. Then *q* he heard a noise
of walking near his dirt-covered house. A man *q* came to his house
and sat inside his doorway. Then *q* the newly arrived man spoke. ¹⁰⁰
Then *q* he said, "I have come to invite you, friend, to witness the
dance tonight," said he *q.* And *q Yā'qoḷasɛmē͎ᵋ* never asked him
who had sent him to invite him, for he felt very uneasy because
he had never met the man, therefore he just arose at once and
followed the man as he went upstream walking along the river of ¹⁰⁵
Ā'ḷᵋaḷxō. And *q* they never had one spoken word as they were
going up the river. And so *q* it was nearly evening when *q* the man
spoke. Then *q* he said, "Let us rest for a while that you may know
why I invited you to come to the house of our chief, this *G·ī'lg·iyāᵋ-
lis,* that you may notice everything what will be done tonight," ¹¹⁰
said he *q.* Then *q* they started. But *q* they had not gone far when
Yā'qoḷasɛmē͎ᵋ heard a man saying, "Now we come to look for
a face," the last inviting to the dance which was heard by him.
And the man also asked *Yā'qoḷasɛmē͎ᵋ* that they should sit down
on the ground. Then *q* they sat down on the ground. And *q* they ¹¹⁵
waited for all the men and women and also *q* the children to go in.
And so *q* as soon as the man heard the inviter saying inside of the
large house which was now seen by *Yā'qoḷasɛmē͎ᵋ,* "Now we are
all in," said he *q* then *q* the man vomited a small round quartz
crystal. Then he asked *Yā'qoḷasɛmē͎ᵋ* to open his mouth. Then *q* ¹²⁰
the man put the crystal into his mouth. Then *q* he said, "Now
swallow it and you will not feel anything when they are trying to
harm you," said he *q.* Then *q Yā'qoḷasɛmē͎ᵋ* swallowed the crystal.
Then *q* the man said to *Yā'qoḷasɛmē͎ᵋ,* "Let us go into the house;
that is where you will sit down, the middle of the right hand side, ¹²⁵
so that you may see distinctly everything that will be seen by
you," said he *q.* Then *q* they started and went into the house and
they stood inside the doorway. Then *q* the man who had invited
Yā'qoḷasɛmē͎ᵋ spoke. Then *q* he said, "This our friend has come,
the one to whom you referred as the one to be invited by me, ¹³⁰
friends, and so he will go and sit down there," said he *q* as he invited
Yā'qoḷasɛmē͎ᵋ to go and sit down in the middle of the right hand
side of the house. Then *q* the speaker of the house spoke. Then *q*
he said, "Now take care, supernatural ones, of what we are going
to do on account of this one who came invited by our chief to come ¹³⁵
and sit by our side, this *Yā'qoḷasɛmē͎ᵋ.* Now take care, friend

Yā'qoḷasɛmēᵋ, take note of everything that will be seen by you,
that is going to be shown, your future treasures, besides this house
with posts carrying beams on their shoulders," said he *q*. And so,
140 it was this *q*, the first in the house, the great (dance) from above,
the one that has one hundred songs, and *q* one hundred teeth
showing forehead masks danced with *G·îlā'laḷit*; and this is his
name *G·i̯'lg·ῑyāᵋlis*. And so *q* as soon as this was finished there was
a snapping sound of another kind of cannibal dancer. He came
145 out of the sacred room on the right-hand side of the house, and he
did not utter the cannibal cry while on his head stood the cannibal
head mask which just kept on making a snapping sound. And
so four times he danced around the fire in the middle of the house
before he went into the sacred room. And this was the name of the
150 cannibal dancer, *ᵋnō'lagɛmālis*. As soon as this was finished a
double-faced *Dzō'noq!wa* came and it had the name Numb-Maker,
and so as soon as this was done a woman came out of the room,
the dance of getting everything *(Äwῑ'lōʟɛlaḷ)*. And she had
four songs. Then *q* her name was Carrying-Everything-in-her-
155 Hands. And so *q* as soon as this was done the speaker of the house
took the baton (and said), "O friend *Yā'qoḷasɛmēᵋ*, this is your
treasure, these four kinds of dances which were seen by you, and
also this house Carrying-on-the-Shoulders and this death-bringing
baton," said he *q*. "And so your name as a chief will be *ᵋmā'x̣ǔla-
160 g·ilis* and *ᵋmā'x̣măwῑsa* turning to *ᵋmā'x·măwῑsagɛmēᵋ* and *ᵋmā'-
x̣ǔyā'lidzē* and *Mō'kwitalasogwiᵋlakᵘ*. And this is your treasure,
friend *Yā'qoḷasɛmēᵋ*. And so you will go home, being a cannibal
dancer and on your head will stand the snapping sounding head
of our world. And you will not utter the cannibal cry. Take the
165 yellow pollen of the fir tree and powder your body with it so that
your body will be yellow, for it will be said by your tribe that you
have come back alive," said he *q* and *q* the house disappeared after
this. And so *q Yā'qoḷasɛmēᵋ* was sitting just alone on the ground
and he felt foolish. Then *q* he saw that it was getting daylight.
170 Then *q* he stood up from the ground and went up a hill on the
ground. And *q* as soon as he came to the top of the hill on the
ground he saw the house of his father *P!ā'sɛlaḷ Hǎ'qǔlaḷ* not far
away. Then *q* he saw many children playing at the foot of the
hill on the ground. Then *q* it occurred to him to go down to their
175 playing-ground to talk secretly with one of them. Then *q* he
arrived near them, when one of the children started towards the
place where *Yā'qoḷasɛmēᵋ* was hiding. And so *q* as soon as
Yā'qoḷasɛmēᵋ saw him, *Yā'qoḷasɛmēᵋ* called him. And so *q*
immediately the boy went near him. Then *q Yā'qoḷasɛmēᵋ* told

his nephew, behold (it was he)! to go secretly and call his father [180]
P!ā'sɛlał Hä'qŭlał to come quickly. "Now no one else will be
told," said *Yā'qoḷasɛmē*ᵋ. Then *q* the boy ran out of the bush
to go to the house of *P!ā'sɛlał Hä'qŭlał*. Then *q* he saw *P!ā'sɛlał
Hä'qŭlał* sitting inside. Then *q* the boy sat down by his side and
whispering said to him, "Get up and let us go inland," said he to [185]
him. And so *q* immediately *P!ā'sɛlał Hä'qŭlał* arose and followed
his grandson, the boy. And *q P!ā'sɛlał Hä'qŭlał* never asked the
boy why he had called him, for he guessed that something important
had been seen by him. Then *q* they came to where *Yā'qoḷasɛmē*ᵋ
was sitting on the ground. And so *q* immediately *P!ā'sɛlał Hä'qŭlał* [190]
spoke to him. Then *q* he said, "Is it you, master? For in vain I do
not believe that I see you." said he *q*. Then *q Yā'qoḷasɛmē*ᵋ replied
to his father. Then *q* he said, "It is I, *Yā'qoḷasɛmē*ᵋ, your prince,"
said he *q* and reported to his father about the four kinds of dances,
his treasures and the house and the death-bringing baton and he [195]
told him how on his head was standing the cannibal head which
was always snapping. "I don't utter the cannibal cry, for I am
different from the cannibal dancer uttering the cannibal cry. My
name will be ᵋnō'lagɛmālis. After four days I shall come and show
myself, and you will tell the tribe to surround me," said he *q* and [200]
they finished talking. Then *q P!ā'sɛlał Hä'qŭlał* told *Yā'qoḷasɛm*ᵋē
that his tribe was having a winter ceremonial, and so *q* immediately
*Yā'qoḷasɛmē*ᵋ disappeared. Then *q P!ā'sɛlał Hä'qŭlał* went home
to his house. Then *q* he secretly asked his two sons to clear the
floor of the house. Then *q* his tribe were much startled why they [205]
were clearing the floor of their house. And so *q* as soon as *P!ā'sɛlał
Hä'qŭlał* found out that his tribe were making fun at his clearing the
floor of his house, then *q* he did not wish to take notice of their
words. Then night came. And so *q* it was not late at night before
many wolves came howling behind the village, but *q* they had not [210]
been howling long before the two sons of *P!ā'sɛlał Hä'qŭlał* and
Mɛlē't, his princess, disappeared. And *P!ā'sɛlał Hä'qŭlał* guessed
that the wolves had come to take his three children, for *Yā'qoḷasɛmē*ᵋ had told his father that he had been called by the wolves.
Therefore *P!ā'sɛlał Hä'qŭlał* was just glad. And so *q* as soon as [215]
four days had passed from the time of the meeting of *P!ā'sɛlał
Hä'qŭlał* with *Yā'qoḷasɛmē*ᵋ, *Yā'qoḷasɛmē*ᵋ powdered his body
with yellow fir pollen. And so *q* he just stopped powdering his
body when his body was very yellow. And so *q* as soon as he
finished, he was just startled by the cannibal head (mask) which [220]
began to make the snapping sound on his head. And so *q* as soon
as the cannibal head (mask) standing on his head made the snapping

sound, the three younger brothers and his younger sister, came.
And *q* (one) was the double-faced *Dzō'noq!wa*. Then *q* one of his
225 younger brothers was (dressed) in a big wolf skin. Then *q* *MElē't*
was *Āwī'lōLElaɫ*. (She had) a thick head ring of red cedar bark
and *q* also a thick neckring of cedar bark. Then *q* *Yā'qoḷasEmēᵋ*
was leading when they came in sight at the upper end of the
village of *Gwa'yēᵋ*. And *q* the cannibal head (mask) made always
230 a snapping noise. Then *q* next to him was the double-faced *Dzō'-*
noq!wa. Last *q* came *MElē't* the *Āwī'lōLElaɫ*. And so *q* as soon as
P!ā'sElaɫ Hä'qŭlaɫ saw them, he asked his tribe to surround them.
And so *q* immediately the first of the *Hăxwā'mis* surrounded the
three that had recently disappeared, and they did not know the
235 cannibal head (mask), which was on the head, that this was
Yā'qoḷasEmēᵋ, the one whom they believed to have died long ago.
And it is said those who surrounded *Yā'qoḷasEmēᵋ* did not recognize
him, for he was very emaciated and his body was very yellow. And
Yā'qoḷasEmēᵋ and his younger brother, the double-faced *Dzō'noq!wa*
240 and *MElē't*, the *Āwī'lōLElaɫ* were caught. And *q* they were taken
into the house of *P!ā'sElaɫ Hä'qŭlaɫ*, and *q* *Yā'qoḷasEmēᵋ* and his
(two) younger (brothers) brother and sister went at once into the
curtained room at the right hand side of the rear of the house.
And the *Hăxwā'mis* never sang for them. And so *q* as soon as
245 the three who had been taken by being surrounded were in the
sacred room, all the first of the *Hăxwā'mis* went out. Then *q*
Yā'qoḷasEmēᵋ asked his father *P!ā'sElaɫ Hä'qŭlaɫ* to call secretly
the song leaders of his tribe, to sit down in the sacred room and
Yā'qoḷasEmēᵋ sang his four songs and the song of the double-faced
250 *Dzō'noq!wa* and also the four songs of the *Āwī'lōLElaɫ*. Then *q*
immediately *P!ā'sElaɫ Hä'qŭlaɫ* called the four song leaders. And
so *q* as soon as they sat down on the floor, *Yā'qoḷasEmēᵋ* started
his four songs. Then *q* he started the one song of the double-faced
Dzō'noq!wa. Then *q* the song of the healing dance was first sung for
255 the *Āwī'lōLElaɫ*. Then *q* he next started the song of the Speaking
Dance for *Āwī'lōLElaɫ*; then *q* he also started the song of *Mē'La*
for the *Āwī'lōLElaɫ*. Then *q* he started the War Dance song for
Āwī'lōLElaɫ for there were four kinds of dances of the *Āwī'lōLElaɫ*.
And so *q* as soon as the four song leaders knew all the songs *q*
260 *Yā'qoḷasEmēᵋ* said that he would be pacified that night as soon as
it would get dark, said he *q*. And so *q* as soon as this was finished
the four song leaders went out of the house and went home to
their houses. And so *q* as soon as they had gone home *P!ā'sElaɫ*
Hä'qŭlaɫ came *q* and sat down. Then *q* he asked *Yā'qoḷasEmēᵋ*,
265 "Where is your youngest brother?" said he *q*. Then *q* *Yā'qoḷasEmēᵋ*

answered the word of his father. Then *q* he said, "Don't talk
about him. Take good care when he will come," said he *q*. And
P!ā'sɛlał Hä'q̆ŭlał was afraid of the words of *Yā'qoᴇasɛmēᵉ*,
therefore he did not speak again. And so *q* as soon as evening
came *Yā'qoᴇasɛmēᵉ* asked his father that a fire should be built ²⁷⁰
in his house and that at once the *Hăxwā'mis* should be gone
for (invited) and all should come into his house to pacify him
and his (two) younger brother and his sister, said he *q*. And
so *q* immediately *P!ā'sɛlał Hä'q̆ŭlał* sent four old men to go for
(call) the tribe, so that all should come to his house. And so *q* the ²⁷⁵
four messengers went. And so *q* immediately all the men, women,
and children came in. And *q* Lɛlā'k̂.înis came, the one who had
bewitched *Yā'qoᴇasɛmēᵉ*. And so *q* as soon as they had all gone in,
the cannibal (mask) on the head of *Yā'qoᴇasɛmēᵉ* began to make a
snapping sound , and so *q* immediately the song leaders sang his ²⁸⁰
song. Then *q* *Yā'qoᴇasɛmēᵉ* came dancing out of his sacred room
and danced around the fire in the middle of the house, and *q* the
cannibal head (mask) was standing on his head. And so as soon
as all his four songs had been sung he went into his sacred room.
Now he had the name ᵉnō'lagɛmālis after this. Out of the room *q* ²⁸⁵
came the double-faced *Dzō'noq!wa*. And so *q* immediately the
four song leaders sang his one song. And so *q* as soon as this was
also finished the *Āwī'lōʟɛlał* came out of the sacred room. Then *q*
she just kept on dancing around the fire in the middle of the house.
And so *q* as soon as her four songs had been sung she went into ²⁹⁰
the sacred room, and now she had the name Carrying-Everything-
in-her-Hands. And so *q* as soon as this was finished, *q* many
wolves began to howl behind the village. It is said they were
coming nearer. It is said they came right on to the seaside of the
house. And *q* the first of the *Hăxwā'mis* heard men singing in ²⁹⁵
front of the house of *P!ā'sɛlał Hä'q̆ŭlał*. Therefore the men came
in at the door of the house wearing the (wolf) showing teeth
(masks) on their foreheads. And so *q* as soon as fifty men wearing
wolf masks had come in, one came *q* dressed in a great wolf skin.
He had the name *G·ilā'lalit*. And so *q* as soon as he came in he ³⁰⁰
went right to the rear of the house and lay down on his stomach.
Then *q* fifty men came also behind him. Now there were one
hundred wolf men who came and brought out of the woods the
youngest brother of *Yā'qoᴇasɛmēᵉ* who had now the name ᵉnō'-
lagɛmālis. And so *q* as soon as all the wolf men had come in, the ³⁰⁵
first of the *Hăxwā'mis* were startled, for all the posts of the house
of *P!ā'sɛlał Hä'q̆ŭlał*, the four posts on each side of the door, were
men wearing red cedar bark rings on top of grizzly bears and the

man stood on the head of a grizzly bear, and the man carried the
310 beam of the house on his shoulder. Therefore the house had the
name House-Carried-On-Shoulders. And so *q* as soon as the wolf
men finished singing the one hundred songs of the dance of the
Great-one-from-above the wolf men disappeared, and *q* it was
getting daylight in the morning. And *q* the men and the women
315 went out of the house for it was indeed finished. And *q* ᵋ*nō'lagᴇmālis*, namely *Yā'qoꞮasᴇmēᵋ* never told his father about the death-
bringing baton. But *q* for four days he was sitting in his sacred
room. Then *q* *P!ā'sᴇlaꞮ Hä'qŭlaꞮ* told ᵋ*nō'lagᴇmālis* that *Lᴇlā'k·înis*
was getting ready to start paddling with his three younger brothers,
320 and so *q* immediately ᵋ*nō'lagᴇmālis* arose and took his death-
bringing baton. Then *q* he asked his father *P!ā'sᴇlaꞮ Hä'qŭlaꞮ* to go
with him to the door of the house. And so *q* as soon as they arrived
at the door of the house he saw *Lᴇlā'k·înis* going seaward. Then *q*
ᵋ*nō'lagᴇmālis* turned the butt end of the death-bringing baton to
325 the canoe that was traveling along and *Lᴇlā'k·înis* and his crew
were dead, and that is the end after this.

K·!ēsx·älis[1]

Told by *G·î'qalas*, a *Gwa'waēnoxᵘ*; a *Haxwā'mis* story

Far-End-of-World *(QwēsᴇnxeᵋIis)* was killed by his fellow chief
Standing-on-Flat *(Ɪaᵋwadzâ)*. He was killed by Running-against-
Tide *(TsōpᴇIas)* on account of the kind of chief of the *Häxwā'mis*
he was. He was bewitched. And so *q* he was greatly troubled
5 being sick. He was dying. And *q* he was advised by his younger
brothers to pretend to be dead; and so *q* they reported to his
wives saying that he was getting weak. Then *q* he pretended
to lie dead on the floor. Therefore they made a box and he was
put into the coffin. Then *q* they called his tribe out. Then *q* they
10 were standing outside and *q* the tribesmen were all together. Then
Not-Reached *(WēxꞮeg·ilitsōᵋ)* arose and spoke, one of his brothers.
Not-Reached *q* did not want his elder brother to be buried, for he
wished that he should be buried in his own country. Then *q* arose
on the ground a chief who had the name Chief and agreed to his
15 word, and so *q* they started to bury their brother at *Ā'Ɪᵋalxō*. They
q were made to go and left the twelve wives of Far-End-of-World.
They were crying *q*. They were not told *q* about their plan. It
was in vain. And so *q* they had not gone far when that what
had bewitched Far-End-of-World was thrown into the water.

---

[1] See p. 94.

As soon as they lifted him up he was dead and he revived when [20] that with which he had been bewitched was thrown into the river. He was taken out of the coffin and sat up in the canoe. Then *q* they arrived at the mouth of the river of *Ā'l*ᵉ*alxō*. Then he spoke (and said) that he would eat a slave later on. "Take now this roasted salmon." And so *q* roasted salmon was taken and given to [25] him. And so *q* he ate it. Three times he lifted (aimed with) it, then he ate the roasted salmon. Then *q* they poled (the canoe). Then they arrived at what is named Cottonwood-Seed-Gathering-Place *(Qāqɛm-xwamaxak·!as)*. Then *q* Not-Reached asked what he would do. Then *q* his younger brother said that he would dig and cover the roof [30] of his house with dirt. Then *q* he dug the sand for a living place of his elder brother. The house was covered with dirt. He was left by his younger brothers. For one month they did not go near. And so *q* it was thus: his younger brothers had not gone near for one month when they went to look at him. And so *q* it [35] was good as they were looking at their elder brother. Then *q* Far-End-of-World spoke, "For two months do not come to look at me." And so *q* it was done that way. Then *q* Far-End-of-World went out of his house and sat down outside of his house. Then *q* he saw something that looked like a salmon. However *q* he [40] thought he would creep down the beach to look at the salmon which, behold! was a steelhead. Then he took it and roasted the salmon. Now *q* he was invited by someone and *q* he was sitting in the doorway. What should it be, an animal! Behold! *q* it was a big grizzly bear that was growling. Then *q* twilight came. He [45] was looking at the mountain. What should it be! It was burning as he looked at the mountain. Now *q* it was two months before his younger brothers came to see him. Now his body had really become alive *q*. Then *q* he asked his younger brothers not to stay away long. "For four days you will not come back." And so [50] *q* they came back after four days. And so *q* Far-End-of-World was really alive. And so, "Go," said he *q* to his younger brothers, "for eight days you will not come back." Now he was left by his younger brothers. Then *q* night came and Far-End-of-World was sitting in the doorway of his house. Then *q* he saw again [55] *q* what was seen by him on the mountain when it was burning. It came *q* coming near, that sound of the cannibal. Then *q* Far-End-of-World did not know *q* that he imitated it. Then *q* he knew that, behold! he also was uttering the cannibal cry. Now he was left by the cannibal. Then night came again, and the cry of the [60] cannibal came again. Then *q* he went out to look at it, "for what can you do, even if it should bring death." He saw it had four

faces. He was taken hold of and the man of the woods flew away with him. Then Far-End-of-World discovered that he had been
65 taken into his supernatural treasure. It had four faces q. Then q he was asked, "What are you doing on the rock?" Then q Far-End-of-World said, "I am trying to get a treasure. He was asked by War-Leader *(K·!ēsx·älis)*, "Go on! Stand up and look at me, that I may test you." Then q he tried him(?). He gave
70 him advice what to do. "Go on, try to utter the cannibal cry." Then q he uttered the cannibal cry. Then q he was told that he did it right. "Now your red cedar bark will be like this. Now you will have the name War-Leader. Now your name will be Great-Cannibal. These will be your names." Now he left him.
75 Now War-Leader flew and arrived at the place *Q!a'xsīdzēᵉ*. He went down to the place *Sādzala*, and so q he came down to *Gwa'yēᵉ* here. He arrived at *Ō'k!ŭnaᵉlis*. He came q and was sitting at the place *Q!ä'ltaᵉlekᵘ* when he saw the old woman Moving-about-in-World *(Yä'lag·ilis)*. Then q he uttered the cannibal cry. Then
80 q the old woman became afraid and told her tribe. She said she had seen something bad. Then q a roof was put over the old woman. They took good care of her (?). However the roof had not been over her for a long time before he appeared again. Then q it was known. It was he, behold! Far-End-of-World, he was a cannibal.
85 Now he found out (?) his wives, the twelve wives, his wives worked trying to get a copper. It is said forty (?). Far-End-of-World q gave a winter ceremonial. Now he held a winter ceremonial. Then q War-Leader was caught. Four songs were song. He was tamed. He ate dry salmon and crabapples and viburnum berries
90 and dry berry cakes.

Drury Inlet Story

Told by *G·ī'qalas*, a *Gwa'waēnoxᵘ*

They were catching fish q. A woman was sent q to go and take the fish out of the salmon weir. Then q she took them out. And so q she did not get all the fish out of the salmon weir. Then q she cut the salmon. Then q she saw a feather in the stomach of
5 a steelhead salmon. Then q she took it. And so q she had not been holding it long before it disappeared from her hands. On her part q she was not long on the rock when she was made sick being pregnant. She went home and was asked by her father, "How is your salmon weir? Is it full now?" Then q she spoke, "It is
10 as though the one with whom I am pregnant was moving." — "Arrange a place for our child," said on his part, her father. Then

q a place was arranged by her mother. And so *q* she was not long
on the ground in her house for giving birth before she gave birth.
She gave birth to two children *q*. The little ones had bent legs *q*.
On their part *q* they were not alive a long time when they were [15]
cut by accident by their mother. It is said the feathers just showed
from the mouths of the children and they were dead. They were
buried. — Only your crooked legs will come at the place where
the children will be put on the ground.

Ghost Story of the Nimkish[1]

(Recorded by George Hunt)

The five numaym of the Nimkish were invited by Smoke-
Owner *(Kwā'x·ilanokŭmēᵋ)* who belonged to the numaym of the
L!ā'L!ɛlamin when long ago that was where long ago they lived,
the village of the Nimkish, *X̣ŭlkᵘ*. And so, as soon as all the guests
were in the inviting-house, a man who had the name *MEdzē'nEwisōᵋ*, [5]
who belonged to the numaym The-Famous-Ones *(Ts!ēts!ɛlwāla-
gămēᵋ)*, spoke, one who was really talkative (which is also called
telling invented stories). He said, "Really I don't believe the
words of our late forefathers when they say that, as soon as we
leave *Ōdzā'ᵋlas*, the ghosts go and change (with us) in our houses, [10]
and that it is their winter house where they have a winter ceremonial. I really do not believe their words," said he. Then all
the men were disgusted with the words of *MEdzē'nEwisōᵋ*, because
he did not believe the words of our past ancestors, for he was a
common man. And *ME'mx·o* was told to go ahead and reply [15]
to him. He said to him, "O man, who is well known to talk without
sense, you were not respected from the beginning when you tell
us about the doings of our late forefathers! Did they not tell
you about the skull which came and wailed in the corner of the
house of *ᵋnEmō'x̣ᵘdzaqwalag·ilis* at *Ōdzā'ᵋlas* which said the (following) [20]
words when this skull cried,

'*Ax·a, ax·a, ax·a, hiye-he*, I think of the time when the marriage gift
was being paid to the one who had me for his princess. But now I am only
empty eyes, (I am only) hollow eyes deep down. *Ax·a, ax·a, ax·a, ax·a, ho.*'

Now do you know this? And also that the ghosts were [25]
the first ones to build the village site at *Ōdzā'ᵋlas*. Our late forefathers lately built a house there for a salmon drying house when it
was near winter, when the November moon appears. And so,
as soon as they finish catching salmon in the river, December

---

[1] Compare III 105; C 447.

8

30 approaches and all the Nimkish come drifting down the river
and go to their winter place Xŭlkᵘ. And so, as soon as they have
all drifted down this river the ghosts all come and assemble and
stay in winter at Ōdzá'ᵉlas; for indeed it is their village site,"
said he. Then MEdzē'nEwisōᵉ spoke again and said, "Now your
35 speech is ended. Still I do not believe it. Now I'll try and purify
myself and I will go to Ōdzá'ᵉlas and try to meet with the ghosts
which you say live there, you liars," said he.

Then ME'mx·o spoke again and said, "Don't call us liars, for
it is not our own word that you don't believe, for it is the word
40 of the man who followed, K!wā'gaxsano. Go! MEdzē'nEwisōᵉ and
purify yourself, but take care that you do not have bad luck.
Oh that you would meet with the ghosts, so that you may believe
what you do not believe now," said he.

As soon as they finished the dispute all the men ate and the
45 feasters all took notice of MEdzē'nEwisōᵉ, for it was as though
he regretted his words here and there, and he hardly ate for he
was downhearted. And so, as soon as the feasters finished eating,
they all went out of the feasting house. Last MEdzē'nEwisōᵉ
went out and entered his house and went to the place where an
50 old man was sitting whose name was Ë'k·!Esqámēᵉ who belonged
to the numaym L!ā'L!Elamin. Now MEdzē'nEwisōᵉ sat down by
his side. Then MEdzē'nEwisōᵉ spoke. Then he said, "Oh my dear,
tell me what would you do if you wanted to purify yourself to
meet with the ghosts?" said he. Then Ë'k·!Esqámēᵉ answered
55 him. Then he said, "Incredible. Have you no sense? Did you
ever know of anyone who met with the ghosts?" said he. Then
MEdzē'nEwisōᵉ told him about his words in the feasting-house.
And that was the reason why Ë'k·!Esqámēᵉ said, "Go on and
keep on rubbing your body with hemlock branches in the morning
60 before our tribe arises. And so, as soon as you have finished
rubbing your body with hemlock branches take the wrappings
of a dead person and dip them in water and rub your body with
it. And so, as soon as it is the time when all the men sleep, then
just repeat what you have done first in the morning," said he.
65 And so, as soon as Ë'k·!Esqámēᵉ had given advice to MEdzē'nEwisōᵉ,
MEdzē'nEwisōᵉ lay down on his back in his bed. But he did not
stay there long before he went out of the house and looked for a
grave. And so, as soon as he had found a grave, he took all the
wrappings, the old yellow cedar bark blankets and hid them at
70 the lower end of the village site at Xŭlkᵘ. Then he also broke
of the tips of hemlock branches and hid them where he had hidden
the wrappings, the old yellow cedar bark blankets. And so, as

soon as he had finished he went home to his house. And so, as
soon as he had gone into his house he heard his wife groaning,
for she had suddenly had pains in her chest. And it was not yet [75]
night when his wife died, whose name was Pearl-Shell-Woman
(K·ō'gwisilaōgwa), the daughter of *K·!äsō*ᵉ who belonged to the
numaym ᵉ*nē'nɛlk·!ēnox*ᵘ of the Nimkish. And so she was buried
at once. And now *Mɛdzē'nɛwisō*ᵉ really resolved to purify himself,
and for four days he purified himself. And it was almost noon [80]
when he took the wrappings of old yellow cedar bark blankets
and made a bundle of it. Then he took it across to the other side
at *X̣ŭlk*ᵘ. And so, as soon as he arrived on the other side he walked
up the river*Gwa'* ᵉ*nē*. And so it was really evening when he arrived
at the other end of the village *Ōdzâ'* ᵉ*las*, and *Mɛdzɛ'nɛwisō*ᵉ heard [85]
much noise of men talking. And so, immediately he went into the
river and rubbed his body with hemlock branches. And so, as
soon as he had done so he took the wrappings of old yellow cedar
bark blankets, put them into the water, and rubbed his body
with them. And so, as soon as he had finished he heard a man [90]
telling the people to beat time, saying, "We beat time, shamans,
so that this one may be resuscitated. Now we endeavor, shamans,
to resuscitate this one. We shall do so in vain downward, shamans,
now we will make him hear, who is known by us, shamans," said
what was heard by *Mɛdzē'nɛwisō*ᵉ; and he went back into the [95]
water, into the river, and again he rubbed his body with hemlock
branches. And so, as soon as he had finished he took the old
yellow cedar bark blanket and dipped it into the water. And
he also rubbed his body twice when he heard speaking in the
house in which time was beaten by the ghosts who said, "We [100]
have all come in, shamans. Now take care on account of what
we came in to do in this supernatural house, for we try to bring
to life Pearl-Shell-Woman," said what was heard by *Mɛdzē'nɛwisō*ᵉ.
And that was the reason why he hurried to look through a hole
if there should be one in the front boards of the house. And so [105]
as soon as *Mɛdzē'nɛwisō*ᵉ approached the house, the fire in the
middle of the house began to die down. And so, immediately the
speaker of the house said, "There is a man behind us. Go friend
Haē'lɛlas, you are the fastest (runner)," said he. Immediately
Haē'lɛlas came out of the house and ran around the house. He [110]
went back into the dark house. Then he said, that no secular
person had been seen. But immediately *Mɛdzē'nɛwisō*ᵉ started
running and quickly he rubbed his body twice with the old yellow
cedar bark blanket. And he had rubbed his body four times at
the lower end of the house site of the ghosts at *Ōdzâ'*ᵉ*las*. And [115]

8*

so *MEdzē'nEwisō*ᵉ had enough time to rub his body with hemlock
branches when he saw the fire in the middle of the time-beating
house blazing up. Then the speaker of the house spoke. Then he
said, "Now get ready, shamans, and beat time that the one
120 whom we try to resuscitate may come out of the room," he
said. And *MEdzē'nEwisō*ᵉ heard his words. And that was the
reason why he started running and stood outside the door of the
house. Then immediately the fire in the middle of the house
was slowly dying down. And so, at once the speaker of the house
125 said, "Really there is a man behind us. Go *Haē'ʟEkᵘ*, go out
and look for him who makes us secular," said he. Then *Haē'ʟEkᵘ*
came and went straight out of the door of the house. And *Haē'ʟEkᵘ*
stood next to *MEdzē'nEwisō*ᵉ. Then *Haē'ʟEkᵘ* said to *MEdzē'nEwisō*ᵉ
"Come and let us go in, and stand in a dark place behind the
130 door posts. And so, as soon as your wife comes walking with
quick steps around the fire in the middle of the house, and so,
as soon as she turns around near the door, then jump out and
try to embrace her," said he. Then *MEdzē'nEwisō*ᵉ hid by the
side of *Haē'ʟEkᵘ* as they went in through the door of the house.
135 And *MEdzē'nEwisō*ᵉ hid opposite the posts. Now *Haē'ʟEkᵘ* stood
inside of the door of the house. Then he said, "Oh, shamans,
nothing was seen by me," said he. And so immediately the fire
in the middle of the house blazed up, and so at once the ghosts
beat time. Then *MEdzē'nEwisō*ᵉ saw his wife Pearl-Shell-Woman
140 coming and walking with quick steps around the fire in the middle
of the house. And so, as soon as she came to the entrance at the
doorway, Pearl-Shell-Woman turned around, and so that was
when *MEdzē'nEwisō*ᵉ jumped out and tried to embrace his wife.
It was just as though his hands cut through the body of his wife.
145 And so, immediately the fire in the middle of the house went out.
That was all that was remembered by *MEdzē'nEwisō*ᵉ and for
a little he was dead after this. And so, as soon as *MEdzē'nEwisō*ᵉ
came back to life he believed the words of *ME'mx·o* who said that
the ghosts were living at *Ōdzá'ᵉlas* in winter. Not one man knows
150 where the ghosts go in summer. And so this was another thing
now believed by *MEdzē'nEwisō*ᵉ, that the ghosts have no flesh
and bones, for it was just like smoke and shadow of the owner
of the soul; that (was) the reason why *MEdzē'nEwisō*ᵉ knew, for
he tried to embrace his wife. Then he never felt (with) his hand,
155 for it was as though it passed through under the breasts of his
wife. And that is the end.

For even I, George Hunt, do not really understand the words
about the ghosts of some Indians, for I say that they confound

it, the ghost and the soul. I mean this, the Cannibal dancer when
he comes carrying a dried dead man which he is to eat, that is [160]
called by the Cannibal dancer "to eat a corpse". Now the hunter
who dreams about a ghost, that is a man who has been dead
for a long time and who is now dry, that is what he means, and
the hunter does not go out hunting for he knows already that no
game will be seen by him. I mean this, the soul of a dead man is [165]
not the same as a ghost, according to my way of seeing it, for
the soul is alive, for they never die and I think that is referred
to by the early Indians as *hai'alilaqas*, for other Indians say that
the soul is flying about. And so that is called by the old men of
the Indians a corpse, a man who has been dead long ago and [170]
whose body is now very dry. And it is called a corpse. When it
is only bones, they just have the name "bones of a man"; for it
is only the whole body of a man long since dead who has the
name corpse. That is the end of the tale told by *Q!ē'q!ɛxʟāla*,
a Nimkish man.   [175]

Marriage with a Ghost[1]

Told by *G·ī'qalas*, a *Gwa'waēnoxᵘ*

(Two) lovers *q* loved each other. Then *q* the man became sick.
Then *q* the woman said she had no way of forgetting him if he
should give up (die) because she loved her lover too much. Too
much *q* she desired her lover. Then *q* the man said, it would not
be long if he should die that he would come back and come to [5]
see her. Then *q* the woman tied something on her lover's hand
that she might recognize him. Then *q* he died. And so *q* after
four days he came back to see his beloved. Then *q* he entered
the house of his beloved. He arrived *q*. And so *q* the woman
just at once felt of what (she had made) to recognize him. She [10]
felt of it; and so *q* at once she just embraced her lover. She lay
down with her lover who was now a ghost. "I only came to see
you," said on his part *q* her lover. "Let me go," said on her part
q the woman. "Don't!" said on his part *q* the ghost. "I want
to go too much," said on her part *q* the woman. "Don't," said [15]
on his part *q* the man. "The place at which I am now, is not
good." — "I want very much," said on her part *q* the woman.
"Go and get ready that we may go," said on his part *q* the ghost,
her lover. Then *q* they started. He advised his beloved, "You
will not touch these berries where we are going." Then *q* they [20]

---

[1] See 35th Annual Report Bureau of American Ethnology, p. 710.

started. It was day for the woman. It was night q for the man.
Different was now the day of the man. What q was day was night
for the ghost. Every time it got day it became night for him.
They saw all kinds of berries, salal berries. The woman q did
25 not know. She would pick berries and put them into the basket.
A small basket was carried by her into which they were put. He did
not watch every time whenever she picked into it. She put them
into her basket. For four days they walked inland. Then q they
arrived at the country of the ghosts. They were going down to
30 this q underground. They arrived and they stood on the ground
on one side of a river q. A river q was at this place. Then q the
ghost asked q his beloved to shout. Then q the woman shouted.
"Come!" said she q. "Call again!" she was told on her part
q by her lover. Then q she spoke again. They never q took any
35 notice. "We do not shout this way," said on his part q the ghost.
"Go on, shout!" said on her part q the woman to her lover. Then
q the ghost shouted. Then q it was just as though he opened his
mouth. He did not speak twice shouting. The young men q got
ready q. They came q to be taken. They went aboard the canoe.
40 They were sniffing q noticing a bad smell. They smelled the
woman. They only smelled q. "They did not see us." They
arrived q on shore q. They stepped out of the canoe. The ghosts
smelled the woman q. They only smelled, they did not see the
woman. She entered the house of her lover. After two years she
45 had a child. The woman had been there four years q when she
became homesick. She wished to see her parents. Then q she
was followed by her lover. Now she had a child. She reached her
mother and entered. Then q she put the child into the arms of
her mother. "Do not uncover his face. Just carry him in your
50 arms in the house." Then q for a long time the old one was in
the house. She was surprised. The child did not move. Then q
she did not watch when she uncovered its face. What should it
be? Its little orbits were empty. Then q she threw it on the floor.
But it did not reach the floor when it was taken by its father
55 the ghost. "Although this one said that you should not touch
it." It was known q that it was dead. The woman just got
twisted q the one who had carried the child and the ghost and
his beloved just went home.

The Ghost Country

Told by *Yā'qoḻas*, a *Naqᴇ'mg·ilisala*

The ghosts[1] live in four houses, each one deeper than the preceding
one. A Koskimo woman was crying on account of her dead father.
They buried him and she was crying under the grave for four
days. The people called her but she refused to leave. On the
fourth day she heard somebody come who called her. "I call you [5]
downward, crying woman *(Lē'laxaᴇnlōl Lᴇ*wag·ilaoqwē')*." Then
she jumped up and the ghost said, "Follow me." He went downward and she followed him. They came to a house called Hemlock-
Leaves-On-Back *(K·!i'mwik·ilᴇls)*. They entered the house and
an old woman was sitting near the fire. She said, "Ah, ah, ah, [10]
ah. Sit down near the fire." They took poles to take down dry
salmon and prepared to roast it. They placed it on a small food
mat and broke it up and gave it to *Lᴇ*wag·ilaōgwa*. Just when
she was about to take it, a person came in and invited her into
another house called Maggots-on-Bark-on-Ground *(Aā'badik·ilᴇls)*. [15]
Then the woman who lived in the first house said, "Ah, ah, ah,
ah. Go with her. They are higher in rank than we are." She
followed the person who had invited her and entered the next
house. She saw an old woman sitting by the fire and she seemed
to be the same one whom she had seen first. She prepared in the [20]
same way giving her something to eat. Just when she was about
to eat, another woman came to her and invited her into her house
which was called Place-of-Mouth-Showing-on-Ground *(Nē'nlᴇxtᴇ'l-
dzas)*. The woman in the second house said, "Go with her. They
are higher in rank than we are." When she entered, the same [25]
old woman seemed to be sitting by the fire. Again they prepared
to give her to eat. When she was just about to begin, she was
called by another person into the fourth house called Place-of-
Never-Return *(Hak!waa's)*. Again the woman said, "They are
higher in rank than we. Go." When she entered she saw her [30]
father sitting at the end of the house. And when he saw her he
became angry and said, "Why do you come here? This is the
place from which nobody ever returns. Whoever enters the first
three houses may return. But if you come here you must stay.
Do not eat what is offered to you and go back." Then he called [35]
the ghosts to take her back. She was lying under the grave tree
like one dead. The ghosts came back singing the following song:

hama yaxaxaxa.

---

[1] See X 36; C 313, 323.

She was like one dead when she came back. When her father
⁴⁰ spoke to her he had said, "When we take you back we will sing
so that the Koskimo may hear our song." They brought her up
alive on a board. The people heard the song but they did not
see anyone. Then they took the board into the winter dance
house. This song belongs originally to the Koskimo and was
⁴⁵ carried from there to the Newettee and to the *Nā'k!wax·da⁵xᵘ*.

Gift of the Ravens.

Told by *Yā'qoɹas*, a *Naqᴇ'mg·ilisala*

At Sea Otter Cove *(Sē'max·)* there lived a man, his wife and
their young son. They belonged to the *Naqᴇ'mg·ilisala*. They
were asleep in the house. When day came the child went to play.
The mother prepared dried mussels for their meal and when the
⁵ child came home she gave them to him to eat. The boy said,
"I am not hungry." The following day the child went out again
early in the morning and stayed away all day long. In the evening
he came home. Again the mother offered him dried mussels
but he refused them saying that he was not hungry. The parents
¹⁰ did not urge him although they observed that he did not eat
anything at all. Every morning the child went out to play and
came home at night; and everytime he refused the mussels which
his mother offered him. One evening the boy said, "Grease keeps
on coming up." *(Lā'laqa⁵yosa)* Then he vomited and his mother
¹⁵ saw that he had been eating grease. The boy said to his father,
"Get up before daylight!" and he told him what to do. The parents
did not ask him why he requested his father to rise. On the following morning when the father rose he saw whales stranded on the
beach. The young man had found a magic treasure. Then the
²⁰ father called the *Gwa'ts!ēnoxᵘ* to a feast. Now the parents learned
that the boy had been playing with ravens and they wondered
why his blanket was always torn as though it had been bitten.
The raven had made a hole in the head of the boy, taken the
brains out and put blubber into it. For this reason he always
²⁵ vomited blubber. Then they called the place, "place of grease
coming up." *(Lā'laqa⁵yō'dzas*, west of Cape Scott). The place
where the whales went ashore is called *Ăx⁵axɹa'*. When the *Gwa'-
ts!ēnoxᵘ* saw that the boy had obtained supernatural power they
called all the people together and said, "We will see whether
³⁰ it is true." They walked to Sea Otter Cove and entered the house
of his parents. The boy said, "Beat fast time for me." When
they started the boy beat his chest and vomited grease. He said,

"Go both ways along the beach and look for dead game." The boy went aboard the canoe and said, "If you do not find a whale where you are going, you may kill me." The people went out and [35] very soon found a stranded whale. They cut it up and carried the blubber to Sea Otter Cove. *(Ma'p!ēq* is the fort of the *Gwa'-ts!ēnox^u.)*

Initiation Story, Triangle Island.

Told by *Yā'qoʟas,* a *NaqE'mg·ïlisala.*

K!ŭk!wās was a man of the *Yū'ʟ!ēnox^u.* He lived at Triangle Island *(Hë'l^εa^εs).* Somebody said to *K!ŭk!wās* "Go to the supernatural rock *(Nau'alak!wa,* a small island near Triangle Island)." Another man took *K!ŭk!wās* who was lame, on his back and carried him there. He carried him through a hole in the rock. [5] When he had passed through he put him down and he said to him, "Now swim across to the small island, *Nau'alak!wa.*" When he was half across something pulled him by his feet and stretched his legs so that they became straight. He continued swimming and something pulled his legs again. It was the supernatural [10] power. The water was dark and he was unable to see what it was. There is a passage with a rock in the center. Then he jumped ashore and his legs were well. When he was on the rock he looked around and he believed to see a house above. There he was given the *G·ā'yaxalak^u,* a *Nō'ʟEm* dance. He looked to the other side [15] and he saw many people wearing red cedar bark. He saw many cannibals wearing head rings. Then he refused to accept the *Nō'ʟEm* and went to the cannibals. For four days he stayed there and his people were waiting for him in vain. They believed him to be dead. He became a cannibal and received supernatural [20] power. Then he showed himself on the inner side of the island where he had first gone into the water. He received the following song:

I am, friend, *mama hamai,* named *Ha^εmaxsa'lag·ïlis,* friend,
I uttered the cannibal cry, friend, I am friend, named [25]
   Xamxaqŭlag·ïlis, friend.

They sent a slave to the place where he was. He killed him and ate the skull and bones. When he came back he ate two slaves. They tried to catch him. Then he bit the nape of his own neck and his back. Therefore the people ran away from him. Now [30] he had been given the name *Ha^εmaxsa'lag·ïlis.* The people went into canoes because they were afraid of him. He was the cannibal in the first winter ceremonial. They sent out a man to get hemlock

twigs to make rings for the cannibal. He found some on the sea
35 side of the island. Figure 42[1] is derived from this. This is
their only cannibal dance. They have no whistles. They do
not cry out "hap." The narrator's grandfather was not yet born
when this happened.

The Sisters
Told by *G·ī'qalas*, a *Gwa'waēnox^u*

Sisters were digging clams *q* at a place named *Bē^εs*. Then
q they put down on the rock their digging sticks and were walking
along. They came back *q* to take their digging sticks. What
should it be? There was nothing there. Their digging sticks *q*
5 were hidden. Then *q* they tried to find out what it was. Then
q she asked her friend where her digging stick was. Then *q* they
quarrelled about their digging sticks. They came to make war
on one tribe, the *Gwa'waēnox^u* and struck each other. They were
hit on the head. They took the digging sticks. Now they are
10 just sitting on the rock and they are called, "Little Girls."

Mountain Woman
Told by *G·ī'qalas*, a *Gwa'waēnox^u*

Mountain-Woman *(NEg·ä'ga)* *q* was making play mountains.
A little mountain *q* was what she made. "Short Neck will be the
name of my mountain. It will have a place for picking berries.
Come," said she on her part *q*, "let us go and pick berries." Then
5 *q* they went picking berries. They arrived at their berrying place.
There were many salmon berries. Then *q* they made jam and they
made berry cakes, very many berry cakes. They were in boxes.
Then *q* again they picked berries. They picked very many currants
q. Then *q* they made jam. They made berry cakes, very many
10 currant cakes. They put them into boxes. Then *q* she called her
tribe, making a feast of berry cakes. The child had the name
of *Pō'^εik·!ā^εlas* and *Lē'l^εElk·!āla*. Then *q* she called again and the
child got the name Inviting-Sound *(Lē'l^εElk·!āla)*. Then *q* the
chief arose, "We will go to our rival, carrying this copper and
15 give away this copper." Then *q* he sold the copper. Now it was
bought. That was the means of giving a potlatch, the price of
the copper given to his rival. Then the chief arose, "Thank you
for what was done by the chief." He answered the speech of
the one who was giving the potlatch.

---

[1] See note on p. 88.

The Steelhead Salmon and the Herring

Told by *G·ī'qalas*, a *Gwa'waēnox^u*

The chief of the steelhead salmon and the chief of the herrings were talking together at the place where the charcoal drifts on the ocean *(Ts!ō'lnax·siwa^elis)*. "Who among us will be the first one to go? Am I not the one? I am skilled in making flesh for those who live landward from us." — "Go on," said the steelhead 5 salmon, "go on." — "I'll go and see those for whom flesh is made by us landward from us." Then the herring started. They arrived at the place where they made flesh. They spawned. The tribes put hemlock branches into the water. Then they made herring spawn which was born of the herrings. The tribes dried the herring 10 spawn, the means of making flesh of the herrings. Then they finished. The herrings went back and met with the steelhead salmon. The herrings spoke, "You will go early, but flesh has been made for the round-faced ones by me." — "Maybe you will really make fat those for whom flesh was made with what you 15 squirt out. I am going to go and set right the body of those for whom you made flesh with what you squirted out." — "Go on, round face," said the herring. They were teasing each other. Then they parted. That is the end.

Clam and Olachen

Told by *Â^ewaxElag·ilis*

"Am I only good being roasted?" said the clam, "for there are many ways that are good." — "What are your good ways?" said the Olachen. "Are my good ways only few?" — "What are your other good ways?" said on his part the Olachen to the Clam. "Is it not a good way when I am put side by side on the fire?" said 5 on his part the Clam to the Olachen. "Is that the whole number of your good ways as you are a clam?" said on his part the Olachen to him. "Is it not a good way when I am put in a row, when I am held by tongs, when it is as though I prettily open my mouth in the house," said the Clam on his part to the Olachen. "Is that the 10 number of ways that you are good?" said the Clam on his part to the Olachen. "What is it if this is the only right thing, when my good ways end. These are my good ways. For four times it goes out of your shells." — "These are all my good ways. That is the number of my good ways as I am a Clam." 15

"Go on, you also Olachen, say the number of your good ways." —
"Is it not a good way for me when I am being picked out? I am
dried on the ground so that my body gets dry. I am taken and I
am roasted in tongs. I stand next to the fire and one is taken, and
20 the fire is lighted on top (like a torch), that is my good way. I am
turned over and over, and I am taken and put on an old mat
and I lie prettily on the floor. That is my good way, you Clam, as
I am an Olachen."

Maggots-on-Water[1]

Told by *NEg·ä'dzē* (Charlie Wilson), a *G·ī'g·îlgăm*

A man had the name Maggots-on-Water *(Āap!alag·îLē^ε)*. Then *q*
he always had wives. And so *q* every time as soon as he had a wife,
then *q* he took the one who had become his wife to an island out
at sea so that they had no way of swimming, those who had
5 become the wives of the man. As soon *q* as his wife had been
for four days on the island, then every time he looked for her.
Every time there were maggots on his wife. Then every time he ate the
maggots. His mouth *q* was small and round. Only maggots fitted
into his mouth. Many *q* he had taken to the island. As soon *q* as
10 he would go with his wife to the island, then *q* for four days he
would not look for his wife. He would go and look, now there would
be maggots on his wife. And so that *q* he would eat, her maggots.

Then *q* Maggots-on-Water said again that he would have a
wife again. Then *q* he wished to have for his wife a pretty girl
15 and so *q* he wooed the woman. Then *q* his tribe *q* found it out.
And so *q* on their part they did not allow the woman to try because
Maggots-on-Water had killed almost all his women. On her part
q the woman did not want to be spoken to. She wished the man
for a husband and so *q* the woman had Maggots-on-Water for
20 her husband. And so *q* he started with his wife to go to the island.
"Go, step out of the canoe," said he *q* to his wife. Then *q* the
woman stepped out of the canoe. Then *q* Maggots-on-Water
only went out seaward. Then *q* the woman said that she would
go to her husband. Then *q* the husband did not wish his wife to
25 come aboard. "Come, that I may go aboard," said *q* the woman.
"Don't," said on his part *q* her husband. "Later you will come
aboard, if you will pull out your hair." Then *q* the woman pulled
out her hair. "Now all my hair is off, come that I may go aboard."

---

[1] See Comox, S 85, compare also S 89, no. 19; Ts 861; Quileute, Journal
American Folklore, 32:255.

— "Don't," said q her husband, "later on you will come aboard
if you pull out your eyelashes," said q the man to his wife. Then [30]
q she pulled out her eyelashes. "Come, turn landward," said she
q to her husband, "now all my eyelashes are off." — "Don't,"
said again q the man to his wife. "Later on you will come aboard
if you will pull out your pubic hair." Then q the woman pulled
out what she had. "Come, now all I had is off." — "Don't," said [35]
q Maggots-on-Water again to his wife, "later on you will come
when you have gone with spread legs around this island." Then
q the woman went around the island. Then q again she said to
her husband that she would go aboard. And so q the man only
paddled away. Now he left his wife. He went home. Now the [40]
woman was just alone. She was naked. The woman cried. Then
she lay down on the rock and cried. She cried for three days.
Then q she had been for four days on the island, then the woman
got tired of crying. Then q she went to sleep at the mouth of the
river. She had not been sleeping long when something came by [45]
which she was awakened, "Don't sleep," she was told q. "You
are called to go to our house," she was told q. It came again
q and she was awakened from her sleep. Then q the woman arose
from the rock and entered. The rock was open. This was the
place where the woman entered. What should it be but a large [50]
house. "Come," the woman on her part q was told. "I know
that you were deserted; and so I am going to see what I'll do
to you that you may arrive going back to the place where you
came from. You will be the owner of this my paddle-side canoe.
Then you will go home." That was given to her by (at) the place [55]
where she was. And q the woman came out; and for four days
she had been on the island. It was not long q before her husband
came to see what had happened to his wife. Then Maggots-on-
Water turned landward. He did not see his wife q and Maggots-
on-Water thought his wife was dead. Behold! he was not afraid [60]
on account of what he was doing. Then q his wife went in that
direction, near the beach on the rock and in vain Maggots-on-Water
looked for his wife. Then q his wife went aboard the canoe of her
husband. Then q Maggots-on-Water discovered his wife. "Oh,
mistress, is it you? You are the one for whom I came who is to be [65]
taken (by me)," said he q to his wife. "Come, that I may go aboard to
you, mistress," said q Maggots-on-Water to his wife. "I do not
wish that you come aboard. Later on you will come aboard if
you will pull out your hair." Then q Maggots-on-Water pulled
out his hair. "Come, mistress, that I may go aboard. Now all [70]
my hair is off." — "I do not wish that you come. Later on you

will come if you will pull out your eyelashes and your beard."
Then *q* the man pulled out his eyelashes and his beard. "Come,
mistress, that I may go aboard. Now all my eyelashes and beard
75 are off." — "I do not wish that you come aboard. Later on you
will come if you will pull out your pubic hair." Then *q* the man
pulled out his pubic hair. "Come, mistress, now all my pubic hair
is gone." — "I do not wish that you come," said his wife, "later
on you will come aboard. Go on and go around the island
80 with your legs turned outward." Then *q* Maggots-on-Water went
around. He went around the island his legs turned outward, and
the woman made turn back (upon him) the bad deed that he had
done to his wife. "You will not come aboard," said the woman to
her husband. "You will die for what you have done to me." — "Do
85 not now say so, mistress," said *q* Maggots-on-Water. He tried to
beg his wife to go and take him aboard her traveling canoe. Then
q the woman raised her mouth; she was on the water, out at
sea, and she called, "Come eagle, peck this Maggots-on-Water."
Then *q* again, "Come eagle, peck this Maggots-on-Water." The
90 eagle came *q*. He flew about and came soaring and was going
to get Maggots-on-Water. Then *q* the man was grasped by the
eagle. Then another came *q* and grasped him. His wife just
stayed on the water *q*. She saw very many eagles coming and
pecking. It was not long before all the flesh of the man was gone.
95 Only *q* his bare bones were on the rock when all his flesh was
finished by the many eagles. Then his wife went home. Now
she had won over her husband. The woman *q* caused surprise because she was not killed by Maggots-on-Water in his house. The woman was questioned. The woman was the cause of surprise for
100 her tribe because she was alive notwithstanding the badness of
her husband and the woman owned the paddle-side canoe. She
talked about it to her tribe.

The Dog[1]

Told by *Lā'bid*. Recorded by George Hunt.

The *A'ᵉwa.iLELa* were living *q* at *Hǎ'nwadē'*. *Hǎ'xomalag·iᵉlakᵘ*
had a large dog. Now *Hǎ'xomalag·iᵉlakᵘ* treated his dog really
well, for he always told his wife to feed the dog when her husband
was away, for *Hǎ'xomalag·iᵉlakᵘ* knew the way of his wife towards
5 the dog when he was away; for his wife never fed the dog; for
she only would always strike him all the time with her fire tongs

---

[1] Compare 35th Annual Report Bureau of American Ethnology, p. 1256.

when the dog tried to come to the house; for the woman really
hated the dog; for she did not want to feed him. The dog also
hated the woman, and the man always quarreled with his wife
when the man asked his wife to feed the dog. Then the woman [10]
just said to her husband, "Oh, do go on and feed your old dog,"
said she. And so only the man fed his dog; and so the dog hardly
ate what was given to him by his master. And the man saw that
the dog was feeling badly, for the dog would just lie down on the
floor in the place where he used to sleep. And so, as soon as [15]
night came the woman said to her husband they would go early to
lie down in their bed. And so, as soon as they were lying down they
fell asleep. And so, as soon as the dog heard his master and his
wife snoring together the dog sat up and made his small bed;
and so, as soon as he had made his bed he started and went to the [20]
place where his master and his wife were sleeping. Then the dog
took off his dog skin and put it on the floor. Then he took off
the man's skin of his master and put it on. Then he took the
dog skin and put it on his master. And so, as soon as he had
finished, the one who was now a man awakened the woman; [25]
and so, as soon as the woman saw that the one who was now a
dog was lying down the woman at once kicked out of the room
the one who was now her dog; but it was he, her husband; and
so the man who was now a dog just started and lay down where
the real dog used to lie down and the dog who had put on the [30]
man's skin of his master lay down by the side of the woman,
and the man turned his back to her. And so the woman tried
to embrace the one who was now her husband, the dog. And so
the man just spoke angrily to the woman, "Do go to sleep, for
I am very sleepy," said he. Then she said, "What is the matter? [35]
Only turn on your part your face towards me," said the woman
to the man. Then the man said, "What would be my benefit
if I on my part turned my face to you? I am well where I am.
Go on, sleep!" said the Dog-Man to the woman when he began
to snore, and the Dog-Man went to sleep, but the woman never [40]
went to sleep, for she was surprised at the way in which her husband spoke to her. And so, as soon as daylight came in the morning
the Dog-Man spoke. Then he said to his wife, "Go on, get up,
woman, and go and feed that poor dog!" said he, while he was
still just lying with his back towards the woman. And so the [45]
woman was afraid of the way he was speaking. That was the
reason why she arose at once to feed the dog. And so, as soon
as she reached the place where the dog was lying the dog sat
up and stared at the woman as though he wanted to talk when

⁵⁰ he was whining. And the woman also was surprised at the manner
of the dog, for the dog had never once done that way, for it was
as if he were waiting for the woman, although they hated each
other. And the woman stood still watching the dog as he came
to her standing, pressing his fore-paws on the breast of the woman.
⁵⁵ And the woman said to him, "Oh, what is the matter with you,
it is as though you wanted to have a word with me ? Pray tell me,"
said the woman to the dog, for now the woman really pitied the dog.
And she forgot that she was going to cook, And the Dog-Man spoke
angrily and said, "What is the matter with you that you stay
⁶⁰ away so long ?" said he to the woman. Then the woman said to
him, "I am very much surprised on account of the way the dog
acts in the house toward me, for he never ate what I gave him
to eat," said the woman. Then the Dog-Man said to her, "He
feels just grateful for what you are doing when you are feeding
⁶⁵ him. Now look out and keep on this way and give him to eat
when we have not (yet) eaten," said the Dog-Man to the woman.
Then the woman said to him, "That is now the way of my mind,
for I pity him very much," said the woman. Then the Dog-Man
said to the woman, "That is what I wish you to say, that you
⁷⁰ will just always pity the poor dog, that he may return the good for
the good done to him. I mean this, that you always feed him first
when we have not (yet) eaten," said he. Then the woman said to
him, "That is what I am going to do as long as I am a woman (as
long as I live)," said the woman. The woman did so for a long time.
⁷⁵ She was really treating the dog well. Then the dog also was always
as though he wanted to have a word with the woman and the
woman would always sit down at the place where the dog was
lying down. And the woman asked the dog to talk and tell the
reason why he was so very fond of her, said the woman to him.
⁸⁰ The dog just whined as though he was trying to speak, and so
the woman pitied him very much. The woman did not understand the ways of the Dog-Man, for he always just talked angrily
to the woman and he had no laugh in the way her real husband
would have who was just always laughing, for he was a very kind
⁸⁵ man, the one who was now a dog, and that surprised the woman
about the Dog-Man that he told the woman to lie down first and
so, as soon as she was lying down the Dog-Man lay down with
his back to the woman, and so, as soon as the woman tried to
embrace him he spoke angrily to the woman. "Don't touch me,"
⁹⁰ said he. Now the woman became used to this. For a long time
the Dog-Man did so, for the Dog-Man now believed that the
woman really pitied the dog and that she fed he dog immediately
when she first got up in the morning. And so that was the reason

why the dog said that he would set right his master, that he should
become a man again and that he also would become a dog again. ⁹⁵
And so, as soon as night came the Dog-Man asked the woman that
they would lie down in their bed, and so, as soon as she lay down she
went to sleep. Then was the time when the Dog-Man arose and went to
the place where the dog was lying. He took off his man's skin in
which he was dressed and put it down, and took off the dog skin of ¹⁰⁰
his master and put it on. Then he put on the man's skin on his
master, and his master became a man again and he also became a
dog again. And so, as soon as he had done so the man went and lay
down at the place where his wife was lying down and his wife was
sound asleep. And so, immediately the man awakened his wife, and ¹⁰⁵
the man told her that he had tried to talk to his wife, "When you
went to feed me I could not get out my words to you, for I under-
stood all your words to me when my dog put his dog skin on me and
when he put my man's skin on himself. I mean this, now treat this
dog well and let him be the first to eat when we have not (yet) eaten; ¹¹⁰
and also, don't get angry at him, for we are afraid of what he has
done to us," said the man to his wife. Then the woman said to
her husband, "Thank you, that you have come back to me, for
I truly suffered, for I was just always scolded by him who, behold!
was a Dog-Man. When we lay down at night he always turned ¹¹⁵
his back on me and when I tried to embrace him he scolded me
and said, 'Go to sleep.' When it was getting daylight in the morning
he awakened me to feed the dog and, behold! it was you. I mean
this, now I will treat this dog well and he will be the first to eat
when we have not (yet) eaten. I mean this, I am now truly grateful, ¹²⁰
my master, that you have come back to me," said the woman
to her husband. Then the man said, "That is the reason why I
say so, mistress, I see the reason why the dog has done this to
us, for he knew that I loved him very much; but you hated each
other. Now he has given advice to you, that you stop maltreating ¹²⁵
him, and that you only treat him well. This is evidently the reason
why this your word is good, as you say that this one will be fed
when we have not (yet) eaten. I mean this, I really am frightened
by what he has done to me. I do not expect that the dog
will do the same to me (again). I mean this, mistress. Let us take ¹³⁰
care together of our supernatural dog that he may protect us as
long as we live, for he is a great supernatural one. See what he
has done to me," said he. And the dog always played with his
mistress. And that is the end.

That is the reason why the Indians do not dare to maltreat ¹³⁵
their dogs and they just die of old age.

9

The Tale of the Dogs
Recorded by George Hunt

"This is not a myth for what I talk about is a tale, for my tale is seven generations old," said *Lā'bid* to me.

All the *Gwē'tɛla* lived at *ᵉyîlē's* and all the men had many dogs. Now the men always took their fire tongs and struck the dogs
5 when they came into the house of the owners. The dogs were always hungry. They were not fed by their owners and therefore they were just emaciated. The dogs were always sleeping outside of the houses of their owners, no matter whether the sun was shining or there was snow or rain or wind. Only one dog owner,
10 *T!ē'qwap*, the chief of the numaym *Kᵘkwā'k!ŭm* of the *Gwē'tɛla*, treated his dog well and the name of the dog was *G·ī'gɛxsta*, for he had for his bed a low box with well shredded cedar bark, and *G·ī'gɛxsta* lay in it at night. And when *T!ē'qwap* arose in the morning he immediately called his dog and fed him and after
15 *G·ī'gɛxsta* had eaten *T!ē'qwap* sat down with his wife *Sɛbɛ'lxēl* and they ate. *T!ē'qwap* never even once forgot to feed his dog first before *T!ē'qwap* and his wife began to eat. It was a fine day, therefore *Yā'yaqoL!ālas* went out of his house and sat down in the summer seat. And he had not been sitting there very long when
20 he saw two dogs going and scratching all the sleeping dogs and immediately the dogs who had been asleep would wake up and they went back into the woods of Alert Bay. Then *Yā'yaqoL!ālas* saw that all the many dogs went into the woods. It had occurred to *Yā'yaqoL!ālas* that he would follow secretly the many dogs.
25 *Yā'yaqoL!ālas* was not long in hiding before he heard a man talking who said, "You have come, all you tribes that we may ask one another why we came here and why we sit on the ground. Now call our chief *Mālᵉid*," — the speaker of the dogs meant *G·ī'gɛxsta* — "that our chief may come and listen to the reason why we came
30 here to where we are sitting; two may go. Do not come without bringing him," he said. Then two small dogs arose and one of them said, "We will go and call our chief *Mālᵉid*," said he as the two small dogs started. They did not stay away long before they came back and sat down. Then they were asked by the
35 speaker of the dogs, "Did you call *Mālᵉid*, the chief?" said he. Then one of the small dogs said, "We were not allowed by *T!ē qwap* and his wife to go near the place where our chief *Mālᵉid*, is sleeping and *T!ē'qwap* and his wife took the fire tongs and struck us and we just ran away," said he. Then the speaker of the dogs said,
40 "Our chief must come. Go back and even if you are struck by

T!ē'qwap and his wife when you reach the bed of our chief, tell him quickly and say to him, 'We have come and call you, chief *Māl*ᵉ*id*, that you go and listen to what they will say. Follow us,' you will say to him," said he. Immediately the two small dogs started and went into the house of *T!ē'qwap* and immediately ⁴⁵ the two small dogs went to the bed of *Māl*ᵉ*id*, namely *G·ī'gɛxsta*. One of the small dogs had just time to scratch *Māl*ᵉ*id*. Then *T!ē'qwap* took the fire tongs and tried to strike the two small dogs. He had no time to strike them before the two small dogs ran out with *Māl*ᵉ*id* and when they came to the place where ⁵⁰ many dogs were sitting *Māl*ᵉ*id* was told by the speaker to sit by himself. And as soon as *Māl*ᵉ*id* was sitting another large dog arose and said, "It would be good, my tribe, if we did not ask permission of our chief in regard to what he intends to do. Now listen, chief, I will tell you that I am maltreated by our masters. ⁵⁵ When I try to go into the house in the morning and when I wish to be fed, then he only takes his fire tongs and strikes me and chases me out of the house. Then I just lie down again the way I always lie down when it is raining or snowing, being very hungry," said he and he sat down. Then still another dog arose and he ⁶⁰ said the same as the first one had said when he spoke and when he had ended his speech he sat down, and still another dog arose and he followed the words of those spoken first. And only one among the dogs had not yet spoken. Then he arose and spoke and said, "O chief *Māl*ᵉ*id*, now you hear what all our tribe say. We ⁶⁵ all are maltreated by our masters, for they strike us with fire tongs. The reason is not that they want to kill us, they only like to hear us cry with pain and laugh watching us when we run away and that must make sick your hearts, my tribe. Now we will take revenge and we will all together kill our masters, my ⁷⁰ tribe," said he. As soon as he finished this speech the man sat down. Then *Māl*ᵉ*id*, the chief arose and said, "I am told that you are maltreated by your masters. I am very well treated by my master, for my bed is well made and I am first fed by them before my master eats. And after I have eaten my master ⁷⁵ eats. My only wish is that you should only not kill my master," said *Māl*ᵉ*id* and he ran home to his house. As soon as he arrived at the house of *T!ē'qwap* he climbed up and went to the roof of the house and barked running about on the roof until it was nearly midnight. Then there was a great earthquake and all the ⁸⁰ houses of the Kwakiutl collapsed. Only the house of the master of *G·ī'gɛxsta* did not collapse and *T!ē'qwap*, the owner of this house, and those who lived in his house were the only ones alive,

9*

and *Yā′yaqoʟ!ālas* who had been hiding listened to what had been
85 said by the dogs. That is the reason why the Indians know that
the dogs take care of the earthquakes for *Yā′yaqoʟ!ālas* talked
about all he had heard the dogs say and therefore the Indians
now treat their dogs well.

Squirrel and Thunderbird

Told by *Wā′k·as*, 1899. Recorded by George Hunt.

The first of the numaym *G·â′p!ēnox^u* lived *q* at Sandstone Place
(Dɛnā′sɛx). Then *q Yā′yaqɛxts!a* was a sea hunter, he who was
said not to be a chief for he was only the harpooneer of the house of
chief Place-of-Getting-Rich *(Q!ōmɛ^εnakŭlas)*. Then *q Yā′yaqɛxts!a*
5 purified himself all the time in the pond far inland. There was *q* a
clear place not far from the shore of the lake. Then *q Yā′yaqɛxts!a*
was wondering what was the reason of its being so, and so *q* that
was the reason why it occurred to him that he would really purify
himself; and he resolved to wash twice in the lake, mornings and
10 evenings. And *q* he resolved to stay there inland for four days.
And so *q* immediately he purified himself in the pond and rubbed
his body with hemlock branches. And so *q* as soon as he had
finished he broke off the supernatural tips of hemlock and made a
bed on the ground in the shelter of a hemlock tree. And so *q* as soon
15 as he had finished his work it was nearly evening. Then *q* he went
again to purify himself in the pond, and *q* again he rubbed his
body with hemlock branches. And so *q* as soon as he had finished
he went to his shelter and lay down on the ground. And so *q* as
soon as it was getting daylight in the morning he arose and purified
20 himself in the pond and rubbed his body with hemlock branches,
and so, as soon as he had finished, he started and went to pray to
all kinds of trees and all the bushes, for he said as he was praying,
he said, "I have come to ask you to take mercy on me, supernatural
ones; please advise me what is best to do that I may get a super-
25 natural treasure on this ground that looks supernatural; please
come to me tonight and make me have a good dream, directing
me to what I refer to as my treasure that I may succeed in the
reason of my coming. Don't let me have bad luck," said he to all
kinds of trees and all the bushes. And so *q* it was evening when
30 he went back and he went *q* and took a short rest where he lay
down that night. And so *q* as soon as it was getting dark he went *q*
and purified himself in the pond and *q* he rubbed his body again
with hemlock branches. And so *q* as soon as he had finished he went
q to the place where he (used to) lie down and lay down. And so *q*

immediately *Yā'yaqɛxts!a* went to sleep. And so *q* immediately [35] he dreamed that a man came and sat down at the place where he was lying down. Then *q* the man spoke to *Yā'yaqɛxts!a*. Then he said *q*, "O friend *Yā'yaqɛxts!a*, I came sent by our friends to let you know the end of their speeches last evening when chief Yew-Tree called in those who have him for their chief, all the trees [40] and all the bushes. And this was the speech of Yew-Tree, 'You have done well to have called for mercy all the trees and all the bushes and also done well that you have purified yourself twice and rubbed your body with hemlock branches in the pond.' Then Hellebore said that you should take its leaves and rub them on your body [45] after you have finished rubbing your body with hemlock branches, that really all the human smell may come off from your body, for something great will be seen by you, a double-headed serpent and a thunderbird, for that is where the double-headed serpent tries to bask in the sun, the well-cleared ground that was seen by [50] you. Only you will take care, friend, when you see the double-headed serpent. It is that, if it changes itself early on the ground you will find something that comes from its scales which are (thus that) there is nothing that is not killed when it is at the end of an arrow," said he as in his dream the man disappeared. And so *q* [55] immediately *Yā'yaqɛxts!a* awoke when it was getting daylight. And so *q* immediately he arose and went into the pond. And so *q* he had not arrived at the pond when he saw one hellebore plant standing on the ground. Then *q* he plucked off four of its leaves. And so *q* as soon as he arrived at the pond, he put on the shore the [60] four leaves of the hellebore plant, by the pond. Then *q* he purified himself and rubbed his body with hemlock branches. And so *q* as soon as he had done so he took the leaves of the hellebore plant and rubbed the hellebore plant on his body. And so *q* as soon as he had done so he again started to go inland and asked for mercy [65] all the trees and bushes. And he just repeated what he had been saying before. And so it was evening and he came back to the place where he used to lie down at night. Then *q* he stopped on the ground and went to pluck off four leaves of the hellebore plant. Then *q* he carried them going towards the pond. Then *q* he put [70] down the hellebore plant close to the shore of the pond and *q* he purified himself and rubbed his body with hemlock branches. And so *q* as soon as he had finished he took the four leaves of the hellebore plant and rubbed the hellebore on his body. And so *q* as soon as he had done so he lay down on the place where he always [75] lay down. And *q* he slept really well that night. And so *q* as soon as daylight came in the morning he arose and went *q* and plucked

off four leaves of the hellebore plant. Then *q* he carried them
going towards the pond. And *q* he again put the leaves of the
⁸⁰ hellebore plant down close to the pond. Then *q* he purified himself
and rubbed his body with hemlock branches. And so *q* as soon as
he had finished, he went *q* and took the four leaves of the hellebore
plant and rubbed the hellebore plant on his body. Now he rubbed
for a long time the hellebore on his body. It is said he only stopped
⁸⁵ when the leaves of the hellebore had dissolved on his body. And
so *q* as soon as he had done so he went *q* out of the water in the
pond and sat down on the ground to dry his body. Then *q* Yā'yagₑxts!a heard a squeaking sound coming towards the place where
he was sitting. Then *q* Yā'yagₑxts!a arose from the ground and
⁹⁰ went into hiding on one side of a tree. And *q* the squeaking increased
and what was heard by Yā'yagₑxts!a was coming nearer. Then *q*
he saw the double-headed serpent. Then *q* a man was standing
in the middle. The double-headed serpent came right on to the
well-cleared ground and stopped moving on the ground, for the
⁹⁵ sun was shining there. Then *q* Yā'yagₑxts!a just fainted, for he
could not plan what to do, for the whole body of the double-headed
serpent was glistening, as the double-headed serpent was just for
a long time keeping quiet on the ground. Then *q* Yā'yagₑxts!a
heard a swift sound above, which came downward, coming from
¹⁰⁰ the upper side of our world. Probably *q* the double-headed serpent
also heard it; and that was the reason why the double-headed
serpent tried to escape. And *q* Yā'yagₑxts!a saw the Thunderbird
coming down shooting lightning ahead. And so *q* as soon as he
tried to catch the double-headed serpent in his talons the double-
¹⁰⁵ headed serpent became a squirrel, and *q* the squirrel just went into
a hole in the ground. And *q* the Thunderbird just went back upward.
Then *q* Yā'yagₑxts!a arose and went *q* to the place where the double-
headed serpent had been lying on the ground, to search for a scale
of the double-headed serpent. Then *q* he found something shining,
¹¹⁰ lying on the ground at the place where the double-headed serpent
had been. Then *q* he took a leaf of a salal bush and wrapped it
around the scale. Then *q* he came home. And so *q* it was getting
dark when he arrived behind his house. That was *q* when he tucked
the wrapped scale in at the bottom of a cedar tree. And so *q* as
¹¹⁵ soon as he had hidden the scale Yā'yagₑxts!a went into his house
and went to lie down on his bed. And so *q* as soon as he lay down
he dreamed *q* of an oldish man who came and sat by his side at the
right-hand side of Yā'yagₑxts!a. Then *q* the man spoke and said,
"You have succeded, friend Yā'yagₑxts!a in what you have done,
¹²⁰ for you did not hurt me, for I am the double-headed serpent, for it

was he, the Thunderbird, who tried to hurt me. He doesn't know which way I went when I became a squirrel. I mean this, you might have obtained a great treasure from me, for I had already seen that you were hiding behind the tree. I mean this, you have succeeded when you took my scale. Now you have a great treasure. [125] Go on! Make an arrow and put the scale at the end of the arrow and nothing will live that is shot by you, even if it were a whale or an animal. When you wish it to become a rock, what is shot by you, say to this arrow that it shall become a rock, and say to the arrow that what is shot by you shall burn. And also that, [130] everything will be obeyed by the arrow what you tell him," said the man and he disappeared. And so, as soon as daylight came in the morning *Yā'yaqᴇxts!a* arose and took his knife and well-splitting cedar wood and went inland through the rear door of the house. Then q he sat down on the ground near the cedar tree [135] where the scale of the double-headed serpent was hidden. Then q he measured two spans and a short span for the length of his arrow. Then q he cut it off. And so, as soon as it was cut off he split q and squared it. Then q he shaved it off well so that it became round. And so q as soon as it was the right size he gathered the [140] small shavings and rubbed them on what was to be an arrow. And so q as soon as it was finished it was smooth. And so, as soon as he had finished he took the scale of the double-headed serpent, and split the end of what was to be an arrow. Then q he tucked the scale in the split end. Then q he took a well split spruce root and [145] did well as he twisted it well around the end of the arrow. Then q the length that was twisted around by the root at the end of the arrow was four finger widths in length, and that was the reason why he put on tightly the twisted root at the end of the arrow, because he did not wish the scale of the double-headed serpent to [150] drop out when he would shoot at something. And so q as soon as the arrow-making of *Yā'yaqᴇxts!a* was finished, he prayed q to it and said, "O friend, you have come, supernatural one, brought to me by your owner, to come and help me in my work; and also that, not to bring misfortune to me, great, real supernatural one, and [155] all the time we shall be together, friend," said *Yā'yaqᴇxts!a* to his supernatural treasure. Then q he hid it again under the cedar tree. Then q he took his knife into his house. Then q he took his bow and went inland through the rear door of his house. Then q he took his death-bringing arrow. Then q he started hunting inland. [160] Then q he saw a black bear. Then q he shot it with his arrow. And so q immediately the bear fell to the ground and q he had killed the bear. And so q immediately *Yā'yaqᴇxts!a* skinned it. And so

q as soon as he had finished skinning it he hung q up the skin at
165 the bottom of the spruce tree. Then q *Yā'yaqExts!a* started again.
Then q he saw an elk. Then q *Yā'yaqExts!a* said to his arrow, "Now
I will shoot with you at that elk and you will turn it into a stone,"
said he q and he shot it. And so q immediately the elk fell down
dead and turned into a rock. And q *Yā'yaqExts!a*'s mind was really
170 good after this, for it was as though he did not believe that his
arrow would do this. Then q he started and saw a hill on the ground.
Then q he said to his arrow, "Now I'll shoot you at this hill, for you
shall set it on fire," said he q as he shot at it. And so q immediately
the trees on the hill on the ground caught fire. And q *Yā'yaqExt !a*
175 came back, and so q he took the skin of the black bear and carried
it on his back as he was coming home to his house. And so q he
was not near his house before he saw a squirrel crying at the bottom
of the cedar tree. Then q it occurred to *Yā'yaqExts!a* to hide his
bow and arrow under the cedar tree. And so q he hid it there. As
180 soon as he had done so he saw the squirrel sitting on a log and q
Yā'yaqExts!a remembered that the double-headed serpent had
become a squirrel. That q was the reason why he prayed to the
squirrel. Then q he said, "Thank you, supernatural one, that we
have met again. Thank you that you have taken mercy on me
185 with this my supernatural treasure, the death-bringing arrow.
Only let me continue to get easily everything that is being hunted
by me, and also that I may not have misfortune as long as I
keep together with you. Take mercy on me!" said he. And q
the squirrel just sat still on the spruce log. And so q as soon as the
190 prayer of *Yā'yaqExts!a* was ended the squirrel squeaked and
jumped about going into the hole in the ground. Then q *Yā'yaqExts!a* came and started and q he really knew that this squirrel
was the double-headed serpent, for that was the way the squirrel
acted, the way it acted on the ground when the double-headed
195 serpent became a squirrel when the Thunderbird tried to take hold
of it. And so q as soon as *Yā'yaqExts!a* entered his house, then q
he hung up the bear skin in the corner of his house. Then q he
ate a little. And so q as soon as he had finished he lay down in his
bed when q it was dark. Then q he fell asleep at once, for he was
200 very tired, for he had been walking far. And q he dreamed of the
double-headed serpent at night and q *Yā'yaqExts!a* saw in his dream
the oldish man who came into the house as *Yā'yaqExts!a* was lying
on his back, and, in his dream he thought of the arrow, his supernatural treasure from the double-headed serpent. Then q the
205 oldish man spoke. Then q he said, "I come to see you, friend
Yā'yaqExts!a. You recognized me, for I am the double-headed

serpent who became a squirrel and I'll be a squirrel when we meet
from time to time. And so I am the squirrel seen by you at the
place where you hide your bow and arrow under the cedar tree.
This is the reason why I wish to come and give you a dream for ²¹⁰
your dream that you will still hide your bow and arrow under the
cedar tree; that I may watch it, for it would give bad luck to you
if you should take it into your house. I mean this, friend, just take
care in everything you are doing and also do not forget to purify
yourself when you go to lie down at night. And also this; don't ²¹⁵
forget your chief, Place-of-Getting-Rich, and give him the greater
part of what you shoot. In case you do so to the chief, you will never
have bad luck," said the man as he disappeared after this. Then *q*
Yā′yaɢExts!a began to be awake. Then *q* he was thinking about
the words of his dream man when he told him to give to chief ²²⁰
Place-of-Getting-Rich the greater part of the animals he killed,
and of all the fish. Then *q Yā′yaɢExts!a* truly acted according to
the words of the dream of the man. And *q* it occurred to *Yā′ya-
ɢExts!a* to go sea otter hunting when daylight would come in the
morning, for he did not wish his tribe to know of his supernatural ²²⁵
treasure, the arrow. And so that *q* was the reason why he arose
when day had not (yet) come and he went inland to get his bow
and arrow and he went and hid it on the rocks near to where he
was going to pass when he was going paddling. And so *q* as soon
as he had hidden it he came back and went into his house and ²³⁰
took his sitting mat and his knee blanket and his paddle, for
indeed, the harpoon shaft just always lies in the small hunting
canoe. Then *q* he went aboard his small canoe. Then *q* he started
paddling and he took his bow and his arrow aboard. And so *q* he
paddled close to the rocks at the place *Ō′yaɢEmᵉla*. Then *q* he ²³⁵
saw many sea otters diving for mussels. And so *q* as soon as they
all came up *Yā′yaɢExts!a* took his bow and arrow and shot at
the many sea otters. And so *q* they were just all killed on the
water, many sea otters. Then *q Yā′yaɢExts!a* took his death-
bringing arrow and put it aboard his small canoe. Then *q* he pulled ²⁴⁰
aboard more than twenty sea otters into his small canoe; and *q*
his small canoe was hardly above the water. And so *q* he started
paddling and went home to his house. And so *q* as soon as he
almost reached the point of Sandstone *(DEnā′sEx)* he went into
the bay of the rock and stepped *q* out of his small canoe, carrying ²⁴⁵
his bow and arrow, as he was running keeping out of sight and
went to hide his bow and arrow at the bottom of the cedar tree
at the place referred to by the double-headed serpent man, where
he was always to hide his bow and arrow. But *q* it was not long

²⁵⁰ before he came back and went aboard his small canoe. Then *q* he started paddling and went *q* to the beach of the house of Place-of-Getting-Rich. The tribe were not all awake *q* when he arrived. Then *q* *Yā'yaɢExts!a* stepped out of his small canoe and *q* he asked Place-of-Getting-Rich to send his men slaves to unload the sea ²⁵⁵ otters from his small canoe. And so *q* immediately his slaves unloaded the sea otters from the small canoe, and *q* *Yā'yaɢExts!a* treated his chief, Place-of-Getting-Rich, as a chief with more than twenty sea otters. That *q* was the first (time when) *Yā'ya-ɢExts!a* did in that way when he treated Place-of-Getting-Rich ²⁶⁰ as a chief with many sea otters, according to the word of the double-headed serpent man to *Yā'yaɢExts!a*. (And thus it began that the first of the *G·ā'p!ēnox*ᵘ treated the head chief as a chief.) And *q* the slaves skinned the sea otters on the beach. And so *q* they were all skinned. Then *q* the slaves took the skins of the sea ²⁶⁵ otters and hung them up in the corner of the house. Now Place-of-Getting-Rich believed that the word of *Yā'yaɢExts!a* was true, who lived in a house different from the house of Place-of-Getting-Rich. Then *q* Place-of-Getting-Rich sent a slave to go and invite *Yā'yaɢExts!a* to eat after his arrival at his house. And so *q* immedi- ²⁷⁰ ately *Yā'yaɢExts!a* arose and followed the slave who was sent to invite him and he entered the house of Place-of-Getting-Rich. Then *q* *Yā'yaɢExts!a* was led to sit down on a new mat spread in the rear of the house. And so *q* immediately dried salmon was given to him to eat. And so *q* as soon as he finished eating the ²⁷⁵ dried salmon, they gave him to eat boiled rock cod. And so *q* as soon as he had eaten with spoons the rock cod, Place-of-Getting-Rich spoke. Then he said *q*, "Great is what you have done to me, child, with these many sea otters. It is unbelievable what you have done. Thank you for your kind heart (to me), child. Now ²⁸⁰ come and move into my house that we may be one in the house here," said Place-of-Getting-Rich to *Yā'yaɢExts!a*. Then *q* *Yā'ya-ɢExts!a* replied to his words. Then *q* he said, "That is your word, chief. It is great. Why should I not treat you as a chief for I have you for my chief, chief Place-of-Getting-Rich, for this is only the ²⁸⁵ first, these sea otters, with which I'll continue to treat you as a chief. Only take care, else it is you who will be overcome by all I (do) treating you as a chief, chief. And also you say that I should come and move into your house, chief. Don't say that now and I will still stay in my house. Later on I'll move to your house, ²⁹⁰ chief, when I have finished treating you as a chief," said he. And *q* *Yā'yaɢExts!a* arose and went home to his house. And *q* the chief Place-of-Getting-Rich guessed that *Yā'yaɢExts!a* had obtained a

supernatural treasure of some kind and that therefore he was unwilling to come and move to his house. Then *q* *Yā'yag̣ᴇxts!a* did not forget to purify himself in the pond every evening. And so *q* he had taken a rest for four days, beginning at the time he had gotten many sea otters. And so *q* it was not (yet) nearly daylight when he arose *q* and took his knee cover blanket and his sitting mat and his paddle and went *q* and put them aboard his small canoe. Then *q* he ran inland and took his bow and arrow. He came *q* and carried them and put them aboard his small canoe. Then *q* he went aboard and started paddling. But *q* he had not gone far when he saw many seals on a rock close to point Open-Mouth-Rock (*Aqălā'laa*). Then *q* he took his bow and arrow and shot them, and many seals just lay dead on the rock. Then *q* *Yā'yag̣ᴇxts!a* loaded his small canoe with many seals. And so *q* as soon as they were all aboard he went home. And so *q* as soon as he arrived at the bay he went in there. Then *q* he took his bow and arrow and went running to hide his bow and arrow at the foot of the cedar tree. He came *q* going back and went aboard his small canoe and started paddling. Then *q* he arrived at the beach of the house of Place-of-Getting-Rich. Then *q* *Yā'yag̣ᴇxts!a* stepped out of his small canoe and went to the house of Place-of-Getting-Rich. Then *q* he asked the chief to send his slaves to go and take the seals out of his small canoe. Then *q* Place-of-Getting-Rich sent four of his slaves, and so *q* immediately the four slaves went and hauled the seals out of the small canoe. And so *q* as soon as they had all been taken out of the canoe Place-of-Getting-Rich asked his slaves to singe all the seals. And so *q* as soon as all the seals had been singed they cut them up. And so *q* as soon as all had been cut up Place-of-Getting-Rich invited his tribe that all should come into his house. And so *q* as soon as they were all in he gave a feast to them with the seals. And *q* *Yā'yag̣ᴇxts!a* went paddling every fourth day and he filled his small canoe with porpoises, and he filled it with sealions. Then *q* last, with four whales and all were given in a feast by Place-of-Getting-Rich to his tribe. Then *q* the tribe dried the meat of the whales and sealions and porpoises and seals and the meat of the sea otters. And so *q* as soon as *Yā'yag̣ᴇxts!a* had caught all that I have mentioned he moved into the house of Place-of-Getting-Rich, and *q* *Yā'yag̣ᴇxts!a* became proud because he caught easily everything, and *q* he also forgot the advice of the double-headed serpent man. And so *q* he made his bedroom in the rear of the house of Place-of-Getting-Rich; and so *q* as soon as he had finished making his bedroom he went inland to go to the hiding place of his bow and

his death-bringing arrow. Then *q* he took the bow and the arrow and came carrying them. Then *q* just for a short time he saw the squirrel as it went into the hole in the ground. Then *q Yā'yagExts!a* did not take notice of it. And so *q Yā'yagExts!a* just went along
340 into his house, the house of Place-of-Getting-Rich, and he went *q q* and hung up his bow and arrow at the head of his bed. And so *q* as soon as he had finished, it was as though he was getting sleepy. Then *q* he lay down. Then *q* right away he fell asleep. And so *q* immediately he dreamed about the double-headed serpent man
345 who came and sat by his side. Then *q* he said to *Yā'yagExts!a,* "What has been done by you ? I tried to advise you never to bring the death-bringing arrow into the house. Now you have disobeyed me, and you have brought it into this house. Now you have spoiled this. Now you will be poor from this day on, for you have
350 become proud," said he and he disappeared. And so *q* immediately *Yā'yagExts!a* awoke. Then *q* he arose and took his arrow and untied the root from its end. Then *q* he looked at the place where the scale of the double-headed serpent had been and *q* he saw that there was nothing there. And so *q* he just took his bow and
355 his death-bringing arrow and threw them into the fire of the house. Then *q* he went back into his bedroom and cried, for indeed he was just going to be always poor. And that is the end.

Lo'ya

Told by Ō'mx·ᵋit

Lo'ya q also was fishing halibut. Then *q* he arrived at his halibut fishing ground. Then *q* he threw his anchor into the water. Then *q* he threw into the water his halibut fish hook. He would then *q* get a bite of halibut. And so *q* he just threw it into the water.
5 He said *q* that he was only fishing (halibut) for the chief of the halibut. Then *q* he obtained by fishing the chief of the halibut. And so *q* immediately he went home when he got in his canoe *Hǎ'nwäla,* the chief of the halibut. Then *q* he came ashore to his house at *Tsā'xwaēsEᵋlakᵘ.*[1] Then *q* he cut what he had caught
10 and dried it. Very fat was what he had caught, *Hǎ'nwäla,* the chief of the halibut. Then *q* he started paddling again to go fishing with a fish basket. Then *q* he caught in the fish basket the chief of the kelp fish. It was *q* really fat. And so *q* immediately he went home to cut the kelp fish he had caught to dry it. It was
15 really fat.[2]

---

[1] A small island about a half mile out at point west of *nEᵋwē'dēᶜ.*
[2] The incident told at the end seems to belong here.

Then *q* he named his child *Yā'yaq!ᴇlg·is*. *Lo'ya* said *q* to his
child, "I am going to give a winter ceremonial and you will be a
cannibal dancer," said *q Lo'ya*. "Go ahead," said on his part *q*
Yā'yaq!ᴇlg·is. "Go and invite our tribe to come and talk over
what we shall do when we have a winter dance." — "I shall go ²⁰
and invite our tribe," said on his part *q Lo'ya*. "Invitation!"
said on his part *q Lo'ya*. He just went *q* to each corner in his house.
There was only one house. They were two, (he and) his child.
Then *q Lo'ya* arose and spoke. "You have come, tribe. We are
going to have a winter ceremonial. Now this *Yā'yaq!ᴇlg·is* is going ²⁵
to disappear," said *q Lo'ya*. Then *q Yā'yaq!ᴇlg·is* disappeared.
And so *q* the house of *Lo'ya* was the winter ceremonial house. And
so *q* he had for food in his house the fat skin of halibut and fat
kelp fish which he had caught. Then *q* they captured his child
and *q Yā'yaq!ᴇlg·is* was a cannibal dancer. And so *q* they just ³⁰
came, two together, (he and) his child when they captured him.
Then *q Lo'ya* went into the house and stood in the door of his house.
"Be careful, friends, now beat time," said on his part *q Lo'ya*.
Then *q* they prepared(?) and it was he *q* who beat time. His son
came *q* who was cannibal dancer. Only the two, *Lo'ya* and his ³⁵
son were in the house.

The nephews of *Lo'ya* came *q* to visit him, coming from *nᴇᵋwē'dēᶜ*.
Then *q Lo'ya* invited them in. "Inviting you, warriors," said *q*
Lo'ya. Then *q* his nephews sat down in the house. Then *q Lo'ya*
spoke. "What may these warriors eat? Come and eat this fat ⁴⁰
skin," said *q Lo'ya*. He himself answered. Then *q* he gave skin to
his nephews. There were three *q* of his nephews. Then *q* his nephews
ate. Then *q Lo'ya* gave them a report, "We are having a great
winter ceremonial. The cannibal dancer *Yā'yaq!ᴇlg·is* arrives on
the roof of this house," said *q Lo'ya*. But *q* (he) and his son were ⁴⁵
two in the house. Then *q* the nephews of *Lo'ya* said, "*Lo'ya* must
be a fool. Why should they have a winter ceremonial when they
are two in the house, (he) and his son? Only many tribes have a
winter ceremonial. Let us go home and tell our father at *nᴇᵋwē'dēᶜ*."
Then *q* the children went home to *nᴇᵋwē'dēᶜ*. ⁵⁰

Then[1] *q* the Bella Bella warriors came. *Lo'ya* on his part *q* had
no way of pulling up quickly his anchor. It is said he just jumped
out of his canoe. "This is the way you will dive, like the diving of
cormorants," said *q Lo'ya* as he dived. And so *q* he only saved
himself in the house of the fishes below. Then *q Lo'ya* saw the fish. ⁵⁵
They were just men sitting in the house. "Take care of this, *Lo'ya*,"

---

[1] The following incident was told independently as belonging to this
story.

said *q* the men. "You will only go to the end of this house and go past the mouth of the sea monster *(ts!ē'gis)* which is open at your beach," ʟo'*ya* was told *q* by the fish. "I shall do so," said on his
60 part *q* ʟo'*ya* and *q* he went outside of the house, walking to the seaside of the fishes around the fire. Then *q* ʟo'*ya* arrived at the mouth of the sea monster. Its mouth was open. Then *q* he walked up the beach to his house. And so *q* in vain the warriors were in their canoes near his former traveling canoe waiting that ʟo'*ya* should
65 come up. Then he went to his house.

Hä'qŭlał
Told by *Ō'mx·ᵋit*

It is said, that the reason why a house was built at *Dzō'dzadē^ᶜ* was *Hä'qŭlał.* And so *q* they lived at Sea-otter-Slide-Point *(Xŭ'm-dasbēᵋ).* Then *q* he was sitting in his house. His brother-in-law ʟ!ā'k!watsōt *q* came and entered. Then *q* he whispered to *Hä'qŭlał.*
5 He said *q* "Kill this man who came to warm himself by your fire, who was sent to come and look at you. Now *q* you will be killed, *Hä'qŭlał*, by *G·îlgāmēᵋstāla.*[1] But *q* he[2] had just come *q* to dry his hair, but *Ë'k·ila* had only been in the water. "You are bad, ʟ!ā'-k!watsōt," said *q Hä'qŭlał.* How shall I go and finish my feasting,
10 if I kill this man? I shall kill him." It is said *Hä'qŭlał* arose and took his stone ax and threw it at *Ë'k·ila.* Then *q Ë'k·ila* was dead and so *q* he just pushed him into the fire and barred his door. And so *q* the relatives of *Ë'k·ila* tried to enter when they learned that *Ë'k·ila* was dead.
15 Then *q* he moved and left Sea-otter-Slide-Point and went to Deer-Place *(Ĝē'wasᴇmēᵋ)* and his whole tribe went across with him, the one numaym, the numaym of the tribe of *Hä'qŭlał.* [But so] *q* that was where *G·îlgāmēᵋstāla* and his numaym were, at Sea-otter-Slide-Point. Then *q G·î'lgāmēᵋstāla*[3] said, "Let us invite *Hä'qŭlał* and
20 take revenge on him who killed him[2]. Go and hunt seals that we may give them to *Hä'qŭlał* to eat." It is said these seals came and he invited *Hä'qŭlał.* It is said *Hä'qŭlał* came and all went in, (he) and his numaym. Then *q G·î'lgāmēᵋstāla* shot with his arrow at *Hä'qŭlał.* Then *q* he missed; that one *q*, the slave, was killed. It is
25 said the arrow really hit the stomach of the slave. Then *q Hä'qŭlał* became angry. He took his knife and struck among the guests. That *q* was his knife, the bone of a whale. And so *q Hä'qŭlał* just went home to Deer-Place. It is said he did not eat of what they

---

[1] The narrator anticipates here the consequences of the murder of *Ë'k·ila.*
[2] Namely *Ë'k·ila.*
[3] The brother of *Hä'pŭlał's* wife *Lă'nuxᵘsᴇxLä.*

tried to give him to eat, when he knew that he had just been deceived
by *G·î′lgămē⁵stāla*, to be killed by his brother-in-law.   30
   Then *q* the children of *Ë′k·ila* said to their mother[1], "Let us
go and see the one named *ʟă′nux̣ᵘsₑxʟä* at Deer-Place." — "Go,"
said *q* on her part the mother of the children. These were the
children of *Ë′k·ila* who were going to *ʟă′nux̣ᵘsₑxʟä*. Then *q* the
children walked along the beach, going to Deer-Place. Then *q* 35
they reached their aunt *ʟă′nux̣ᵘsₑxʟä*. The men *q* were feasting
invited by *Hä'qŭlał*. Then *q* the seals were being steamed, *q* they
were done. Then *q* they took them out with tongs. Then *q Hä'qŭlał*
took the flippers and bit them once. Then *q* he threw them across
the house to the children. "Take this," said *Hä'qŭlał*. "Eat this, 40
children," said *q Hä'qŭlał*, "so that you may quickly grow up if
you will strike back at me," said *Hä'qŭlał q*. And so *q* the children
just went out and went home to Sea-otter-Slide-Point. Then *q*
they told their mother, "What was the word of *Hä'qŭlał* to us?"
said *q* the children. "What did he say?" said *q* their mother. "He 45
bit the flippers and threw the flippers at us. 'Eat this, children,
that you may quickly grow up, if you will strike back at me,'
said *Hä'qŭlał* to us," said *q* the children to their mother. And so *q*
their mother just cried on account of the words of her children.
It is said, *G·î′lgămē⁵stāla* came and asked his sister, "Why are you 50
crying?" Then *q* the woman told her brother about the words of
Hä'qŭlał, when he bit the flipper and threw it at the children.
"We will go across to *nₑ⁵wē′dē⁵*," said *q* on his part *G·î′lgămē⁵stāla*,
"and leave this bad man." Then *q* they moved, all, he and his
numaym. They made a house at *nₑ⁵wē′dē⁵*; and so *q Hä'qŭlał* also 55
just moved and went to *⁵mₑgwī′g·ē⁵*, he and his whole numaym;
and they also went and made a house at *⁵mₑgwī′g·ē⁵*. Then *Hä'qŭlał*
q went to River's Inlet *(Ăwī′k·!ēnox̣ᵘ)* to try to get a wife from
Yā′yawi⁵nâg·i⁵laḳᵘ and so *q* he came to have two wives with
ʟă′nux̣ᵘsₑxʟä. Then *q* he went to *Mₑ⁵lō′bax·* to go and take sockeye 60
salmon. Then *q* they were done. Then *q* his brother-in-law,
G·î′lgămē⁵stāla, walked along the beach to go and see *Hä'qŭlał*.
And so *q ʟă′nux̣ᵘsₑxʟä* gave to eat to her brother. It is said, the
heart of *G·î′lgămē⁵stāla* was really sore when he saw that *Hä'qŭlał*
had two wives, and *q* he did not really like his sister. It was she 65
who was liked by *Hä'qŭlał*, the River's Inlet woman. "Let us go
hunting," said *q Hä'qŭlał* to *G·î′lgămē⁵stāla*. "Let us (go)," said *q*
on his part, *G·î′lgămē⁵stāla*. Then *q* they went along the beach.
Then *q* he saw a seal. Then *q* he shot with his arrow. It is said,
he really hit the seal. Then *q* it floated on the water. "Go on, 70
swim," said *q Hä'qŭlał* to *G·î′lgămē⁵stāla*. Then *q G·î′lgămē⁵stāla*

[1] A sister of *G·î′lgămē⁵stāla*.

swam towards the seal. Behold, *Hä'qŭlaɬ* was just deceiving him
(when he told him) to swim. Then *q* he threw at him with a stone
and so *q G·î'lgămē ˤstāla* every time just dived. Then *q G·î'lgămē ˤstāla*
75 arrived. Then *q* they took hold of each other, "Behold, you only
deceived me," said *q G·î'lgămē ˤstāla*. "We are going to fight."
Then *q G·î'lgămē ˤstāla* went home to *nɛ ˤwē'dē ˤ*. Then *q Hä'qŭlaɬ*
also went home to *Măgwī'g·ē ˤ*. Then *q G·î'lgămē ˤstāla* called his
numaym to tell them that he would go and pole up *Mɛ ˤlō'bax·*
80 with the children, the children of the late *Ë'k·ila*, that they should
grow up at the lake of the river of *Mɛ ˤlō'bax·*. He was going to
put them all the time into the water; that was what was told to
his numaym. "Go on," *G·î'lgămē ˤstāla* on his part was told by his
numaym. Then *q* they poled up, the three, *q G·î'lgămē ˤstāla* and
85 the two children. Then *q* they arrived at the lake. An island *q*
was in the lake. That is the place where their house was built, to
be their house. Then *q* the children went bathing in the water *q*
always four times every day. Then *q* it was one year. Then *q* he
measured the size of the children on the flat rock. Then *q* he laid
90 the children down on their backs and took a stone to hammer out
the sizes of their heads. It is said, he always did so, measuring
them for one year. It is said, the children grew up quickly. It is
said, he always made the children fight when they played. For
this reason the children became very strong.
95 Then *q Hä'qŭlaɬ* went to River's Inlet to go and add on (to his
ceremonials) the cannibal dance. Then *q Hä'qŭlaɬ* was a novice
at River's Inlet. It is said *Hä'qŭlaɬ* came paddling secretly to
Mɛ ˤlō'bax·, the place of the children at the mouth of the river.
Hä'qŭlaɬ was searching for something to be killed by him. "Let
100 us go with torches to hunt loons," said *q* on his part *G·î'lgămē ˤstāla*
to the children. Then *q* they drifted down the river at night.
Then *q* they lighted the fire in the canoe. Then *q* they shot loons.
Then *q* cried a loon. "Go on, extinguish the fire in our canoe,"
said *q G·î'lgămē ˤstāla* to the children who were with him in the
105 canoe. Behold! *Hä'qŭlaɬ q* was coming and almost took hold of
the stern of the canoe of *G·î'lgămē ˤstāla* and he wished to kill him.
And so *q G·î'lgămē ˤstāla* just hid and quickly went up the river.
He was not found by *Hä'qŭlaɬ* on account of the dark night, and
G·î'lgămē ˤstāla remained alive when he was lost. And so *q G·î'l-*
110 *gămē ˤstāla* just kept on going to his house on the lake. And so *q*
Hä'qŭlaɬ just went home to River's Inlet to be surrounded in his
character of cannibal dancer. Then *q Hä'qŭlaɬ* finished the dance.
It is said, he came back home to his country in *ˤmɛgwī'g·ē ˤ*. Now *q*
he was a novice. Now *q* he was wearing his blanket. A bearskin *q*

was his blanket. An artificial man *q* was made on the back of his [115] blanket of red cedar bark and imitations of bones were on the back of his blanket. And so that was the reason why *Hä'qŭlaɫ* was much feared, on account of his red cedar bark. It is said, his name was *Ɫā'manē* in his character as cannibal dancer.

It is said he was always sitting on the roof of his house. "I shall [120] go visiting *Ɫā'manē*," said *q* on his part *A ᵋmā' x·âg·ila*. He came home from *nᴇᵋwē'dēˈ*. "Take care," *A ᵋmā' x·âg·ila* was told *q*, "of that bad man." — "You will just see me, I will just come and make fire on the beach at *ʟᴇ'mwas* if I should be killed by the bad man." [125]

And so *q G·î'lgămēᵋstāla* came drifting down with the children. It is said, the children were really strong. Then *q A ᵋmā' x·âg·ila* arrived on the beach in the country of *Hä'qŭlaɫ*. Then *q* he was met and he was asked for his news. Then *q A ᵋmā' x·âg·ila* spoke, "These are my news, they have grown up and *G·î'lgămēᵋstāla* is [130] coming drifting down the river. Really strong are the children." — "What are your news?" said *q* on his part *Hä'qŭlaɫ*. He was sitting on the roof of his house. "This is the news, they come drifting down *q* who have grown up. It is said, they are really strong," *Hä'qŭlaɫ* was told on his part *q*. Then *q Hä'qŭlaɫ* became [135] angry. "Why do you make this a great news?" said he *q*. *Hä'qŭlaɫ q* arose and took his war ax to go and kill *A ᵋmā' x·âg·ila* and he cut open his stomach and threw him into the water on the beach. Then *q* he went back and sat down on the roof of his house.

Then *q* the children said, "Let us pull up the beach our late [140] friend on the other side," said *q* the children. Then *q* they tied (a rope) around his neck and towed him to the far side and pulled him up the beach to high water mark. Then *q* it was almost evening. There came *q* very many wolves. Then *q* the children said, "Let us go and watch how they eat our friend *A ᵋmā' x·âg·ila*." It is said [145] very many wolves came to eat him. Behold! *q* they did not eat him. Behold! *q* they just licked the cut in his stomach and revived him. Then *q* the wolves left. Behold! *q A ᵋmā' x·âg·ila* had revived. Then *q* it became dark when *A ᵋmā' x·âg·ila* arose from the beach to go to *ʟᴇ'mwas* and make a fire on the beach at night. Then *q* [150] the fire on the beach was seen by those who lived at *nᴇᵋwē'dēˈ*. "Behold! now our friend has been killed," said on their part *q* the tribe of *A ᵋmā' x·âg·ila*. "Let us take him," they said *q*. Then *q* they went and took *A ᵋmā' x·âg·ila*. Then *q* he reported to his tribe how he had been killed by *Hä'qŭlaɫ*. And so *q* he was just pitied by the [155] wolves.

Then *q* the tribe of *Hä'qŭlaɫ* made ready to go and visit *G·î'lgămēᵋ*-

10

stāla. Then *q* the whole tribe of *Hä'qŭlał* went to the *Łā'wits!ēs*
at *Ḡāk·!ɛxsdɛ'ls*. Then *q* *ʟă'nux̣ᵘsɛxʟä* carried her daughter and
160 sent her to go and visit *G·î'lgămē⁵stāla*. Then *q* *ʟă'nux̣ᵘsɛxʟä*
whispered to her child, "'Come and make war against my father.
His whole tribe went to the *Łā'wits!ēs*,' you will say to your uncle,"
said *q* *ʟă'nux̣ᵘsɛxʟä* to her child. Then *q* her child went aboard.
Then *q* she arrived in the country of *G·î'lgămē⁵stāla*. Then *q*
165 *G·î'lgămē⁵stāla* was called to come and take out of the canoe his
niece. Then *q* his niece told him, "Go and make war against my
father," said *q* the girl. "Then the whole tribe *q* has gone to the
Łā'wits!ēs." And so immediately *q* *G·î'lgămē⁵stāla* made ready
with his numaym to go to the *Łā'wits!ēs*. He tried to believe the
170 words of the girl. Then *q* the wife of *G·î'lgămē⁵stāla* took blood
and smeared her face with blood and *q* she lied when she said that
G·î'lgămē⁵stāla was dying. And then just quickly she bought
wrappings for *G·î'lgămē⁵stāla*. But he just said that he believed
the words of the girl. And so *q* he believed (her) when he saw the
175 numaym of *Hä'qŭlał* really going to the *Łā'wits!ēs*. He came *q*
quickly returning to Bull Harbor *(Ḡē'⁵ya)*. It is said, there was
just one canoe builder, an old man at Bull Harbor. Then *q* *G·î'lgămē⁵stāla* spoke, "I came to have my knife sharpened, that you may
sharpen it, old man. This is what I will use to cut open *Hä'qŭlał*,
180 if I kill him." — "Give it to me, that I sharpen it." Then *q* the
old man sharpened it. "Now evidently your knife is sharp," said
q the old man. Then *q* he cut his hip. "Behold! sharp is the knife
of your children. Go and kill this bad man. As soon as a canoe I
am building is finished, then every time *Hä'qŭlał* takes it away."
185 Then *q* *G·î'lgămē⁵stāla* went to the beach and hid on the side of the
house of *Hä'qŭlał*. He knew that he always went across to bathe.
Hä'qŭlał *q* came across with his slaves. Then *q* he took off his
dress of elkskin. Then *q* he washed in the wash basin. Then *q*
G·î'lgămē⁵stāla was afraid that he might not have enough time to
190 kill him, whenever he went into his wash tub. Then *q* *Hä'qŭlał*
went home, and *q* *G·î'lgămē⁵stāla* was afraid. "Let his tribe be
killed first," said *q* *G·î'lgămē⁵stāla*, "and we will go to Deer-Place
to wait for his tribe when they come and call at Deer-Place, for
that is their other village site," said *q* *G·î'lgămē⁵stāla*. Then he
195 started and went aboard his traveling canoe to go to Deer-Place.
And then *q* he hid on the side of a flat rock on the water. There
came *q* a large canoe. It came in sight at the point. "These are
the ones for whom we wait," said *q* on his part *G·î'lgămē⁵stāla*.
"Be ready now when they arrive." It is said they were coming.
200 Then *q* they paddled and ran into them. Then *q* was upset the

tribe of *Hä'qŭlaɫ*. They were killed by the children. "Save that
ʟ!ā'k!watsōt," said *q* on his part *G·î'lgămēᵉstāla*. Then *q* the feet of
ʟ!ā'k!watsōt were tied with a stone and he was stood up in the water.
Then the whole tribe of *Hä'qŭlaɫ* were dead. "Now let us go to
Hä'qŭlaɫ and go there and kill him this night," said *q* *G·î'lgămēᵉ-* 205
stāla to his tribe. Then *q* they arrived *q* behind *ᵉmɛgwî'g·ēᵉ*. It
was dark and *q* they just walked on the rock going to the house of
Hä'qŭlaɫ. Then *q* they heard a noise of crying. Then *Hä'qŭlaɫ*
heard the noise. "Heh," said *q* *Hä'qŭlaɫ*, "our visiting canoe will
not stay away in vain," said *q* *Hä'qŭlaɫ*. He was expecting his 210
tribe. However, they all had been killed.

"Question this one who is crying," said *q* on his part *G·î'lgămēᵉ-*
stāla. Then *q* one man secretly went to ask the woman, "Why
are you crying?" — "*Hä'qŭlaɫ* has killed my husband. We are
* Łā'wits!ēs*," said *q* the woman, "therefore, I am crying." Then *q* 215
spoke *Hä'qŭlaɫ*, "Why do(n't) you, little one, stop making your
crying noise?" said *q* *Hä'qŭlaɫ*. "Am I not just getting tired of
crying?" Then evidently *Hä'qŭlaɫ* went to sleep. *G·î'lgămēᵉstāla* said
q "Let us enter his house." Then *q* the left-handed strong child lifted
the door. That door was one side of a cedar tree. Then *q* the 220
warriors entered. They took hold of *Hä'qŭlaɫ*. Then *q* *Hä'qŭlaɫ*
scolded. "Don't in vain treat me too roughly. Now you will strike
back at me. Let the cut in my stomach be crooked that it may be
that way in later generations," said *q* *Hä'qŭlaɫ*. "You shall be that
way," said *q* *G·î'lgămēᵉstāla*. Then they cut up *Hä'qŭlaɫ*. Then *q* 225
spoke the younger brother of *Hä'qŭlaɫ* in the next house. "Now
you have done everything to your late uncle," said *q* the younger
brother of *Hä'qŭlaɫ*. Then *q* *G·î'lgămēᵉstāla* spoke, "Now he has been
cut in two in the house," said *q* *G·î'lgămēᵉstāla*. "Well," said the
younger brother of *Hä'qŭlaɫ*, "now our days will become calm. 230
Come, load my goods that we may go and be again one tribe," said
q the younger brother of *Hä'qŭlaɫ*, and that is the end.

X·ā'nElkᵘ[1]

Told by *Yā'qoʟas*, a *NaqɛE'mg·ilisala*

In the beginning the *NaqɛE'mg·ilisala* and Koskimo lived at
Ǥō'sēᵉ. Both had the same winter ceremonial which belonged
to them. Both tribes were hungry at *Ǥō'sēᵉ*. Therefore, they
left the place. Their chief had the name *X·ā'nElkᵘ* and *ᵉnā'ᵉnɛ-*
mōgwidzaᵉlas and his son was *Nūn*. They settled everywhere 5

---

[1] S 163; C 176.

10*

where mussels occurred. The father of *Nūn* settled in *Ā′sdɛlɛm*. Only two old people were living there.

The wife of *ɛnā′ɛnɛmōgwidzaɛlas* tried to find mussels. After they had gone some distance she saw a dead whale. Now they 10 had plenty to eat. She threw away her mussel basket and went home. Her husband was warming his back. She went in and kicked her husband. She said, "Don't stay this way." The man turned around. The woman was sitting on the other side of the fire and her genitalia were uncovered. Then he said, "Ah, ah, ah, 15 that indeed is yours!" Then they went and called all the tribes together which were scattered about and they were going to give a feast with the whale.

Now they went to Winter Place *(Ts!ɛɛwŭ′nxas)* where her son was. *X·ā′nɛlkᵘ* and his wife were asleep in the house and suddenly 20 in the night they found that their son had disappeared. They did not know what had happened to him. For four years they waited for him. They did not know where he was. After four years, they heard a noise in the woods and they said, "Maybe he is coming back." Then they saw many wolves and their son was standing 25 on the back of one of the wolves. He was wearing a head mask. Hemlock was around his forehead and on his head. Four times he came and showed himself. The first time he had a wolf mask, the second time a hemlock ring. Every time he was ornamented differently. The wolf who had made the head dress of the young 30 man had no hands. They had been cut off. Then his father went to catch his son on the fourth day; and the son came. The son obtained a treasure from the wolves. He had received the *nō′nlɛm* ceremonial. He brought the head mask *(g·ilgɛmł* New; *x·ī′siwēɛ* Kwa) and the hemlock ornaments for the *nō′nlɛm*. From now on 35 his name was *Nūn*.

Ya′x·st!ał¹

Told by *Yā′qoʟas*, a *Naqɛ′mg·ilisala*

On the west coast, behind *K·!ēɛyaī′ł* lived *ʟaō′laxmut*, the father of *Ya′x·st!ał*. He had three sons. *Ya′x·st!ał*'s body was full of sores. The *Xoyā′las* made war against them and only he and his three sons were left alive. The bodies of the tribe were 5 lying along the beach of *G·ildɛdzo′lis*. They were not buried. Therefore the place was called *Dǎ′ldzolis* (stretched out on the beach). Their heads had been cut off. Every day the wolves

---

¹ S 205; compare C 177.

would come out of the woods and feed on the bodies. ʟaō'laxmut
said to his children, "How do you feel? I feel troubled on account
of the way in which we are. Let us move to the small hill (fort) [10]
nearby here." The father thought, "My sons shall receive supernatural power from the wolves. Let me test my children early
in the morning to see whether they are strong of mind." There
was a rock covered with barnacles near the beach. And he called
his sons and made them lie down on their backs. He held them by [15]
the feet and pulled them around the rock so that their backs were
scratched by the barnacles. When his eldest son was being pulled
around the rock he moaned for pain because his back was scratched
down to the bone. Then he called his second boy and pulled him
in the same way around the rock. He pulled him a little farther [20]
along and then the boy began to cry out so that he had to give up.
The youth could not stand it any longer. Now he called the next
one, *Ya'x·st!at*, whose body was full of sores. He took him by
the feet pulled him all around the rock. Although the boy's back
was cut to the bone by the sharp barnacles he said, "Now let me [25]
lie down on my stomach and pull me around." ʟaō'laxmut did
so. Then he felt happy because his boy was strong and he was
sure that he would not be afraid of anything. The father sang
his sacred song because he had been successful. He instructed
Ya'x·st!at, "Lie down among the bodies of our slain tribesmen [30]
and wait for the wolves to come. Be careful! Lie on your stomach
so that you may breathe without being observed. The wolves
will carry you away. When one of them throws you on his back
breathe cautiously and if the wolf should notice that you are
breathing he will throw you down. Then try to fall on your stomach [35]
so that you may breathe without being noticed." He left his son
and went home with his two elder sons who were almost dead
from being pulled around the rock.

ʟaō'laxmut was sitting on the roof of his house every evening.
It was not long before he saw the wolves coming out of the woods [40]
at the head of the bay. They ran down to the dead bodies. One
of the wolves ran about among them and smelled of all the bodies
until he came to *Yā'x·st!at*. Then the wolf threw him on his back
and ran back carrying him along. When he thought he felt that
Ya'x·st!at was breathing, he threw him down and *Ya'x·st!at* fell [45]
on his stomach. The wolves examined him and when they found
that he did not breathe they took him up again and ran on. Thus
they finally reached their village and they threw him down outside.
Now *Ya'x·st!at* heard them talking in the house. The man who
had carried him said that he was a sea otter. The people asked [50]

him to bring him in. The wolf man who had brought him took
him and carried him into the house. They put him on a board
and the man whose office it was to carve the game was called
to cut him up. He blew upon his neck so as to open up the hair.
⁵⁵ When he did so *Ya′x·st!al* jumped up and said, "Don't be in
such a hurry." The wolves were trying to put on their skins
but they had no time to do so. And they all were seen in their
human form. Then they talked together. One of them said, "Let
him stay here for four years." But the speaker of the house said,
⁶⁰ "Do not let him stay here too long. Let us ask him why he has
come here. Let him speak and let him tell us what he wants. Truly
he has come only to get something from us." Then *Ya′x·st!al*
replied, "I came to get supernatural power." The Wolves said,
"We'll give him the means of making canoes so that he may be
⁶⁵ able to make four canoes in one day." *Ya′x·st!al* thought, "That
is not what I want." The listener of the house heard his thoughts.
They asked, "Do you want to have a spear?" And he thought,
"That is not what I want." Again the listener of the house heard
his thoughts. Then he saw hanging in the house the thing he wanted.
⁷⁰ The people said, "Let him be careful with what he wants." They
asked him, "Do you want the death bringer?" and he said, "That
is what I want." They took it down and told him to be careful
with it. It is also called the fire bringer *(k·!i′lk·!ilxalag·ila)*. They
gave it to him. Then he said, "Now let the people come to take
⁷⁵ him home." Thus said the speaker of the house. They were all
sitting in the house and they called their speediest runner to invite
the wolves living in the other villages. The runner asked for a
stone hammer. He stood up and they gave him the hammer.
Now he was ready to go inviting. He threw the hammer up and
⁸⁰ jumped out of the house and before it fell down he was back. He
said, "I have gone all around the world." Then he threw the hammer
up again and ran out again inviting. Before the hammer fell
down he had run all around the world. He said, "I have been
everywhere." They did not believe him. Then the runner said,
⁸⁵ "Look at these four stones which I am carrying here. I picked
them up in *Xŭ′mdasbēᵋ*." They recognized these stones and now
they believed him. Now the wolves took *Ya′x·st!al* back to Hope
Island. They came down to the sea. He was walking among the
wolves. He was carrying his supernatural power. It sounded
⁹⁰ as though the world was breaking to pieces when the wolves came
down. They took him down to the beach and the wolves went
back. Then his father, his mother and his brothers were ready
to catch him. When he saw his father coming; the death bringer

began to move in his hands. He said, "Don't move. That is my
father." He moved it against the mountains on the other side ⁹⁵
and all the trees caught fire. Then he went home. He sat down
next to his father.

He had not been there for two days when the *Xoyā'las* came
to attack them. Then his father sat down on the roof of his house
and sang his sacred song. The warriors of the *Xoyā'las* said, "Now ¹⁰⁰
he has his last good time before we are going to kill him." The
warriors jumped out of their canoes to attack him. When they
were walking on the beach *Ya'x·st!al* came out of the house with
his death bringer. He swung it against them and they were all
burned. Then *Ya'x·st!al* went to the dead people of his tribe ¹⁰⁵
who were lying on the beach and sprinkled his water of life over
them and some of them came back to life. Then his death bringer
said to him, "Make war against the *Nā'k!wax·da*ᵋxᵘ." He started
and when he came to Newettee *(nɛᵋwē'dēˤ)* he saw smoke. His
death bringer said, "Attack them." *Ya'x·st!al* said to it, "Do ¹¹⁰
not move. That is my tribe." But he could not hold it. It began
to move and burned Bull Harbor *(ʟɛ'mwas)*. Then it flew out
of his hand and he lost it.

Yax·st!al was given the *Nō'nʟɛm* ceremonial by the wolves at
K·!ēᵋyai'l. During the four days of the ceremonial the people use ¹¹⁵
"backward talk".[1]

*Hamā' lak·awē*ᵋ[2]

Told by *Kwa' xsēᵋstala*

They were going to have a winter ceremonial at *Ō'qwiyōwas*
at *Hǎ'nwadēˤ*. Then *q* his children purified themselves. They
kept the taboos. They did not eat. For four days *q* they did
not eat. There were four brothers, *q* the children of *Hamā'lak·awē*ᵋ.
*Hamā'lak·awē*ᵋ was the name of the father of the children. "Don't, ⁵
dear ones," said on his part *q Hamā'lak·awē*ᵋ to his children. "I
come to see our salmon. Take care, children," said on his part *q
Hamā'lak·awē*ᵋ. "Let your minds come!" Then *q* the brothers
got ready and were about to start. As soon as they arrived at
*K·ā'tǎlē*ᵋ, "When you look up you see what is told about our salmon. ¹⁰
It is one thing which will be told to them." Then *q* the brothers
started. Then *q* they saw what was referred to by their father
and they saw something stretched out white at the end of a
ridge of a mountain. "I see," said *q* the middle one of the
brothers, "that is evidently what was referred to by our father." ¹⁵
Then *q* he started and he passed upward to what was seen by him

---

[1] See p. 12.   [2] See C 8.

and he went to find out about it. Then q he reached it. Really
q it was lying on the belly in its large size. Very large q it was in
the way it showed in the sun. "Come, dear ones," said q the
20 youngest one. "Behold! this was referred to by our father." Then
q the youngest one advised his elder brothers. "Take care, dear
ones," said he q. "Remember the words of our father. Do not
be too eager. That only will be the place where we cut it, the
right side of its body." Then q he cut it. Then q four times he
25 aimed with his knife at the right side and he cut it and they just
listened to the advice (given) to them by the youngest brother,
and he followed the words of his father to him, that youngest
one. And only he q really remembered the advice of his father
to them. "Four times you will take it in the middle of its right
30 side." Then q the elder brothers of the youngest one did not
remember the words (spoken) to them. Then q the elder brothers
began to cut and they were very desirous only for this which
was still q (?) and the elder brothers forgot the words of the
youngest one and q only this youngest one followed the advice
35 (given) to them by their father. "Go on quickly. You are making
a mistake!" Now q the youngest one saw a fog and q the fog
rolled down the mountain. "Quick, now you who are making
mistakes. Now we have bad luck." Then q quickly they tied
up their meat obtained from the mountain goat. That was q
40 One-Horn-on-Forehead. That was a large mountain goat, One-
Horn-on-Forehead. "That was told to you, you who are making
mistakes." Now there came a great deal of snow. It was snowing.
It did not last one day when the gorge was full. Then they started
going down. And q the dog owners were stuck to (followed closely)
45 their dogs, for they were four. And they started going down.
Now the eldest brother was unfortunate. He did not know the
place where he was going to, on account of the snow. He did
not see our world on account of the thickness of the snow on the
rock. He just waded through the snow, for now the tops of the
50 bushes were covered. The eldest one together with his dog fell
down. Now he also started. And the next one to him was also
unfortunate. He also q was just urged on by his dog. "That
was told to you who are making mistakes," said on his part q
the youngest one to his elder brothers, the one who remembered the
55 words (given) to them by their father. Then two were now alive.
He started. Then again he was unfortunate, and he also went
down in the gorge. He also q just followed his dog and his dog
also urged him. Now he followed the trail. The one who was
now alive started, that youngest one. Then q this dog made a
60 trail. The dog was wading. And so q the owner of the dog just

followed him on the trail made by the dog for him. Then *q* the
dog would start. Now *q* the one who was alive did not act carelessly
for he only followed the dog when the dog made a trail for his
master. Now indeed *q* it was almost as though the dog were talking.
Then *q* the dog started again. Now it was a long time and he [65]
came back to his master and *q* it was indeed as though the dog
were talking. He embraced the neck of his master well and he
turned his face to his master. He also whined *q* and licked the
face of his master. Behold! he almost arrived at the place found
by his dog for a hiding place for his master, and he started and [70]
arrived at his future hiding place, a big house. It is said, indeed
it was a great covered rock like a large house *q*, a large covered
rock *q*. Now the dog dug out the soil and sat next to his master
in the place where he was digging. He covered the place around
him with soil and sat in the hole. Only *q* his mouth showed over [75]
the soil. That was the reason *q* why he was alive, what he had
obtained by cutting from the mountain goat. He stayed *q* this
way the whole length of the winter. He stayed in what had been
dug by his dog. Then his dog started and left his master on the
floor. Then *q* the dog went back. And so *q* he licked the face [80]
of his master. Now *q* the dog was not long in the house when he
started again. The dog started again. Behold! every now and
then *q* he would go down and behold! he made a trail for his master.
Behold! he would come to the river. Then *q* his dog went back
again. And so he would come again to his master and embrace [85]
his master's neck and lick his face. Now the dog really tried
to make alive his master. He curled his body around the face
of his master for it was cold when it was really winter. Then the
dog came again *q* and started. He went out of sight where he
was going and he came back. And so *q* he did so again. In vain [90]
q he again embraced the neck of his master. That also *q* he did
again. In vain *q* he licked again the face of his master.

Now their father knew that his children had evidently met
misfortune on account of the bushes at *Hǎ'nwadē*ᶜ for not one
tree was showing over the snow. Not one mountain was showing. [95]
That was just the reason *q* why their father just guessed that
they had met with misfortune. That was just the reason *q* that
his house showed out on the ground, the winter dance house of their
father (which he had made) on behalf of his children. That *q*
was the reason why they tried to give food to those who intended [100]
to give the winter dance.

Now we will go back to the one who was left alive among his
elder brothers. He saw a small *(sᴇ'nxa?)* on top of his hiding

place. Then his mind became a little better and he thought that
¹⁰⁵ summer was coming. And *q* the dog started again. He came
now and then going down the river. Now behold! the dog reached
the house. They always used to live at a place called *Q!aᵋwa'k·as.*
Then the dog went back to the place of his master. Then *q* he
embraced his neck to warm (?) him. Now it was as though
¹¹⁰ he was almost talking. Then the mind of his master became
strong. He came leading his master downward, straight down *q*
the river. That was *q* the trail obtained by the dog for his trail
when he went right down to the river, the river of *K·ā'tâlēᵋ.* And
they reached the house. That *q* was the time when the dog spoke
¹¹⁵ on the roof of the house. When behold! he came, going out of
sight. When, behold! he dug the snow on the roof of the house
and he tried to get to the floor of the house. Then *q* again the
dog dug on the right hand side of the door of the late fireplace
in the house, and again he put his master into the hole into the place
¹²⁰ he had dug. And *q* he covered him again with soil to make him
warm with it in his little digging which had now his size. He had
no strength. He had no flesh, only *q* bones, on account of the
time he had not eaten. Now *q* he had not eaten for one year. Then
his dog started again. He left his master. The dog went out of
¹²⁵ his sight. Behold! sometimes he went down on the bank of the
river, on the river of *Hǎ'nwadēᶜ* and he went back to his master,
and he licked his master again and *q* he also curled himself around
his face trying to warm his master. Then *q* the dog started again.
He started again *q.* Again he went down on the river and again
¹³⁰ he passed far beyond his stopping places and again he went back
to the place of his master, for he knew that he was now very weak.
He had hardly any breath. Now the dog started again going
down the river. Now again he passed far away beyond the place
where he had first stopped, and again he went back to the place
¹³⁵ of his master for he observed that he was very weak. Now it
came to be known that the tracks of the dog were seen. "It is
important, what was seen by me. Indeed, it is a dog. There are
tracks on the bank of the river," and *q* the tracks of the dog came
to what is named *Mā'ts!ɛs.* It was the village site *q* of the early
¹⁴⁰ tribe. Then the first of the *A'ᵋwa.iʟɛla* talked among themselves.
"What may it be, slave, if these are the ones who went mountain
goat hunting." Then were sent five men and the five men went
poling. They tried to observe the tracks, the dog tracks, and
they observed that they were the tracks of a dog. "Behold! we
¹⁴⁵ reached our mountain goat hunters." Then *q* *Hǎmā'lak·awēᵋ*
called his tribe. They talked about this matter. Then *q* they

tried to get *Łā'x̣ᵉŭnāla* and *Łā'x̣ᵉŭnāla* was seated in front, and
he was asked, he was prayed to go and try to observe the actions
of the dog. Then *Łā'x̣ŭnāla* spoke. Then *q* he asked that boards
should be tied end to end with cedar withes. Two flat boards *q* 150
were used. They were like shoes of the one who was going to try
to observe the place of the dogs. Then *q* he asked that he might
carry a basket. It was a large basket *q*. And *q* he started. He
carried boards like scoop nets (?). He did not sink into the snow
q for he was walking on the boards. He was walking along *q* 155
and he just followed the tracks of the dog. Now he almost reached
the place of the child, that is (the place) named *Q!aᵉwak·as*. Now
he started. He met with the dog as it came starting down the
river. And so *q* the dog turned back to the place where it had come
from. Now he followed the one who searched for their place 160
and he arrived at their place and so *q* the dog only moved right
on his trail and went to his master. Then *Łā'x̣ᵉŭnāla* followed
the dog and *q* he saw the child. He was only bones *q*. There
was no flesh on his face. He was hardly breathing on account
of his weakness. "Oh dear," said *Łā'x̣ᵉŭnāla q*. The child *q* just 165
made jump out his breath, when he was addressed by *Łā'x̣ᵉŭnāla*.
The child did not speak on account of his weakness and he was
put into the basket. Now *Łā'x̣ᵉŭnāla* passed down the river
carrying on his back the child sitting in the basket. And *q* he
arrived at (the place) named *Ō'qwīyōwas*. Then *q* his father got 170
ready. He called the early *Ā'ᵉwa.iᴸᴇla* and a house was made
by them and *q* a house was built on the ground, and the early
Ā'ᵉwa.iᴸᴇla were assembled. Then time was going to be beaten for
the one who was left alive among the brothers. The great dance
from above was the supernatural treasure of his father *Hămā'lak·a-* 175
wēᵉ. The song was sung for him. This *q* is still the grandfather's
song of the *Ā'ᵉwa.iᴸᴇla*.

> *Ye heyata ye heyata*
> "Come, do not walk on four feet," was said.
> "Walk around in a circle," was said.   180
> Come out safely walking on four feet, the supernatural one.
> *Yeheeya.*

Now *q* he came to life when they finished beating time. Then
his body become strong.

The Dwarf Tribe[1]

Told by *G·ī'qalas*, a *Gwa'waēnoxᵘ*

It is said *Q!ē'q!ᴇx·ᴸāla*, the chief of the numaym *Q!ō'mk·!ūt!ᴇs*
of the *Gwaᵉsᴇla* was living at *Ǵwē'k·ᴇlis*. Then *q* the mind of

---

[1] For distribution see Ts 867 and the following story.

Q!ē′q!ᴇx·ʟāla never felt happy for he knew that his wife had for
her lover the prince of *Sē′saxâlas* the chief of the numaym *G·ī′-*
5 *g·ilgᵃm* of the *Gwaᵉsᴇla*. Then *q Q!ē′q!ᴇx·ʟāla* asked his wife to
go somewhere with him late at night, said he *q*. And so *q* as soon
as the whole tribe had gone to sleep they secretly launched their
small canoe and loaded their small canoe with their property
and their traveling provisions. Then *q* they went aboard and
10 started paddling and they were going to *Ǵwāḷgwaʟ!ālaᵉlis*. And
so *q* daylight nearly came when they arrived there. And so *q*
as soon as they arrived there *Q!ē′q!ᴇx·ʟāla* carried his load immediately *q* into a small house which always was at *Ǵwāḷgwaʟ!ālaᵉlis*
and *q* he said to his wife, "We will never go home again, for I
15 am jealous of you on account of the prince of *Sē′saxâlas* who is
your lover," said he *q*. "Now I shall have the name Always-Jealous
on account of your foolishness," said he *q* to his wife. And so
q his wife never answered, and that was the name of *Q!ē′q!ᴇx·ʟāla,*
Wī′wŭnak·o according to the word of the one who told me the
20 tale, for it is not a myth, for *Wī′wŭnak·o* owned a gun. And so
q the jealous *Wī′wŭnak·o* stayed for a long time at *Ǵwāḷgwaʟ!ālaᵉlis*.
Then *q* it was a fine day without a ground-swell. Then *q Wī′wŭnak·o*
asked his wife to sit with him on the summer seat in front of their
little house. And so *q* they went and sat in the summer seat.
25 They on their part *q* had not been sitting in the summer seat
a long time when *Wī′wŭnak·o* saw two men coming out of the
woods on the south side of the small house. Then *q* one of them
carried on his back something like a box. Then *q* they walked
right down to the beach and so *q* as soon as they came to the sea,
30 the one who carried something like a box took this load from his
back and put into the water a small canoe made of the bark of
balsam fir. Then *q* the two men went aboard and *q* one of them
stood in the bow. Then *q* the other was in the stern as they were
paddling seaward with their paddles. On their part *q* they had
35 not gone far seaward before they put down their paddles in their
small canoe and at the same time (both) jumped into the sea.
And so *q* they stayed under the water a long time and they came
up. Then *q Wī′wŭnak·o* and his wife saw that there were four
halibut carried in each hand of the two men and they had thrown
40 sixteen halibut into their canoe which was growing larger. Then
q Wī′wŭnak·o asked his wife, "Let us be ready to steal their halibut
when they go down diving again," said he *q*. And so *q* as soon
as the two men dived *Wī′wŭnak·o* and his wife launched their
small canoe and went to throw the sixteen halibut into their
45 small canoe. It is said, they came ashore and quickly threw the

halibut out of the canoe and hauled the small canoe up the shore.
Then *q* they had time to carry up all the sixteen halibut. And so
q as soon as they finished hiding them *Wī'wŭnak·o* and his wife
also went into hiding on the ground. It is said the two men came
and emerged. Then *q* that was again the same number of halibut *q*, [50]
sixteen again, which they carried which were thrown by them into
their small canoe. Then *q* they went aboard their small canoe and
stood up in it and together they were staring at their halibut,
and it seemed that they missed those stolen by *Wī'wŭnak·o* and
his wife. And so *q* the two men were standing in their small canoe [55]
for a long time, when the one standing in the bow stretched out his
right hand, holding the hand shoreward, as though he were feeling
inland. Then *q* he put his hand to his nose and smelled of it; and
so *q* as soon as he finished smelling of it he stretched out his right
hand again, and again went along feeling. And so *q* as soon as [60]
his hand with which he felt about came to the hiding place of
Wī'wŭnak·o and his wife the man smelled of his hand. Then *q*
immediately the small canoe started and went ashore to the south
of *Wī'wŭnak·o*'s small house. Then *q* the two men at once stepped
out of their small canoe. Then *q* one of them folded up his small [65]
canoe, carried it on his back as they were going up the beach, and
went into the woods. Then *q* *Wī'wŭnak·o* asked his wife to be
careful and not to be afraid, "for I will follow the two men," said
he *q* as he took his ammunition bag and his gun and went out of
his small house and followed the tracks of the two men. On his [70]
part *q* he had not gone (far) inland when he caught up with them
and so *q* *Wī'wŭnak·o* kept on close behind them. Then *q* it seems
that the two men did not see him. Then *q* they arrived at the
shore of a long lake. Then *q* *Wī'wŭnak·o* saw many houses on
the other side of the place where the trail which was followed by [75]
him showed itself. Then *q* one of the two men shouted, "Come
and take us across, something has gone wrong with us," said he *q*.
Then *q* an old man answered him who said, "And so already I
have tried to advise you two not to overdo it," said he *q*. That
is what he tried to say. It is said, the two men came in a small [80]
canoe. Then *q* *Wī'wŭnak·o* saw that they paddled under a cedar
tree that lay across a narrow neck of water on the shore of the
lake. Then *q* *Wī'wŭnak·o* started and sat down on the place under
which he supposed the small canoe would paddle. It is said, the
small canoe came and in the stern was seated a man who went [85]
just under the place where he was sitting. Then *q* it went right
on to the place where the two men were standing and took them
aboard. It is said, he came back again; and so *q* as soon as they

arrived right under the place where *Wī'wŭnak·o* was seated he stood
⁹⁰ up from where he was sitting and jumped down into the middle
of the small canoe and *q* there were four as they arrived on the
beach of the village; and *q* the three men never took notice of
Wī'wŭnak·o as he jumped down into the small canoe. They also took
no notice of him when he stepped out of the small canoe on the
⁹⁵ beach of the village. Then *q* it occurred to *Wī'wŭnak·o* that he
would just follow the three men when they went up the beach,
and *q* one of the three men carried on his back the small folding
canoe wrapped around the sixteen halibut; and *q* *Wī'wŭnak·o*
was behind the three men as they went into the house. And so
¹⁰⁰ *q* as soon as *Wī'wŭnak·o* entered inside of the door of the house
he heard someone saying, "Come for a while, my dear, that we
may talk together," said *q* what was being heard by him. Then *q*
Wī'wŭnak·o went to him and he saw a handsome young man
sitting on the floor. And so *q* as soon as *Wī'wŭnak·o* came to the
¹⁰⁵ place where the man was sitting the man said to *Wī'wŭnak·o*.
"Why did you come to this bad tribe? Now only take care else
you will also be as I am. I am rooted to the floor. Do not eat
what is given you to eat else you will stay away forever," said
he *q* while the one rooted to the floor gave him a long basket.
¹¹⁰ "Now you will hide this (under the blanket) and so, as you are
given to eat, pretend to eat and just drop what you pretend to
eat into this basket, and also when you will be questioned and
they say to you, 'to what tribe do you belong?' you will say that
you are *Lē'gwiłda* *xᵘ*. Don't say that you are a Kwakiutl, else
¹¹⁵ you would be treated the way I was. I was struck all over. Look
at my body," said he *q* as he showed him many scars. And so *q*
as soon as the one rooted to the floor finished giving advice to
Wī'wŭnak·o, he sent him to sit down in the rear of the house.
And so *q* immediately *Wī'wŭnak·o* went and sat down in the
¹²⁰ rear of the house still carrying his gun. Then *q* another man came
into the house. Then *q* he sat down on the floor near where *Wī'wŭ-
nak·o* was seated. Then *q* the man who had just come asked
Wī'wŭnak·o, "To what tribe do you belong?" said he to him *q*.
Then *q* *Wī'wŭnak·o* replied to him. Then *q* he said to him, "I
¹²⁵ am a *Lē'gwiłda* *xᵘ*," said he *q*. And so *q* immediately the man who
had just come went out of the house and reported that he said
he was a *Lē'gwiłda* *xᵘ*. It is said, the tribe came and entered
the house and they talked kindly to *Wī'wŭnak·o*, and so *q* as soon
as they finished talking kindly to him the other men went
¹³⁰ out of the house. Then *q* the woman sitting on the floor of the
house arose and took down an open work, small basket which

is called clam button receptacle. Then *q* she took a small dish
and put it on the floor where she was sitting. Then *q* she took the
little basket and poured (in) the clam buttons into the small
dish and put it down in front of *Wī′wŭnak·o*. And *Wī′wŭnak·o* 135
saw that they were all small toads which moved about alive.
As soon as the small dish with toads was put down, *Wī′wŭnak·o*
took them at once and pretended to put them into his mouth
and he threw them into the basket which opened up on his chest.
And so *q* as soon as he had taken all out of the small dish the woman 140
took the small dish and put it away; and he was given food once
only. On his part *q Wī′wŭnak·o* had not been sitting down for a long
time before there was the cry of a man outside of the house where
Wī′wŭnak·o was sitting. "Behold! a large elk is walking along
the other side," said he *q*. And so *q* immediately the hunters 145
took their bows and arrows and launched their small canoes;
and *q* they were going to shoot the elk. And so *q* they had not
started paddling when *Wī′wŭnak·o* stood up, took his gun and
went out of the house and he looked at what was the cause of
the talking of the tribe. Then *q* he saw the elk. Then *q Wī′wŭnak·o* 150
thought he would shoot it, for he thought he could hit it. Then
q he sat down and took aim with his gun. It is said, many men
stood on the ground behind him. Then *q* he shot. Then *q* all the
men fell down dead and they died of the sound. He also hit the
elk and it was also dead. Then the tribe became afraid of *Wī′wŭ-* 155
nak·o after that and *q* he was sent to go home to his house.
It is said, *Wī′wŭnak·o* came being taken across by two young
men traveling in a small canoe of the bark of balsam fir. And
so *q* as soon as he arrived at the end of the trail he stepped out
of the small canoe. It is said, he came and started walking. And 160
so *q* it was evening when he arrived at his house at *Gwālgwaʟ!āla⁵lis*,
and *q* all the halibut were cut up, for his wife *q* began at once to
cut the halibut when he started away. And *Wī′wŭnak·o* found
out that he had now the name *Q!ē′q!ɛx·ʟāla*, on account of the
tribe from which the two men had come who were seen diving 165
seaward from his house at *Gwālgwaʟ!āla⁵lis*. And that is the end.

The Dwarfs

Told by *Nɛg·ä′dzē*, a Koskimo

It is said, *Yā′qayalēsɛmē⁵* lived at *Yū′ʟ!ē⁵* with his tribe the
first of the *Yū′ʟ!ēnox^u*. Then *q* he had for his one of the opposite

¹ See Ts 867 and the preceding story.

side (rival) *Yā'qaḷɛnlis*, chief of the numaym Dirty-Teeth. Then
q Yā'qayalēsɛmēᵋ had three younger brothers (all men). They
⁵ were all sea hunters, *Yā'qayalēsɛmēᵋ* and his rival *Yā'qaḷɛnlis*.
And so *q Ya'qayalēsɛmēᵋ* with his three younger brothers always
went night hunting every night, spearing sea otters and seals.
Then *q* his hunting canoe was always full of sea otters and
seals. Now *Ya'qaḷɛnlis* always had no game and *Yā'qaḷɛnlis*
¹⁰ was beaten by *Yā'qayalēsɛmēᵋ* and *Yā'qaḷɛnlis* was ridiculed by
his rival and so *q* that was the reason why *Yā'qaḷɛnlis* hated
Yā'qayalēsɛmēᵋ. And *Yā'qaḷɛnlis* secretly *q* went *q* and tried
about to find the place where *Yā'qayalēsɛmēᵋ* went hunting sea
otters and seals. And so, as soon *q* as he had found it he took
¹⁵ (rotten) alder wood and carved it and his carving imitated a sea
otter. And so, as soon *q* as it was evening *Yā'qaḷɛnlis* finished
his carving. And so *q* immediately he started paddling and put
the carved alder wood that pretended to be a sea otter on a rock
on the side of the island between Landward *Yū'ʟ!ēᵋ* and Seaward
²⁰ *Yū'ʟ!ēᵋ*. And so *q* as soon as he had finished he came home. And
so, as soon as it got dark at night *Yā'qayalēsɛmēᵋ* started sea
hunting with his three younger brothers and went night hunting
for sea otters and seals. And so *q* as soon as he arrived at the
island, *Yā'qayalēsɛmēᵋ* saw the carved sea otter lying on the
²⁵ rock point of the island. And so *q* immediately he speared it.
Then the imitation sea otter jumped into the water and swam
out seaward and it never came up. Then *q* day came, when the
youngest brother, the steersman, spoke and *q* he asked his eldest
brother *Yā'qayalēsɛmēᵋ* to let go of his harpoon line. And so *q*
³⁰ immediately *Yā'qayalēsɛmēᵋ* tried to let go of his harpoon line.
And so *q* the harpoon line just stuck to his palms. Then *q Ya'ɂa-*
yalēsɛmēᵋ at once just cried, for he guessed that *Yā'qaḷɛnlis* had
planned the way of doing of the sea otter. Then *q* he told his
three younger brothers about the harpoon line which stuck to his
³⁵ hands, and *q* the four brothers all cried, for *q* the tops of the
mountains were not to be seen now. Then *q* they exceeded
ten days being taken out to sea by what had been speared.
Then *q* the four brothers slept. Then *q* the youngest one heard
half awake the canoe rolling on a sandy beach. Then *q* he
⁴⁰ looked. Then *q* he saw a smooth beach. Then *q* he awakened
his elder brothers and so *q* immediately they all got up in their
traveling canoe and stepped out of the canoe and hauled up
their small canoe and put it among the bushes. And so *q* as
soon as they had finished hiding their small canoe, they sat down
⁴⁵ under the trees. However, *q* they had not been sitting on the

ground long when a canoe came in sight at the point and sitting
in the stern was a small man. It is said he came right along and
anchored near to the seaward from the place where the four brothers
were sitting under (the bushes). Then *q* the little man took his
halibut club and a rope and jumped into the water at the side [50]
of his canoe. Then *q* for a long time he stayed under water before
he came up. Then *q* he went aboard his canoe. Then *q* he hauled
aboard his halibut, strung up. Then *q* he pulled out his stringing
rope. Then *q* he jumped again into the water and dived. Then
q the one next to the youngest one among the younger brothers [55]
of *Yā'qayalēsᴇmēᵉ* spoke. Then *q* he said to his elder brothers,
"Let us launch our traveling canoe and steal the halibut of the
boy," he said *q*. And so *q* immediately the four brothers carried
at the ends their canoe and put it on the water on the sea. Then
q the one next to the youngest went aboard the canoe and he [60]
alone in it went *q* seaward to the place where the canoe of the
small man was floating. Then *q* he pulled out one halibut and
came ashore. Then *q* the four brothers at once *q* carried the canoe
up the beach and put it down among the bushes on the ground
so that the place where it was on the ground was really sheltered. [65]
And so *q* as soon as they had finished the four brothers sat down
on the ground. The little man came up *q*. Then *q* he went aboard
his canoe and hauled aboard halibut strung up. Then *q* four
times he dived before *q* he stopped. Then *q* the little man hauled
up his anchor. And so *q* as soon as he had tied the anchor in the [70]
canoe he came paddling ashore and came to the beach of the
place where the four brothers were sitting. Then *q* the little man
walked up the beach and went *q* to the place where the four brothers
were sitting. And so *q* as soon as the little man saw the four brothers
q he spoke. Then *q* he said, "Who among you stole my halibut?" [75]
said he. And so *q* immediately *Yā'qayalēsᴇmēᵉ* replied to him.
Then *q* he said to him, pointing to the one next to the youngest
one, "He, my younger brother, took your halibut," said he to
him *q*. Then *q* the little man went to the one to whom he referred
as the one who had stolen the halibut and clubbed him on the [80]
head with his halibut club. And *q* the one next to the youngest
was dead. Then the little man started and went aboard his canoe
to go home to his house which was seen by *Yā'qayalēsᴇmēᵉ*. And
so *q* as soon as the little man arrived he went *q* and immediately
told about the four men seen by him, and so *q* also that he had [85]
clubbed one of them on the head. And so *q* immediately the chief
of the tribe sent four little men to go and invite the three brothers.
And so *q* immediately those who were sent went. Then *q* they

11

arrived at the place where *Yā'qayalēsᴇmē*ᵋ and his younger brothers
⁹⁰ were sitting on the ground. Then *q* the four little men stepped
out of their traveling canoe and went to invite *Yā'qayalēsᴇmē*ᵋ
and his two younger brothers. And so *q* *Yā'qayalēsᴇmē*ᵋ immediately asked his younger brothers to launch their canoe and
so, as soon as it was on the water they went aboard. Then *q* they
⁹⁵ paddled following those who had been sent to invite them. And
so *q* as soon as they arrived at the beach of the house of the chief
*Yā'qayalēsᴇmē*ᵋ and his two younger brothers stepped out of the
canoe and went *q* behind the four men who had invited them
and they entered the house. That was as large as a taboo house
¹⁰⁰ of the first people. And so *q* as soon as the three brothers had
sat down on the floor, the wife of the chief went *q* immediately
and cooked food to be eaten upon their arrival by the three
brothers. Three courses were served to them. And so *q* as soon as
they had finished eating upon their arrival the chief *q* asked his
¹⁰⁵ tribe to prepare their weapons, for *q* they were expecting all the
birds to make war on them, the swans and cranes and geese and
all their kinds. And *q* *Yā'qayalēsᴇmē*ᵋ found out that the dwarfs
were being attacked by all the birds and *q* *Yā'qayalēsᴇmē*ᵋ found
out that it was the north end of our world; and *q* the dwarfs
¹¹⁰ sharpened all the points of their spears and clubs and poles. And
so *q* they had recently finished preparing their weapons when it
was time to sleep. Then the little ones all went to sleep, for they
were expecting war to be made against them. And so *q* as soon
as daylight came in the morning the beginning of the swans came
¹¹⁵ in sight and all the birds sat down on the wide, level place where
the dwarfs always fought with all the birds. And so *q* as soon
as all the birds were all on the meadow at what was to be the
battle ground, and *q* the swans kept together, and the true geese
also kept together, and also *q* the laughing geese and cranes, and
¹²⁰ little geese and all the various kinds of large birds. And so *q* as
soon as this was finished, all the birds uttered the war cry and
q all the dwarfs went out carrying their weapons, and they also
uttered the war cry. Then *q* the dwarfs attacked. And so *q* as
soon as they arrived at the place of the birds then *q* the place
¹²⁵ of the birds became foggy; and *q* they threw their down, and
they speared the dwarfs with the quills (of their wings). And
that *q* was the reason why many of the dwarfs were killed for
q they breathed in the down. Then *q* they were suffocated. Now
many on both sides were killed. And so *q* as soon as it was evening
¹³⁰ *q* all the birds started flying to the north side where they had
come from. Those of the dwarfs *q* who were left alive also came

home. And *q* *Yā'qayalēsEmē*ᵋ and his two younger brothers just
were seated on the ground outside the chief's house watching their
ways on the meadow. And so *q* *Yā'qayalēsEmē*ᵋ listened to the
chief as he now *q* gave advice to his tribe, to be ready and not to [135]
give in to their enemies, the birds, if they should come again the
next day, said he *q*. Then *q* *Yā'qayalēsEmē*ᵋ spoke. Then *q* he
said, "O chief, will the birds come again to make war against
your tribe?" said he to him *q*. Then *q* the chief who had the name
Only-One *(*ᵋnEmō'gwis)* replied to him. Then *q* he said, "Yes, [140]
they will come again tomorrow, for they will come for one moon
every day to make war against us, until it will be the time when
the birds will go home to the Upper End of our World," said
he to him *q*. Then *q* *Yā'qayalēsEmē*ᵋ said, "Now let your tribe,
chief, take a rest for a while. And so it will be good if they will [145]
be ready if we should be beaten, for we will go and fight the warriors
when they come tomorrow," said *q* *Yā'qayalēsEmē*ᵋ. Then *q* the
chief was really thankful for his speech. And so *q* *Yā'qayalēsEmē*ᵋ
and his two younger brothers went to sleep early. And so *q* as
soon as daylight came in the morning, they arose and went into [150]
the water in the river. And so *q* as soon as they had finished, they
heard the birds that came and sat down on the meadow on the
regular battle ground. And so *q* as soon as they were all on the
ground, they uttered the war cry. Then *q* the dwarfs also uttered
the war cry. Then *q* the three brothers attacked them. They [155]
ran *q* among the swans and twisted their necks. They only stopped
when all the birds took to flight. The three brothers *q* came back.
Then *q* Only-One, the chief of the dwarfs invited his tribe, that
all should enter his house. And so *q* as soon as all were inside
q *Yā'qayalēsEmē*ᵋ and his younger brothers were invited to come [160]
in. And so *q* as soon as they sat down in the house, then *q* the
chief of the dwarfs spoke. Then *q* he said, "Now look at them,
tribe, and let us reward the kind heart of the visitors, for they
have put to flight those who made always war against us. And
so we have the name of victors over them. I mean this, let the [165]
shaman go to where the one left behind by them lies dead that
he may come here," said he *q*. And so *q* immediately the shaman
went out of the door of the house and went to the place where
the one next to the youngest brother of *Yā'qayalēsEmē*ᵋ had been
clubbed by the little man. But *q* it was not long before the shaman [170]
came in again followed by the man who had been dead. Then
q he sat down among his brothers. Then *q* the chief spoke again.
Then *q* he said, "Now I try to feel your hearts. (Now I reward
you for your kindness), *Yā'qayalēsEmē*ᵋ and your crew, and so this

11*

[175] my former house will go to them, these sea lion posts and the *g·ī′gēs* next to the door.[1] Four sea lions are the posts of the house. Now go home! You will just have the sun on the left-hand side of your faces every morning," said he *q*. And so *q* as soon as his speech was finished they went out of the house. And so as soon [180] as daylight came in the morning *Yā′qayalēsɛmēᵋ* launched his canoe. Then *q* they went aboard. They came *q* and started by canoe. Then *q* the place where they were paddling had a very strong tide, therefore they were coming home very fast. Then *q* for four days they were coming landward before they arrived [185] at *Yū′ʟ!ēᵋ* in the night. And *q* they went straight home. And so *q* they were just told that *Yā′qatɛnlis* was dead, it was said that he had been killed by the uncle of *Yā′qayalēsɛmēᵋ*, for the first *Yū′ʟ!ēnoxᵘ* guessed that he was the one who had planned the way in which *Yā′qayalēsɛmēᵋ* and his three younger brothers [190] had disappeared. And *Yā′qayalēsɛmēᵋ* was the only head chief of the *Yū′ʟ!ēnoxᵘ* after this. And that is the end of this which is not a myth, for it is only an old story of a not far distant day.

Scab[2]

Told by *Nɛg·ä′dzē* (Charlie Wilson), a *G·ī′g·îlgăm*

There were many tribes *q* who had as chief one man who was respected. He had seven sons *q*. Then *q* one of the children had a sickness. The child was scratching himself, the youngest one. It was *q* the last one of the children. Then *q* the heart of the [5] wife of the chief became sore on account of her child. Ah, his body was really full of boils. Then *q* the child was struck by his mother with tongs that he should not too much scratch his body. But on his part *q* the child could not be forbidden, for the scratching of its body felt sweet. On her part *q* one night the wife of the [10] chief spoke, when the married couple were lying down. Then *q* spoke his wife, "How is your mind, for too sick is my mind on account of the ways of our child. This bad sickness has come to him. I think we should think not minding that we are even cruel to our child. Not good might be your name among our tribe [15] on account of the way our tribe treats you, that we go and desert our youngest child." Then *q* replied her husband," And so, on your part, true is your word, my dear," said he *q* to his wife. "Even

---

[1] See M. figs. 19. 20, p. 379.
[2] S 160, 189; C 38; see also the following tale. This is the same story as C 38, retold by the same narrator after an interval of thirty-two years. For distribution see Ts 734, 779. See note p. 229.

if we treat cruelly our child, we will invite our tribe that we may tell about the bad sickness of our child." Then q on the next day he sent his house men (attendants). Then q his house men [20] invited his tribe for the morning, all, with their wives and their children. The great many, all came q into the house, many tribes. Then q arose the chief and spoke, "Welcome tribe," said on his part q the chief. "Not this is what I called you for, as I usually invite you, tribe. This is why I invite you, tribe. I might not [25] be well named by you, if it were thus for this bad sickness which has come to this youngest one of my children. This is the reason why I called you, tribe." Then q one chief arose. "Thank you for your word, chief," said q one chief. "Never mind now if we really treat cruelly our youngest child. Let us load today all [30] your (our) canoes and take all your property." Then q they made ready to load (their canoes). Then q the tribes loaded (their canoes).

The child had a grandmother q an old woman. Then q all were aboard. The old woman was unwilling to go aboard to her tribe for she wished to stay with her grandchild. On their part q they [35] did not allow her to sit on the beach; and the old woman was going to put fire into a shell and tied it into it; and also a little dried salmon. Then q she hid it under a stump. Then q she said to her grandchild, "Remember the fire which is under the stump and take it, master." The old woman was crying on account [40] of her grandchild. One man came q and took the old woman on each side to throw her aboard the canoe. Then they started.

Then the child sat on the beach deserted. He was a little boy q and his tribe disappeared and the child was sitting on the beach all alone. Good q was the mind of the child. He did not make [45] much of the doings of his tribe; therefore he did not make much of the doings of his parents, for the child wished that he might have his own way scratching his body. Then q a little longer after his sitting on the beach, then at last he took the fire and came and made fire on the beach where he was sitting. He had no [50] house q. There was nothing on the village site. And q the child scratched his body. Well q flew the blood from his body when he was scratching because it felt sweet. Then q the child really scratched his body. It felt sweet. Then q he became quiet with his scratching and the stomach of the child moved. The stomach [55] of the child was moving q. Then q the child tried to stand it. Then q he scratched his body. Then q the moving in his stomach became quiet. Then q he tried to stop scratching and he tried to (with)stand the (desire to) scratch. Then q he stopped scratching his body and he was quiet and again his stomach moved. Then q he (with)- [60]

stood the scratching. Again *q* moved the body of the child. Verily *q* he (with)stood (the temptation) so as not to scratch. There came *q* a hand and showed itself on his stomach. It is said the child wanted very much to scratch himself. Then *q* he gave in
⁶⁵ and scratched himself again. Then *q* the hand drew back again and the child scratched himself. It felt sweet. In vain *q* he grunted at the same time. Then he stopped scratching himself. And *q* the hand showed itself again on the stomach of the child. Then *q* the hands came out moving on the stomach of the child. Now
⁷⁰ again the child (with)stood (the temptation) that he did not scratch himself and *q* he gave in and scratched himself. Then *q* the hand drew back again and *q* he became quiet again with his scratching. Then *q* he tried to make himself strong that for a long time he should not scratch, and so he stopped scratching himself. He
⁷⁵ became quiet. Then *q* the hand came out again. Then a little boy jumped out. Behold! that was the reason why the child was scratching himself. Then *q* the child which came out of his stomach spoke. Then *q* he said, "Oh," said *q* the child, "I am the reason why you had boils on your body. Look at your body. There
⁸⁰ are no scars on your body," said *q* the one who had jumped out of his stomach. Then *q* spoke the one whose body had been full of boils, "Welcome child, did I not get you by good luck ?" said *q* the child. Now you will have the name Scab, child," said he *q*. Then *q* for a long time they were sitting on the beach (he) with
⁸⁵ the one who was now his child. Then *q* Scab, his child, spoke, "I am going to walk along the beach to the far side. Do not wait for me," said he *q* to his father. "Go, master," thus said *q* his father. Then *q* Scab started to go and he went to his goal on this side of the head of the village site. Then *q* Scab walked along
⁹⁰ the river and went right to the graves on the inland side. Then *q* he gathered up hemlock needles and went down to the beach. Then *q* he turned around. Four times he turned around and poured out the hemlock needles. Then *q* he said, "You will be steelhead salmon, " said he *q*. Then *q* he went again where he
⁹⁵ had gone before and again picked up hemlock needles, and again he went down to the beach where he had gone before. And so *q* he did again the same thing. Four times he turned around and spoke again, "You will be cohoes salmon," said he *q*. Then *q* he went back again to pick up some hemlock needles. And so
¹⁰⁰ *q* he went again to the beach where he used to go. Then *q* he turned around again four times and threw the hemlock needles into the water. "You will be spring salmon," said he *q*. Then *q* he went into the woods again and took up some hemlock needles,

and he went again to the beach. And so *q* he turned around again
four times before he poured out the hemlock needles. "You will [105]
be dog salmon," said he *q*. Then *q* he went again to the place
where he used to go to the graves to pick up again. Then *q* he
turned around and poured out the hemlock needles, "You will
be red cod swimming on each side of the mouth of the beach
of my river." Then *q* he heard a thundering noise. Behold! those [110]
were the salmon. They were the salmon, the salmon that came
going to the mouth of the river. Then *q* Scab started to go and
tell his father. "Come and let us go and start by canoe and build
a house on the other side of this river. My work has come and
showed itself, many salmon." And what was to be taken across [115]
by father and son, for they had no property in the house. And so
q only their fire was taken up and that is what was moved by them,
and so *q* they took the fire to the place referred to where they
were to build a house on the bank of the river. Then *q* he went
inland with his father to go and get bark of the cedar to build [120]
a house. They pulled off this bark and so *q* they began to make
a house. Really large *q* was the house. Then *q* they finished and
so *q* Scab called his father. "Now you will cut and watch the
roasting and let me fish with the hook for you. The salmon are
coming up our river." Then *q* Scab fished with the hook for [125]
salmon. Then *q* his father roasted and looked after the cutting.
They were not doing this way for a long time *q* before they filled
their house. Then *q* they were tired of their work when it began
to get dark. Then *q* they went to sleep. They were sleeping a long
time for they were tired. Father and son were sleeping. He was [130]
happy because they had got much fish.

Then *q* in the morning Scab arose. Then *q* he looked after
the fish he had caught. What should it be? There was no fish
that he had caught. Then *q* he awakened his father. "Get up!
Important is what has happened to our fish. Not one of our [135]
fish we caught is there." — "Important is your word, master,"
said on his part *q* his father. Then *q* his father arose. They had
no breakfast *q*, for none of what they had caught was there. Then
were downhearted father and son because they had no breakfast.
"Stop being of sore heart, father, for you will go fishing and I [140]
will roast and cut, that we may make our house full again. Then *q*
his father went down to the beach to catch salmon. There were
very many salmon. The river was full. And so *q* Scab cut and
watched the roasting. Not long and they made the house full,
and they finished working. Now it was past noon. "Make a bow [145]
for me, father," said *q* Scab to his father, "and four arrows,"

said he *q*. Then *q* his father made a bow. Then *q* he finished it.
Of nice bone were the arrow points. And so he finished. Then *q*
night came. Then he said to his father. "I am not going to sleep
150 this night, soon something might be seen by me. You will just
sleep sweetly," said he *q* to his father. Then *q* night came.
The moon was full; and so early in the night it was dark. And
so *q* Scab was sitting on the ground behind the house, but his
father was asleep. And so *q* the moon came and showed itself.
155 Then *q* it was light on the beach. The smoke went out to sea *q*,
the smoke of the house and Scab was sitting on the beach. In
vain he was looking at what was being looked for by him in vain.
And so *q* it had been night for a long time when there came a
black (shadow) out of the woods to the beach side, inland. It
160 came and walked right on and reached the house of Scab. And
so *q* it came near to the place where Scab was sitting and *q* he
recognized what kind of a thing it was. Behold! it was a *Dzō'noq!wa*
for she was carrying a basket on her back. Then *q* she entered
and he scratched the feet of his father. Then *q* there was no sound
165 of moving of his father. She came *q* and stretched her hand through
the sides of the house and took the roasted salmon. Then *q*
she continued to put the roasted salmon into her basket. And so
q with one hand she was still taking the roasted salmon. And so
q the breasts of the *Dzō'noq!wa* hung through the house. Scab
170 wished *q* that the whole breast of the *Dzō'noq!wa* should hang
through. Then *q* they hung through entirely inside of the house.
Then *q* Scab spanned his bow and shot at her. Now all his fish
were gone. The *Dzō'noq!wa* used both hands putting the roasted
salmon into her basket. And so *q* Scab arose and shot the breast
175 of the *Dzō'noq!wa*. Then *q* he shot again the other breast. Then
q again he took one arrow. Then *q* again he shot one and all the
four arrows were gone. They all got into the *Dzō'noq!wa*. The
Dzō'noq!wa *q* had time to pull through her hands, and to turn
her face landward and she cried, "Oh!" and she felt the arrows.
180 "Ah!" the *Dzō'noq!wa* cried for pain. Then *q* she came to a tree.
Ah! The *Dzō'noq!wa* *q* pushed over the trees as she was going
inland and the *Dzō'noq!wa* went home to where she may have
come from. Then *q* Scab spoke. He said *q*, "That must be what
took our first catch," said *q* Scab. Then *q* his father said, "Behold,
185 it must be that way, master," said he to his child. Now it was
past noon.

"Make red cedar bark for me," said *q* Scab, "and a neck ring."
Then *q* his father made red cedar bark and made a neck ring according to the words of his child, and the red cedar bark was done.

Really good *q* was the red cedar bark, the head ring which his 190
father had made and really good was his neck ring. Then *q* Scab
took the red cedar bark and put it around his head. He took
q his blanket and put it on. Then *q* he put on his neck ring of red
cedar bark. Then *q* Scab took charcoal and blackened his face.
Then *q* he took down and put down on his head, all of it with 195
his red cedar bark and so *q* he finished. Then *q* he said to his
father, "I will go along the beach, inland," said he *q* to his father.
"Do not in vain worry about me." — "Go on, master," said *q*
his father, "shall I not watch for you?" Then *q* Scab started inland.
Oh! Scab scattered about the down *q* as he was going inland, 200
and *q* Scab arrived at a tree. And so *q* Scab saw the tree. A great
tree had fallen down where the *Dzō'noq!wa* had pushed it over.
And so *q* for a long time he walked inland. Then *q* Scab saw a
round water *q*. And so *q* he saw a trail, a really straight trail.
"What may it be?" said *q* Scab. "This may be the reason of our 205
going, the trail of the sick one who came on account of this water."
It was as though the water went right through below. "Let me
try!" said *q* Scab. "Let me sit down on the ground that I may
discover who may be the owner of this water." Then *q* Scab
raised his head and looked at the face in the water which was 210
like a looking glass. And so *q* for a long time he was sitting on
the ground until *q* a shadow passed the long trail. It came quickly
q walking along going to draw water. Then *q* Scab spoke and he
recognized it was the little *Dzō'noq!wa* woman. Then *q* Scab
said, "For whom are you drawing water?" said *q* Scab to the 215
little *Dzō'noq!wa* woman. "Ah," said the *Dzō'noq!wa*, "I am
drawing water for mother. She is very sick." — "Yai," said
q Scab. "Go on and ask her, there is no way *q* for a shaman to
arrive who will heal you," said *q* Scab to the little *Dzōnoq!wa*
woman. Then *q* the little *Dzō'noq!wa* woman went back. She 220
just threw down her bucket on account of the importance of the
word of Scab. And so *q* the little *Dzō'noq!wa* woman entered her
house and so she told about where she had come from. "This
shaman *q* asked whether there are shamans here; and he has
come to heal you." "Oh!" the *Dzō'noq!wa* was groaning. "For 225
what might be our payment to him, mistress?" said *q* the *Dzō'noq!wa*.
"Go on, bring him." Then *q* the little *Dzō'noq!wa* woman went
back to tell Scab who was still sitting by the water. "I told your
words to my father. How much should he pay you?" — "Yai",
said on his part *q* Scab. "And so there may continue to be nothing 230
in your house. Go again. Tell him my words." Then *q* the little
Dzō'noq!wa woman went back again to tell the words of Scab.

"And so there may be nothing in our house." Ah, very much suffered the *Dzō'noq!wa* of her sickness. "Go," said *q* the *Dzō'noq!wa*
235 to the little *Dzō'noq!wa* woman. "Only take care that you do not cause misfortune in our house. A death bringer is the quality of our house." Then *q* the little *Dzō'noq!wa* woman went back. "You are to come," said *q* the little *Dzō'noq!wa* woman. "Only *q* take good care of our house. Not right is our house." — "Well,"
240 said on his part *q* Scab, "and do I also continue to be an ordinary man?" And so *q* Scab started. The little *Dzō'noq!wa* woman went ahead. Then *q* Scab heard the noise of the shutting (door) of the house, and he arrived at the house. Then *q* the little *Dzō'-noq!wa* woman went ahead when the door opened. Then *q* it fell
245 down again. Then *q* Scab tucked into his mouth hellebore, trying to frighten them. Then *q* the door opened. Then *q* Scab entered the house. Then *q* he squirted out in both directions of the door of the house and the double-headed serpent in both parts of the house became drunk on account of the hellebore which did it,
250 which was taken in the mouth by Scab; the cause of the house being a death bringer (was) the double-headed serpent. Then Scab was standing on the door side of the fire of the house. Ah, they were lying down, lying down near the sick *Dzō'noq!wa*. Then *q* Scab started and went and stood on the outside of the sick
255 *Dzō'noq!wa*. She did not know that Scab was standing in the house. Then *q* he sat down at the outer side of the sick *Dzō'noq!wa*. "Where do you feel it?" said *q* Scab. "Oh," the *Dzō'noq!wa* was groaning. "Here it is," said *q* the *Dzō'noq!wa*. Then *q* Scab felt of the breast of the *Dzō'noq!wa*. And *q* Scab just at once felt
260 his arrow. "Ah," said *q* Scab. He thought this was the one he had shot. Then *q* Scab said, "Behold! great is your sickness," said *q* Scab to the *Dzō'noq!wa*. "I am going to try to find it," said *q* Scab. Then *q* he bent his head down to the chest of the *Dzō'noq!wa* and bit his arrow. Then *q* he bit the end of one of the arrows
265 and pulled it out from the chest of the *Dzō'noq!wa* and hid it on his stomach. Then *q* again the other one. He also pulled out the one and hid it in his lap. It was not seen by the *Dzō'noq!wa* and the others in the house what Scab had done and Scab bent down his head again to the one who was being cured by him, and
270 so *q* he pulled out another arrow and he also hid it. There was one left which he had not got. Then *q* again he took the one arrow and he had obtained all four. Then *q* Scab asked the *Dzō'noq!wa*, "How are you?" said he *q*. And so *q* the *Dzō'noq!wa* said, "I am getting well." Then *q* Scab blew on the chest of the *Dzō'noq!wa*.
275 Scab finished in the house healing the *Dzō'noq!wa*. Then *q* the

Dzō'noq!wa sat up in the house and expressed thanks for what
Scab had done. "Thank you," said *q* the *Dzō'noq!wa.* "I have
already said that you are a great shaman who came to enter
my house, for nobody dares to do so to my house. Death bringer
is my house. Take these bones outside. Now let me try to feel [280]
you (return your kindness). Do not hurt my child. Now you will
have her for your wife with this house and this water where you
were sitting down. Even whenever anybody has been for a long
time (dead) on the ground he will be sprinkled on the ground
by you. This has the name water of life. Now you will take this [285]
box of your wife. It is never at an end. It cannot be emptied."
Then Scab wanted to go home and he went home with his wife.
"Yai," said *q* the *Dzō'noq!wa* to her husband, "Lift my box from
the floor." Then *q* Scab went to the box of his wife. Small was
the box of his wife. Then *q* Scab was too weak for the small box. [290]
As soon as the father of the *Dzō'noq!wa* should know that Scab
was too weak for the box, Scab would not have gotten his wife
and everything in the house. Then *q* Scab whispered to his wife
that he was too weak for the box and the little *Dzō'noq!wa* woman
loved Scab and she helped her husband. All those who were [295]
sitting in the house did not know that Scab was too weak for the
little box. And so the little *Dzō'noq!wa* woman alone carried
in one hand the box and went outside and they took following
them the house which he had obtained. And so he took following
him the water of life. Four days *q* he had been inland in the house [300]
of the *Dzō'noq!wa.* And so *q* Scab and his wife arrived in their
house, (his) and that of his father. What should it be? His father
was now dead. Only *q* bare bones were on the floor. "Behold!
my father here is dead," said *q* Scab to his wife. "Where is he?"
said *q* the wife of Scab. The little *Dzō'noq!wa* woman could not [305]
see. Then *q* Scab took his wife, "This is it," said Scab. Then *q*
the little *Dzō'noq!wa* woman took some water of life and sprinkled
it over the father of Scab. And so *q* the father of Scab arose.
"Ah, it has been made very sweet in my sleep," said *q* the father
of Scab. Then *q* Scab spoke, "No, you were not asleep, you were [310]
dead," said *q* Scab to his father. "You were only now revived
by my supernatural treasure. I obtained my supernatural treasure,
this water of life, and also the house, and also this my wife."
Then his father talked gratefully, "Welcome, child," said *q* his
father. "Now you have again obtained a supernatural treasure, [315]
child," said *q* his father. "Thank you!"
    And so *q* for a long time Scab was married and he loved his wife.
Then *q* evidently he got tired of his wife. Then *q* in the morning

Scab rose to go down to the beach. He stepped into the water
320 at the beach and he saw somebody sailing on the sea. "Come
ashore that I may go aboard." The Goose came. "Too bad, there
is no place to sit. We have too many clover roots." Again *q* one
canoe came. "Come ashore that I may go aboard." The Gull
came *q* also. "There is no place to sit. Our tails are sticking up."
325 Then *q* he was left. There came another one. "Come ashore, that
I may go aboard." — "Too bad, there is no place to sit. Too deep
is our stern," said *q* the Loon. Another one came *q* sailing along.
"Come ashore, that I may go aboard." — "Too bad, our canoe
is cranky," said *q* the Albatross. Way out at sea Scab hardly
330 saw. Then way out at sea, "Come ashore. Let me go aboard."
They came ashore *q*. "Go on," said *q* the one sitting in the bow,
"Ask our friend where he is going." — "I want to marry the
daughter of our chief." — "Welcome," said *q* the Bufflehead duck.
Then *q* Scab went aboard. "Let us begin. Let us try to find out
335 the strength of our friend," said *q* the Bufflehead duck. "Let
us here go down that we may try to find out the length of the
breath of our friend, for we are going to dive through this large
mountain." Then *q* they dived. Behold! he said *q*, "I shall only
scratch you when my breath gets short." Then *q* they dived.
340 Then *q* Scab scratched his friend to raise his head. "Hardly long
enough is the breath of our friend," said *q* the Bufflehead. "Oh!
that it would be longer before our friend scratches (us)," said he
q, "for we (shall) take him through this great mountain." — "Just
go on," said *q* Scab. Then *q* they dived. They dived. They tried to
345 be quick. Scab never *q* scratched his friend. He just *q* raised his
head now, and so *q* he just saw distinctly. He saw brightly on the
water the house of the chief. "Do you see now?" Scab was told
q. "That is where you will reach it, that light." Then *q* they
went towards the house. Then *q* the Bufflehead spoke, "How
350 will we do with our friend?" said *q* the Bufflehead. Then *q* one
Bufflehead said, "Let us search for dry firewood, for our chief is
always hard up for firewood." — "Well," said one of the Buffleheads, "I know a good piece of firewood. There at the end of
the beach is an alder tree." Then *q* they went to it. Then *q* they
355 found really good firewood. The firewood was good to be cut
into three pieces *q*. There was a hole *q* at the end of the firewood
"Here our friend will go into this hole at the end of the firewood."
Then *q* he went into the hole at the end of the firewood. Then *q*
the Bufflehead towed the firewood and towed it to the beach
360 of the chief. It was just not yet [a little] ebb-tide. The firewood
q would drift to the shore. The little Buffleheads towed it back

to the place where it floated on the beach. The little Buffleheads watched their friend, when it should drift ashore. They dived on the beach of the chief, watching their friend. Then *q* it was morning and *q* the tide turned. The chief *q* came out of the house [365] to look at his beach. The chief came down the beach *q*. He saw the firewood lying on the beach on the road leading from the house down. Then *q* he went back to take his ax. He came *q* to chop the firewood. "That on its part is very dry," said *q* the chief. He cut the wood in two places. Then *q* he carried it on [370] his shoulder. He did not know that Scab was hidden in it. Then *q* he carried it on his shoulder. That *q* was first carried, the one in which Scab was. Then *q* he went down the beach again and he carried another one. And so *q* that was when Scab came out and hid in the house in a corner. It is said Scab just saw [375] distinctly the one whom he wanted for his wife. She was right in the middle of the rear of the house, but *q* the chief continued to carry the firewood and Scab was sitting in the corner of the house.

Now the Moon came *q*. He sat down in the house. "Ah," said [380] *q* the Moon, "I saw one man in one country; *q* his name is Scab. I only wish to have him for the husband of our dear one, for *q* he is called Scab, the one who *q* has for his wife the little *Dzō'-noq!wa* woman," said the Moon. Then *q* it got dark. The Sun *q* came and sat down in the house. That *q* was also the word [385] of the Sun, the former word of the Moon. "I saw this child named Scab *q* who has for his wife the little *Dzō'noq!wa* woman. I do wish our dear had him for a husband." Ah, very good was the mind of Scab that he was thus referred to. Then *q* he went in the house to go near to the one who was referred to as his wife. Then [390] *q* Scab lifted the bed cover of the child. Then *q* he was driven away and it was said that it was a dog running about. Then *q* again he lifted the bed cover of the child. Then *q* he was kicked again. "Don't kick me," said *q* Scab, "It is as though I have been told that I shall have you for my wife. I am Scab." Then [395] *q* the child called him that he should lie down with her and *q* he lay down and so he was glad. He was laughing with the one who was now his wife. Then *q* the parents of the child heard it *q*. "What is the noise you are making, my dear?" They were never *q* answered by their child. Then *q* it was night again. Then *q* they played [400] again that night. Then *q* she was again told by her mother, "Drive away that dog," said *q* her mother and her mother said it was a dog who was playing with her daughter; but it was he, Scab, who was playing with her. Then *q* it was night again. "Who is

405 it with whom you are always laughing?" said *q* the wife of the chief. "You are funny," said on her part *q* the child. "It is as though you said that I should have Scab for my husband. This is Scab who is lying down with me." Then *q* day came. "Arise, and come into the house to eat breakfast with your husband,"
410 said *q* the chief. "What are you going to do?" said *q* the woman to her husband Scab. "That is the reason that you are being told to get up to sit down on my seat. The points of devilfish are on it. As soon as you lie back on it you will be dead. What will you do?" Scab *q* was told by his wife. "What shall I do?" said
415 on his part *q* Scab, "Behold, I shall just die, for what can I do?" His wife on her part said *q*, "I love you. Turn your back this way, that I press on your back," said *q* the woman to her husband, and she was afraid that her husband might die. Then *q* she rubbed the back of her husband. "Now you are ready. Now you will
420 go on my seat. Don't be in vain afraid, when you lie back on my seat." — "Go on, start!" said *q* Scab to his wife. Then *q* he went out of the room to sit down in the seat. "Come, mistress," said *q* the chief to his child and his son-in-law, "Sit down in this seat of your wife," said *q* the chief to Scab. Then *q* Scab leaned
425 in what was referred to by his father-in-law. Only *q* the death board fell down. It dropped down on the floor when Scab leaned back on what was referred to. Then *q* the chief looked in vain at his wife, surprised that Scab was not dead on the floor in the seat, and so *q* the wife of Scab was of good heart when her husband
430 was not dead. And so *q* the chief just said he would give up because Scab was not an ordinary man. And so *q* it was a long time before Scab became homesick. Then he remembered his father and his wife. Then *q* the woman asked *q* her husband, "Are you homesick now?" said she *q* to her husband. "I am really homesick," said
435 *q* Scab. "And so you wish to go home?" said *q* the woman to her husband. "I do," said on his part *q* Scab. "How shall I do that you may go home?" — "How shall I do it?" said *q* Scab, "Maybe my friend may take me back." — "Don't be in vain of sore heart," said *q* the woman to her husband, "We will go to your house
440 to see your father and your wife, the little *Dzō'noq!wa* woman." Then the woman told her father. She told her mother and her brothers. These were her brothers, the Moon and the Sun. They were the brothers of the woman. Then *q* the father of the woman said, "Go mistress!" said he to his daughter. I wish you would
445 not only measure the length of your stay." Then *q* she made ready her flying-garment for she was only going to fly across the large mountain. And so *q* she went out with her husband.

Then *q* the child put on her flying-garment. Then *q* the woman said to her husband, "You will just lie down flat on my back and embrace my neck. We are going to fly. Do not go to sleep!" [450] said she *q* to her husband, and *q* she flew up and arrived over the large mountain. And so *q* the woman just saw the smoke. "Evidently, that is the smoke of the house," said *q* the woman to her husband. "That is it," said on his part *q* Scab to his wife. Then *q* they were soaring, and they arrived inland of the house of her [455] husband. Then *q* they reached the country. She took off her flying-garment and folded it up and she only squeezed her flying-garment. Then *q* they entered the house. And so *q* his father and his little wife, the little *Dzŏ'noq!wa* woman were sitting there.

"I am going to try to throw on the floor against your friend, your [460] wife," said *q* the woman to Scab. Then *q* the woman threw (her power) against the little *Dzŏ'noq!wa* woman. At once *q* the little *Dzŏ'noq!wa* woman flew about in the corner of the house. She was made into a red-headed woodpecker by our lady. It was not long *q* that on her part she moved about in the house. She became [465] a person again. And so *q* the little *Dzŏ'noq!wa* woman also made our lady into a bird. Then *q* she threw on the floor her power against our lady; and at once *q* our lady flew about in the corner of the house and she had become a woodpecker of the house. Our lady *q* was a woodpecker when she was treated with supernatural [470] power by the little *Dzŏ'noq!wa* woman. And so *q* it was not long before she made her right and took it back and now they sat down well in the house. They did not *q* do again as they had done. They just threw against each other, the extraordinary women. [475]

And so *q* for a long time he was married with his wives. Then *q* for a long time our lady was in the country of her husband. And so *q* our lady became jealous. She wanted to go home. Then *q* our lady told her husband Scab, "I wish to go home," said *q* our lady to her husband. "And I shall go," said *q* Scab to his [480] wife. And so *q* she made herself ready to go home. She went to the rear side of the house of her husband. And so *q* Scab went, following his wife. Then *q* our lady put on her dress and so *q* she had it on. "Will you go?" said *q* our lady to her husband. "Indeed I will," *q* said Scab. "Go on, lie down on my back in the [485] same way as before. Do not go to sleep!" said she *q* again to her husband. Then *q* the married couple flew. Not long watched Scab their going, when he fell asleep on the back of his wife. Then *q* he fell off and Scab was dead. Then she, his wife, went along. Then *q* the father of Scab was paddling. Then *q* the man saw [490]

something drifting about. "What may it be?" said *q* the mind
of the man. Then *q* he went to the one drifting about. He arrived
there. And just there *q* he recognized his son. "What happened
to you, child?" said he *q*. He took his child, put him aboard
⁴⁹⁵ and went home. And so *q* he carried his child up. "I just came
and found your husband on the water floating about," said the
man *q* to the little *Dzŏ'noq!wa* woman, "Now he is dead." — "Where
is he?" said on her part *q* the little *Dzŏ'noq!wa* woman. "This
is he," said on his part *q* her father-in-law, for the little *Dzŏ'noq!wa*
⁵⁰⁰ woman could really not see, therefore the man showed his daughter-
in-law, showing where the husband of the little *Dzŏ'noq!wa* woman
lay. Then *q* the little *Dzŏ'noq!wa* woman took the water of life
and sprinkled it over her husband. And so *q* he said also, "Oh,
on my part it has been made sweet in my sleep." — "You have
⁵⁰⁵ not just been asleep," said the little *Dzŏ'noq!wa* woman to her
husband. "You have been dead. I have just washed you with
this water of life," and Scab and the little *Dzŏ'noq!wa* woman
were again a married couple.

Told by *Yā'qoʟas*, a *NaqE'mg·îlisala*[1]

Once upon a time there was a girl whose body was covered
with sores. Therefore she was called Scabby-Body *(ʟEmk·!în)*. Her
parents and all the people deserted her. She had no house because
the people had gone away with all the roof boards and wall boards.
⁵ Only the grandmother of the girl pitied her and left a little fire
in a mussel shell. The girl picked up some old mats that were
left on the ground. She hung them over a board and used this
as a shelter. She was very sick and lay there, her body covered
with sores. She took a mussel and let it bite off one of her sores.
¹⁰ Then she put the mussel with the scab in it under a tree where
the rain would drip on it. She did so four times. After a few
days she went to look at it and what should it be? The shell
had increased in size and was closed. And all the scabs had disappeared from her body! Then she looked for a larger mussel
¹⁵ shell. She took the scab out of the smaller one and put it into
the larger one. After four days she went to look at it and she found
a small child in it. It was not complete. There were only arms
and legs. After four days more she went back, and she found
that it had become a real child. She put it into a still larger mussel
²⁰ shell. After four days more she went back to it and she found

---

¹ S. 160, 189; C 38; see also the preceding tale. For distribution see Ts
734, 779.

a little boy whose feet and hands stuck out of the mussel shell.
Then she took him out and carried him home. She looked after
the child and called him Scab.

One day he began to cry and asked for a bow. Therefore his mother
went and got a hemlock branch for a bow and bones for arrow [25]
points. The boy asked for food. Then his mother cried and said,
"We have nothing here. I will go and see whether there is anything
in my father's salmon trap." The boy went with her and they
saw that there was one sockeye salmon in it. They took it home.
She smoked the salmon, cut it up and roasted it. The boy ate [30]
one half of it. The other half they put up intending to eat it the
next morning. The next morning it was gone. They went back
to the salmon trap and there were two salmon in it. She cooked
them quickly. They ate the one and put up the other one. On
the following morning the salmon had disappeared. Every day [35]
they went to the salmon trap and found salmon in it. But what-
ever they put away at night had disappeared the following morning.
One day the boy said, "I am going to watch to see what is taking
away our salmon." The mother went down to look after the
salmon trap and the boy was sitting alone in the house. Then [40]
he saw something lifting the door flap. He was holding his bow
and arrow ready to shoot. Now what should it be ? A *Dzō'noq!wa*
came in. She had very large breasts. She stretched out her arms
and took the roasted salmon. Then she turned back to go out
of the door. At that moment the boy who was sitting in the corner [45]
of the house, shot her breast with his arrow. The *Dzō'noq!wa*
shouted and ran back into the woods. When the mother of the
boy came back he told her what had happened. He said, "I like
my arrow. I am going to follow the *Dzō'noq!wa* and get my arrow
back." He started following her tracks. When it became dark [50]
he sat down in the woods. While he was sitting there he heard
a humming noise behind the place where he was sitting. He went
into hiding. He knew that this proceeded from the one he had
shot. When day came he found the tracks of the *Dzō'noq!wa*
and followed them. They led up a mountain and down to a lake. [55]
He saw that she had walked along the lake. He followed her,
found her house and sat down at the place where they used to
draw water. Now three children of the *Dzō'noq!wa* came to draw
water. They saw him sitting there and they were so much scared
that they did not dare to draw water and went back. They told [60]
their mother that they had seen somebody sitting at the water.
Their mother replied, "Important is what you tell me. Go back
and ask whether he is a shaman. Maybe he comes to cure me".

12

Then the youngest daughter went back and asked the boy. "Are
65 you a shaman ? If you are one, please, come and cure our mother."
He said, "I am a shaman." The girl went back and told her mother
who asked her to fetch the boy. She said to him, "If you cure me
you shall marry her." The boy replied, "Is that what you say ?
I do not want to marry your youngest daughter." The girl went
70 back and reported to her mother what he had said. The speaker
of the sick *Dzō′noq!wa* said, "Important is what you say. Let
him come anyway. Tell him that he may marry my second daughter."
When they sent the message the boy said he did not want her.
Then the speaker of the *Dzō′noq!wa* sent the youngest daughter
75 to ask him whether he wished to marry the eldest daughter. The
boy said that she was the one he wanted. He went into the house
of the *Dzō′noq!wa* to cure her. When he entered he saw a large
Bull-Head sitting next to her trying to cure her. But the Bull-Head
could not find the arrow. The boy sat down next to her, took
80 hold of the arrow and pulled it out. Then the *Dzō′noq!wa* said,
"I feel that you have pulled out my sickness." Neither the Bull-
Head shaman nor anyone else could see the arrow. Then he married
the eldest daughter of the *Dzō′noq!wa*.

After four years he felt homesick. He lay in bed covering his
85 head with his blanket. Then the mother *Dzō′noq!wa* asked her
daughter, "What is the matter with your husband ?" And his
wife asked him, "Are you homesick ? Mother wants to know."
The young man replied, "I fear my mother may be dead. I should
like to see her." Then the mother *Dzō′noq!wa* said, "Get ready
90 to go to his home. I'll give you presents to take along." The
daughter of the *Dzō′noq!wa* was given a supernatural blanket.
It was to be her husband's supernatural power. It was made
of the skin of the *Xō′los*, the younger brother of the Thunderbird. She gave this to her husband. On one side of the blanket
95 were skins of the tomtit *(ts!ō′saxs)* and of the humming bird. She
also gave him the water of life. Then they went home the same
way he had come.

When they reached the house of his mother there was no smoke.
He went in with his wife, wearing the blanket which he had received
100 and which he wanted to show to his mother. But what should
there be ? There was only a pile of bones. She had died weeping
for her lost son. Then he spread the blanket over her bones, sprinkled
the water of life over it and his mother came back to life. She
rubbed her eyes and said, "I slept for a long time." — "No," said
105 her son, "you were dead."

Now the three lived together in the house. Then the young

man said to his mother, "I want to take another wife." His wife
agreed. Then his mother asked, "Whom do you want to marry?"
He replied, "I want to marry the daughter of The-One-Shining-
Down *(SEpaᵋxā'lis)*, The-One-Prayed-to *(A'myaxēt)*. Then he 110
engaged the myth animals to go with him and get his wife. He
engaged all the quadrupeds and birds to accompany him. The
way led upward, like a ladder. They reached the place from where
they were to ascend. The deer was the first to be sent up. He
wanted to be their guide. But a strong wind blew down against 115
him. He could not go up and was blown back. Next *Ō'ᵋmäł* said
he wanted to try. But he did not even go as far as the deer and
was blown back. Next the wren *(kwi'łk·â* Newettee; *xwā't!a* Kwakiutl)* tried to go up. He flew right and left evading the wind
and succeeded in getting up. When he reached there all were 120
able to go up, for he made the wind stop. They climbed up the
ladder and when they reached the upper world they sat down.
Then they deliberated what to do. *Ō'ᵋmäł*, the raven, said, "I
think Scab should go into the house." But all the others objected
to it. Then *Ō'ᵋmäł* said, "Let us look for some rotten stump. 125
(ts!ē'mos)." They went and found a dry alder. They pushed
it into the water and Scab went into it. Then they pushed it
off and it drifted away. The young man thought, "I wish the
wind would drift it towards the shore of the house." At once
the wind started and the log drifted ashore.   130
   Soon the daughter of the chief saw the rotten alder wood. She
went into the house and told her father. Her father replied, "Important is what you say. I have been a man for a long time and
never did any wood drift to this shore. Go and get it." Then
she carried it under her arm and carried it in. Her father said, 135
"Put it upon the fire." He did not know that the young man
was hidden in it. The girl threw it upon the fire and a piece of the
fine ashes from the wood flew into her room. It was Scab who
retransformed himself. The girl was in her room. He lifted her
blanket and the woman asked, "Who are you?" He said, "I am 140
Scab. I came to marry you." She replied, "Our minds meet.
I wish to have you for my husband." When her father heard
them talking he asked, "With whom are you talking there?"
The girl replied, "It is Scab. He came to marry me."
   Then her father said, "Come out with him. You shall eat with 145
him." Then they were sitting there. Scab was wearing his thunder-
bird blanket. They put a kettle on the fire without water in it.
The kettle became red hot. When it was hot the chief threw
Scab into it. Scab's wife became very angry. Scab transformed

12*

150 himself into a flake of light ashes and flew into his wife's room.
Then he retransformed himself into a man. When he was talking
to his wife the chief asked, "To whom are you talking there?"
His wife replied, "It is my husband." The chief went into the
room and said, "Don't let your husband sleep so late. He shall
155 come to help me get my stone hammer which dropped into a
cedar tree." Scab arose and they went out to get the hammer.
The chief went behind Scab who was walking very fast. The
chief had split a cedar tree and put in a trigger. He had thrown
his hammer into the crack. Now he asked Scab to go in to get
160 it and as soon as he was inside he knocked out the trigger. Then
the tree closed over him. "Serves you right," said the chief. "You
came to disgrace me." He saw what seemed to be Scab's blood
coming out of the crack. But he had come back to life and stood
there a little distance away. Scab went back to his wife and said
165 to her, "Tell your father to give up. He cannot kill me. I have
supernatural powers." Then her father gave up trying to kill
his son-in-law.

After a while Scab became homesick. His wife asked him,
"Why are you so downcast?" He replied, "I am afraid my mother
170 is dead." Then the chief sent him back. "I give you a salmon
for your provisions. And take along a fish hook." The salmon of
which he spoke was a whale and the woman caught it with the
hook. She lifted it as though it were a small salmon. The woman
said to her husband, "You will have to catch the next one." Scab
175 did it and lifted the whale out of the water easily. Then they
went back home. He had obtained as supernatural gift the ability
to catch whales in this manner.

The old chief sent them to look at his canoe which they were
to use to go home. They went along the beach but Scab did not
180 see any canoe, only something that looked like a ship. He came
back to the house and said to his wife, "I do not see a canoe.
I only see something that looks like a ship." His wife said, "That
is what my father means." His wife took hold of the bow of the
ship and hauled it to the house. Then they started and they
185 arrived at the house of his mother and his first wife.

They went up the beach. There she saw the *Dzō'noq!wa* woman
sitting in the house. His new wife sat down holding her forehead.
She said to her husband, "Why did you bring me here if you have
a wife already?" And the two wives began to quarrel. The daughter
190 of the heavenly chief took the *Dzō'noq!wa* woman and tore her
to pieces. She said, "You will be the blue jays of later generations."
The pieces became blue jays and hopped about. Then Scab collected

all the blue jays, put them under the blanket and sprinkled them with the water of life and the woman came back to life. Now the *Dzō'noq!wa* woman jumped upon the daughter of the sun and [195] tore her to pieces. She said, "You will be the squirrels of later generations." Then Scab collected the pieces, put them under the blanket and sprinkled them with the water of life. And she came back to life. The two women, however, were angry and both went home. [200]

Then Scab lay on his back. He was very sad because both his wives were gone. He thought, "What shall I do? I am going to get back one of my wives. I like the daughter of the Sun best. I will go up to the sky." So he followed her to get her back. He saw her walking over the water and Scab followed her. When he [205] was not very far behind her he stepped on a bad place and sank. His wife saw it. She went on and reached her father's house. Her father asked her, "Why didn't you stay with your husband?" She replied, "He had another wife." Her father asked, "What did he do?" She answered, "He followed me and he stepped [210] into the mouth of a monster and sank." Her father inquired, "Do you know where he sank?" — "Yes," she replied. Her father said, "I will try to save him." The young woman showed him the place. Then her father took a rope to the end of which a hand was tied and he let it down. The hand went down and searched [215] for him and found his bones. But one of the bones was missing. And the hand went down again to find the missing bone. The hand found it. Then the chief in the upper world sprinkled him with the water of life and he came back to life. His wife took him into her house and he stayed there. [220]

Marriage between the Nimkish and Kayoquath

Told by *Ālē'was*, a *Kayoquath*

TaneneL!a, chief of the Kayoquath had one son, who was about thirteen years of age. One day the old chief was lying alongside the fire with his naked back toward the fire; and while he was there he went to sleep. When his son came in he asked his mother to roast some salmon spawn, for he said that he was hungry. His [5] mother split roasting tongs out of a piece of red pine and roasted two pairs of spawn for her son. She put the tongs into the ground on the same side where the old chief was sleeping. The young man was sitting by the side of the fire waiting for the salmon spawn to be done. Suddenly the roasting spawn burst and some of it flew [10] against the old chief's back. He was very angry with his son, and

said to him, "I am ashamed of you, for you don't seem to think
of what you have to do to get into my high seat, for I have never
seen you go to bathe for good luck, in order to be a great chief
¹⁵ like me." He took the hot roasted salmon spawn and threw it into
his son's face and burnt it badly. The young man went into his
bedroom and lay down. After midnight he got up and went
stealthily to where his mother kept her dentalium shells. Then he
took two small baskets full of shells and also two sea otter skin
²⁰ blankets and put small abalone shells on his ears. After he had done
all this, he went out of his father's house and went up *T!ā'sis* river.
He kept on walking all that night, and all the next day and all the
next night until daylight. Then he took a rest. He walked again
the rest of that day until the next morning. Then he found some
²⁵ tracks of human beings near a small stream running down towards
the east coast of Vancouver Island. In the stream was a new salmon
trap. Then the young man said to himself, "I will wait here to
see if this man will come to look after his salmon trap." So he took
one of his sea otter skin blankets, and spread it out on the river
³⁰ back. Then he went to pick some salal berries. He had not been
away long when he heard someone speaking at the place where the
salmon trap was. He went and he saw a man and a woman standing on the river bank. They were looking at the sea otter skin
blanket spread on the gravel. The young man spoke first, and
³⁵ said, "Brother and sister, why are you looking at my sea otter
skin blanket?" and the man replied, "Brother, where did you come
from? What brought you here, and who are you?" and the young
man said, "I came from *T!ā'sis* and I am the son of *TaneneL!a*.
I am sent by my father to come to see if I can find a chief who has
⁴⁰ a daughter whom I might marry." Then the man answered, "I am
chief *L!ā'sotiwalis* of the *ᵋnēᵋnᴇlk·!ēnoxᵘ*, and my wife is the
daughter of chief *YaxLᴇn*. We have a daughter who is old enough
to be married now. *L!ā'sotiwalis* did not take the salmon out of
his trap; he only told the young man to go aboard his canoe; and
⁴⁵ as soon as he was aboard *L!ā'sotiwalis* paddled home. It did not
take them long to go downstream. Then they came to the beach
of the village *ᵋnē'ᵋnᴇlg·as*, and all the *ᵋnēᵋnᴇlk·!ēnoxᵘ* saw the
stranger in their chief's canoe. As soon as they arrived *L!ā'sotiwalis*
with his wife stepped out of the canoe, but the young man was
⁵⁰ told to stay until he was called out by the speakers. *L!ā'sotiwalis*
went into his house and ordered his slaves to clear it. He sent his
speakers to call his tribe. When they were all assembled in the
house *L!ā'sotiwalis* sent his speakers to invite the young man who
was still in the canoe. When he was called he followed the speakers

into the house. He was led to the rear of the house. When he [55] was seated ʟ!*ā'sotiwalis* called his daughter, ʟ!*āxʟElēdzEmga* and made her sit down by the side of her husband. Then the young man gave two small baskets of dentalia and the two otter skin blankets as a marriage gift to ʟ!*ā'sotiwalis*. In due time the woman gave birth to a boy who was named *YaxʟEn*. Soon they had [60] another child, a girl; they gave her the name of *Ō'ᵋmag·ilis*.

Then the young man became downcast, and his father-in-law asked him if he was homesick; and he said that he would like to go and see his parents. So his father-in-law called all his people in and told them that his son-in-law was going home with his wife and [65] his two children, and that he would give him a whale house dish and a seal house dish and the Cannibal dance, with its name *Nawīs*, and also lynx-skin blankets and grease. Twelve young men had to carry on their backs these presents. In two days' time they came to the mouth of *T!ā'sis* river, where the *Ga'yok!wadExᵘ* [70] lived; and when the young man arrived in his father's house, they were startled to see him, for they had thought him dead long ago. He gave the lynx skin blankets and a feast of grease to his people; and ever since that time the names and the dances of the Nimkish and Kayoquath are in part the same. [75]

Sī'wit[1].

Told by *G·ī'qalas, a Gwa'waēnoxᵘ*

All the *Qwē'qᵘsōt!ēnoxᵘ* q and the *Gwa'waēnoxᵘ* were together q at a place named *Gŭ'mgŭmlig·a*. Then q the children were playing. They were shooting upward with their bird arrows to a tree trying to beat one another, trying to get from one another their bird arrows. They were using bows. Then q *Sī'wit* was beaten by his [5] friend *Ts!â'gŭlis*. *Ts!â'gŭlis* obtained all the bird arrows of *Sī'wit*. Then q *Sī'wit* became angry and broke his bow and gave it to his friend. Then q *Ts!â'gŭlis* also broke his bow on account of his friend. And so q *Sī'wit* was just beaten again by *Ts!â'gŭlis*. Then q he took kelp and broke it in pieces. And so q again they [10] tried their strength. Then they threw spears at the kelp. And so q *Sī'wit* was beaten again. Then q they changed what they were doing. *Sī'wit* q grasped the top of a cedar to twist it. And so q he went to the top (but) he hardly twisted it. And so q *Ts!â'gŭlis* was just playing on the ground and quickly just twisted the cedar. [15] Then q again he twisted a cedar. And so q he went to the top

---

[1] See X 60.

again as he twisted the cedar. Then *q Sī'wit* was beaten again.
Then *q* he gave up and he was beaten by his friend. *Sī'wit* was
the cause of shame of his father. He started by canoe and built
²⁰ a house outside at *Hē'gₑms*. Then *q* the child just lay down. He
would not eat *q* for he was sick at heart being beaten by his friend.
A bear skin *q* was his bed cover. Then *q* his mother asked her
husband *ᵉmā'x̣ŭlag·ilis*, "Wake up our child, else he will stay
too much in the house, that he may go and try and search a place
²⁵ to sprinkle his body." — "Why should he not be ashamed of
being beaten by his friend?" Then *q* he awakened his son. And
so *q* the child only fixed himself in the way in which he was lying
down. He pulled up his bed cover. Then *q* he was again awakened
by his father to go and search for a place that would do him good.
³⁰ And so *q* the child again never moved. Then *q* he was scolded
by his father. "Get up and just go away. I am too much ashamed
of the reports about you." — "Do not just speak too badly to
our son or it might not be well, what you do." Then *q* his father
rushed at his son to uncover him. What should it be? Nobody
³⁵ was lying there. "Slave at the head of the house, there is nothing
where our child lay. He must have gone out early."

Then *q* the child started *q*. He arrived at a pond. He sat down
by the water of the pond. On his part *q* he had not been long
sitting on the ground by the pond when a loon emerged and sat
⁴⁰ on the water. Surprisingly sounded *q* the loon on the water. Then
q the loon dived. Then, a little porpoise came *q* and emerged.
Then *q* the porpoise went down. Then a whale came *q* and emerged.
Then *q* it went down again. Then *q* the lake began to rise. And
so *q* the child just went towards the water. On his part *q* he had
⁴⁵ not been sitting near the water for a long time before he felt
something on his back. It came up *q* moving through under his
arms on both sides of his neck. What should it be? A devilfish.
Then *q* the devilfish lay on his head. Then *q* he did not even
move. He just tried to say to his manhood that he might as
⁵⁰ well die on account of what they might do to him. That was
being looked for by him, that he might really die on account of
the shame of being beaten, because he had no strength against
his friend. He was taken under water, sucked under water by the
devilfish. On his part *q* he had not been taken down long by
⁵⁵ the devilfish, before he was made to breathe by the devilfish.
He was made to arrive at a house below. He was made to enter
by the devilfish into the house. Then *q* he was invited in and went
and they talked together. *Sī'wit* only thought *q* that he would
try to get a supernatural treasure because he was too much defeated

by his friend. Then he wished in his mind to be given a large [60]
knife that he might really kill his friend. "Behold, it will be so,"
it is said. Then *q* he was taught the ways of the knife. With
it was killed what was tried in the corners of the house. "Strike
with it a seal. You will do that way. Now you will go striking
along with it." Then *q* he went out. He started going northward. [65]
He went downward. Then he arrived at the place called Old-
Man *(Nŏ'mas)*. Then *q* he saw the one called *ᵋnɛmxx·a'lig·iyu.*
He saw the men on its edge. Then *q* he killed it. He killed with
his knife the men on the edges of the *ᵋnɛmxx·a'lig·iyu.* Then *q*
the men on the edges of the *ᵋnɛmxx·a'lig·iyu* were all dead. He [70]
turned over the middle part and struck the *ᵋnɛmxx·a'lig·iyu.* However *q* he did not kill it. The *ᵋnɛmxx·a'lig·iyu q* was alive when
he left it. He went southward and arrived at the place named
K!wīt. He saw the place called Logs-Piled-up *(Xwā'laqɛm).* They
were the foundation of a large house. Behold! *q* this was the one [75]
named *Q!ŏ'mogwa.* Then *q* he chopped off some of what are said
to be many hands. On his part *q* he had not been chopping long
when he was dead. Then *q* he left him. He turned towards *Hā'da.*
He arrived at the place called *K!wā'xŭm* when he saw large fish.
Then *q* he struck them with his knife. He killed them. Then [80]
he left them. Then *q* he arrived at the mouth of the place named
Xā'wag·ē. Then *q* he saw a snag. He struck it with his knife.
Then *q* he saw something sitting in the mouth of a cracked rock.
Then *q* he said, "Yah." Then *q* he said again "Yah." On its
part *q* it never turned its head. Then *q* he spoke again, "Why [85]
may it not turn its head. So it is of a different kind. You are
of a different kind," said he on his part *q.* He rushed to the beach
and stabbed it. He stabbed it with his knife. What should it
be ? It lay flat on the beach. Then *q* the waters just rose. Behold!
it was just blood. It was only blood. Now he had made bad all [90]
the shellfish of the country of the *Qwē'qᵘsŏt!ēnoxᵘ.* For four months
he did not allow them to eat the shellfish on the other side. Then
q he left them. He entered the place *Hā'da.* Then *q* he saw one
named sea monster *(Hā'naq!ăts!ă).* Then *q* he killed a whale to
feed it to the one called sea monster. Then *q* it ate it. And so [95]
q he did not (eat) it all when *Sī'wit* turned to it and cut its wind-
pipe, so that the one called sea monster was dead. Then it was
dead. Then he left it. Then *q* he arrived at a place named *Q!ē'q!ɛl-
sɛla.* Then *q* he saw what was only *q* hands. There was no owner
of the hands. *Sī'wit* went to it and struck it with his knife. Then [100]
q he killed it. Then he left it. He arrived at *ᵋyā'x·ᵋyak·ilīt.* He
saw many dolphins jumping about. It is said *Sī'wit* went towards

them and killed them. *Sī'wit* had hard work *q*. It took him a
long time *q* striking them with his knife. Then *q* he left them
¹⁰⁵ when he had killed all the dolphins. He came back out of the
inlet to the place *Hā'da*. He gathered all the fish and gathered
them at the place *Ts!ē'gwats!ᵉ*. Then *q* he left them. Then *q* he
entered the place *Gwa'yēᵋ*. He saw different kinds of wonderful
things. It was their way to bury themselves from time to time
¹¹⁰ and *q* he became afraid. Then *q* he went back. His heart was
angry and he arrived there. He killed them. However, *q* there
was no way in which he could cut off the wonderful ones in their
way. Their bodies were seal flippers *q*. They only lay on the
beach buried *q*. Behold! that was the way of the place *Tᴇ'lg̣wis-*
¹¹⁵ *(aᵋla)*. Then *q Sī'wit* gave up striking them. Then *q* they only
dug in their other ends. Then he just left them. Then *q* he tried
to enter *Gwa'yēᵋ*. It is said he did not dare to walk there for the
soft ground was very muddy at *Gwa'ᵋyē*. Then *q* he just went
out and went towards where he had come from to go and see his
¹²⁰ parents. Then *q* he arrived at *Ł'k·!ᴇg̣ᴇmāla*. It is said he was
not walking on the ground. Then *q* he went back to go to the place
where he formerly had been fighting with his friend *Ts!ā'g̣ülis*.
Then *q* he sat down and looked up. Then *q* he saw his father.
He moved on the ground. Then *q* his younger brother talked
¹²⁵ to his mother. He wanted to imitate snares for bullheads *q*. Then *q*
the child was crying *q*. He wanted to pull out a hair of his mother.
Then *q* his father spoke, "Do take some of your hair for your dear."
Then *q* this was the reason why his mother spun the hair. The
child *q* felt good when it had a snare (made) of the hair of his mother.
¹³⁰ Then *q* he went down the beach among other children. He tried
to snare bullheads. A bullhead came *q* painted prettily *q*. Then
q Tō'x̣ᵘʟawig·iᵋlakᵘ tried to snare it. Then *q* he was pushed down
on the rock by the other children. He was maltreated by the
other children. Then *q* again the bullhead got into the snare. And
¹³⁵ so *q* he was just pushed down again on the rock. He was maltreated
by the other children. Then *q* he snared again the bullhead. Then
q the bullhead was taken away from him. It is said the bullhead
just *q* went through the snare of the others except that of his
younger brother. Behold! *q* that was *Sī'wit*. Then *q Tō'x̣ᵘʟawig·iᵋ-*
¹⁴⁰ *lakᵘ* again *q* snared the bullhead. Then *q* the snare of *Tō'x̣ᵘʟawig·iᵋ-*
lakᵘ took good hold. Then *q* it was as though he did not begin
to pull. And so *q Sī'wit* just left on the rock his bullhead mask.
Then *q* he sat down on the rock and he transformed into birds
the many children. Then *q*, "Is it you?" said on his part *q Sī'wit*.
¹⁴⁵ "Are you my younger brother?" — "I am *Tō'x̣ᵘʟawig·iᵋlakᵘ*." —

"Come to me that I may try to ask you about our parents. Are
they alive?" — "Indeed, although we are no longer men, we are
only thus treated by them. Only dirt is thrown upon us by our
tribe. We are not men now. Nothing, we are the poorest. We
have for our firewood toilet sticks that were thrown away." — 150
"Go and call our father to come that I may talk with our father.
Come here quickly!" Then *q* the child called his father. "Come
and go to the one who has (you for) a dog, *Sī'wit*. Behold, it is
he who came below there. He has come and is sitting on the
rock where I am." Then *q* he was told by his father, "Don't. 155
Do not obey the one who sent you to come and make fun. That
is the reason why we are just poor now." The child was struck.
He was hardly alive *q*. Then *q* it was so, *q* the child cried while
he was walking going back to his elder brother. "I was only
struck by our father. He said I only first made fun of him. I am 160
hardly alive." — "Never mind if you are dead. Go and call our
father. 'You shall come quickly *q* to *Sī'wit*.'" And so *q* the child
was only struck again by his father. "Will you be dead now obeying
those who make a fool of you that you come to make fun of what
happened to us?" Then *q* the child just rolled out of the house. 165
He was hardly alive now. He just crawled *q* going to his elder
brother. Then *q* he told his elder brother, "I have hardly strength
enough to move on account of being beaten." Then *q* his elder
brother blew on the body of the younger brother and his body
became alive again. Then *q* *Sī'wit* spoke again to his younger 170
brother, "Go and call our father. 'You are to come, come at once
quickly to the one who has (you for) a dog, *Sī'wit*. He says that
if you do not come, he will at once just go back again *q* below,
where *Sī'wit* came from, into the sea.'" Then *q* this mother spoke,
"Do try to see what this Short-Life-Maker *(Wā'wanᴇmg·ilaǥa)* 175
refers to that what he may have found, whether it is really so."
Then *q* his father arose to look. What should it be? *Sī'wit* was
sitting on the rock. Different was his head. And it was that *q*
the old man in vain rushed down to his child. As soon as he appeared
at the door *Sī'wit* just measured that he should not rightly touch 180
his father. *Sī'wit* turned round and rushed again into the sea
and he became different. A sea otter *q* was lying on the back
on the water, the mask of *Sī'wit*. On his stomach on the water
crawled *q* about young sea otters; *q* they were little sea otters.
Then *q* he went down again and when he came and emerged he 185
was a large whale. There rolled about little whales around the
large whale. Then *q* he went down. Then the *Gwa'waēnox*ᵘ
talked about his ways. Then *q* *Sī'wit* came up again in different

ways. He was a dolphin *q*. Foam of breaking waves *q* was just
¹⁹⁰ on the beach on account of the dolphins. Very many *q* went
down. A big hand came up again *q*, emerged and showed itself.
Then *q* it went down again. He came *q* up again and showed
himself. Then *q* *Sī'wit* was standing in the doorway in the wide
door of what is called *Q!ō'mogwa*. There were four doors *q*. Then
¹⁹⁵ *q* *Sī'wit* moved back and forth on the side of the wide door which
was snapping *q*. Then *q* *Sī'wit* went down again. He was standing
on the water when he came again and he emerged a man. Now
Sī'wit was just standing on the sea. Then the tribes launched
their canoes. They took their bows and their arrows. *Sī'wit*
²⁰⁰ went down. He came *q* and emerged and he was different. Then
q he was a young seal. There were four little seals *q*. Then he was
shot with arrows. He was not hit when they tried to shoot him.
"Let us try to snare him." Then *q* they tried to snare him. And
so *q* again he was not to be gotten. Then *q* he changed his face
²⁰⁵ when he went down. When he emerged he was a little loon *q*.
The feet of the loon were up on the water. It was he, *Sī'wit* who
went down *q* as a loon. When he came again the house came
up of the one named *Q!ō'mogwa*. On his part *q* he was not long
on the water when he went down and *Sī'wit* just stood on the
²¹⁰ sea and walked on the surface of the water and now they tried
to snare him. They did not get him. Every time *q* he just went
through the snare. There was nothing that they did not do to
him. They tried *q* to shoot him with arrows. He was not hit.
Then *q* the chief of the *Gwa'waēnoxᵘ* spoke that they should go
²¹⁵ ahead to drive him in. Then *q* they drove him into the inside of
ᴌā'ᴌodaᵉlas. Then *q* he stood on the rock. Then *q* *Sī'wit* was
sitting on the rock; he was a bird *q*. Then *q* he just flew up from
the rock. Then *q* the song leaders were ready. Now he was *Mā'dɛm*.
They sang the *Mā'dɛm* song. They sang for him. Then *q* the
²²⁰ rack was taken and they went to take it to *Sī'wit*. *Sī'wit* was
made to sit on the rack. Then *q* the song leaders sang for him.
Then *q* *Sī'wit* turned around on the rack and the *Mā'dɛm* song
was sung for him and he was *Mā'dɛm*. And so *q* the tribes just
in vain spread out the *Mā'dɛm* rack, as *Sī'wit* just flew away and
²²⁵ went aboard canoes tied together and he was just taken. Then
his father just made a winter ceremonial. Then *q* the *Gwa'waēnoxᵘ*
were singing when they went towards the shore. They were singing
for *Sī'wit*. Then *q* the tribes were too few and too small was the
ground. Then *q* those who went to take *Sī'wit* stayed in the same
²³⁰ way on the water when the ground was dug across. The *Gwa'waēnoxᵘ* made the country, but the house of a menstruating girl

was just dug across at each end. *Qwā'qwisbalaōgwa q* was menstruating *q*. And so *q* the land was just a rounded point, the place where *Qwā'qwisbalaōgwa* was living. Then *q* the former soil of *K!wā'xŭlawat* was carried across on canoes. Then *q* they unloaded the [235] soil at a place named *Gŭ'mgŭmlig·a*. Then *q* *Sī'wit* put on the ground his house, which he had obtained as a supernatural treasure for the winter dance house of his father. Ten platforms *q* were the dugout floor of the house. Now the house was finished on the ground and time was beaten for *ᵋnā'lanokŭmg·iᵋlakᵘ* in the canoe. [240] Then *q* he was made to stand on the rack. Then *q* the tribe said, "Go ahead!" They said *q* four times, "Go ahead in the canoe!" Then *ᵋnā'lanokŭmg·iᵋlakᵘ* sang the *Mā'dɛm* song. Then *q* he went up on the roof of his house. That kind of squeaking noise made his head. Then *q* the chief was asked to hold the line tied to the [245] *Mā'dɛm*. Then *q* he *ᵋnā'lanokŭmg·iᵋlakᵘ* spoke and requested his younger brother that he should hold the *Mā'dɛm* line. He answered the speech of the chief who asked him to hold the *Mā'dɛm* line. Then *q* *ᵋnā'lanokŭmg·iᵋlakᵘ* blew water on his younger brother, on *Tō'x̣ᵘLawig·iᵋlakᵘ*. It was *q* *Sī'wit* himself that stood on the [250] *Mā'dɛm* rack and rapid time was beaten for him.[1]

> *Wowē!* Yow are getting poor on account of the supernatural power. That is really your way, your head is squeaking.

It is said it was as though it was just the way of the movement of the younger brother *Tō'x̣ᵘLawig·iᵋlakᵘ*. It is said [255] it was as though *Tō'x̣ᵘLawig·iᵋlakᵘ* really performed the winter ceremonial of his elder brother *Sī'wit*. They sang at times *q*. The songs were sung for *Sī'wit*. The songs were sung. Four times *q* time was beaten for him. Then *q* he was purified. Then *q* he was placed in the center of the rear of his house, and *q* it was done the [260] right number of times (four times). Then *q* arose the friend of *ᵋnā'lanokŭmg·iᵋlakᵘ*. Then *q* *Ts!ā'gŭlis* spoke. Don't continue too much to sing for your supernatural one who was coming down the river, *Gwa'waēnoxᵘ*. Let us know the supernatural treasure of the supernatural one who was coming down the river, *Gwa'*- [265] *waēnoxᵘ*," said he *q*. He tucked up his sleeves to pull down *ᵋnā'*-*lanokŭmg·iᵋlakᵘ*. "Do not act roughly, friend," said on his part *ᵋnā'lanokŭmg·iᵋlakᵘ* to his friend *Ts!ā'gŭlis*. And so *q* he just disobeyed and pulled his hair. The quartz of his head was squeaking *q*. He forbade him *q* to treat him roughly. Then *q* *ᵋnā'lanokŭmg·iᵋ*- [270] *lakᵘ* arose being pulled by his friend *Ts!ā'gŭlis*. Then *q* *ᵋnā'lanokŭmg·iᵋlakᵘ* became angry. He put his arms through to pull both

---

[1] The following is his *mā'dɛm* song.

sides of his hair and tore it open. It is said steam just came out
of it when it was torn apart by *ᵉnā'lanokŭmg·iᵉlakᵘ*. Then he
275 tore to pieces *Tṣ!ā'gŭlis*. Then *q* the tribe of *Sī'wit* tried to rush
out. Then *q* they became afraid of what he was doing when he
tore to pieces his friend. Then *q* snapped the door, *q* it was a
snapping door. The double-headed serpents on both sides of the
door of the house were putting out their tongues and he barred
280 the door and locked in his tribe. There was no wife *q* that was
not offered to *ᵉnā'lanokŭmg·iᵉlakᵘ* (to induce him) to open the
door. But *q* he did not open. And so *q* his tribe tried every way.
And so *q* *ᵉnā'lanokŭmg·iᵉlakᵘ* sold the *Qwē'qᵘsōt!ēnoxᵘ*. He asked
for fire tongs. He asked for baskets from some of the *Qwē'qᵘsō-*
285 *t!ēnoxᵘ*.

The sister of *ᵉnā'lanokŭmg·iᵉlakᵘ* had a husband among the
Nimkish. She was *Qwē'sg·ilidzɛmga*. Then *q* *ᵉnā'lanokŭmg·iᵉlakᵘ*
gave as a marriage present *q* boxes in which the *Qwē'qᵘsōt!ēnoxᵘ*
were and he gave them as a marriage present to *Lɛlā'k·!inx·ᵉīt*.
290 He was the husband of *Qwē'sg·ilidzɛmga*. The *Qwē'qᵘsōt!ēnoxᵘ*
were talking inside when they were given as a marriage present.
Then *q* they were standing under the *Mā'dɛm* rack. They were
alive under it when the one named *ᵉmā'xᵘmɛwīdzɛmga* was dead.
Then *q* spoke *Tṣ!ɛ'ndɛg·îmg·iᵉlakᵘ*, "Do not please kill *L!ā'sotiwalis*."
295 Then *q* *L!ā'sotiwalis* was left alive among his tribe.

Another version.

(Recorded by George Hunt)

The first of the *Gwa'waēnoxᵘ* lived *q* at *Hē'gɛms*. Then *q* they
had for their chief *Hä'kwitawēᵉ* who had for his wife *Tsē'naga*.
Then *q* they had a son *Sī'wit*, a foolish boy. Then *q* he had for his
sister *Qwā'qwisbalaōgwa*. Then *q* the youngest one of the three
5 children of *Hä'kwitawēᵉ* and his wife was Made-to-be-Raindrop-
on-Tree *(Tō'xᵘLawig·iᵉlakᵘ)*. And *q* *Sī'wit* was a young man who
was very lazy, for he was just always sleeping. Now *q* one man
who came from the tribe of *Hä'kwitawēᵉ* came who had gone to
Ġwa'ᵉyasdɛ'ms. He came home to *Hē'gɛms*. Then *q* the man who
10 had the name Gliding-to-and-fro-in-the-World *(K·!ā'x·iᵉlälag·ilis)*
reported about *Tṣ!ā'gŭlis* who had found a treasure and who,
therefore, was the only strong man, for *Tṣ!ā'gŭlis* would just pull
off the head of a person whom he wanted to be killed. And so *q*
as soon as the man finished his report *Hä'kwitawēᵉ* arose, took up
15 the fire tongs and carried them as he went into the room where
Sī'wit was lying down. Then *q* he said as he struck *Sī'wit* with the

tongs, "Take care! you who are asleep, sleepy-head, you ought to go
every night into the woods to purify yourself in the ponds to try
to obtain a treasure, you man who are (like) a woman making me
ashamed. Look at the treasure of *Ts!ā'gŭlis*. It is said, he just [20]
pulls off the head of whomever he wishes to be dead among his
tribe," said *q Hä'kwilawē*ᵉ to his child *Sī'wit* as he went out of the
room. And *q Sī'wit* thought of the words of his father, for it was
true that he was just always asleep. He never thought of helping
his father, for he just always was working, trying to get food; and *q* [25]
it occurred to him to go to the pond inland when [all] his parents
went to sleep at night, said *q* his mind. And so *q* as soon as
night came [all] his parents lay down on the floor with his younger
brother and so *q*, as soon as *Sī'wit* heard that they were all snoring
he was quiet when he arose from his bed and went secretly out of [30]
the door of the house of his father. And so *q* as soon as he had
gone out of the door of the house he started and went to the place
where a pond was inland from the house; and so *q* as soon as he
arrived at the pond he at once broke off hemlock branches. Then *q*
he took the hemlock branches, when he sat down in the water of [35]
the pond and washed his body so that all the dirt of the body was
off. And so *q* as soon as all the dirt was off the body he rubbed
his body with hemlock branches; and so *q* as soon as he had finished,
he went home to his house and lay down on his bed; and his parents
never knew that *Sī'wit* had gone inland. And so *q* as soon as day [40]
came in the morning [all] his parents and his two younger brothers
arose, and so *q* as soon as the cooking of *Tsē'naqa*, the mother of
Sī'wit was done, *Hä'kwilawē*ᵉ, the father of *Sī'wit* arose and took
the fire tongs and struck *Sī'wit* with the tongs. Now *Hä'kwilawē*ᵉ
just repeated his former words to *Sī'wit*. And so *q Sī'wit* only said [45]
that he was not hungry, and his father gave up (calling) him and
*Hä'kwilawē*ᵉ went out of the bedroom of *Sī'wit* and began to eat.
Now *Sī'wit* was not thinking about food, for he had made up his
mind to purify himself so as to have a treasure, and he never came
out of the bedroom. And so *q* as soon as night came again and [all] [50]
his parents and their children had gone to sleep, and so *q* as soon
as *Sī'wit* heard that all were snoring, he arose and went out of the
door of the house. And he started and went again to the pond.
And so *q* as soon as he arrived there he sat down in the water and
washed his body, so *q* as soon as he had finished washing his body [55]
he rubbed his body with hemlock branches; and so *q* as soon as
he had finished he went home to his house to lie down in his bedroom
when it was nearly daylight. And so *q* as soon as day came in the
morning *Sī'wit* heard his father arise and build up the fire, and

[60] now his wife began to cook and so, as soon as the food was done the father of *Sī'wit* took the fire tongs and went into the bedroom of *Sī'wit* and he again struck his child with the tongs and again he called *Sī'wit* to come to eat; and again *Sī'wit* just said that he was not hungry. Now his father gave it up and he began to eat [65] with his wife and his two children. And *Sī'wit* again never came out of his bedroom all day. And so, as soon as night came and [all] his parents and his two younger brothers had gone to sleep, and so *q* as soon as he heard them all snoring, *Sī'wit* arose and went out of the door of the house. Then *q* he started and went to the pond. [70] And so *q* as soon as he arrived there he sat down in the water and washed his body, and so *q* as soon as he had finished washing his body he rubbed his body with hemlock branches. And so *q* as soon as he had finished he went home to his house and lay down in his bedroom when day nearly came. And *q Sī'wit* never went [75] to sleep for he heard his father get up and make a fire when daylight first came. Then *q* he heard his mother when she began to cook. And so *q* as soon as the cooking was done his mother called her husband to go and call *Sī'wit* to come to eat with them. And so *q* immediately *Hä'kwilawēᵋ* took with him the tongs. Then *q* he [80] said to his wife, "Now I will truly strike this bad man, that he may die," said he *q* as he went into the bedroom of *Sī'wit*. And so *q* as soon as *Hä'kwilawēᵋ* came into the bedroom of *Sī'wit* he struck him with the tongs, and so *q* he only finished striking him when the tongs were broken to pieces. Now *Hä'kwilawēᵋ* never called [85] *Sī'wit*, for he thought he was dead. It is said *Hä'kwilawēᵋ* came out of the bedroom of *Sī'wit* and sat down to eat with his wife and his two children. Now the mind of *Sī'wit* was really strong and he was not going to go home to his house when he would go out of the house again, said his mind. Now night [90] came, and so *q* as soon as his parents with his two younger brothers had gone to sleep, and so *q* as soon as *Sī'wit* heard them all snoring he arose and took two cedar sticks and put them upright under his quilt so that they looked like his knees so that his father should think that he was still lying down when day would come. And [95] so *q* as soon as his work was finished it was this way, for what he made looked as though he was lying on his back; and *Sī'wit* went out of the door and went to the pond; and so *q* as soon as he arrived there he at once broke off hemlock branches and he carried them and sat down in the water. Then he washed his body, and so *q* [100] as soon as he had finished washing his body he rubbed his body with hemlock branches. And so *q* as soon as he had finished, the pond began to rise on the ground; so *q* as soon as it covered the

knees of *Sī'wit* the pond went down again. Then *q* the pond rose
again and so *q* as soon as it reached his navel the water went down
again. Then *q* the pond rose again and so *q* as soon as the water [105]
reached his chest the water went down; and the pond rose again
and so *q* as soon as it reached the chin of *Sī'wit* he felt something
coming and winding its body around him. And *q* he was covered
by a large devilfish; and he was dragged into the pond and was
taken into the great house of *Q!ō'mogwa*. And now *Sī'wit* was [110]
asked by the speaker of the house of *Q!ō'mogwa* to sit down on the
floor on the right hand side of the door inside of it. And *q Sī'wit*
saw *Q!ō'mogwa* sitting on the floor in the middle of the rear of the
carved house, and so it was that many seals and sea otters and
sealions were creeping about the floor of the house, and so it was [115]
that two grizzly bears were seen by him. Then *q* the speaker of
the house spoke. Then *q* he said, "Welcome, friend *Sī'wit*. I know
why you came, and so you will take care and do not stay here long.
For four days you will stay in the house of this my chief," said
he *q*. Then *q* when night came, the speaker of the house went [120]
and sat on the floor next to *Sī'wit* and whispered to him and said,
"Do take care, friend *Sī'wit*. Don't feel uneasy about going back
to your home, for you are getting a treasure from this chief,"
said he *q*. Now *Sī'wit* felt happy, for now he knew that he would
get a treasure, as he had entered the house of *Q!ō'mogwa*. [125]

And now I will talk about his father *Hä'kwilawēᵉ*. It is said, as
soon as day came in the morning, at the time when *Sī'wit* stayed
away, then *q Hä'kwilawēᵉ* arose and built a fire in his house. And
so *q* as soon as the fire he made was blazing up his wife began to
cook; and so *q* as soon as her cooking was done *Hä'kwilawēᵉ* arose [130]
and went into the bedroom of *Sī'wit* carrying the clam digging
stick; and so *q* as soon as he came in he saw *Sī'wit* lying on his back.
Then *q* he struck him with the digging stick. Then *q* the cedar
sticks broke through the bed cover, those that imitated the knees.
Then *q Hä'kwilawēᵉ* lifted the bed cover and saw that no *Sī'wit* [135]
was lying there. Then *q* in vain *Hä'kwilawēᵉ* searched around the
bedroom of *Sī'wit*. Then *q* he went out of the bedroom to tell his
wife that *Sī'wit* was not lying on the floor in his bedroom. And *q*
the wife of *Hä'kwilawēᵉ* in vain was angry and *q* she blamed her
husband because he would always strike *Sī'wit* with the tongs in [140]
the morning. And *q* the first of the numaym *G·ī'g·ilgăm* of the
Gwa'waēnoxᵘ came and listened to the conversation of *Hä'kwilawēᵉ*
and his wife *Tsē'naga*. Then *q* the hearts of the first of the *Gwa'-
waēnoxᵘ* were really sore when they found out how *Hä'kwilawēᵉ*
had treated his son *Sī'wit*, and that *q* was the reason why they all [145]

13

drove away *Hä'kwilawēᵋ* who had to leave *Hē'gₑms* (which is called by the White people, Nimmo Bay on Mackenzie Sound). Then *q Hä'kwilawēᵋ* and his wife became scared, for they were threatened with death by the *Gwa'waēnoxᵘ* and that *q* was the
150 reason why *Hä'kwilawēᵋ* at once *q* loaded his canoe with his belongings; so *q* as soon as they had loaded the canoe with all his belongings he went aboard with his wife and his two children to go to a place near *Gwa'yēᵋ*, a country which has the name *K!wā'xŭlawat* and *q* he built a house there (at a place called Hayle Point by the White
155 people). It was now the living place of *Hä'kwilawēᵋ*, that *K!wa'-xula ᵋwat*. And so *q* as soon as the following year came the other *Gwa'waēnoxᵘ* also built houses at *K!wā'xŭlawat*. And *q* there were many tribe-fellows of *Hä'kwilawēᵋ* after this. On his part *q* it was now four years that *Hä'kwilawēᵋ* had lived at *K!wā'xŭlawat*, and *q*
160 he forgot about *Sī'wit*, for he thought that he was dead. Therefore *Hä'kwilawēᵋ* and his wife never thought of *Sī'wit*. Then *q* it was a fine day in the morning when *Tō'xᵘʟawig·iᵋlakᵘ*, the youngest son of *Hä'kwilawēᵋ* came into the house. Then *q* he asked his mother to make a fish line for him to go fishing for kelp fish on the other
165 side of the point of the village site of *K!wā'xŭlawat*. And so *q* immediately his mother plucked out some of her hair for the fish line; and so *q* as soon as she finished the fish line, *Tsē'naga* gave it to her son. And so *q* immediately the boy ran out of the house carrying the fish line and went to the other side of the point of
170 *K!wā'xŭlawat*. And so *q* as soon as *Tō'xᵘʟawig·iᵋlakᵘ* arrived where he was going to fish, *q* he stood at the shore of the sea. Then *q* he saw a great bullhead on the rock under water turning landward, and so *q* the boy was just standing there on the rock looking at it, for it seemed strange that the large bullhead should not swim
175 away. Then *q* it opened its mouth and *Sī'wit q* came out of its mouth. And so *q Tō'xᵘʟawig·iᵋlakᵘ* recognized at once his eldest brother. It is said, *Sī'wit* came out of the water and sat down alongside of his younger brother. And so *q* that was when *Sī'wit* spoke for the first time. Then *q* he said, "Are our parents well?"
180 said he *q*; and *Tō'xᵘʟawig·iᵋlakᵘ* said that they were all well. Then *q Sī'wit* asked his younger brother to call his father, "for I came to talk with him," said he *q*. And so *q* immediately *Tō'xᵘʟawig·iᵋlakᵘ* ran and went into his house. Then *q* he sat down on the floor by the side of his father, as he was sitting on the floor. Then *q Tō'xᵘʟa-*
185 *wig·iᵋlakᵘ* said to him, "Father! I am sent by *Sī'wit* to come and call you that you may talk to him on the other side of the point," said he *q*. Then *q* his father was very angry. Then *q Hä'kwilawēᵋ* said, "That is the only thing that you do not make fun of, my dead

child," said he *q* as he struck him with the tongs. Then *q* *Tō'x^uLa-wig·iᵋlak^u* cried as he was going to tell *Sī'wit*. Then *q* *Sī'wit* asked ^190
his younger brother to go and call his mother. Then *q* *Tō'x^uLa-wig·iᵋlak^u* ran again and went into the house. And so *q* *Tō'x^uLa-wig·iᵋlak^u* was just standing on the floor. Then *q* he said, "Mother,
I am sent by *Sī'wit* to come and call you that you talk to him on
the other side of the point," said he *q*. Then *q* his mother asked ^195
her husband to follow their child, "for it might be true what he is
saying," said she *q*. And so *q* immediately *Hä'kwiławēᵋ* arose from
the floor and followed his child. And so *q* as soon as he arrived
Tō'x^uLawig·iᵋlak^u did not see *Sī'wit* sitting on the rock where he
had been sitting. Then *Tō'x^uLawig·iᵋlak^u* saw the great bullhead ^200
where it was still lying where he had first seen it. Then *q* *Tō'x^uLa-wig·iᵋlak^u* said to his father, "That is where *Sī'wit* came out of its
mouth," said he *q*. Then a sea otter came and raised its head.
Then *q* *Tō'x^uLawig·iᵋlak^u* said to his father, "That is *Sī'wit*." Then
q the sea otter went down and a sea grizzly bear raised its head, ^205
then *q* the sea grizzly bear went down. Then *q* a seal raised its
head. Then *q* the seal went down. Then *q* a sealion raised its
head. Then the sealion went down. Then *q* a killerwhale came
and spouted. Then *q* the killerwhale went down. Then *q* *Sī'wit*
came out of the water. Then *q* it was he, *Sī'wit* who first spoke. ^210
Then he said *q*, "This is the reason why I wished you to come.
Now you will dig out a house in the ground with four platforms,
which is my treasure house. And this, that you will surround me,
as I am a *Mā'dEm* (dancer). After four times I may come," said
he *q* as he disappeared. Then *q* *Hä'kwiławēᵋ* was just standing ^215
on the rock. A large house came *q* up out of the sea water seaward,
and the front was painted with a killerwhale (design) and two
whales stood on each side of the door of the house. Then *q* five
birds were sitting on top of the board-holding poles of the house
and *q* the large house of *Q!ō'mogwa* went down again. And so at ^220
last *Hä'kwiławēᵋ* went home with his son *Tō'x^uLawig·iᵋlak^u*. And
so *q* as soon as he had entered his house, he reported to his wife.
Then *q* he said to his wife, "O slave, the word of *Tō'x^uLawig·iᵋlak^u*
is really true, for I have talked with my son *Sī'wit*, and I have
seen all his treasures and the large house which came out of the ^225
water. For four days we are not going to surround him, for he is
the great *Mā'dEm* (dancer)," said he *q*. Then *q* he at once called
in his tribe so that all should go into his house at *K!wā'x̣ūlawat*.
And so *q* as soon as the first of the *Gwa'waēnox^u* had all gone in,
Hä'kwiławēᵋ engaged them to dig out (the ground) for a house ^230
with four platforms. And so *q* immediately his tribe-fellows and

13*

their women dug out the soil. Then q he sent the cedar splitters
to go and split boards from a cedar tree for the upholding boards
of the house and *Hä'kwilawē*ᵋ never told his tribe the reason why
²³⁵ he had this done to the ground. Then q his tribe never asked the
reason why it was done. And so q as soon as they had worked for
four days they finished in the morning. And so q as soon as it
was noon *Sī'wit* showed himself at the lower end of the village, at
K!wā'x̣ŭlawat and q he sang the sacred song. And so q as soon
²⁴⁰ as his sacred song was ended his head was heard to squeak and
his hair was just shining on account of the quartz crystals which
were among his hair. And q the first of the *Gwa'waēnox*ᵘ [fell down]
lost their minds, for they were much afraid of what was being
seen by them. Then q *Hä'kwilawē*ᵋ spoke. Then q he said, "Now
²⁴⁵ take care, tribe and let us surround *Sī'wit*," said he q; and q the
*Gwa'waēnox*ᵘ found out that it was *Sī'wit* whom they had thought
to be dead. Then q the first of the *Gwa'waēnox*ᵘ surrounded *Sī'wit*,
and so q as soon as they came near him he disappeared and he
emerged seaward from the village site. And q *Sī'wit* walked on the
²⁵⁰ water. And so q the first of the *Gwa'waēnox*ᵘ launched their canoes
when *Sī'wit* came shoreward. And so q as soon as all the men
came near again to *Sī'wit* he disappeared. Then q he showed
himself at the lower end of the village site at *K!wā'x̣ŭlawat*. And q
Qwā'qwisbalaōgwa, the sister of *Sī'wit* was menstruating and so
²⁵⁵ *Qwā'qwisbalaōgwa* ran around her brother *Sī'wit*. And q *Sī'wit*
was taken after that. And q for a while *Sī'wit* became secular on
account of his sister *Qwā'qwisbalaōgwa* as she was menstruating;
and so q as soon as *Sī'wit* was caught on the beach on the lower
end of the village site, the large house came to be on the ground
²⁶⁰ with a painting on the front of a killerwhale and two whales on
each side of the door of the house; and also the five birds sitting
on top of the board-holding poles of the great house. And q
*Hä'kwilawē*ᵋ asked his tribe all to go in, for the fire had built
itself in the large house with four platforms. And so q as soon as
²⁶⁵ the first of the *Gwa'waēnox*ᵘ and *Sī'wit* had gone in, *Sī'wit* taught
his one song to the song leaders of the tribe of his father *Hä'kwilawē*ᵋ.
And so q as soon as all the song leaders knew the song, the song
leaders really sang it. And q *Sī'wit* danced. And so q as soon as he
finished dancing he lay down on his back in the rear of the carved
²⁷⁰ posts of the house which were all sealions, carved on each of the
four posts. Then q there were two sealions on the ends of the
beams of the house. And so q as soon as the ancestors of the
*Gwa'waēnox*ᵘ were all inside *Sī'wit* went in, and q he sang his
sacred song. And so q as soon as his sacred song was ended, the

song leaders of the *Gwa'waēnox*[u] sang the sacred song of *Sī'wit*, [275] for now they knew it. And this is the song of *Sī'wit*:

Wonderful, very wonderful is the way of this your wonderful head; now your wonderful head has a screeching mask, now the face of your head is steaming. Wonderful, very wonderful.

And so *q* as soon as the song of *Sī'wit* was finished he started [280] and lay down on his back in the rear of the large house, his treasure, as I said before, and so *q* it was not long before the first of the *Gwa'waēnox*[u] went out and all the men shouted, for a canoe was seen paddling in. It came *q* to the beach of the village. Then *q* it came from *Gwa'ᵉyasdᴇ'ms*, which is called by the White people, Camp [285] Bay, for that was the village of the first of the *Qwē'qᵘsōt!ēnox*[u], for that was the tribe of *Ts!á'gŭlis*, praised (as) the only strong man among all the tribes. And so *Ts!á'gŭlis* came ashore. Then *q* the young men of the *Gwa'waēnox*[u] went to the beach to meet *Ts!á'gŭlis*. And so *q* at once *Ts!á'gŭlis* spoke. Then he said *q*, [290] "Is it true, *Sī'wit* has come home?" said he *q*. Then *q* the young men said that it was true. "Look at this great house and he is a great *Mā'dᴇm* (dancer). Now you will witness it tonight when he will dance," said *q* the young men to *Ts!á'gŭlis*. And *q Ts!á'gŭlis* and the three men of his crew were invited to eat on their arrival [295] in the house of *Hä'kwiławēᵉ* which was another one than the house which *Sī'wit* had obtained as a treasure. And so *q* as soon as *Ts!á'gŭlis* sat down with the three (men of) his crew he was given to eat at once. And so *q* it was evening when they finished eating on their arrival. And *q* four men went (to call) for the dance of [300] *Sī'wit*, *Sī'wit* who after this changed his name and the four men, the (walkers) inviters said, "We came to invite that all may go in to pacify *ᵉnā'lanokŭmg·iᵉlak*[u] in the great winter ceremonial house. "Shamans, go quickly!" he said *q*. "We are told that the visitors shall witness him," said *q* one of the inviters. Then *q* all the tribes [305] with the women went in. And so *q* as soon as they had gone in *Ts!á'gŭlis* and the three (men of) his crew went in and sat down on the right hand side inside the door. And so *q* as soon as they were sitting, the one who had now the name *ᵉnā'lanokŭmg·iᵉlak*[u] sang his sacred song and the quartz crystals screeched on his head; and [310] *q* he arose from the floor and went around the fire in the middle of the winter ceremonial house. And so *q* as soon as his sacred song was at an end the song leaders sang and *q ᵉnā'lanokŭmg·iᵉlak*[u] began to dance. And so *q* as soon as he had danced he stood (still) on the floor in the middle of the house. Then *q Ts!á'gŭlis* arose. [315] Then *q* he spoke. Then *q* he said, "Now listen, *Gwa'waēnox*[u], I wish to test the strength of my friend here. We'll strive to outdo each

other [with him],'' said *q Ts!ā'gŭlis*, as he went to where *ᵉnā'lano-
kŭmg·iᵉlakᵘ* was standing on the floor. Then *q* they wrestled.
320 Then *q ᵉnā'lanokŭmg·iᵉlakᵘ* took hold of the head of *Ts!ā'gŭlis*
and pulled it off. And so *q* as soon as *Ts!ā'gŭlis* fell down on the
floor, for indeed he was dead, then *q ᵉnā'lanokŭmg·iᵉlakᵘ* broke
his head in two and threw one half to the right hand side of the
house. Then *q* he threw the other half to the left hand side of the
325 house. Then *q* he asked his younger brother *Tō'x̣ᵘʟawig·iᵉlakᵘ*, for
now he changed the name of his younger brother *Tō'x̣ᵘʟawig·iᵉlakᵘ*,
and he had the name *X̣wē'x·x̣wēlɛmg·iᵉlakᵘ* after this *q*; and *q
ᵉnā'lanokŭmg·iᵉlakᵘ* asked *X̣wē'x·x̣wēlɛmg·iᵉlakᵘ* to take the three
men, the crew of *Ts!ā'gŭlis* for his slaves and thus the *Qwē'qᵘsŏt!ē-
330 noxᵘ* were disgraced by the *Gwa'waēnoxᵘ*. And *q* the first of the
Gwa'waēnoxᵘ rushed out, for they were afraid of what had been
done by *ᵉnā'lanokŭmg·iᵉlakᵘ* to *Ts!ā'gŭlis*. And that is the end
after this.

This was told by *G·ī'qalas* of the numaym *G·ī'g·îlgăm* of the
335 *Gwa'waēnoxᵘ*.

Then *G·ī'qalas* the story teller said, "I forgot this, that *ᵉnā'lano-
kŭmg·iᵉlakᵘ* said when all the *Gwa'waēnoxᵘ* went out of the house,
"You cannot continue to see me if you don't wash off my supernatural power in the morning, for I have this song for washing off
340 from me (the supernatural power) which I teach you," said he *q*
to his father. And so *q* immediately *ᵉnā'lanokŭmg·iᵉlakᵘ* sang the
song for washing off (the supernatural power). It said,

    1. Ah, it is said not entirely came out, not came out your super-
    natural power that came off and went away.
345   2. Ah, your supernatural power will not make poor; woai, woai, woai.
    3. Ah, it is said not entirely came out what I was told by the great
    helper, ai howa a.

And so *q* as soon as *Hä'kwitawēᵉ* and his youngest son *Tō'x̣ᵘʟawig·iᵉ-
lakᵘ* who had now the name *X̣wēx·x̣wēlɛmg·iᵉlakᵘ* had learned the
350 three songs for washing off (the supernatural power) *Hä'kwitawēᵉ*
secretly called eight respected men to go to his house when *q*
midnight was finished. And so *q* as soon as it was past midnight
the eight men went *q* and sat down in the rear of the house of
ᵉnā'lanokŭmg·iᵉlakᵘ and now they just followed the ways of the
355 Kwakiutl when they purify those who have disappeared and who
first come out of the woods. Only the purification song was
different. Now at last this is the end.

Gambler

Told by *Ǧaa'xsta^εlas*, a *Sēnʟ!ɛm*.

It is said very different were the children of two chiefs. It is said that they quite agreed that they would gamble. They always bet everything against each other. Then, it is said, the one always lost; and so, it is said, he caused everything to be gone. And so, it is said, just last of all he gambled (staking) his wife. And now ⁵ he lost her. Then, it is said, his father became ashamed when his child lost in his gambling. Then, it is said, he called in his tribe and he said that he would leave his child. Then, it is said, day came in the morning and now the whole tribe were aboard (ready) to go (and) move to another country; (and) now they lived there. ¹⁰ And so, it is said, as soon as the child was entirely left he dug up the ground and put a bedding of moss into it. Then, it is said, he laid on top bark. And so, it is said, as soon as he had finished on the ground he lay down in it on the ground in what he had dug, and he put the moss over his body. And so, it is said, he was ¹⁵ for a long time that way. He never arose, for he wished that he might really die on the ground there. Then, it is said, it became winter. Now it was snowing. Now the snow was deep on the ground and he hardly had any breath because he had become weak on account of the time that he had not been drinking. Then, ²⁰ it is said, night came and now, it is said, day almost came when he heard the snow settling. Then, it is said, he opened his eyes and he saw a pretty woman, it is said, approaching, and so, it is said, she moved towards him and spoke to him, "What is your condition here?" said, it is said, on her part the woman. "I am ²⁵ committing suicide now," (he said) in his way of talking. "Arise from the ground now," said on her part, it is said, the woman. "I cannot do it," said, it is said, on his part the man. "I am now too weak." Then, it is said, the woman took off the moss from his body and took a small, covered box. Then she smeared his ³⁰ body with what came out of the covered box. Then, it is said, she put into his mouth something coming from it. Now his body became a little alive, and so, it is said, again, it is said, she took it and again increased his strength. Then again, and, it is said, again his strength was increasing and he sat up on the ground. ³⁵ Then, it is said, the woman smeared his body again and he stood up on the ground. Then, it is said, the woman spoke, "Come, follow me that we may go to my house." Then, it is said, he arose from the ground and went following the woman. Then,

⁴⁰ it is said, they arrived at a mountain, and so, it is said, as soon as they went down to a prairie he saw smoke and they were also walking on the prairie in a nice country until the end of the day and, it is said, it was evening when they arrived and, it is said, behold! her whole tribe had come into the house. Then, it is ⁴⁵ said, the woman said to the one who was now her husband, "I shall go ahead going in, and so you will only be observant when I sit down. You will enter. Not by any means will you turn your head, and you will only turn your eye to the right side of the house. I on my part shall smile at you. You will start and go ⁵⁰ across to sit down in the house by my side." And now the woman entered and went to sit down on the floor at (the place) she had referred to. Then, it is said, the man entered and so he just turned his eye to his wife when she was smiling. Then he started to go and sat down at her side on the floor and he and the child of the ⁵⁵ chief were married. And now his tribe went out. Behold! that was the reason why they had all come in. It was their way when they married. And now where he was staying all the time, behold! were the wolves, it is said. And so, it is said, it was a long time before he was called out of the room by his parents-in-law and ⁶⁰ there was spread on the floor a lynx skin on which they were to be seated, and so, it is said, they were given to eat. Then, it is said, his father-in-law spoke and asked him for the reason why he was in this way. Then, it is said, he replied. He said that this was the reason that he was left by his tribe, shame when he lost ⁶⁵ to his friend when he was gambling with him. Then, it is said, he was given by his father-in-law gambling sticks. "Now you will never lose when you gamble." And so, it is said, he was asked whether he did not wish to go home. Then, it is said, he said that he did. Then, it is said, he sent his sons to go and hunt ⁷⁰ mountain goats for future traveling provisions of their sister and her husband when they should go home. Then, it is said, his wife was ready when she sewed a wolf body for her husband. Then, it is said, she finished it and she engaged her husband to go also to hunt mountain goats with her and he started. It is said she ⁷⁵ told her husband, "Do not be seen by your brothers-in-law when you wear my work here. You might be killed." And so, it is said, he did so and, it is said, he was just hiding. He did not allow himself to be seen by his brothers-in-law, and so, it is said, was obtained all the game with his wife; namely mountain goats. ⁸⁰ Then, it is said, they went home and so, after that he had met with his brothers-in-law back of the house they went in. And so at once they skinned their game. Then, it is said, they dried

it and now the wife of the man had a child. A boy, it is said, was
born by her and now they were ready to be taken out by his brother-
in-law. It is said it was night. Then, it is said, the father-in-law [85]
said to her husband, "What is it, son-in-law? I give you this from
which your wife is to drink and whenever you will draw water
you give this to her. Everytime she will put into the water this
back sinew of a deer, everytime she will drink. You will treat
your wife carefully. You will not allow her to be smoked (touched [90]
by smoke), else she might not stay; and you will continue thus; and
as soon as you will hurt her your child on his part will not stay."
Now, it is said, it was evening when he called his son-in-law to
smear the calves of his legs with tallow from the inside of a small
covered basket. When this was done, it is said, he was sent to go [95]
among his brothers-in-law when they were going to play on the
seaside. "As soon as you will get their toy it will be yours," said,
it is said, his father-in-law to him and so he went out and went.
Then, it is said, one of his brothers-in-law was holding the quartz,
and that was to be his toy. And so, it is said, they threw it at [100]
one another in their way (as they were accustomed to do). From
time to time it was thrown to one, and so, it is said, that was the
place when the child tried to catch it. And so, it is said, they
were for a long time on the beach when the child got it and so,
it is said, it was now his after that. And he went home; and he [105]
was going to be taken out the next morning. It was morning
when he got up and got ready and his traveling provisions were
dried meat. Many were his companions and he started with his
wife and his child; and it was the end of the day when he arrived
in his country. And, behold! he had come returning to his tribe [110]
at the village site. And he entered the house of his father; and so
it is said, he did not (?) recognize that he was his own child and,
it is said, he was just surprised when he came. He entered; however
it is said, it has just been placed outside on the ground what came
with his wife, back of the village site. Then, it is said, he asked [115]
his father to engage his tribe to go and move to the place of his
wife. Then, it is said, his father started (called) his tribe and so,
it is said, they all came. They tried to move the load of the wife
of his child and he was gratified when he saw his child and he
invited his tribe to come and eat with his child, for he was grateful [120]
for his daughter-in-law and for his grandchild. And he was told
what was gained by his child. It is said he was told on his part
to invite one tribe, and so he wished to invite (them) and so, it
is said, he invited one tribe. Well, and so it is said, those who
were invited came and so, it is said, immediately he sent an invita- [125]

tion and gave to eat dried mountain goat, because that was obtained from his daughter-in-law. Then he distributed skins among his guests and now it was done. Then, it is said, he was sent by his wife to go and draw water to be drunk by her. Then, it is
130 said, he drew water for her from the river. It is said he came back and carried what was given by his father-in-law. Then, it is said, he gave it to his wife. Then, it is said, she took the sinew and put it into the water there. Nothing, it is said, on its part happened to the water, and she drank. Then, it is said, it became
135 night when she wished that the man should go and try to gamble with his friend with his new gambling sticks. Then, it is said, he entered and said to his friend, "Come, let us gamble, friend." —
"Oh, don't say now that we gamble again for you are not clever," said his friend to him, "else you might again lose your wife." —
140 "Nevertheless I will do so. Come, let us try." Then, it is said, his friend called him to sit down in his house and they began to gamble, and he gambled with what was given to him by his father-in-law, and so, it is said, it began to happen that his friend was losing, the one who was challenged by him. It is said, he on
145 his part, had not been long in the house (when he said), "Now let us stop, friend." It was the gambler who said it. "I only wished first to try, for I thought that he might now be a gambler." Then, it is said, he went home. He carried home the former ornaments of his friend and he got back what he had lost, and night came.
150 Then day came. Then his wife arose, and so at once, it is said, she sent her husband to go and draw water again for her. Then, it is said, her husband started and went to draw water. It is said, he came back. Then, it is said, he gave the water to his wife. Then, it is said, she took it and took her sinew and put it
155 into the water, and, so it is said, again nothing happened to the water. Then, it is said, day came. Then, it is said, it came to be evening again and he was going to challenge his friend again. Then, it is said, he entered his house and so at once, it is said, he said to his friend, "Come, friend, let us gamble again." On his
160 part, it is said, his father would not allow it. "Don't now gamble with your friend who evidently has got a supernatural treasure where he went." And so, it is said, the son just disobeyed his father and he sat down in the house and gambled, and his friend won again all his ornaments. He was at an end with his former
165 ornaments. Then, it is said, they continued. Then, it is said, his friend again obtained his wife whom long ago he had gambled away and he got back his wife. On his part, it is said, he said that he would not take his other wife because he was afraid of his

new wife. He said, it is said, that his friend should take care
of his wife. Then, it is said, he asked his friend, "Now we will [170]
stop." — "Let us start again," said on his part his friend. Then,
it is said, they gambled again and he gambled for the former
wife, namely his friend's, and he obtained everything that belonged
to his friend and he stopped. Then, it is said, he went home and
went to sleep. Then, it is said, it was morning. Then, it is said, [175]
his wife arose and she sent her husband again to go and draw
water for her. Then, it is said, he drew water. It is said he came
back again. Then, it is said, he gave it to his wife. Then, it is
said, she took it and again she put the sinew into the water and
so again, it is said, nothing happened to the water, and day came [180]
and they ate and his wife was happy, for she knew that she was
treated well by her husband. And now his former first wife kept
on talking that she would go back to her husband. It is said,
on his part the man did not wish for her for he loved his wife
on account of his child. Then, it is said, night came again and so, [185]
it is said, he tried to say that he would go and gamble with his
friend, for what might be done by his friend after he had gotten
all his former ornaments and his former wives? On his part he
did not refuse in vain and he only went home, and, it is said, he
just continued to be bothered by his wife whom he had obtained [190]
again in his gambling, and the mind of his friend was also sore
on account of his being beaten, for now he was just poor and
they went to sleep again. Then, it is said, it was morning when he
arose with his wife, and so, it is said, at once his wife again gave
him her basket to go again and draw water for her. Then, it is [195]
said, her husband took the basket and went to draw water. Then,
it is said, he arrived at the water. Then, it is said, he saw his
wife. Then, it is said, he was taken by her and was asked, "Why
don't you like me?" he was told by his other wife. "I do not wish
to hurt my wife here. She will know when I go back that you [200]
came to speak to me," and he was let go by his wife. Then, it
is said, he went home. Then, it is said, he gave the water to his
wife. Then, it is said, she took it. Then, it is said, she put the
sinew into the water. Then, it is said, the water became thick.
On her part, it is said, she did not drink it and, it is said, she just [205]
poured it out by the side of the fire. Then, it is said, she arose
and led her little child (away) in the house, and it went with her and
lay down in the house with her. Then, it is said, her husband
followed her and went to see her. What should it be? They had
gone into their wolf skins in the house. Then, it is said, her husband [210]
tried to beg her, that she should not do this, that she should not

go home, for he did not like his other wife. On her part, it is said, she never made any noise moving. It is said, the heart of the man was really sore for he knew that his wife would now go home. 215 It is said, she never arose in the house that day. Then it got night and so, it it said, she was still staying in the house. It is said, the man never went to sleep. He watched his wife (to see) whether she would start. Then, it is said, day came, and so, it is said, she still was staying in the house. It is said, she went into her 220 dress in the house with her child. It went to the end of the day. Then, it is said, night came again, and so, it is said, in vain he talked to his wife for her not to go home. She on her part, it is said, never replied to him, and, it is said, the man was just again sitting on the floor the (whole) length of the night, for he was 225 watching (to see) whether she would start. Then, it is said, day came, and, it is said, it was that again, she just stayed in the house. It is said, she and her child never ate. Sometimes her father-in-law tried to beg her not to go home. It is said, she never answered him. Then, it is said, night came and so, it is said, 230 again the man never went to sleep to the end of the night and he just continued watching (to see) whether she would start. Then, it is said, day came and so, it is said, she was still staying in the house. From time to time her husband tried to ask his child to arise and eat, but, it is said, he never arose. It is said, it went 235 to the end of the day. Now night came again when it was four days that her husband had not slept, watching her. Evidently, it is said, the woman wished that her husband should go to sleep. Then, it is said, the man fell asleep. Then, it is said, day was coming, when the woman arose with her child and started and 240 she was going to go home to where she had come from. Then, it is said, she saw the tracks of her husband and his other wife because snow was on the stone on the ground and the mind of his wife became really angry. Then, it is said, she reached the trail at the foot of the mountain and so, it is said, she passed 245 through, as soon as she (had) burrowed through it, so that it could not be passed through by her husband, and her husband was sick inside (sad) and he knew that he had no wife and no child. And so, it is said, at once he arose and went trying to walk and, it is said, he saw her tracks in the snow and he walked 250 in their tracks. Then, it is said, he arrived at that trail at the foot of the mountain. What should it be? The trail was closed. Then, it is said, he sat down at once on the rock and cried, and, it is said, he had been a long time on the rock when a sound of talking was coming. "Why are you crying on the rock here?"

Then, it is said, he wiped his eyes and looked at it. Oh, behold! [255] it was a beaver. "I am trying to walk (to get) my wife, but I have no way to get through because this my trail is closed." Then, it is said, the beaver said, "I shall dig it up here." And he dug it up. Then he started and went through there and now he went along in a nice country. Then, it is said, he went along. Then, [260] it is said, he came to the shore of a pond on a prairie. However, it is said, there was no way of crossing it. He tried, it is said, to go to the end to cross it, but there was no way of doing it. Then, it is said, he sat down and began to cry, for he thought of giving up, and so, it is said, he was sitting on the ground for a long time [265] when a sound of speaking came, "Why are you crying on the ground here?" Then, it is said, he raised his head and looked at it. Oh, behold! it was the panther. "That is the reason why I made a noise. I am trying to walk (to get) my wife, but there is no way of crossing this water on the ground." — "And I shall [270] show you that you have a way of doing it with this water on the ground," said the panther. "Go into the water. Only you will keep your eyes shut all the time when you go and your eyes are covered in this water." Then, it is said, he arose and followed the advice as to his way of doing. And when first, it is said, his [275] eyes were covered in the water, he went through on the trail in the water and, it is said, he came across. Then, it is said, he started again. It was a long time before he came to the shore of a water on the ground, and it was here, it is said, his wife's wish that the country was this way, that her husband should [280] not arrive at her house, and so, it is said, he just sat down again on the ground and cried again and he felt again like giving up, and, it is said, for a long time he was on the ground again when the panther came and spoke, "Why are you crying on the ground? You are foolish. Do you not remember what I told you? Go on [285] and do according to my former advice (given) to you and cross." Then, it is said, he remembered it and so at once, it is said, he arose and went into the water, and so, it is said, when first his eyes were covered in the water he went through on his trail. Then, it is said, he went across. Then, it is said, he started and for a long [290] time he had walked when he arrived again at a water on the ground, and, it is said, he just went right into the water and did in this way as he had done before. Then, it is said, he went across. Then, it is said, he started again. Now again, it is said, he reached a water on the ground and again he just sat down on the ground [295] and he thought of giving up. It is said the panther came. "What is the reason that you are again just sitting here on the shore,

since you have almost arrived at the house of your wife here ?" —
"This is the reason, I was waiting for you to come and give me
300 advice regarding my way of getting my wife." — "You will
go straight to the house of her grandparents at one end of the
beach and at once then you will see your child. Go across," said,
it is said, on his part the panther to him. Then, it is said, he arose
from the shore and went into the water and he followed his word.
305 He spoke to him full of pity, and so, it is said, he moved along
according to his advice and it was evening. Then, it is said, he
entered the house of the grandparents of his wife. Then, it is
said, he met them when they were arranging their fire in the
house, and, it is said, they only felt about. Behold! the grand-
310 father and his wife were blind [with his wife]. Then, it is said,
he helped them fix their fire. Then, it is said, the old man spoke
gratefully. "What is the matter with you, can't you see ?" said
on his part, it is said, the man to the old man. "No, I do not." —
"Now I shall make you see." Then, it is said, he took his small
315 covered box and took out some tallow and chewed it. Then, it
is said, he smeared a little on their eyes. Then, it is said, he asked
them, "How are you ? Do you not begin to see ?" — "I begin
to see a little." Then, it is said, he did so again. Then, it
is said, he asked again, "Do you not begin to see ?" — "Now
320 I begin to see. It would be good if you would take pity on us
again." And so, it is said, immediately he smeared it on their
eyes again and now he said that he was beginning to see. Then,
it is said, he did the same also to his wife and, it is said, she also
began to see. When his little child came in, it is said, he just
325 went right to his father. "Did you just come ?" said he to his
father. "I just came to take you and your mother." — "You
will never get my mother. She is not allowed by her parents
to go back to you," said he on his part, it is said, to his father.
"Go on, help me," said he on his part, it is said, to his child. "Indeed
330 I shall try, for really my mother is not allowed to go out of the
house, and it is just that she is always in the room." — "Go on,"
said he on his part, it is said, to his child. "You will just cry,
say that you wish that your mother follow you and you go and
ease yourself on the beach. Do not allow anyone else, whoever
335 it may be," said he on his part, it is said, to his child. "I shall
go." Then, it is said, he took some of his tallow that was in his
small covered box and he gave it to his child, and he went home.
Then, it is said, he went to his mother. And so immediately, it
is said, his mother asked him, "Where from is what is held by
340 you ?" — "It was his who came, the old man's." — "You lie,"

said she on her part, it is said, to her child. "Indeed, it is his,
your father's, I recognize it." — "No," said on his part, it is said,
the child to his mother, "It is his, the old man's." On her part,
it is said, the woman did not speak again in vain to her child.
On his part, it is said, the child was not long in the house when [345]
he asked his mother, "Come follow me that I ease myself on the
beach." — "Go, engage one of your aunts," said on her part, it
is said, the woman to her child. Then, it is said, the child became
angry. Then, it is said, he was still crying wanting her, his mother,
to go and follow him. His grandparents came, it is said, and said [350]
that she should follow him but, it is said, she did not wish it, and
that one was always referred to, his mother, and she was to follow
him. It is said she did not want to agree because she knew that
it was the plan of his father and, it is said, he was just annoying
his mother on account of his continual crying, and his mother [355]
arose, "Come, bad child, that I may follow you." Then, it is
said, he arose and they went out. Behold! it is said, he came to
the place where his father was standing on the ground at the
seaward side. And so, it is said, he at once took his wife, as soon
as she went out of the door. Then, it is said, the child kept on [360]
laughing. "That is the reason why I wished you to come out,"
said he, it is said, to his mother, and they just went with her husband into her house. It is said, her parents, on their part, did not
say anything to their son-in-law when they came back and, it
is said, they only warned him and his wife. Then, it is said, it [365]
was the fishing season. Then, it is said, her husband wished to
go fishing on the river with his parents-in-law and his sisters-
in-law, and so, it is said, his wife agreed and her husband went,
and now she had again a child, and her child, it is said, was again
a little boy. Then, it is said, they started by canoe and went [370]
to their future fishing place and his wife with her children stayed
at home. They arrived at their future fishing place and so already,
it is said, his mind and that of one of his sisters-in-law were different.
It is said, he did not feel troubled about his wife and he was just
one at heart with his sister-in-law. For a long time they stayed [375]
fishing on the river and, it is said, they finished and they tied
in bundles what they had obtained by fishing and they went
home. However, it is said, he was told time and again by his
father-in-law, for he knew in regard to his child that she would
know what was being done by his son-in-law and his sister-in- [380]
law. Then, it is said, they went home and they arrived on the
beach at the village site. Then, it is said, they unloaded their
canoe; and so, it is said, as soon as their load was out of the canoe

he was given food by his wife. Then, it is said, his wife sent him,
385 "Go and draw water for me to be drunk." And so, it is said,
already the man was afraid. Then, it is said, he took the bucket
of his wife. Now he drew water with it. Then, it is said, he went
back and gave it to his wife. Then, it is said, she took it. Then,
it is said, she put the back sinew of the deer into the water and
390 so, it is said, the water got thick. Then, it is said, she threw down
by the side of the fire everything and (even) the back sinew. Then,
it is said, she arose and led her children into the house and she
went into her wolf skin with her children and they started and
she again left her husband, for she knew what he had done with
395 his sister-in-law when he was fishing. And so, it is said, the man
arose and went trying to get his wife and his children by walking.
And so he still saw, it is said, their tracks; but, it is said, not very
far he arrived at a place where he was stopped by a great mountain. Now, it is said however, there was a great cascade under
400 which she had gone and so, it is said, the man tried to search
for a place of finding her, for he desired his children. But, it is
said, he never found her and he gave it up. He came and just
went back. On his part, it is said, he did not go in vain to his
former house, he just passed it and went home to the country
405 of his father. And so, it is said, as soon as he arrived he went
back to his former wife and now he had two wives with the former
wife of his friend which he came to obtain when he gambled with
his friend. And that is the end.

Night-Hunter and Day-Hunter

Told by ʟ!ā'bid, an A'ᵉwa.iʟEla story. Recorded by George Hunt

That one *q* Head-Copper-Maker *(ʟ!ā'qwag·ilagEmēᵉ)* and his
numaym, the First-Ones *(G·ī'g·ĭlgăm)* were living in a village,
those who were called by the first of the A'ᵉwa.iʟEla the Big Ones
(Ăwā'wa) for *q* it was recently since they changed the name to
5 "the first ones". When the late True-Copper-in-House *(ʟ!ā-
qwaiʟq!anakᵘ)* came and had for her husband Shelter *(T!ā't!Ents!ĭd)*
who came from the numaym the First-Ones of the Great Kwakiutl.
Then *q* True-Copper-in-House had two sons. Then *q* the father
of True-Copper-in-House, Spreading-Dancer *(ʟapalaɬ)*, died. Then
10 *q* Spreading-Dancer had no other child besides True-Copper-in-
House; and so *q* that was the reason why True-Copper-in-House
took her small son and she went and put him into the former seat
of her father Spreading-Dancer and so *q* he carried the name of the

numaym of his father Shelter, The-First-Ones; and q the Big-Ones were (called) First-Ones after this. And so that is the beginning [15] of the name of the First-Ones for the numyam Great-Ones of the *A' ᵋwa.iᴌᴇla*, those who came down (first) at Hump-Back-Salmon-place *(Hă'nwadē')*. Then q that is when the numaym, the First-Ones lived at *Ē ᵋawē'g·a ᵋlis*. Then q Head-Copper-Maker had as children four sons, and so q Head-Copper-Maker was sitting on [20] his summer seat with his four children when q the eldest spoke. Then q he said, "What shall I do for our father? I will be a harpooneer that he may always butcher for our tribe," said he q. And then q the one next to him also spoke. Then q he said, "I also will be a harpooneer and I will have our youngest brother for my [25] steersman; and your steersman will be my younger brother. You will be Night-Hunter," said he q to his eldest brother, "and I shall be Day-Hunter so that our father may just keep on butchering for our tribe," said he q. And q it was the first time that the eldest brother had the name of Night-Hunter after this. Then q the [30] younger brother had the name Day-Hunter after this. Then q Head-Copper-Maker was glad on account of the words of his children for that was what was desired by Head-Copper-Maker for the work of his four sons, (to be) seal hunters.

And so q immediately Night-Hunter made ready with his [35] steersman, the middle brother, and q he singed off the bottom of his hunting canoe, and q as soon as he had done so, he went with his steersman inland and they dug up hellebore. And so q as soon as they had obtained the hellebore they broke off the magic tip of hemlock. Then q they went to the water at the head [40] of the river of *Ē ᵋawē'g·a ᵋlis*. Then q he took two hellebore (roots) and gave them to his steersman. Then q two hellebore (roots) he rubbed q on his body; and so q his younger brother, the steersman, imitated the way of doing of his eldest brother. And so q as soon as they had finished with the hellebore, then q he took [45] hemlock boughs and they rubbed their bodies, (both) at the same time. And so q as soon as they had finished they sat on the ground on the bank of the river and, q they waited until evening to go out of the woods and start sea hunting. And so q as soon as it got somewhat dark in the evening, they went out of the woods and [50] went to where their hunting canoe was. Then q they carried it down and went aboard it. Then q they went to Skull Rock *(Qā'g·ᴇk!waa's)*, the point below *Ē ᵋawē'g·a ᵋlis*. Then q they steered for Open-Point *(Ăxē'lba)* and so q as soon as they arrived at Open-Point they heard the seals crying on top of a great mountain, the [55] name of which is *Ga'tstaēs*, which is not far from Open-Point. Then

14

q Night-Hunter started paddling and *q* the canoe stopped at the foot of *Ǥa'tstaēs*. Then *q* they kept quiet listening for the seals to cry again; but *q* it was not long before the seals cried again there
60 above, and so *q* immediately Night-Hunter went ashore at the foot of *Ǥa'tstaēs*, for there was the crying of the seals from the terrace seen before from time to time by Night-Hunter. Then *q* he stepped out of his traveling canoe and went up to the terrace on the mountain and *q* he carried his cedar withe rope, the long
65 anchor line of his canoe and his seal club. Then *q* when he arrived half way up the terrace of the mountain, which was another terrace, Night-Hunter saw a round fire burning. Then *q* he went up to it and what was seen by him? A great seal lying on the ground and on the back of his head was a quartz crystal. This is what
70 was seen by him burning, the quartz in the nape of the great seal. And so *q* as soon as the great seal saw Night-Hunter it jumped down into the mouth of the sleeping place of the seals. Then *q* there was much noise of seals fighting among themselves inside of the cave, which behold! was the road down, the breathing hole
75 of the sleeping-place of the seals. Then *q* Night-Hiunter started and looked down into it. Then *q* a strong wind was blowing into his face out of the sleeping place of the seals. Then *q* Night-Hunter put down his cedar withe rope on the rock. Then *q* he held his club as he went down, and he called his younger brother, his
80 steersman whose name was *Q!ēgēd*. Then *q* he arrived at the place where his canoe was. Then *q* he said to his younger brother, "I have found by good luck the sleeping-place of the seals. You will not talk about it to our brother Day-Hunter; if you tell anyone about this, even if you tell our father, I shall kill you with this
85 club," said he *q* as he aimed the club at his younger brother. Then *q* his younger brother pleaded with his elder brother and said he had no way of telling anyone about the sleeping place of the seals, which he had found by good luck; and so *q* as soon as his speech was finished, then *q* Night-Hunter told his younger brother that
90 they would go up the mountain that night. Then they went up and *q* Night-Hunter was still carrying his club. Then *q* he arrived at the hole, the mouth of the sleeping-place of the seals. Then *q* Night-Hunter took the cedar withe rope and tied the end to a tree standing by the side of the hole, the mouth of the sleeping place
95 of the seals. Then *q* he asked his younger brother, that when first he tugged at the rope, "then you will pull me up," said *q* Night-Hunter as he took hold of the rope and went down. Well, but *q* it was not long before he tugged at the rope and *Q!ēgēd* hauled up the rope which was very heavy (on account of) a large seal. Then

q he untied the rope from the seal. Then *q Q!ēgēd* let down the [100] rope again, and *q* again Night-Hunter tugged at the rope and *q* again *Q!ēgēd* hauled it up. Then *q* four large seals were hauled up by *Q!ēgēd*. Then *q* he hauled up Night-Hunter. Then *q* they rolled down the four seals. Then *q* Night-Hunter told *Q!ēgēd* to wash the seals and the inside of their mouths and their eyes so that the [105] soil and hemlock needles should come off. And so *q* as soon as he finished washing off the soil and needles *q* they put them on board of their traveling canoe; and so *q* as soon as the four large seals were all on board the traveling canoe they went home.

And so *q* they arrived at Hump-Back-Place *(Hǎ'nwadē')* when [110] *q* daylight came. Then *q* they arrived on the beach of their house at *Ē'awē'g·a'lis* and *q* he saw Day-Hunter as he started paddling out, going toward Knight Inlet. And so *q Q!ēgēd* unloaded the four seals, for *q* already Night-Hunter had gone up the beach and had entered his house. And so *q* immediately Head-Copper-Maker [115] went *q* and made a fire on the beach to singe off (the hair of) the four seals, and so *q* as soon as he had finished he cut up the seals, and *q* he steamed them. And so *q* as soon as the seals were done he invited his tribe, and this was the first seal feast that Head-Copper-Maker made with the seals first caught by his son Night-Hunter. [120] And so *q* when it was evening Day-Hunter came to the beach, but *q* he had only one sleepy-eyed seal (as) his game. Then *q* he was much ashamed when he heard that four large seals were the game of his elder brother. Then *q* when it was evening Night-Hunter started sea hunting with his younger brother *Q!ēgēd*. And so *q* [125] they just went right to *Ġa'tstaēs*. Then *q* they arrived at the foot of the sleeping place of the seals. Then they stepped out of their traveling canoe and *q* Night-Hunter carried his club. Then *q* they arrived at the sleeping place of the seals. Then *q* he took hold of the cedar withe rope and *q* he went down. However, *q* it was not [130] long before he tugged at the rope. Then *q Q!ēgēd* hauled it up. Then *q* he untied the rope from a large seal. Eight large seals *q* were hauled up by *Q!ēgēd*. Then *q* he hauled up Night-Hunter and now the place where the seals were piled up has the name "The throwing down of seals". Then they rolled down the eight seals. Then [135] *q Q!ēgēd* washed off the soil and hemlock leaves from the bodies of the seals and from their mouths and eyes. And so *q* as soon as they finished Night-Hunter took his harpoon and speared the outside of the seals, pretending that they had been speared. And so *q* as soon as he finished he put the seals aboard his traveling [140] canoe. It is said, he came going home. And so *q* as soon as he arrived at Hump-Back-Place it began to be daylight. Then *q* he

14*

arrived at his house in $\bar{E}^{\varepsilon}aw\bar{e}'g\cdot a^{\varepsilon}lis$ and q Night-Hunter saw his younger b rother, Day-Hunter, when he started sea hunting; and
145 so q as soon as Day-Hunter saw the traveling canoe of his elder brother Night-Hunter lying really deep in the water, then q he went up the beach again and went into his house, and q he felt ashamed on account of the many game (animals) of his elder brother. And q Night-Hunter stepped out of his traveling canoe and entered
150 his house and went to sleep. Then q his father, Head-Copper-Maker, went down to the beach and unloaded the eight seals from the traveling canoe of his son. Then q Day-Hunter asked his younger brother, *Wālɛwid*, whispering to him to go secretly, to look into the mouths of the seals and into their eyes for needles
155 and soil that might be in the mouth or sticking in the eyes of the seals, for Day-Hunter and his whole tribe guessed that he had found by good luck the sleeping place of the seals. And so q that was the reason why Day-Hunter sent his steersman *Wālɛwid* to go and look at the seals. And so q *Wālɛwid* pretended to help his
160 father, Head-Copper-Maker, when q he was unloading the seals out of the canoe. Then q *Wālɛwid* saw at once q the soil in the eyes of the seals and he also discovered the hemlock leaves in the mouths of the seals. and q *Wālɛwid* took the hemlock leaves and gave them secretly q to his elder brother, Day-Hunter. Then q
165 Day-Hunter said, "Do not have a place of telling (tell anyone) that I have discoveresd that Night-Hunter has found by good luck the sleeping place of the seals," said he q to his younger brother, and q the mind of Day-Hunter was good, because q he had found it out. And q Head-Copper-Maker singed the eight
170 seals; and so q as soon as he finished he cut them up q. And so q as soon as he finished he invited his tribe; and so q as soon as they had all come into his house Head-Copper-Maker gave out raw seal to his guests; and so q as soon as he had finished, all the guests went out. Then q Night-Hunter and his steersman
175 *Q!ēgēd* went out and went to sit down in the summer seat at the seaside of this house. And so q they had not been long on the ground when Day-Hunter and his steersman *Wālɛwid* came out of their house and he came q and they also sat down in the summer seat, and q Day-Hunter and his elder brother, Night-Hunter,
180 were close together. Then q Night-Hunter spoke to his younger brother, Day-Hunter. Then q he said to him, "What is your reason for not starting to paddle today, Day-Hunter," said he q to him. Then q Day-Hunter replied to him. Then q he said, "O master, the reason why I did not start paddling is that I confess
185 that I am really ashamed, for you alone get many seals here and

I just got one sleepy-eyed seal; and I pray you that our names may go to each other, that I may have the name of Night-Hunter and you may have the name of Day-Hunter," said he *q* to his eldest brother. Then *q* his eldest brother laughed. Then *q* he said, "Go on! be Night-Hunter, for now you wish to have it for your [190] name. Go out tonight and you will still go to where you always go. Now I shall have the name Night-Hunter; and so I will start by canoe tomorrow morning and go day hunting where I always go with this little one," said he *q*. And so *q* as soon as it got dark in the evening the new Night-Hunter started by canoe, the younger [195] brother, and *q* that is where they went, towards Knight Inlet, and so *q* as soon as daylight came they went home, and *q* two seals were their game. Then *q* his eldest brother started sea hunting, the one who now had the name Day-Hunter, and *q* he went towards *Qā'g·ɛk!waa's* and so *q* as soon as they had gone out of sight at the [200] point of *Ē̆ᵉawē'g·aᵉlis*, *q* the new Night-Hunter *q* went aboard his canoe with his steersman *Wālɛwid*. Then *q* they started paddling and went towards *Qā'g·ɛk!waa's*. And so *q* as soon as they came to its point they saw their eldest brother steering for Open Point *(Ă̆xē'tba)*; and so *q* as soon as their eldest brother was out of sight at Open- [205] Point the new Night-Hunter started paddling. Then *q* he arrived at Open-Point. Now *q* he paddled along close to the rocks, and *q* nothing was seen. And so *q* he came near *Ǥa'tstaēs*, and now *q* he discovered the traveling canoe of his eldest brother, being tied at each end at the foot of *Ǥa'tstaēs*. But, it is said, not long [210] before he reached the canoe, he stepped out of his canoe carrying his club of crabapple wood. Then *q* he went up; but *q* he had not gone up high when he went on a trail, a trail of animals. Then *q* he followed the trail going towards the place straight above the place where the canoe lay on the water. But *q* he had [215] not gone far before he saw one hauling up with hard work the rope out of the cave. That was *Q!ēgēd, the* steersman of the one who had now the name Day-Hunter. And so *q* the one who had now the new name Night-Hunter went right up to him while what was being hauled up by him had not yet appeared, and went [220] and stood behind him. It is said a large seal tied in the middle to the rope came up. Then *q Q!ēgēd* put the seal on the pile and, *q Q!ēgēd* did not see Night-Hunter as he stood behind him. Then *q* Night-Hunter struck him with his club and *q Q!ēgēd* was dead. Then *q* the new Night-Hunter took hold of the rope and let it [225] down into the breathing-hole of the sleeping place of the seals. But *q* it was not long before the new Day-Hunter tugged at the rope. Then *q* the new Night-Hunter hauled up the rope. Then

q he saw that it was he who was being hauled up by him, his eldest
²³⁰ brother, the new Day-Hunter. Then *q* Night-Hunter saw him.
And so *q* immediately he stopped hauling him, and so *q* the new
Night-Hunter spoke first to his eldest brother, the new Day-
Hunter. Then *q* he said to him, "You who has (made) mistakes,
would it be bad if you just had asked me, as I am your younger
²³⁵ brother, to come and only help you with your great treasure,
the sleeping place of the seals, this which is not often obtained
by men? Now you will go and become a seal," said *q* the new
Night-Hunter there to his eldest brother, the new Day-Hunter.
And so *q* Night-Hunter was cutting the rope, while Day-Hunter
²⁴⁰ spoke. Then *q* he said to him, "Don't be in a hurry in doing
what you intend to do to your brother. It would be good if you
only look ahead that only we together are owners of this what
I found by good luck, this sleeping place of the seals," said he
q. And *q* that was his word (said in vain), as the new Night-Hunter
²⁴⁵ cut the rope and *q* his eldest brother fell down and, *q* he was dead.
And *q* Night-Hunter did not take (any) of the seals that came
lying on the ground, for he did not want them to think that he
had killed his eldest brother. And for that reason he loaded his
traveling canoe with fire wood and *q* went home. Then *q* he was
²⁵⁰ asked by his father, Head-Copper-Maker, what had been done
by him when he started paddling. Then *q* Night-Hunter said
that he had gone to get fire wood, for the first of the numaym
The-First-Ones of the *A'ᵉwa.iʟɛla* guessed that he had killed his
eldest brother. Then *q* it was evening and *q* the time had passed
²⁵⁵ for Day-Hunter to come home. And so *q* he never came on the
following day; and *q* all the men not only guessed that he had
been killed by his younger brother, and so *q* it was that the new
Night-Hunter was very happy.

Now I will stop for a while talking about Night-Hunter and so
²⁶⁰ I will talk about his elder brother, Day-Hunter, who was said
to be dead in the inside of the sleeping place of the seals. It is
said, it was this, when the rope which was held by Day-Hunter
had been cut by Night-Hunter, he fell upon the rocks, upon the stone
floor in the sleeping-place of the seals. Then *q* Day-Hunter knew
²⁶⁵ that his belly burst, for his intestines were just scattered over
the rocks, but his mind was whole inside, and *q* he lay on the rocks
at the place where he fell down. Then *q* he heard many men
talking among themselves, talking about his way when he had
fallen down and now all the men were glad about the one to whom
²⁷⁰ they referred as "Making-Awake-on-the-Rocks" *(Tsʼɛx·tsʼɛk·ʼag·i-*
la), as he was dead, killed by a fall, said *q* what was heard by him.

And *q* many men came and stood around him. Then *q* Day-Hunter heard someone call out loud, saying, "Why are you gathering around there?" said *q* the sound a long ways off. Then *q* replied one man that was standing alongside of the place where Day- 275 Hunter lay on the rock. Then *q* he said, "Making-Awake-on-the-Rocks fell down into our house, and so he is dead here," said he *q*. Then *q* the one who had asked, "Why are you gathered around?" said, "Serves him right that he is dead," said he *q*. And so *q* that was the reason why the heart of Day-Hunter became strong 280 so that he stood up quickly on the rocks and *q* some of the seals had no time to put on their seal masks. Then *q* many had time to put them on. And so *q* Day-Hunter just stood on the floor waiting for the words that the men might speak to him, or kill him. Then *q* the chief, who had the name Seal-Face *(Mē'gwatᴇm),* 285 spoke. That was the largest one of all the seals, the one on whose nape was the round quartz crystal. Then *q* he said, "O tribe, now we have become secular for our friend, Making-Awake-on-the-Rocks, for he has seen that we are men here the same as he is. Go on! Ask him! Does he not wish us to cure him?" said *q* 290 the chief. Then *q* one man who stood [together] on the floor (by the side) of Day-Hunter came. Then *q* the man spoke. Then *q* he said, "That is wished by him here, that you should do so, chief," said *q* he who, behold! was the listener who now *q* was standing by the side of Day-Hunter. Then *q* one man in the 295 corner of what was now a large house with carved posts came *q* carrying something like a dish full of water of life. Then *q* the man sprinkled it over the body of Day-Hunter, and *q* he was set aright and *q* his hurts were cured. Then *q* the chief spoke again. Then *q* he said, "What is wished by our friend for his treas- 300 ure? Does he not want the Material for Potlatches?" said he *q*. Then *q* Day-Hunter thought that he did not want it. And so *q* immediately the listener said, "He does not want it." Then *q* the chief spoke again. Then *q* he said, "Does he not want the carved posts and the Water of Life in the corner here?" said he 305 *q*. Then *q* Day-Hunter thought, "What is the use of it?" And so *q* immediately the listener said, "What is the use of it?" said he *q*. And so *q* the chief became angry about him. Then *q* he said, "Does our friend not want the Death-Bringing-Baton?" said he. Then *q* Day-Hunter thought, "That is what is wanted 310 by me, the Death-Bringer." And so *q* immediately the listener said, "He says that 'is wanted by our friend here, the Death-Bringer, that he may take revenge on his younger brother," said he *q*. And Day-Hunter obtained by good luck the Fire-Making

315 Death-Bringing-Baton, for that was the name of the Death-Bringer. Then q the chief said, "Later on I shall engage (somebody) to take our friend (home), after he has been here for four days in our house, you tribe," said he q. And q Day-Hunter was just walking about among the seals, who were all men when they came home 320 to their houses, "where I now stay, to the sleeping place of the seals." The seal men call it" Place of Wealth" *(Q!ṓmx·dᴇᵉms)*, for q as soon as night comes, when q the tribes hold a winter ceremonial. And so q these are the dances, the sea grizzly bear, and the grizzly bear, and the war dance, and the laughing goose dance, 325 and also the killerwhale dance, and the cannibal dance of the seal men, for they are really afraid of him when he is in a trance. Then q these dances were seen by Day-Hunter, and Day-Hunter did not know that this, behold! would be winter, when it was night and that therefore the seal men held the winter ceremonial 330 at night. And so q for this reason there are few seals in winter. Then q summer is day for them. And q Day-Hunter was always called "Making-Awake-on-the-Rocks", the time he walked among the seal men. And so q the chief invited his tribe in the morning. Then q Day-Hunter was asked to go and sit among the guests. Then 335 q he was told to go to the rear of the house; and so q as soon as he sat down, then q the chief arose. Then q he spoke. Then q he said, "This is the reason why I called you, tribe, on account of our friend here, Making-Awake-on-the-Rock, that he may go home to the place from which he came. And so I engage someone 340 to take him home; and so the one we obtain by engaging will be our friend Going-in-One-Day-to-the-End-of-the-World *(Hayîlbalisᴇla)*, for he has a long breath when he dives, for the entrance to our house is far away. I know that our friend, Making-Awake-on-the-Rock is anxious to go home for he has been for 345 four days in our house. Now come, friend Going-in-One-Day-to-the-End-of-the-World, and take our friend home," said he q. Then q a really (well) dressed man came and arose. Then q he said, "Now come, friend Making-Awake-on-the-Rock, let me try the length of your breath," said he q. And so q immediately Day-350 Hunter stood up and went to him. And so q he was given by the chief the Death-Bringer. Then q Going-in-One-Day-to-the-End-of-the-World asked him to lie down on his back and to just scratch his sides when his breath was at an end, said q Going-in-One-Day-to-the-End-of-the-World. And so q as soon as the man was 355 ready to dive he became a loon. Then q he dived, but q he did not stay below a long time before Day-Hunter scratched him, and so q immediately he came up. Then q he dived again and q

he stayed down a longer time before Day-Hunter scratched him.
Then *q* he came up and *q* he stayed down a long time. Then *q*
Going-in-one-Day-to-the-End-of-the-World spoke. Then *q* he said, 360
"Now my heart is good, for your breath is long. Go on, now!
Try to make your breath really long," said he *q*. Then *q* he went
down again and dived. And *q* Day-Hunter never scratched Going-
in-One-Day-to-the-End-of-the-World until he came up, as he was
still coming up repeatedly on the beach of the village of the seal 365
men inside the sleeping place of the seals. And *q* the breath of
Day-Hunter was (even) longer than the breath of Going-in-One-
Day-to-the-End-of-the-World. Then *q* Going-in-One-Day-to-the-
End-of-the-World spoke. Then *q* he said, "Now my breath has
been beaten by your breath. Now I am satisfied that we shall 370
arrive at the opening of our place. Now be ready, for we will
soon go out," said he *q* as he dived. Then *q* Day-Hunter knew
that they had come out of the opening of the sleeping place of the
seals, for the light under the water was different, for the daylight
in the sleeping place of the seals was dark. It is said, he came 375
and emerged outside of Egg Island *(Ē'bɛkᵘ)* and that was *q* the
time when Going-in-One-Day-to-the-End-of-the-World, the loon,
spoke, "You, friend, Making-Awake-on-the-Rocks, I know your
younger brother, Night-Hunter, for it is he who hurt you. I wish
you to take revenge on him. We shall engage the sea monster 380
(ᵋnɛmxx·a'lig·iyu) who lives at Charcoal-at-the-Mouth-of-the-
River *(ts!ōlnax·siwē)* to come going at the same time with him,"
said he *q*. Then *q* he asked Day-Hunter, the one referred to as
Making-Awake-one-the-Rocks, to take in his breath, for now
they were going really far away, said he *q*. And *q* he dived and *q* 385
he went out seaward to the sea here. Then *q* he came up at Charcoal-
at-the-Mouth-of-the-River and *q* Day-Hunter saw much charcoal
floating there. Then *q* Going-in-One-Day-to-the-End-of-the-World
spoke. Then *q* he said, "Now take care, friend, now we will go to
this house of the sea monster underneath the sea, for there is 390
another world," said he *q*. Now *q* he dived straight down, but
q they had not been going down long, going through the sea, and
q they arrived at a good place. And that *q* was where the house
of *ᵋnɛmxx·a'lig·iyu* was. And Going-in-One-Day-to-the-End-of-
the-World became a man when they went into the house. And *q* 395
there a stout man was sitting on the floor. As soon *q* as *ᵋnɛmxx·a'li-
g·iyu* saw Going-in-One-Day-to-the-End-of-the-World he talked
kindly to him, and immediately Going-in-One-Day-to-the-End-
of-the-World just spoke to him. He said, "We come to engage
you, friend, to go and take revenge on the younger brother of 400

Making-Awake-on-the-Rocks," said he *q*. Then *q* *ᵉnɛmxx·a'lig·iyu*
was really glad on account of their word. And *q* immediately he
got ready. Then *q* he called what he referred to as his dogs,
the many seals, which were crawling about in the house. It is
⁴⁰⁵ said the seals came to him. Then *q* he took a small seal. The one
referred to by him had the name Dirty *(Nɛsa')*. Then *q* he took
off his seal mask. "I will take this along in case I should want
it, this your seal mask, Child Dirty," said he *q*. And so *q* immediately he got ready. It is said, he came and left his house. They
⁴¹⁰ came up to our world here and *q* Going-in-One-Day-to-the-End-
of-the-World became a loon again and also *ᵉnɛmxx·a'lig·iyu*
became a large halibut. Day-Hunter lay on the back of Going-
in-One-Day-to-the-End-of-the-World and *q* they did it at the
same time, when they dived. And *q* they relied on the sameness
⁴¹⁵ of their magic power. Therefore it was a short time before they
came landward from Charcoal-at-the-Mouth-of-the-River, which
is not far from the edge of the upper world. Then *q* they came up
at Cascade *(Tsɛxŭ'la)*. Then *q* *ᵉnɛmxx·a'lig·iyu* took the seal
mask of Dirty and put it on Making-Awake-on-the-Rocks, Day-
⁴²⁰ Hunter. Then *q* *ᵉnɛmxx·a'lig·iyu* said to Making-Awake-on-the-
Rocks, "Now go, friend, and show your head seaward of the
house of your father. And so, as soon as your tribe see you they
will send your younger brother, Night-Hunter, to go and spear
you, and so, as soon as he comes near you, you will dive and go
⁴²⁵ out seaward to where I am going to stay. And so, as soon as he
will go on my flat surface, I will pull him into the water. And so,
as soon as the sea is running a strong tide you go aboard his traveling
canoe and you will stand up in the canoe and aim about with the
Fire-Bringer that you obtained by good luck," said he *q*. Then
⁴³⁰ *q* Day-Hunter dived. Then *q* he went across and emerged seaward
from his house. And so *q* immediately the men who were sitting
on the ground saw the seal. Then *q* Night-Hunter was asked to
spear it. And so *q* immediately he went out to it, traveling in his
canoe. Then *q* (when) he came near the seal, Night-Hunter took
⁴³⁵ his harpoon, and so *q* he was trying to spear it when the seal dived.
But *q* it did not stay under water a long time when it came and
emerged seaward from where the canoe of Night-Hunter was
floating. Then *q* he started paddling and again tried to spear
the seal. And *q* the seal dived again, and again *q* it went not far
⁴⁴⁰ and there was the place where it emerged. Then Night-Hunter
went again *q* and started paddling and went after it. Then *q* he
tried again to spear it when the seal dived. Then *q* it hardly went
further seaward when it came and emerged again. And so *q* Night-

Hunter tried to go there when the sea began to run. Then *q* Night-Hunter saw that the water was shallow where his canoe lay on [445] the water. Then *q* he poled with his harpoon on the surface of the *ᵋnᴇmxx·a'lig·iyu*, and *q* he was too weak for the tide that began to run. And *q* the harpoon stuck to *ᵋnᴇmxx·a'lig·iyu*. Then *q* his hands also stuck to the harpoon. And so *q* Night-Hunter was just standing in his canoe. Then *q* Day-Hunter took off the [450] seal mask of Dirty and went aboard the traveling canoe of Night-Hunter. Then *q* Day-Hunter spoke. Then *q* he said, "You are Night-Hunter among my brothers. Now you will go where you wished me to go," said he to him *q*. On his part *q* Night-Hunter had no time to speak when he was pulled into the water by his [455] harpoon. And *q* he was really dead after this, for as soon *q* as he stepped on the sand beach that ran across where it was now shallow the distance across from *Ēᵋawē'g·aᵋlis* to Cascade. (The water) is only knee deep and now the tide was running very strong. That is the back of *ᵋnᴇmxx·a'lig·iyu*, the sandy gravel on the surface. [460]

(It is said that *ᵋnᴇmxx·a'lig·iyu* was in this way whenever he showed himself to the first of the Indians and therefore the hunters of the first Indians said when they saw *ᵋnᴇmxx·a'lig·iyu* when they came home, then the hunters were asked, "Have you no news?" being told by their tribe, then they often said, "I was [465] met by the shallow water of *ᵋnᴇmxx·a'lig·iyu*.) Now *q* the sea was smooth when Night-Hunter had sunk .And *q* the loon, that is Going-in-One-Day-to-the-End-of-the-World was sitting on the water not far from the place where the canoe of Night-Hunter was floating and in which Day-Hunter was now standing. Then [470] all the first of the *A'ᵋwa.iʟᴇla* came out. They were surprised on account of what had happened to Night-Hunter and on account of the one who came standing up in his former canoe who was not known being a different man, for the first of the *A'ᵋwa.iʟᴇla* had forgotten about the time when Day-Hunter had first disappeared. [475] Then *q* the loon cried, the same as though he was awakening Day-Hunter. Then *q* Day-Hunter sang this sacred song:

1. I was brought back to life by the magic power, and I was made alive by the magic power. *Hai hai hai hai.*
2. I was given supernatural power, supernatural power by the excellent [480] tide woman the supernatural one. *Hai hai hai hai.*
3. It was given into my hand the burning fire of the excellent supernatural power. *Hai hai hai hai.*
4. Therefore I am going to burn up everything with my. burning fire you miserable secular people. *Hai hai hai hai.* [485]

And so *q* as soon as he had ended the last words of his sacred song he stretched out his right hand, holding the Death-Bringing-

Baton, turning the end towards *Qā'qētɛn*. And so *q* immediately
the mountain took fire. Then *q* he pointed to Cascade. It is said
490 the mountain also caught fire. Then *q* he pointed his hand towards
*Mā'g·it!anē*ᵉ. Then *q* the mountain also caught fire. Then *q* he
pointed his hand up the river from *Ē*ᵉ*awē'g·a*ᵉ*lis*. Then *q* immediately
it also all caught fire. And *q* he stopped after this. This *q* was
the reason why he did so, that his father should know that he was
495 still alive and that he had obtained by good luck the supernatural
treasure, the Death-Bringing-Baton. Then Going-to-the-End-of-
the-World-in-one-Day, the loon, cried, for he was still sitting on
the water. Then *q* he dived. Then *q* he went down under the
canoe, the standing place of Day-Hunter and pressed his back
500 against the bottom of the canoe while he carried him to the beach
of the house of his father, Head-Copper-Maker. And so *q* as soon
as he arrived on the beach Head-Copper-Maker went to meet
his son, Day-Hunter, and *q* he called him out of the canoe and
they went into his house. And *q* the first *A'*ᵉ*wa.iLɛla* were much
505 afraid of Day-Hunter, for they had all seen how (the country)
burned when he stretched out his hands. Therefore his tribe gave
all their property into his house and he was really treated as a
chief by his tribe. And that is the end.

A Koskimo version, recorded by George Hunt

The first of the numaym *Naɛ'nsx·a* of the Koskimo, lived *q*
at *Xŭtē's*. The sea hunters of sea otters and hair seals and fur
seals were rivals. The one had the name "Night-Hunter", the
one who came from the numaym *Naɛ'nsx·a*. The other one came
5 from the numaym *G·ēxsɛmx·s*ᵉ*ānaɫ*, namely Day-Hunter, and
Hunter always got many seals every day when he started in the
morning, and it was not (yet) near noon when he came back, his small
hunting canoe filled with seals. And so that was also what Night-
Hunter did, when he started hunting when it first began to get dark
10 in the evening, and he came home in the morning, his small hunting
canoe filled with seals which he had obtained by spearing in the
night, and so *q* they did so for a long time. Then *q* Night-Hunter
was beaten by his rival Day-Hunter. Therefore, Night-Hunter
tried to discover the place from which his seals came. Then *q*
15 Night-Hunter was told that there was soil on the teeth of the
seals, and so, therefore, Night-Hunter guessed that Day-Hunter
had found by good luck the sleeping place of the seals, and so *q*
Night-Hunter thought he would watch which way Day-Hunter
would go when he would start paddling again in the morning.

Then *q* Day-Hunter started paddling with his steersman when [20] daylight came in the morning, and he did not see Night-Hunter as he was sitting on the ground watching which way he would go. Then *q* Night-Hunter saw that Day-Hunter paddled behind the tide, which was running out in the morning and he steered for Limestone Island, for its east end. Then Night-Hunter went [25] into his house and awakened his two younger brothers that they should get up quickly and *q* the three brothers were going to paddle, following Day-Hunter. Then *q* they crossed over to *Kwā'kwaᵋno* and kept close in shore as they paddled along there. Then *q* they arrived at the point and *q* they crossed over to the east end of [30] Limestone Island. Then *q* they arrived at (Rocky) Point. They kept close in shore *q* as they paddled along inward. Then *q* they passed the point and went into the bay. But then *q* the youngest brother of Night-Hunter saw a small canoe under water, with many stones in it to keep it under water. Then *q* Night-Hunter [35] saw a slide on the front of a mountain on the ground, and so *q* immediately Night-Hunter guessed that this was the place where the seals rolled down. Then *q* Night-Hunter took his seal club and *q* he stepped out of his small hunting canoe. Then *q* he found a trail leading up, so, *q* as soon as he reached the top of the slide [40] he saw the steersman of Day-Hunter hard at work hauling up a cedar withe rope, and so *q* that was the moment when Night-Hunter ran up and clubbed him and, *q* the man fell down into the sleeping place of the seals way inland, for there are two names, sleeping place and retreat(?). And so *q* as soon as the man fell [45] down into the sleeping place, Night-Hunter saw two cedar bark ropes leading down into the sleeping place. He untied it *q* from the place where it was tied to the butt of a tree and he threw it down into the sleeping place, and, *q* Night-Hunter came away after that and hauled up the small canoe that had been Day- [50] Hunter's, and broke it to pieces. And so *q* as soon as he had done so *q* he paddled away and he tried to get (waited for) night (to come) at the outer side of Limestone Island; and so *q* as soon as night came he speared seals and so *q* he had the right (number) for seals harpooned by him; and so *q* when it was getting daylight [55] in the morning, he went home to *Xŭtē's*. And *q* Day-Hunter was the cause of uneasiness of his numaym, because he always came home when it was not (yet) nearly evening, and *q* Night-Hunter was glad because his rival, Day-Hunter, was dead, for he was now the only one to give seal feasts to the first of the Koskimo. [60]

And now I will talk again about Day-Hunter; and he just sat down on the rock inside the sleeping place, as he gave up trying

to find a way to get up. However q he stayed there for four days,
but q in the morning a Loon came sitting on the water in the inner
65 corner of the sleeping place. Then q the Loon cried, and so q it
was Day-Hunter's place of speaking to him. Then q he said, "Oh,
that you would become a man and help me out of this place where
I have to stay," said he q to the Loon. Then the Loon replied to
him. Then q he said, "What am I if not a man? How do you
70 wish me to help you?" said q the Loon. Then q Day-Hunter said
to him, "Go on and go on to take me out from this place where
I must stay on account of my friend Night-Hunter!" said Day-
Hunter to the Loon. Then q the Loon came to the place where
Day-Hunter was sitting. Then q the Loon said, "Come friend,
75 lie face down on my back and try. You will try to make your breath
long, for the entrance to the sleeping place is long. You will just
scratch me if your breath should come to an end," said the Loon
to Day-Hunter. Then q he stood up and lay face down on the
back of the Loon. Then q Loon said, "Be ready now for me to
80 dive!" said he as he dived down; and so he did not stay down a
long time before Day-Hunter scratched him. Then q he came
up inside the sleeping place. Then q the Loon said to Day-Hunter,
"Don't do this, for your breath is too short, for the entrance of
the sleeping place is very far. Try now to take a long breath and
85 let us dive again," said q the Loon. Then q he dived again and q
stayed down longer when Day-Hunter scratched Loon. He came
up q; but q it was not long before he dived again and now he
stayed down a long time before Day-Hunter scratched the Loon.
He came up q. Then q the Loon spoke. Then q he said, "Now
90 try to take a really long breath, for now we will try to succeed
and go out of this sleeping place. Go on, gather your breath,"
said q Loon to Day-Hunter. Then q he dived. He came up q
outside of the sleeping place. Then q the Loon went ashore and
so q as soon as he arrived on the rocks the Loon asked Day-Hunter
95 to go and get rotten wood to carve an (imitation of a) seal; and so
q immediately Day-Hunter went and took a small piece of rotten
wood and carved it, and q in imitation of a seal. And so, as soon
as his carving was done, then q the Loon told Day-Hunter to go
and put the carved imitation of the seal on the point, for that was
100 where Night-Hunter paddled every night, said q the Loon. Then
q Day-Hunter put the carved rotten wood seal on the point, and
q the imitation seal was facing seaward. And so, as soon as he
had done so q the Loon called Day-Hunter. He came q and again
lay face down on the back of the Loon, and q he was going to take
105 Day-Hunter across in the evening q to *K·!ā'gɛkᵘ*, and it is not far
from *Xŭtē's*.

And now *q* the Loon caused Day-Hunter to become a shaman
and so *q* for that reason Day-Hunter did not go *q* at once into
his house in *Xŭtē's* and *q* for four days he stayed in the woods,
before he was heard singing his sacred song; and *q* time was beaten [110]
for him by the first of the Koskimo, and *q* Day-Hunter had the
name Made-to-Walk-Ahead *(Toǥomēǥ·ilitsɛ^ɛwē)*, being a shaman.

Now I shall talk about Night-Hunter. And *q* Night-Hunter
asked his two younger brothers to go sea hunting with him at
night, at the time when Day-Hunter came out of the sleeping [115]
place. Then *q* that way they were passing to Limestone Island;
and so *q* as soon as they arrived outside the sleeping place, Night-
Hunter saw a large seal on the rock on the point. Then *q* Night-
Hunter speared it, and so *q* immediately the large seal jumped
into the sea and went straight out of the inlet of the Koskimo. [120]
Then *q* they came to *G·ɛxwī't.* It never came up; and so it was
the time when the middle one of the younger brothers of Night-
Hunter spoke. Then *q* he said to the eldest brother, "Let go of
the spear line, my dear, for a supernatural thing has been speared
by you. See! it has never come up," said he *q.* And so *q* immediately [125]
Night-Hunter wanted to let go of the spear line, and so *q* the spear
line just stuck to the side of the small canoe. Then he took his
knife and cut the spear line, and so *q* it just stuck under the cutwater
of the small canoe. And *q* Night-Hunter gave up after this, and
he was taken straight out into the ocean by the great seal which [130]
had been speared by him which was called Seal-Face *(Mē'ǥwatɛm).*

Then *q* for four days they were taken out seaward by the seal
speared by him, before they came to the floating driftwood. Then
q for four days they passed through the driftwood before they
came to the charcoal, which is called Charcoal-at-the-Mouth-of- [135]
the-River and they were really carried fast by the Seal face, which
hauled along Night-Hunter's small canoe. Now *q* it was as though
the sea was higher than the gunwales of the small canoe on account
of the way they were going. Then *q* it was four days after they
passed Charcoal-at-the-River, before they came to the feathers, [140]
which are called Floating Feathers. (I think that is what Stone-
Body called Feather-Point.) Then *q* it was four days after they
had passed through the floating feathers before they came to the
floating sand. Then *q* the youngest brother of Night-Hunter began
to get tired and *q* he stood up in the small canoe and jumped on [145]
the sand, and *q* he went down, and *q* one was left behind, his past
youngest brother. Then *q* it was four days after they had passed
through the floating sands, before *q* they came to the place where
the post of heaven was standing on the water, which is said to

150 be the post which holds up the upper world; and so q that was the place where Night-Hunter saw sealions and seals and killerwhales and whales, many that looked like house dishes at the foot of the post of the world. Then q they heard the cannibal cry there. Then q it was four days after they had passed the post of heaven
155 before they arrived on the rocks on Sand Stone Island $D_{E}{}^{\epsilon}n\bar{a}'x_{E}$-*k!wa*), and, it is said, the harpoon line just, in a way, sawed the Sand Stone Island, and q there were many sealions and seals and sea otters on it. Then q four days after they passed through it they arrived at a large island with trees. That was the house of
160 Copper-Maker *(ʟ!ā'qwag·ila)*. Farther north q was the village of salmon *(mēnâyoxwana)*; and so q as soon as they arrived the manufactured seal of rotten wood floated up; and, so q immediately Night-Hunter was invited on behalf of Copper-Maker. Now q Night-Hunter and his younger brother went up the beach and they
165 went to eat upon their arrival at the house of Copper-Maker. Then q Night-Hunter saw the house with a sea monster on the front. Then q the snapping door was the mouth of the sea monster. Then q one whose office it was to invite, advised them to jump in when it opened its mouth, and q they went in and sat down in the
170 rear of the large house of Copper-Maker, and so, q there were many seals walking about in the house, which were called by the tribe the dogs of Copper-Maker. Then q the people asked one another what they would give to eat to Night-Hunter and his younger brother. Then q the younger brother of Night-Hunter
175 thought he would really like to eat many seals if they should be given to him to be eaten on their arrival. Then q a man who was sitting in the corner in the house spoke. Then q he said, "He would really like to eat many of the dogs of our chief, Copper-Maker, if they were given to be eaten to visitors," thus said q the
180 listener of the house. And so q immediately they clubbed on the head a small seal. Then q Night-Hunter was asked to cook it himself, for the tribe of Copper-Maker did not know what to do with seals, for they did not eat the meat of seals, and so q therefore Night-Hunter asked his younger brother to take charge of it. Then
185 q his younger brother took the dead seal and put it on to the fire of the house and q he singed it, and so q as soon as he had finished singeing it, he cut it open. Then q he cut it up. Then q he steamed it, for there were many stones on the fire of the house and so q the tribe of Copper-Maker just looked on (and saw) what they were
190 doing, and so q as soon as the seal was steamed Night-Hunter and his younger brother ate it, and q the tribe of Copper-Maker turned up their noses from the eating of what they called the

flesh of the dogs of their chief, Copper-Maker. And so *q* as soon
as they had eaten the steamed seal *q* Night-Hunter saw the posts
of the great house, that they were all sealions; and so *q* the [195]
feasting dishes, a killerwhale and a sealion and a sea otter and
a seal and a whale, were in the house of Copper-Maker; and so
q the cannibal pole was thus. Then the cannibal uttered the cannibal
cry behind the house. All [around] this *q*

was seen by Night-Hunter at the post of [200]
heaven and *q* Night-Hunter wished to get
all the things in the house of Copper-Maker.
Then *q* the listener who was sitting in the
corner of the house spoke. Then *q* he said,
"This Night-Hunter is wishing to get all the privileges in the house [205]
of Copper-Maker," said he *q*. Then *q* the attendant of Copper-
Maker spoke. Then *q* he said, "Our friend got everything wished by
him from Copper-Maker, for it will follow you when you go home to
your country, on the inland side of the world. You will just steer
sun in the morning," said he *q* and *q* Night-towards the place of [210]
appearance of the Hunter thanked him for his words.

FLOOR OF HOUSE

For four winters *q* he stayed in the house of Copper-Maker,
and *q* the younger brother of Night-Hunter was always *q* walking
along the curved beach, clubbing sea otters which came *q* to sit
on the beach. Then *q* among them came the mother of the sea [215]
otters among the clubbed ones, for Night-Hunter *q* was told by
Copper-Maker that he should club enough sea otters, and that
what he obtained by clubbing should be just enough to fill his
small canoe. Then *q* Night-Hunter just skinned the sea otter
and stretched (the skins), and so *q* as soon as he thought the sea [220]
otters were enough to fill his small canoe *q* he stopped clubbing
them and *q* he stayed for four days in the house of Copper-Maker,
and he did not know that he had stayed four years; and Copper-
Maker asked Night-Hunter to get ready to come home to this
inland side of the world. Then *q* Night-Hunter spread the sea [225]
otters in his small canoe and so *q*, as soon as he had finished *q*
Copper-Maker spoke. Then *q* he said, "Go, friend Night-Hunter
and your treasure, my former house and everything in it will be
taken by our friend Whale, when it is as though you had arrived
at your house, for I will help you and you will have really good [230]
weather. Don't forget to steer for the place of appearance of the
sun in the morning, so that you may really strike the place from
which you came. Now good bye friend, and your name will be
Copper-Maker as your chief's name, friend," said he *q*. Then
q Night-Hunter came paddling with his younger brother; and [235]

15

q they were for a long time on the water coming landward. Then
q it was night when they arrived at the beach at *Xŭtē's*. However,
the first of the Koskimo had not gone to sleep. Then *q* they were
met by the young men. One of the young men *q*, on his part,
240 recognized Night-Hunter. Then *q* the young man *q* ran up the
beach and went to knock at the door of the house of the parents
of Night-Hunter. Then *q* the young man said, "Come! open your
door! Night-Hunter has arrived on the beach, his small traveling
canoe full of these sea otters." That was *q* the word of the young
245 man, when *q Yā*ᵉ*yāg̣Exts!a*, the father of Night-Hunter, said, "Confounded, that was the only (thing) that you have not said to me
in your making fun of my dead children," said he *q* while they
came carrying in many skinned sea otters and *q Yā*ᵉ*yāg̣Exts!a*
believed it, and so his children came home, and now Night-Hunter
250 and his younger brother came and entered the house, and Night-
Hunter reported to his father, *Yā*ᵉ*yag̣Exts!a*, on the future coming
and bringing of his treasure, the former house of Copper-Maker
and everything in it. And *q Yā*ᵉ*yāg̣Exts!a* was really glad on account
of the treasure of his children. Then *q* for three nights Night-
255 Hunter slept in his house; then *q* he dreamt of the whale that was
coming straight to the beach of his house and so *q* that was the
reason why he knew that the whale would now come in the morning,
when it would be daylight again. And *q* night came again and *q*
Night-Hunter dreamt again about Copper-Maker who asked him
260 to go ahead and finish a house ground for the great house, "for
it will be brought to you when day comes," said *q* the dream of
Night-Hunter about the words of Copper-Maker to him. Then *q*
Night-Hunter awoke. What should it be; it was getting daylight
and so *q* it had not been daylight a long time when a whale
265 came in sight there at *Āmā'g·i*ᵉ*na*. On his back was the cannibal pole
in this way. Then *q* (eagle) down was what it spouted. Then *q*
red cedar bark was hanging on the cross
piece of the cannibal pole there and that
was the means of covering with (eagle)
270 down the cannibal pole and the cedar bark
on it with eagle down, the spouting of
the whale. It came *q* right to the beach of the house of Night-
Hunter and Night-Hunter just went down to the beach and went
and stood on the whale. Then *q* he held a small bundle and he
275 went *q* and put it down by the side of his house. And so *q* as
soon as he put down the house, the house grew up. Now *q* it was a
large house. The painting on the front boards was a sea monster.
Then *q* Night-Hunter went down again to the beach. Then *q* he

pulled out the cannibal pole and put it up in the rear of the great house. Immediately q he invited the tribes and q he gave a winter [280] ceremonial and q his younger brother was a cannibal. Then q he had the name *Gwayokulag·ilis*, and q he gave away sea otters to the tribes, and q the whale went back seaward, and q Day-Hunter was beaten by Night-Hunter. And that is the end.

Now what may it be? What is the whale about which the story [285] teller told me, on the back of which the cannibal pole was standing, that came carrying the house and the many house dishes? What may it have been? a Japanese ship or a real whale? I guess it was a ship, for it went back out to sea.

The place to which Night-Hunter went first was driftwood [290] on water after he had been out four days from Limestone-Island. Then four days after he had passed the Driftwood-on-Water he came to the Charcoal-at-the-Mouth-of-the-River. Then four days after he had passed charcoal at the mouth of the river he came to Floating-Feathers. Then four days after he had passed Floating- [295] Feathers (what is guessed by me that it was Stone-Body's Feather-End), he came to Sand-on-Water. Then four days after he had passed the Sand-on-Water he came to the post of our world. Then, four days after he had passed the post of our world he came to the sandstone island. Then four days after he had passed the [300] sandstone island he came to the village of Copper-Maker, the Rich one *(Q!ō'mogwa)*, for Copper-Maker has two names.

Copper-Body

Told by *K·!ä'maxālas*, a *Gwa'waēnox^u G·ī'g·ilgăm* woman

Copper-Body *(ʟ!ā'qwag·idɛk^u)*, the head chief of the family *G·ī'-g·ilgăm* of the *Gwa'waēnox^u* was living q at *T!ɛ'mx^{u}sɛm*, the island inside of the mouth of Clay *(ʟ!ē'q!a* Drury Inlet). Then q Copper-Body had one child, a woman who had the name Skin-Dresser-Woman *(Ălak·ilaōgwa)*, his only begotten princess. And so q [5] they were all sitting on the summer seat, Copper-Body and his wife Copper-in-House *(ʟ!ā'qwăl)* and his princess and his tribe, on the summer seat on the seaside of his house, for it was a really fine day. And so q it was not (yet) nearly noon when a large canoe came in sight at the point of *T!ɛ'mx^{u}sɛm* with really many [10] men as a crew. Then q one man arose in the middle of the canoe holding the paddle on his shoulder; and so q as soon as they reached the beach of the house of Copper-Body the man standing in the middle, holding the paddle on his shoulder spoke. Then he said q,

15*

¹⁵ "I have come I, Cloudy *(Ă'nxwit)* to try to get for my wife your only begotten Princess, Skin-Dresser-Woman, chief Copper-Body; for (the) only (thing) we have always heard is this princess-pole which is screeching," said he *q* as he took up a blanket of bear skin to give it as a marriage present to Copper-Body on account
²⁰ of his princess. Then *q* the man, the speaker of the canoe, spoke again taking hold of another black bear skin blanket also. Then he said *q*, "With this I call my wife," said he *q*. And so *q* immediately Copper-Body arose outside and asked his tribe to go into his house with his princess, that she should sit on her princess seat,
²⁵ that they should take her down to the canoe of his son-in-law. Then *q* all his tribe went in with his princess. It was *q* not long before they came out of the house carrying among them the princess seat of the princess of Copper-Body, set all around with skulls, and *q* Skin-Dresser-Woman was sitting on her princess seat as she
³⁰ was put aboard the traveling canoe of her husband and many privileges and red cedar bark (ornaments) of four kinds of dances for the winter ceremonial were in the large box, the privileges given in marriage to Cloudy, and four large drums. And so *q* as soon as this was finished *q* Cloudy never *q* thanked for
³⁵ the privileges given to him in marriage; for he just started at once steering for Pointed Beach *(Ă ᵋwī'lbaᵋlis)*. And *q* they just steered towards Deserter's Island *(Ō'k!ŭnēᵋ)*. And so *q* as soon as they approached it they steered for Cox Island *(Yū'L!ēᵋ)*. And so *q* as soon as they approached it they steered for Triangle Island *(Hë'lᵋaᵋs)*.
⁴⁰ And so *q* as soon as they came near it they steered out into the ocean. And *q* no land was to be seen. And *q* the heart of Skin-Dresser-Woman was bad after that. That *q* was the reason why she asked her husband, "Oh! is it far where we are going?" said she *q*. Then *q* her husband said, "It is far," said he *q*. And so *q*
⁴⁵ Skin-Dresser-Woman just lay down in the canoe and cried. Then *q* Skin-Dresser-Woman said again, "Have we not almost arrived?" said she *q*. Then *q* her husband said, "We have almost arrived," said he *q*. And *q* Skin-Dresser-Woman cried again. And so *q* the men had been paddling a long time when the steersman said that
⁵⁰ he could see the mountains of their country. And so *q* immediately Skin-Dresser-Woman spoke and said to her husband, "Have we not yet almost arrived?" said she *q*. Then *q* her husband said, "We have almost arrived," said he *q*. Then *q* Skin-Dresser-Woman sat up in the canoe and looked, and *q* she saw a long steep rock
⁵⁵ running down to the water being steered for by the canoe. And so *q* as soon as they arrived, the steersman took hold of the anchor line of the canoe and tied it to the end of a root extending down

from a spruce tree which stood on top of the hill running down to
the water. Then *q* the steersman stood up in the canoe and climbed
along the root and went up. And so *q* all the men did the same. 60
Then *q* Skin-Dresser-Woman said to her husband that she could
not go up that way. Then *q* her husband said, "Come and lie
on my back," said he *q*. And so *q* immediately Skin-Dresser-
Woman lay on the back of her husband, and *q* her husband took
hold of the root, and so *q* as soon as he reached the top of the place 65
that fell steep down to the water, her husband put her down on
the ground and started following a good trail. Then *q* Skin-Dresser-
Woman went after him, for her husband never turned his head
towards her. And *q* Skin-Dresser-Woman could not overtake her
husband, but *q* she saw her husband going down into a cave at the 70
foot of the steep mountain. And *q* Skin-Dresser-Woman was
really out of breath, and that was the reason why she was not
walking fast. Then *q* she saw an old woman sitting on the ground
where water was dripping down from the end of a root just above
the woman. And so *q* as soon as Skin-Dresser-Woman arrived 75
near where the woman was sitting, then *q* the seated woman spoke.
Then she said *q*, "Do stop for a while, mistress, so that I may
advise you; for these who brought you here are not men. Are they
not bears? Do not by any mean's eat when you are fed by them,
else you might always stay away; and that also, do not let yourself 80
be kissed by your husband; and also do not allow him to cohabit
with you, else you might stay away. Take this!" said she *q* as
she gave a small basket to Skin-Dresser-Woman, "Hide it, and
as soon as you will be given to eat pretend to eat it; but secretly
put what you are given to eat into this little basket." Then *q* 85
she also gave her white moss to be chewed when she pretended
to eat and, "Look at me! This is the reason why I am rooted to
the ground; for long ago I ate what was given to me to eat. And
so *q* as soon as night came I cohabited with my husband. And so
daylight came in the morning. Then I was sent to come and draw 90
water at the place where I am now rooted to the ground. And so
q as soon as I sat down on the ground I came to be rooted to the
ground and I am still sitting here on the ground since that time.
And as soon as you have pretended to eat come and give me the
small basket when it is full of the food you pretended to eat. Now 95
go! else it might be suspected that I am giving you advice," said she
q. And so *q* immediately Skin-Dresser-Woman started and went into
the cave house of the bear, and went and sat down by the side of
her husband. And so *q* immediately her husband asked his two
sisters to go and pick crabapples for food (to be eaten) after arrival 100

by his wife. And so *q* immediately the two women, the sisters
of Cloudy, took their bear skins and put them on. And *q* they
were two bears who walked out of the inside of the cave house. On
their part *q* they had not been away long when the two bears
¹⁰⁵ came back. And it was that *q*, the two bears took a new mat
and spread it in front of Cloudy and his wife, Skin-Dresser-Woman.
Then *q* the two black bears turned their backs towards the mat
spread out on the floor and squirted out of their backsides cleaned
crabapples. And so *q* as soon as all the crabapples were out the
¹¹⁰ two bears took off their bear skins and hung them inside on the
right hand side of the doorway. They came *q* and sat down with
Cloudy to eat the crabapples. And *q* Skin-Dresser-Woman pretended to eat the crabapples, for she only threw the crabapples
into the small basket. And so *q* as soon as the basket was full
¹¹⁵ of crabapples Skin-Dresser-Woman arose hiding the small basket
with the crabapples in it and went to the Woman-Rooted-to-the-
Ground. And so *q* as soon as she arrived there, Skin-Dresser-
Woman gave the small basket to the Woman-Rooted-to-the-
Ground. And so *q* immediately the Woman-Rooted-to-the-Ground
¹²⁰ poured out the crabapples and she gave back the empty basket to
Skin-Dresser-Woman. Then *q* the Woman Rooted-to-the-Ground
said, "Don't by any means sleep tonight when you go to lie down
with your husband, else he might cohabit with you; and do not
let yourself be kissed by him. And that, if he should cohabit
¹²⁵ with you, you will stay in this country, and if you eat what will
be given to you to eat, you will also stay here," said she *q*. "Now
go home else it might be suspected that we are talking together,"
said she *q*. And so *q* Skin-Dresser-Woman just hid the small
basket and she arose and went to the house of her husband, Cloudy.
¹³⁰ And *q* they ate (only) once in the day. And so *q* as soon as night
came Cloudy said to his wife, Skin-Dresser-Woman, "Come! let
us lie down!" And so *q* immediately Skin-Dresser-Woman arose
from the floor and followed her husband and lay down in bed. And
so *q* immediately her husband wished to cohabit with her. And so *q*
¹³⁵ Skin-Dresser-Woman just cried to the end of the night and Cloudy
did not speak again. And *q* daylight came in the morning. Then *q*
Cloudy asked his wife to rise. And so *q* immediately they arose
and went to sit down alongside the fire in the house. Then *q* Cloudy
asked his two sisters to go and get viburnum berries for breakfast
¹⁴⁰ (for him) and his wife. And so *q* immediately the two sisters of
Cloudy took their bear skins and put them on, and *q* they were
two bears as they went out of the cave house. On their part *q*
it was not long before the two bears came back into the house
through the door of the cave. And *q* they did again as they had

done with the crabapples, and the two bears turned their backs [145]
to the mat•spread on the floor and squirted viburnum berries out
of their backsides. And so *q* as soon as they had finished, the
two bears took off their bear skins and hung them on the inside of
the right hand side of the doorway. They came *q* and sat down
with Cloudy and ate with him the viburnum berries. And *q* Skin- [150]
Dresser-Woman pretended also to eat the viburnum berries, and
she only put the viburnum berries into the small basket. And
so *q* as soon as the basket was full of viburnum berries, Skin-Dresser-
Woman arose and went out of what was referred to by the bears
as their house, to go to the Woman-Rooted-to-the-Ground. And so [155]
q as soon as Skin-Dresser-Woman arrived she gave the basket
of berries to the Woman-Rooted-to-the-Ground. Then *q* the
woman took the small basket and poured the viburnum berries
on the ground. Then *q* the Woman-Rooted-to-the-Ground said,
"Never mind if I speak often giving you advice, child! Don't [160]
fall asleep, else your husband might cohabit with you; and that,
do not by any means allow yourself to be kissed. Just cry at once
when he tries to cohabit with you, for this is not allowed (that)
bears hear crying; for this is the reason I am rooted here that
I allowed him who is now your husband to cohabit with me when [165]
we first lay down at night. That is it. Go! Else we might be
suspected," said she *q*. And so *q* immediately Skin-Dresser-Woman
took the small basket and went home and sat down at the place
where she always used to sit. And *q* night came again. Then *q*
Cloudy asked Skin-Dresser-Woman, "Let us lie down!" said he *q*. [170]
And so *q* immediately Skin-Dresser-Woman arose and she lay
down with her husband in the bed. And so *q* immediately her husband wished to cohabit with her. And so *q* Skin-Dresser-Woman
only cried. And so *q* immediately her husband turned around and
lay back to back with his wife as they were lying down; and also he [175]
never cohabited with her. And so, as soon as day came in the
morning Skin-Dresser-Woman and her husband, Cloudy, arose
and went to sit down where they were always sitting down. Then
q Cloudy asked his two sisters to pick berries inland for breakfast
(for him) and his wife. Then *q* the two women put on their bear [180]
skins. Then *q* the two bears went out of the house. On their part
q it was not long before the two bears came in and took the food
mat and spread it before Skin-Dresser-Woman. Then *q* the two
bears stood facing both ways and *q* squirted out of their backsides
currants. And so *q* as soon as all the currants were out of their [185]
backsides, the two bears took off their bear skins and hung them
up. The two women came *q* and sat down to eat the currants and
Cloudy also ate the currants with his wife Skin-Dresser-Woman

who only pretended to eat currants. And so *q* as soon as the little
¹⁹⁰ basket was full she stood up at once and went out of the house
and went to the Woman-Rooted-to-the-Ground. Then *q* she gave
the small basket with currants to the Woman-Rooted-to-the-
Ground. And so *q* immediately the Woman-Rooted-to-the-Ground
poured the currants on the ground. Then *q* the Woman-Rooted-
¹⁹⁵ to-the-Ground said, "Now take care and do not fall asleep tonight.
And this, if you should fall asleep your husband would cohabit
with you and then you would never go home to your parents the
way I am; and this, do not allow yourself to be kissed. I mean
this. As soon as you will not cohabit tonight then you will go
²⁰⁰ home tomorrow. This will be your traveling canoe, the canoe of
your husband, for it is the only one among the bears, this canoe.
And that is the reason why they cannot try to paddle after you,"
said she *q*. "Now go, else your husband may suspect that I am
advising you," said she *q*. And so *q* immediately Skin-Dresser-
²⁰⁵ Woman took the small basket and went home. Then *q* night came.
Then *q* she lay down in her bed with her husband. And so *q* daylight almost came when Skin-Dresser-Woman became really
sleepy and she fell asleep for a short time, and so *q* Skin-Dresser-
Woman only woke up when she was beeing kissed by her husband.
²¹⁰ And so *q* immediately Skin-Dresser-Woman began to cry. And *q*
daylight came in the morning. Then *q* they arose and sat down
where they were always sitting every day. Then *q* Cloudy asked
his two women to and pick fruits for breakfast for (himself)
and his wife. And so *q* immediately the two sisters put on their
²¹⁵ bear skin blankets and went out of the house. On their part *q*
it was not long before they came back. Then *q* the two bears took
the food mat and spread it in front of Cloudy and his wife, Skin-
Dresser-Woman. And so *q* the bears stood facing both ways and
squirted out of their backsides the elderberries of the bears; and
²²⁰ so *q* as soon as all the elderberries of the bears were out, the two
bears took off their bear skin blankets and hung them up where
they always hung them up. They came *q* and sat down to eat
with Cloudy when he was eating the elderberries with his wife,
Skin-Dresser-Woman who only pretended to eat the elderberries.
²²⁵ And Skin-Dresser-Woman had whiskers which reached down to
below her chest from being kissed by her husband. And so *q* as
soon as Skin-Dresser-Woman had finished eating the elderberries
she arose at once and went out of the house to go to the place
where the Woman-Rooted-to-the-Ground was seated. And so *q*
²³⁰ immediately the Woman-Rooted-to-the-Ground spoke, and Skin-
Dresser-Woman had not reached her. Then she said *q*, "Why
did you allow yourself to be kissed by your husband? Now you

have whiskers," said she *q*. "Give me the small basket and go
right to the canoe and go home to our country. Just untie the
anchor line of the canoe at once and paddle. You will always [235]
steer the way the bow of the canoe is heading and be not afraid
of your husband, for he cannot try to paddle after you, for there
is no other canoe. Now go!" said she *q*. And so *q* immediately
Skin-Dresser-Woman went running to go to the place where the
canoe was tied and she went aboard. Then *q* she untied the anchor [240]
line from the end of the root. Then *q* she started paddling and q
to the end of the day she steered the way the canoe was headed.
Then *q* night came. But *q* it was past midnight when Skin-Dresser-
Woman saw something like fire coming out of the door of a house
straight ahead of (the direction) steered for by her. Then *q* she [245]
saw many men walking about inside. Then *q* it was as though the
house was drawing the canoe of Skin-Dresser-Woman, for it was
going very fast. Then *q* the canoe went in through the wide door
of the house and it went and lay on the floor at the right hand
side of the great fire in the middle of the large house. Then *q* [250]
Skin-Dresser-Woman was still sitting in the canoe, and not a person
was seen walking in the house except many seals, but at last she saw
a man lying on his back in the rear of the large house who spoke
and said, "Come and get a supernatural treasure from me. You
have done well to come into my house. Now come out of your [255]
traveling canoe and come and sit down by my side, for I wish to
have you for my wife," said *q* the man to Skin-Dresser-Woman.
Then *q* Skin-Dresser-Woman thought, "Let me have him for my
husband," said *q* her mind. Then *q* Skin-Dresser-Woman arose
from the canoe and stepped out of it and went to sit by the side [260]
of the man who was not known to her. And so *q* as soon as she
was sitting on the floor the man spoke to her again. Then he said
q, "I know that you do not recognize me, I am *Q!ō'mogwa* and
my house has the name House-of-Happiness *(aix·ᵉaix·dă̆ᵉmĭl)*, for
always are happy the many tribes who come to it from time to [265]
time. Now you also will be happy, Skin-Dresser-Woman on account
of my coming to have you for my wife for a short time," said he *q*.
And *q* Skin-Dresser-Woman's mind was good on account of this
speech and *q* *Q!ō'mogwa* and Skin-Dresser-Woman were husband
and wife now. And *q* Skin-Dresser-Woman never thought of her [270]
parents, for she was really treated well by her husband, *Q!ō'mogwa*.
And so *q* immediately Skin-Dresser-Woman became pregnant.
Then *q* she gave birth to a boy. (I forgot that when Skin-Dresser-
Woman first lay down with *Q!ō'mogwa* that night, then *q* when
day came in the morning, then *q* they arose. Then *q* Skin-Dresser- [275]
Woman saw that she had no whiskers for *Q!ō'mogwa* had taken

them off.) And so *q* as soon as she had given birth *Q!ō'mogwa* gave the name Copper-Maker *(ʟ!ā'qwag·ila)* to the boy, his child. Then *q* the next year Skin-Dresser-Woman gave birth again to a girl.
²⁸⁰ And so *q* immediately *Q!ō'mogwa* named his daughter Copper-Maker-Woman *(ʟ!ā'qwag·ilaōgwa)*. And *q* Skin-Dresser-Woman was always really happy on account of her children who were really growing up fast, and also on account of her husband *Q!ō'mogwa* who treated his children and his wife really well. That was the
²⁸⁵ reason why Skin-Dresser-Woman did not think of her parents. Then *q* it was the next winter when she gave birth to a son. Then *q Q!ō'mogwa* called the boy Potlatch-Giver *(ᵉmā'xwa)* and the following winter Skin-Dresser-Woman gave birth also to a girl. Then *q Q!ō'mogwa* called his youngest daughter Potlatch-Giver-
²⁹⁰ Woman *(ᵉmāx·mawēdzɛmga)*. And *q* Skin-Dresser-Woman remembered her parents after this. And so *q Q!ō'mogwa* noticed that his wife was down-hearted every day. Then *q Q!ō'mogwa* asked his wife, "Are you not anxious to go home to your parents?" said he *q*. Then *q* Skin-Dresser-Woman said that she was thinking
²⁹⁵ about her parents. Then *q Q!ō'mogwa* said, "Now behold! you will go home quickly," said he *q*. And so *q* as soon as night came *Q!ō'mogwa* asked his wife to lie down in their bed. And so *q* as soon as *Q!ō'mogwa* and his wife Skin-Dresser-Woman were lying down then *q Q!ō'mogwa* spoke as he was lying down with his wife. Then
³⁰⁰ *q* he said *q*, "Now you wish to go home to your house. I shall take you to your parents. Only you will obey me in one thing I tell you. Shut your eyes and go to sleep and never mind anything you hear, the kinds of sounds. Do not open your eyes and do not try to see what will be heard by you, else you will have hard luck,"
³⁰⁵ said *q Q!ō'mogwa* to his wife. And so *q* immediately Skin-Dresser-Woman shut her eyes. Now she was made to sleep by *Q!ō'mogwa*. Then *q* she had not been asleep long when Skin-Dresser-Woman was aroused by a rumbling all around the house. Then *q* she woke up. Then *q* she remembered the words of her husband when
³¹⁰ he had said that she should never open her eyes. And so *q* she just kept her eyes shut although she did not sleep. Then it was as though the rumbling passed. Then *q Q!ō'mogwa* awakened his wife and she opened her eyes. Then he said *q*, "Now you are home, now I shall also go home to my own house, for this will be the
³¹⁵ house of our children, the house with four platforms dug down into the ground," said he *q* as he disappeared when *q* it was getting daylight in the morning. And *q* Skin-Dresser-Woman heard her princess-pole when the eagle sitting on top of it was screeching. And *q* Skin-Dresser-Woman saw the privileges given in marriage
³²⁰ by Copper-Body to Cloudy the bear man, for they were all hanging

in the rear of the great house of *Q!ō′mogwa*. And so *q* as soon as it was broad daylight in the morning Skin-Dresser-Woman recognized the voice of her father who was talking in front of her house. Then *q* immediately Skin-Dresser-Woman arose from her bed and went to open the door of her house and called in her [325] father, to come and sit down. And so *q* Copper-Body just sat down for a short time and when they stopped talking, (he) and the princess Skin-Dresser-Woman, he went out of the door of the house to awaken his tribe, for they were all still asleep. And *q* he told the news to the tribe that his princess Skin-Dresser-Woman [330] had come. And so *q* immediately the whole tribe of Copper-Body came to see clearly his Princess, Skin-Dresser-Woman. And so *q* as soon as all had come in Copper-Body discovered the four large boxes at the right hand side of the large house. Then *q* he opened them. Then *q* coppers were in one of the boxes; then *q* blankets [335] were in another box; then *q* smoked and dried whale meat was in another box; then *q* four house dishes were in one of the boxes. One *q* was a sea otter house dish; then *q* one was a killerwhale house dish; then *q* one was a whale house dish, and so *q* one was a sealion house dish. And so *q* as soon as Copper-Body had finished [340] looking at them, he called his tribe and all sat down. Then *q* he gave a feast of dried whale and dried sea lion and seal, as he put into it the four house dishes. And *q* the first of the *Gwa′waēnoxᵘ* ate. And so *q* as soon as they finished, then *q* Copper-Body took the four coppers and gave them one each to the four chiefs of the [345] first of the *Gwa′waēnoxᵘ*. And so *q* as soon as they had finished the tribes went out of the house of Copper-Body. Therefore the grandson of Copper-Body was called Copper-Maker.

The Woman Carried away by a Skull.[1]
Told by *Gŭyō′sdēdzas*, a *Wā′ᵋwŭlibâᵋyē*.

I asked *K·!ē′sēlas* who came, for I tried to be informed regarding the word about the White man, for it was that, that I might talk about it, being informed in regard to the story. I said to him, "Go on, tell me, that I may listen to what is known by you." — "I shall tell you." — "Let me listen." [5]

A pretty woman *q* was wooed (by many) against one another. The whole tribe vied wooing her [wooed her against one another]. But no one was good enough for her. Then *q* she was wooed by another tribe. Then one was good enough for her and she desired him, and he was right in her mind. Then the minds of her tribe [10] fellows were sore, for she desired one of another tribe. Then *q*

---

[1] See Quileute, Columbia University Contributions to Anthropology, XII 183.

her tribe fellows talked among themselves. "Let us just make war on them that the whole tribe may die." And so q they made war upon the tribe. They killed them. They destroyed the whole
15 tribe. They cut off their heads. Now they came home to their houses. Then q they took the heads of the men and put them on a scaffold on the beach. Then skulls were on the beach. The heart of the woman was sore. The woman arose and looked at the skulls. She went down to the beach. Right there she saw in the
20 middle of the beach the skull of the one whom she had desired for her husband. The woman cried. The woman spoke, "What is the way in which you are? Does the way in which you are perhaps make alive? Come skull, the one who was in vain desired!" And so q the woman went straight to her house and lay down in
25 her bed. Then her heart was sore on account of the one whom in vain she wished for a husband, and night came. Then q somebody knocked at her door when daylight was coming. "Open for me." The woman arose and opened. She saw at once that it was the man whom she desired for a husband. She rushed and embraced
30 him. "You are the one for whom I come," said he q, "that we may go and start paddling. Go on, fold your bedding, and let us go on and start paddling." Then q the woman took her bedding and her clothing. "Take everything now!" Then q she folded it and gave it to the man and they started. And so q they went
35 aboard the canoe. The man q took the bedding and spread it out in the canoe. "Lie down here in the canoe. Now we will start paddling," and the woman lay down in the canoe. He paddled. The woman was asleep. She slept in the canoe. The man was paddling. Day came. The woman raised her head and sat up in
40 the canoe and awoke. She looked around. No land was to be seen; no mountain was to be seen, no island. Then the man spoke, "I only want you to know about what you said when you made fun of the way in which I was. And so I shall go home." .The man jumped into the water and a skull was rolling over the water.
45 Now he had again become a skull. And what should the woman say? And so q she continued not to know the way she was heading. In vain she was drifting about for a long time, day after day. A (great) number of years she was still drifting. Then q the woman saw a round thing at the side on the water, foam on the water.
50 She took her paddle and lifted it aboard and put it in the canoe. Indeed, although it was in the canoe it was not melting. Day came. What should it be? Clothing. It was calico and much thread. And she was still adrift. Still she was in this way on the water, but now she became glad, for now she had clothing. There
55 was noise of (the bow of the canoe) striking land. She raised her

head and looked. What should it be, but a nice country! She stepped out of the canoe and pulled her traveling canoe after her. Then she unloaded it. She unloaded her clothing. There was much of it. She sewed and made a house and her house was made of canvas. No person was seen. Although the house was on the [60] beach nobody came to meet her. Then *q* there was a sound of shooting. Then *q* she went out and looked for it. And so *q* nothing was seen by her. Without her seeing them, two men, walking together, saw her. The men came to the front of her (tent). And so *q* they came and stood at the door. "Come in!" said the woman *q*. [65] These were White men. Then *q* the woman spoke to them, "Why is your clothing so bad ?" said *q* the woman. Deerskin was their clothing and their hats and their shoes. "That is our clothing," said *q* the men. "Don't you wish that I give you some ?" said on her part *q* the woman. "You will be good," said *q* the White [70] men. Then *q* she called them and she dressed them with her clothing and she took clothing and gave it to them. It is said the clothing was red and they put it on. Then *q* the woman asked them, "Is this your number ?" — "We are many." — "Is your village far away ?" — "It is not very far. It is quite near." — [75] "Go and tell your chief that I come to talk to him; and let him come and carry my clothing." And they started, and told their chief. He came *q* steering. They towed the ship. He came and arrived where she lived. And so *q* their chief came and she gave him the clothing to be loaded in the ship. They tried to fill the [80] ship and it just swelled up and became much. Then the woman went aboard the ship. Now she was taken to their village. That woman became chief of the tribe. She was the queen of the tribe.

NOTE TO THE STORY OF SCAB

A number of the stories contained in the present volume were told by the same narrator at various times. The story of Scab was told to by *Neg·ä′dze* in 1900 (Version 1) and again in 1932 (Version 2). When he first told it to me he said that it was the one story which his grandmother, a *Dɛna′x·da*ᵉ*x*ᵘ woman, used to tell him when he was a boy and that he used to go to sleep over the story. The two versions are essentially the same in content except on two points. According to (1) when Scab marries the daughter of the chief above he is at once accepted by his father-in-law. In (2) the usual test themes are introduced by which the son-in-law proves his supernatural power. A still earlier version told about 1890 in Alert Bay also omits the tests (S 161). In (1) Scab falling from the back of his wife who is flying with him to the sky is drowned, in (2) he is revived by his first wife. Neither of these endings seem to correspond to the plan of the story as told in other places. When the chief above learns of Scab's death, he fishes his bones up from the bottom of the sea and revives him. (See the following story, p. 173, and Ts 780).

The two versions differ in wording and in the elaboration of details. In (1) the father of Scab is called *Hawĭ'lkŭlał*, chief of the *Tsłō'tslₑna* at *G·ₑyō'x^u* (C 39). In (1) the numaym has many children, in (2) the unnamed chief had seven children. In (1) the father deserts the sick child because he fears infection, in (2) the mother induces the father to desert him, because the child's sickness is a cause of shame. The latter is more in keeping with Indian ideology. The whole incident is spun out in (2) and very bare in (1). The attitude of the deserted child is different in the two versions. In (2) the narrator dwells on the satisfaction of the child who can now scratch his body without interference, in (1) he cries on account of his unhappy condition. In (1) the scab boy asks to be named Scab, in (2) the sick person gives him the name. Salmon are created in both versions by throwing into the water hemlock needles taken from graves; in (1) it is specifically said that these were the graves of the deserted child's sisters (C 43). The various kinds of salmon and bull heads (1) or red cod (2) are created in both versions. When they build their house their poverty in household goods is dwelt on in (2). In (1) Scab asks his "father" to make a spear; in (2) he uses a hook (159, C 45;). When Scab is waiting for the appearance of the thief who steals his salmon, (2) gives one of the few descriptions of nature that occur in the texts (160). A few of the words used here occur also in (1). Here the *Dzō'noq!wa* is called a man, but only because on p. 50 he is called "father" by his daughter. By analogy with all other tales she should be a woman. Probably the address on p. 50 refers to the *Dzō'noq!wa* chief while the narrator had in mind the woman who was shot in the breast *(dza^ₑm* nipples). In (2) the making of the cedar bark rings for Scab is described. The scene at the pond is also more fully, though not clearly, described in (2). I presume in a more complete version he would have hidden in a tree and been discovered by the reflection in the water. Here the remark that the water was like a looking glass seems uncalled for. In (2) the little *Dzō'noq!wa* woman is so much frightened by Scab's appearance that she drops her bucket, in (1) she is more appropriately shocked by the demands for payment he makes. In (1) we are told that the house was so full of people that Scab could not be seen, which explains the remark in (2) that people were "lying down, lying down" near the sick *Dzō'noq!wa*. The procedure of healing is described more fully in (1) than in (2) where the tormenting of the patient by pushing the arrows to and fro is entirely omitted